# Britain, France and Appeasement

# Britain, France and Appeasement

## Anglo-French Relations in the Popular Front Era

**Martin Thomas**

**BERG**

*Oxford • New York*

First published in 1996 by
**Berg**
Editorial offices:
150 Cowley Road, Oxford, OX4 1JJ, UK
70 Washington Square South, New York, NY 10012, USA

Berg is an imprint of Oxford International Publishers Ltd.

**Library of Congress Cataloging-in-Publication Data**

A CIP catalogue for this book is available from the Library of Congress.

**British Library Cataloguing-in-Publication Data**

A CIP catalogue record for this book is available from the British Library.

ISBN 1 85973 187 2 (Cloth)
1 85973 192 9 (Paper)

Typeset by JS Typesetting, Wellingborough, Northants.
Printed in the United Kingdom by WBC Book Manufacturers, Bridgend,
Mid Glamorgan.

# Contents

# Acknowledgements

During the research and writing of this book I have been reliant upon the support of several organizations, libraries and individuals on both sides of the Channel. It is a pleasure to acknowledge this help here. I completed the early research for this work as part of my D.Phil. studies at Oxford. During this period I was assisted by overseas research grants from the Arnold, Bryce and Reed fund, the Zacharoff fund, and the Exeter College research grant committee. The British Academy also provided funds which allowed me to travel regularly to the Public Record Office.

Work in archives tends to pose almost as many questions as it answers. Hence, the search for research support has to be a continuing one. I am grateful to the Scouloudi Foundation for providing grants for research in Paris and Aix-en-Provence. The British Academy also gave additional support to this end. The Université d'Aix-en-Provence generously provided me with excellent accommodation. Finally, the Humanities Faculty Research Committee at the University of the West of England has provided indispensable help on several occasions.

Throughout my work, I have been capably assisted by the professional staffs of archives and libraries. I am indebted to the archivists and staff of the Public Record Office at Kew who increasingly work under considerable pressure. Quotations from Crown Copyright material are with the permission of the Controller of Her Majesty's Stationery Office. I am also grateful to the Keeper of Western Manuscripts at the Bodleian Library, and to the staff of the Room 132 archive, for permission to quote from the Viscount Simon, the Francis Hemming and the Horace Rumbold papers. I also thank the University of Cambridge Library for its support, and for permission to quote from the Stanley Baldwin and Viscount Templewood papers. At the Special Collections Library of the University of Birmingham I was guided in work upon the Neville Chamberlain and Earl of Avon papers by Dr B.S. Benedikz. The archive staff at Churchill College, Cambridge were generous with their time and encouragement. My thanks for permission to quote from the many collections in their care. I am grateful to the National Maritime Museum Archive for sanction to quote from Lord Chatfield's papers, and to St Antony's College's Middle East Centre in Oxford for authority to quote from the papers of the First Baron Killearn. The librarians at the University of the West of England, St Matthias Library have also been unfailingly helpful.

## Acknowledgements

In France I have been assisted by a number of people. The personnel of the Archives du Ministère des Affaires Etrangères at the Quai d'Orsay have always been welcoming. On the other side of town, I have found work at the Services Historiques of the Château de Vincennes a great pleasure. My thanks to all the personnel of the three Services Historiques Archives for their advice and support, not least in producing heavy *cartons* without complaint. At the rue de Bercy archive, the staff of the Service des Archives Economiques et Financières helped me find my way through the Finance Ministry records. Everyone at the Archives Nationales Centre des Archives d'Outre-Mer proved equally helpful during a sweltering July in Aix-en-Provence. Work at the Centre des Archives Diplomatiques in Nantes was also made much easier by the affability of everyone I met there. For their assistance, accommodation and friendship I am deeply grateful to Collette Martignon, Annie Moerlon, and Christine and André Frézal and their family.

Many friends and colleagues have helped me to complete the writing of this book. My thanks to Kathryn Earle at Berg for much sound advice and free beer, and to Nigel Hope for his meticulous copy-editing. For agreeing to look over drafts, my thanks go to Zara Steiner, Martin Alexander, Anthony Adamthwaite, Mike Dockrill and Robert Boyce. Alan Sharp also provided much kind encouragement. Through his comments and suggestions, Peter Jackson has added considerably to my understanding of the concerns of French army intelligence. At the University of the West of England I have been fortunate enough to work with friends who have also been able critics. Kent Fedorowich, Glyn Stone and Christian Leitz have all helped me a great deal in completing this project. Alistair Parker of the Queen's College, Oxford, set me off on my research travels. His insight and enthusiasm continues to be an inspiration.

Writing can be a lonely affair. That this has not been the case for me is primarily due to my wife and family. I owe my parents an enormous debt for their constant support and good humour. To Suzy my debts are priceless, and it is to her that I dedicate the book.

# Abbreviations

## Ministries/Organizations

| | |
|---|---|
| ADM | Admiralty |
| AIR | Air Ministry |
| CAB | Cabinet Office Papers |
| CGPF | Confédération générale du patronat français |
| CGT | Confédération générale du travail |
| CO | Colonial Office |
| FO | Foreign Office |
| IIC | Industrial Intelligence Centre (Department of Overseas Trade) |
| NIC | Non-Intervention Committee |
| PCF | Parti communiste français |
| SFIO | Section française de l'internationale ouvrière |
| WO | War Office |

French ministries were frequently identified by their location within Paris. Those most commonly used in this study are as follows.

| | |
|---|---|
| Boulevard Victor | Air Ministry |
| Hôtel Matignon | Prime Minister's Office |
| Quai d'Orsay | Foreign Ministry |
| Rue de Rivoli | Finance Ministry |
| Rue Saint Dominique | War Ministry |
| Wilhelmstrasse | German Foreign Ministry |

## Military – British

| | |
|---|---|
| CID | Committee of Imperial Defence |
| CIGS | Chief of the Imperial General Staff |
| COS | Chiefs of Staff |

| DPR | Defence Policy and Requirements Committee |
| DRC | Defence Requirements Committee |
| D(P)C | Defence (Plans) Committee |

## Military – French

| CPDN | Comité permanent de la défense nationale |
| CSA | Conseil supérieur de l'air |
| CSDN | Conseil supérieur de la défense nationale |
| CSG | Conseil supérieur de la guerre |
| CSM | Conseil supérieur de la marine |
| EMA | Etat-Major de l'armée (army staff) |
| EMAA | Etat-Major de l'armée de l'air (air staff) |
| EMM | Etat-Major de la marine (naval staff) |
| HCM | Haut comité militaire |

## Archives/Published Documents

| ANCOM | Archives Nationales Centre des Archives d'Outre-Mer |
| BDFA | British Documents on Foreign Affairs |
| CADN | Centre des Archives Diplomatiques, Nantes |
| DBFP | Documents on British Foreign Policy |
| DDB | Documents Diplomatiques Belges |
| DDF | Documents Diplomatiques Français |
| DGFP | Documents on German Foreign Policy |
| MAE | Ministère des affaires étrangères archive |
| PRO | Public Record Office |
| SAEF | Service des Archives Economiques et Financières-Finance Ministry |
| SHAA | Service Historique de l'Armée de l'Air |
| SHAT | Service Historique de l'Armée de Terre |
| SHM | Service Historique de la Marine |

## Journals

| *EHQ* | *European History Quarterly* |
| *EHR* | *English Historical Review* |
| *FHS* | *French Historical Studies* |
| *HJ* | *Historical Journal* |
| *JCH* | *Journal of Contemporary History* |
| *JMH* | *Journal of Modern History* |

## Abbreviations

| | |
|---|---|
| JSS | *Journal of Strategic Studies* |
| IHR | *International History Review* |
| INS | *Intelligence and National Security* |
| RD | *Revue Diplomatique* |
| RHA | *Revue Historique des Armées* |
| RHMC | *Revue d'Histoire Moderne et Contemporaine* |
| RHDGM | *Revue d'Histoire de la Deuxième Guerre Mondiale* |

# Introduction

Between May 1936 and April 1938 France was governed by Popular Front coalitions. This two-year period was pivotal in shaping the nation that went to war in September 1939. As a coalition the Front populaire was distinctive: a parliamentary grouping of Socialists, Radical-Socialists and – to varying degrees at differing times – Communists, backed by a diverse range of anti-fascist non-parliamentary groups from unions to literary guilds. At its inception, this governing bloc evoked anticipation and dread in similar measure across French society as a whole. The number of senior Popular Front ministers paraded before the Vichy regime's supreme court at the Riom show trial in March and April 1942 bore witness to an anti-republican consensus which regarded the nadir of *la Troisième* as Léon Blum's first ministry of May 1936 to June 1937. Accused of questionable patriotism, vilified for the inadequacy of its defensive preparations and pilloried for its decadence, the Popular Front was cast as the harbinger of French defeat.[1] In certain respects, the Riom judgments make one intention of this book quite simple. It is hoped to show that far from being 'guilty' of a deliberate or misconstrued neglect of France's strategic plight, the Popular Front led France towards a more comprehensive preparation for war.

This is not, however, a study of French rearmament. Rather, it is an investigation of the Anglo-French diplomatic relationship during the Front populaire years. Writing a generation after the release of British governmental documents from the late 1930s, any study of the entente cordiale in the age of appeasement carries a weight of accumulated historical baggage with it. Over recent years, numerous scholars have also worked extensively within the more diffuse French archival record. Such research has transformed our understanding of French foreign and defence policies in the pre-war period. Yet France still fits uneasily into the historical debates over the appeasement of Germany and Italy during the 1930s. Not surprisingly, the varied definitions of appeasement policy have been formulated primarily with the British government in mind, usually with the shadowy figure of Neville Chamberlain looming from the text. In comparative studies of the entente powers this may be dangerous. Defining a policy applicable to the Baldwin and Chamberlain administrations does not put one in a position to graft that definition of appeasement onto French governments of the day.

Ironically, in one sense, to perform such a graft has a sound logic. During the 1970s and 1980s much of the debate concerning French appeasement policies drew upon François Bédarida's memorable image of an English governess keeping France at her beck and call.[2] In their opening remarks to indispensable books on French foreign policy, Robert Young and Nicole Jordan, two outstanding historians of Popular Front diplomacy, have both stressed the distortive potential of the concept of *la gouvernante anglaise*.[3] At the root of Bédarida's phrase was the idea that France, with its eastern allies exposed, its economy slow to recover from depression and its defensive preparations incomplete, lacked the wherewithal to pursue an independent foreign policy towards Nazi Germany. To build an assessment of French foreign policy on this view may produce one of two consequences. Either a British definition of appeasement could be equally applicable to French administrations from Albert Sarraut's in March 1936 to Edouard Daladier's in September 1939, because these governments were attached firmly to British coat-tails. Alternatively, if France lacked initiative in its German and Italian policies, then perhaps one need not worry about a suitable definition of French appeasement because, *ipso facto*, France lacked a coherently formulated foreign policy.

This book contends that a more nuanced approach is required. To analyse British and French appeasement in the Popular Front era, three crucial differences between the two countries' positions must be borne in mind. First and foremost, the German government objected to direct conversations with French ministers. Hitler preferred the British to represent a 'joint' Anglo-French position. This suited German efforts to split the entente powers. It also met the British preference to keep the initiative in the London–Paris relationship where possible. As premiers, Léon Blum and Camille Chautemps usually let the British government take the reins in this manner with good grace. Hence the second difference: the *Front populaire* governments tended to influence the course of negotiations with Germany and Italy by exerting diplomatic pressure upon London rather than Berlin. The French Ambassador to London throughout the late 1930s, Charles Corbin, was as much an agent of French appeasement policy as his colleague in Berlin, André François-Poncet. This is perhaps easier to understand given the final element in the differing approaches to appeasement between the entente powers. Despite their ready co-operation, the French governments of the Popular Front period remained pessimistic that talks with the fascist powers would yield lasting results. In these circumstances, only unstinting collaboration with the British in the negotiation effort was likely to overcome the residual suspicion of French foreign policy that characterized the Whitehall establishment in 1936.

The British government attempted to appease Germany and Italy in the expectation that a settlement could be achieved. The Front populaire governments co-operated in these efforts, hoping that such a settlement would be arranged, but expecting that it could not be. In that eventuality the fundamental purpose of this French co-operation could still be realized through a full defensive alliance with Britain. Having proved that the fascist powers were bent on confrontation through no fault of the French themselves, Popular Front foreign policy would reap its ultimate reward by turning the entente into a peace-time alliance.

This is clearly a highly reductive interpretation. Studying the machinations of French ambassadors, ministerial envoys and military missions across eastern Europe, it is difficult to see the hand of a policy for western alliance at work. Similarly, the minutes of the senior French civil–military liaison committee, the comité permanent de la défense nationale (CPDN), and of its nearest British equivalent, the committee of imperial defence (CID), reveal how limited was the Anglo-French defensive co-ordination achieved during 1936 and 1937. It would be a tautology to argue that because alliance with Britain was often pursued surreptitiously, there is evidence for it implicit in other aspects of French diplomacy. It is also important to avoid the inference that a lack of optimism about the prospects for a negotiated peace with Germany or Italy meant that the Popular Front governments did not make a genuine effort to achieve a 'general settlement'. France would naturally benefit from a comprehensive, negotiated agreement which settled Nazi Germany's place in a reordered, peaceful Europe. Yet the fact remains that for the Front populaire administrations, co-operation in appeasement carried an additional motive – the revitalization of the entente cordiale with a view to eventual military alliance.

Germany's reoccupation of the Rhineland zone in March 1936 destroyed the 1925 treaties of Locarno, leaving the eastern borders of France, and especially Belgium, dangerously exposed. For over a year after the Rhineland crisis both the British and French governments worked to formulate a replacement western non-aggression pact. The Blum government was also closely involved in attempts to find another route to comprehensive negotiation with Germany by means of economic or colonial appeasement. This involved an amalgam of financial and trade concessions capped by the possible return of one or more of Germany's former imperial possessions. Many of the early steps towards discussions with the German Economics Minister, Hjalmar Schacht, were made in Paris, not London. These initiatives almost coincided with the Quai d'Orsay's formulation of a policy of non-intervention in the Spanish civil war in the first weeks after the rebellion began in late July 1936.

Again, with French encouragement, this policy was seized upon by Great Britain.

The nub of the appeasement effort was the attempt to achieve a lasting peace in eastern Europe. This required a general reduction in armaments and a binding German commitment to remain within eastern frontiers delimited as part of a final general settlement. Ironically, this stage in the appeasement process was not reached during the lifetime of the Front populaire. The Popular Front era ended within a month of Germany's *Anschluss* with Austria in March 1938. By this point, the entente with Britain had acquired additional importance because the French had failed in their attempt to re-mould their eastern alliances with Poland and the three states of the Little Entente into a strategically coherent bloc.

When the first Blum government took office in May 1936 there was a consensus within Stanley Baldwin's Cabinet that fruitful negotiation with Germany and Italy remained possible. Though complicated by events in the Rhineland and Mussolini's empire-building in east Africa, British appeasement was not a policy of last resort. The Foreign Secretary, Anthony Eden, received most of his advice on Germany, France and much of central Europe from the Foreign Office central department. In 1936 this burgeoning ministry section was led by Ralph Wigram, an outstanding diplomat close to the Permanent Under-Secretary, Sir Robert Vansittart. Both men were sceptical that Hitler would agree to comprehensive talks while France's eastern alliance system remained nominally intact. Yet the central department, supposedly a fortress of opposition to Chamberlainite appeasement, was, on balance, in favour of a negotiation effort between 1936 and 1938.

In early 1936 the choice facing the British government was not seen to lie between dialogue with Germany or the construction of a viable collective security network. Faced with an intractable Japanese menace and opportunistic Italian threats to various regions of the Empire, neither the British government nor the general staff saw any benefit in leading a coalition of non-revisionist powers so long as there remained no more pressing danger to the territorial integrity of western Europe. Leadership of an anti-German coalition might precipitate a European war from which Britain had little to gain and much to lose, especially if, as expected, the conflict became globalized by Japanese intervention. With the stakes so very high, the British tendency to be impatient with French involvement in eastern Europe is perhaps understandable. Set against the backcloth of worsening continental tension, the French achievement in consolidating the Anglo-French entente between 1936 to 1938 should not be lightly dismissed.

# Notes

1. Henri Michel, *Le Procès de Riom,* Paris, 1979, pp. 123–225; see also *Léon Blum Before his Judges at the Supreme Court of Riom, March 11th & 12th, 1942*, London, 1943.
2. François Bédarida, 'La "gouvernante anglaise"', in René Rémond and Janine Bourdin (eds), *Edouard Daladier, Chef de Gouvernement, Avril 1938–Septembre 1939*, Paris, 1977, pp. 228–40.
3. Robert J. Young, *In Command of France. French Foreign Policy and Military Planning, 1933–1940*, Cambridge, Mass., 1978, pp. 1–5; Nicole Jordan, *The Popular Front and Central Europe: The Dilemmas of French Impotence, 1918–1940*, Cambridge, 1992, p. 1.

# Sources of Tension in Anglo-French Relations, 1918–1936

**I**

In November 1918 Britain and France emerged victorious from the First World War. For both the British and French, the wartime experience of military alliance was chequered. In spite of the shared hardships of the Great War, mistrust lingered. The community of interest between the two western powers was obscured by persistent disagreements. During the war the two high commands argued over strategy. The British army staff did not adapt easily to its junior role alongside France's senior military commanders. Even the arch 'westerner', the British Chief of Imperial General Staff, General William Robertson, found it difficult to co-operate with French colleagues who shared his enthusiasm for the concentration of resources in France and Flanders. Between 1914 to 1916, this situation was not made easier by the imprecise nature of British and French war aims.[1] The military relationship on the western front was strained by wave after wave of seemingly pointless losses, such as those incurred at Passchendaele where British and Canadian troops had borne the brunt following the French army mutinies provoked by General Robert Nivelle's earlier abortive offensive in April 1917.[2]

From 1915 the British and French Treasuries clashed frequently over war financing and inter-governmental loan policy. The British government resented the hoarding of gold by the Bank of France. In turn, Alexandre Ribot's Ministry of Finance criticized the British decision to keep sterling on the gold standard. The Finance Ministry seemed envious of Britain's greater ability to raise loan finance through the London money market, especially after French credit collapsed in 1916.[3] As the war neared its close, the two premiers, David Lloyd George and Georges Clemenceau, displayed an equal ability to irritate one another. Their relationship was further complicated by the rising influence of the American president, Woodrow Wilson. After the United States' Congressional rejection of the Versailles Treaty in 1919, Britain did not renew its wartime alliance with France. Instead, it keenly reverted to the more elastic commitments of the entente cordiale.

Many of those who were to govern Britain and France in the late 1930s had fought on the western front. Anthony Eden, future Foreign Secretary and erstwhile British rifle corps major, had witnessed the horrors of war at close range. Eden also saw the realities of defeat during his service with the allied army of occupation in the Rhineland. Lord Halifax, his successor at the Foreign Office in 1938, had spent three years as a cavalryman in Flanders, even being assigned to bury the dead. The experiences of these men were not dissimilar to those of Edouard Daladier, future premier and one-time infantry lieutenant – a Verdun veteran cited three times for bravery. Like so many of his political and bureaucratic contemporaries – avid appeaser, Georges Bonnet, among them – Daladier received his call-up papers in August 1914.[4] If nothing else, many of Britain's inter-war MPs had acquired a particular knowledge of France through military service or the loss of sons, brothers and friends in the trenches. Britain was the only great power to remain at France's side throughout the war. As such, French deputies in the *Union Sacrée* coalition necessarily took an interest in British politics. Even Marius Moutet, a committed pacifist who would become Minister of Colonies within the Popular Front coalition, acquired an excellent knowledge of British foreign policy as a newly elected deputy during the First World War.

For the British military caste that had long been a forcing ground for the country's politicians and administrators, the war was a unique experience. Never before had a conflict been so indiscriminate in meting out death to foot soldiers and junior officers alike. It is hard to believe that Eden or Daladier's experience of trench warfare had much in common with the Boer war adventures of the young Winston Churchill, though as First Lord of the Admiralty in 1915, Churchill too was deeply marked by the bloody failure of the Gallipoli campaign. For the 1914–18 generation, the memory of war was truly haunting. Not surprisingly, the Great War was unprecedented in its lasting impact upon public attitudes in Britain and France. Among the most persistent clarion calls to public opinion in both countries between the wars were the campaigns against preparation for, or participation in, armed conflict. In Britain, revulsion at the thought of another European war nourished Lord Robert Cecil's League of Nations Union, and produced the remarkable Peace Ballot in 1935. In France, Théodore Ruyssen's pacifist Association de la paix par le droit expanded in the 1920s before being outstripped by the more uncompromising 'integral' pacifism of the following decade. In both countries, throughout the inter-war period, there was determined opposition to military spending and old-style balance of power diplomacy.[5]

The slaughter of 1914–18 hung over the deliberations of the Paris Peace Conference in 1919–20. Peace planning had gathered momentum during the last eighteen months of the war. In consequence, the British and French delegations to Paris had built up a wider knowledge of each other's needs. As if to symbolize this, the Conference proceedings were conducted in English as well as French, an unprecedented break in diplomatic convention.[6] The Foreign Office Political Intelligence Department (PID), the engine of British peace planning, was closely involved in the demarcation of the new states of eastern Europe. These states quickly identified their security requirements with those of France. Although the PID planners were guided by the principle of ethnic self-determination, they understood the transparent French strategic interest in the constitution of powerful Polish and Czechoslovakian states.[7] For all their arguments over detail, British and French politicians agreed that some form of reparations settlement could legitimately be imposed upon the infant Weimar Republic. The American withdrawal from the Paris settlement strengthened this consensus by adding importance to reparations as a means to limit German power. Britain and France should share the blame for reparations policies which attempted 'to obscure and, if possible, evade the domestic financial consequences of the war'.[8]

Though there were certain common lines of approach to the creation of new European states and the imposition of reparations, over the course of the Peace Conference Anglo-French strategic and economic interests diverged. During 1919 the United Kingdom and its Empire acquired unprecedented security against Germany. This was the product both of decisions made in Paris and of events outside it. The redistribution of Germany's colonies, the demilitarization clauses of the Versailles Treaty, the self-destruction of the German fleet at Scapa Flow and the emergence of a liberal democracy in the former *Kaiserreich* – all of these factors tended to diminish British interest in a continental alliance. In the short term at least, the crippling costs of the war and the gathering strength of the United States economy posed a greater threat to lasting British power. Britain's peace-makers could afford to be dispassionate about a German strategic threat but could not ignore the potential German role in a British and European economic recovery. In spite of the increasing state management of Britain's wartime economy, post-war reconstruction was initially seen in terms of a return to a liberal, free market. The British faith in the restorative power of private enterprise was matched by a recognition of the importance of Anglo-German trade, especially after sterling was returned to the gold standard at its pre-war parity. It was imperative to bring British economic performance into line with the high value of its currency.[9]

In the French case, these strategic and economic priorities were more or less reversed. Apart from being less industrialized than its British counterpart, the French economy was not so clearly export-driven. Less agitated by trade requirements, and lacking the enthusiasm for Empire of French colonial lobbyists, Clemenceau's dominant concern was for the physical safety of metropolitan France against a German nation superior in manpower, industrial capacity and strategic raw materials. Where German trade would be vital to British economic power in the long term, German money and materials were essential to rebuild France's north-eastern industrial base in the short term. The French civil and military leadership was neither consumed by revenge nor insensitive to the perpetuation of Franco-German hostility. Rather, French policy-makers were confronted with a depressing truth. Across numerous indices, from demographic strength to industrial production, France remained weaker than Germany. Crucially, it became apparent that neither the United States nor Great Britain would be prepared to compensate for this with binding pledges of military support.

The collapse of the projected Anglo-American guarantee of France's eastern frontier added to the strategic importance of French policy in the Rhineland between 1919 and 1924. After the election of the 'sky blue' Chamber in November 1919, France embarked upon a rigorous enforcement of German disarmament and reparations obligations. Over the next three years, additional French troops were at various points deployed in the Rhineland zone. This culminated in the Franco-Belgian control of the Ruhr valley in 1923, and the subsequent, abortive attempt to create a buffer Rhenish Republic. Throughout 1921, Aristide Briand, the apostle of Franco-German reconciliation in the mid to late-twenties, was the agent of a harsh policy of Treaty fulfilment born of the failure of the Seydoux Plan of reparations demands. Soon after Briand was succeeded as premier by the former President of the Republic, Raymond Poincaré, in January 1922, the looming impasse in Anglo-French reparations policy turned into an intractable deadlock.[10] Though masked by joint signature of the Dawes Plan in 1924 and the Treaty of Locarno in 1925, entente disagreement over policy in the Rhineland had diminished French strategic independence by precluding a further unilateral occupation of German territory. It had also strained the patience of those British politicians sympathetic to France. The Ruhr occupation was regarded as malevolent and counter-productive. It compounded the British tendency to confuse legitimate French security concerns with an unwarranted malice towards Germany.

## II

Disputes over the fulfilment of reparations demands nourished the mutual suspicion which characterized Anglo-French relations for much of the inter-war period. But between 1924 and 1928, while the Dawes Plan of rescheduled reparations payments was in operation, Anglo-French financial disputes reopened the wounds inflicted by earlier arguments over war loans. Animosity between the British Treasury and the French Finance Ministry, and between the central banks of both countries, was perpetuated by their divergent approaches to currency stabilization and gold reserve policy. In the late 1920s, successive French governments concluded that their financial influence across eastern Europe was compromised by British-sponsored schemes for currency reform in several Danubian states.[11] After his appointment as Governor of the Bank of France in 1926, Emile Moreau was frequently at odds with the Bank of England chief, Montagu Norman. Treasury officials in London were disparaging of French financial acumen. Paradoxically, the Treasury's finance department was resentful of the impressive French economic recovery stimulated by Poincaré's bold devaluation of the franc to one-fifth of its pre-war value in December 1926.[12]

Adherence to the *franc Poincaré* helped delay the impact of depression in France. It also facilitated the continued accumulation of gold reserves which so exasperated the British. As commodity prices fell, and the volume of international trade declined in the early 1930s, so the French commitment to massive gold reserves, expenditure cuts and protectionist tariffs increased. Both Ramsay MacDonald's second Labour government, and the National Government coalition which replaced it in September 1931, regarded French gold accumulation and protectionism as palpably selfish.[13] During reparations talks in December 1931, Sir Frederick Leith-Ross, soon to be appointed government Chief Economic Adviser, vented his fury at French monetary policy upon Jacques Rueff, a respected Finance Ministry mandarin who had been Financial Attaché to London. Leith-Ross had no doubt who was to blame for Britain's enforced devaluation in September 1931: 'It seemed to us that the monetary policy pursued by France was largely responsible for the world crisis which had led to the reparations difficulty, and to the abandonment of the gold standard and we could not be expected to re-stabilize till we had some assurance that gold prices would remain stable in future.'[14] That Rueff did not apparently regard this accusation as extraordinary bore witness to the general tenor of Anglo-French financial discussion.

To the dismay of the British Treasury, France, though itself in the trough of depression in 1935, still possessed enormous gold stocks totalling over 66 billion francs.[15] These were economic sins to compare with the alleged French intransigence over all matters affecting European security policy and a possible revision of Versailles. In Whitehall it appeared that French politicians chanted *franc Poincaré* and *sécurité* like a mantra in a vain bid to stave off economic calamity and German recovery. The *franc Poincaré* was abolished under the first devaluation undertaken by the Popular Front coalition in September 1936. As we shall see, the trauma and bitterness this measure provoked within France was not offset by the marginal improvement in Anglo-French financial relations which followed it.

In the early 1920s, Anglo-French competition in the settlement and redistribution of Turkey's Middle Eastern Empire was a lesser, though not insignificant, cause of entente friction. The imperial rivalries of the Fashoda age resurfaced in arguments over the internationalization of the Moroccan port of Tangier, and the delimitation of frontiers between the French Mandate of Syria and British-controlled Iraq. Across the Middle East, the transition to an era of British and French dominance was complicated by the conflicting wartime promises made by politicians in both countries to their future Arab clients and subjects.[16] In subsequent years, there was little common cause between the two great imperial nations. Seen from a British perspective, French colonial policy was marred by the continued prevalence of military administration, the severe repression of colonial rebellion in Morocco, Syria and Indo-China, and the heavily centralized character of French colonial rule in black Africa. Above all, imperial possessions appeared to strengthen the French attachment to protectionism. Seen from Paris, the British Empire was the primary cause of Britain's refusal to immerse itself more deeply in European affairs. The British were frequently exposed as imperial hypocrites. French methods of imperial policing were criticized, though the British too were quite capable of systematic brutality in pursuit of colonial order. Similarly, Britain's adoption of imperial tariffs following the Ottawa conference in July 1932 made a mockery of Whitehall irritation over French Empire protectionism. At least in the French case there was little doubt that access to colonial manpower would add to the country's strength in a war with Germany. For Britain, the need to defend far-flung territories threatened to expose the inadequacy of British naval and military power in Europe.[17]

## III

Occasional disagreements over Empire were less significant to Anglo-French relations than differences over eastern Europe. Like the arguments over imperial policy, these disagreements originated in the immediate aftermath of the First World War. Within months of Hungary's signature of the Treaty of Trianon in May 1920, Czechoslovakia signed defensive conventions with both Yugoslavia and Romania in an effort to preclude any Hungarian attempt to recover lost territory. In June 1921 the Romanian and Yugoslav governments signed a further defensive agreement, spurred by their alarm at the attempted restoration of Charles IV to the Hungarian throne in March of that year. The tripartite grouping produced by these arrangements was soon being referred to in the European press as the Little Entente. Only after Philippe Berthelot replaced Maurice Paléologue as Secretary-General at the Quai d'Orsay later in 1921 did the French Foreign Ministry look upon this alliance combination with favour.[18] Over the next six years France too constructed a series of security pacts with the successor states of eastern Europe, beginning with the secret Franco-Polish military agreement of February 1921, and ending with treaties with Romania and Yugoslavia in 1926 and 1927 respectively.[19] This obscured the fact that the entente with Britain remained the cornerstone of French diplomacy. Aristide Briand's signature of the Locarno Treaty in October 1925 delimited a mutually recognized Franco-German border. Henceforth, France was reluctant to shape its foreign policy and strategic planning in strict accordance with the wishes of its eastern clients.

The French diplomatic and military establishment was, for example, dismissive of Polish pretensions to great-power status. The Locarno pact was signed within months of a new Franco-Polish treaty of August 1925 which had diluted the provisions for automatic mutual assistance built into the previous 1921 accord. Writing to a correspondent in the French military archive in 1955, General Maxime Weygand recalled that neither he nor Marshal Ferdinand Foch were enthusiastic about the 1921 agreement: 'Neither Marshal Foch nor I favoured the conclusion of a treaty, on terms of parity, with a power which still had neither frontiers, finances nor an army.'[20] After Locarno, the many francophile generals within the Polish regime were hard-pressed to defend French actions. Following the closure of the French military mission to Warsaw in 1932, it fell to the French Ambassadors, Jules Laroche and Léon Noël, to defend French strategic policy as best they could.[21] This task was made harder by the reluctance of the French Finance Ministry to underwrite Polish defence expenditure in the early 1930s through the provision of preferential loans.[22]

From the Paris Peace to the Russo-Polish war, France had played a major part in the creation and consolidation of the Polish state. But after his *coup d'état* in May 1926, the Polish leader, Marshal Jósef Pilsudski, increasingly looked upon the French as only fair-weather friends. Yet, in spite of the conclusion of the chimeric Franco-Soviet pact in May 1935,

Poland was technically France's principal military ally. The inconsistent French view of Poland after Locarno, when taken in conjunction with the often discordant relations between the eastern allies themselves, meant that the French alliance system always amounted to less than the sum of its parts.

The deterioration in Franco-Polish relations caused by the Locarno settlement helps explain why the pact would prove so beneficial to Germany. Foreign Minister Gustav Stresemann's 'diplomatic counter-offensive' against France's Ruhr diplomacy and reparations demands had led to a western European security pact which implicitly acknow-ledged Germany's right to pursue the revision of its disputed eastern frontiers with Poland and Czechoslovakia.[23] The treaty created new sources of Anglo-French division by highlighting Britain's limited interest in either eastern European security or the effectiveness of the French alliance system. It was final confirmation that Britain saw no interest in the lasting restriction of German economic power. A peaceful revisionist perhaps, Stresemann had none the less illuminated the way forward for more unscrupulous German nationalists. In order to undo the Versailles system and recover Germany's lost eastern territories, it was first essential to divide Britain from France.[24]

By 1930 the optimism of the so-called 'Locarno spring' had dis-appeared. But the competitive rearmament which superseded it was for a while delayed by the impact of economic depression upon Europe. In 1930 the new French chief of army staff, General Maxime Weygand, put forward an eight-year military re-equipment programme based upon a thorough upgrade of army *matériel*. Mauled by a series of budgetary cuts, following the collapse of the Disarmament Conference in the spring of 1934, this modernization programme was at last expanded.[25] The sound strategic rationale behind the army's rearmament schemes in the early 1930s has been obscured by a more famous element in French defence spending. Strongly backed by Marshal Philippe Pétain, during 1928 and 1929, Minister of War, Paul Painlevé, struggled to obtain parl-iamentary funding for what was to become identified with his successor at the rue Saint Dominique, André Maginot.

The Maginot line – a system of fixed frontier defences, subterranean tunnels and fortified emplacements – has resided in the popular imagination as ultimate proof that France's war planners lacked initiative. The Maginot line was surely the ultimate trench network, affirmation of the French expectation of a more or less static war of attrition. It was the concrete equivalent of the army command's blink-ered opposition to the creation of a fully independent French air force throughout the 1920s. Recalling the enormous construction costs involved, and the apparent ease with which German panzer columns avoided the Maginot defences in May 1940, it is easy to overlook a basic point. The decision to build the Maginot line was a product of the allied agreement at Locarno to evacuate the Rhineland some five years ahead of schedule. The Anglo-Italian guarantee of France's eastern frontier would count for nothing if French armies could not hold that line in the first weeks of war. As insurance against a successful German invasion, in the early 1930s the Rhineland zone was a fast-diminishing resource. The Maginot defences made sense as a replacement, with one crucial qualification. Since the Maginot line only covered the Franco-German frontier, it was essential that French and British forces could protect Belgium adequately in order to prevent a German descent on France from the north. This in turn demanded that the Belgians continue to trust in French military effectiveness. In 1936, this element of the Maginot strategy fell apart. Belgium became a neutral power and terminated its overt military co-operation with France.[26]

Apart from contributing to delays in French army modernization, the effect of the depression across Europe was dramatically illustrated by catastrophic increases in unemployment, the growth of political extremism in Germany and the final collapse of the reparations settlement. In September 1931 Britain enacted a severe devaluation and came off the gold standard. The resultant creation of a coalition National Government helped ensure the dominance of the Conservative Party in British politics for the rest of the inter-war period. The Conservatives were the driving force of the National Government. Their parliamentary dominance was not accurately reflected in the distribution of Cabinet seats between Tories, National Labourites and the leading figures of the Liberal Party factions. As National Government Prime Minister between 1931 and 1935, MacDonald did not have much of a parliamentary party behind him. As his deputy, the Conservative leader, Stanley Baldwin, headed the largest parliamentary party but was obliged to limit his claim to Cabinet posts in order to preserve the appearance of a coalition administration. Baldwin's closest Conservative lieutenant was Neville Chamberlain, Chancellor of the Exchequer between September 1931 and May 1937. Chamberlain initially built his domestic reputation, not upon foreign affairs, but upon his role as architect of Britain's gradual economic resurgence.[27]

## IV

The depression had a perverse effect upon Anglo-French relations. Although the strength of the franc and the size of its gold stock initially shielded France from economic collapse, the country plunged into deep recession in 1934. As Britain's industrial recovery gathered pace, the

French economy stagnated. By the time the Front populaire took office in May 1936, the financial and economic imbalance between the two countries was particularly marked. The time-lag between the British and French domestic economic crises made Britain's voice within the entente relationship stronger as the decade wore on. Furthermore, British foreign policy drew upon the financial might of the British Empire. This was the one respect in which Britain, though strategically over-extended and with minimal land forces, was none the less more formidable than Germany or Italy. If these states were to respect British naval power – and the ability to impose blockades that went with it – they had also to be convinced of Britain's ability to exploit its greater financial resources in order to win a long war.

There was thus a growing difference between French and British attempts to project their international power in the 1930s. From Moscow to Berlin, perceptions of French continental power rested upon the country's military capability. Reductions in the margin of French military superiority immediately compromised the projection of French strength in Germany or Italy. By 1934, however, Britain's influence in Europe derived less from armaments than from the regeneration of its economic and financial capacity. Britain was not a significant land power. Nor did it yet possess a powerful, modern air force. France's influence upon German policy-makers hinged upon its actual military power and alliance connections. British influence derived less from the turrets of its battleships than from its financial strength, and the greater defensive potential that this implied. Only with regard to Japan did British influence rest squarely upon a military deterrent – in this case the battleship task force that was the core of the Singapore strategy of Far Eastern reinforcement.

The discrepancy in British and French financial strength was reflected in the era of intensified rearmament in the later 1930s. For both countries, massive increases in defence spending were an enormous burden. But, insofar as the adoption of long-term re-equipment programmes were to have a deterrent effect, the British was the more successful, because there was less doubt that the country's economy could withstand it. Even so, this argument can be turned on its head. Numerous historians of British appeasement policy have stressed that the need to conserve Britain's financial strength set limits to defence expenditure. This made the adoption of a conciliatory foreign policy more likely. Impelled by Chamberlain, the British government also came to regard air force expansion as the most economical form of deterrence. There would be no expeditionary force remotely comparable to that of 1914, nor were there sufficient funds available to guarantee an impregnable defence of Empire.[28]

The rapid development of air power in the 1930s diminished the security afforded by fixed land defences. The British were not alone in supposing that the bomber would always get through. In 1934 the French aviation writer, René Chambre, painted a graphic, though not untypical, picture of aerial bombardment, 'We will not prevent the enemy from coming to bomb our towns. This idea must be understood. If the enemy wishes to pass, he will pass. He will drop on our cities tonnes of incendiary devices, toxic gases . . . or biological weapons. Nothing will stop him.'[29] But, unlike Britain, France did not give top priority to the expansion of its air force. French exposure to aerial attack was simply another worry to be placed alongside the fear of land invasion. Even the young strategic theorist, Colonel Charles de Gaulle, did not regard air power as a determining factor in a future Franco-German conflict.[30] For Britain, however, aerial bombardment destroyed the notion of an invulnerable island fortress protected by the Royal Navy. It was feared that massive bombing would so debilitate British cities, public morale and the British economy that the conservation of financial power in preparation for a long war would become irrelevant. Having opted for a strategy of aerial deterrence in 1934, by 1936 it was increasingly evident to the British government that this had not affected the German or Italian determination to build up offensive air forces.[31] By the time the Popular Front took office, Britain and France had not produced an effective defensive strategy against Germany.

The rearmament of the entente powers was induced by the failure of multilateral disarmament in 1934. Here too, the effort to limit German military strength promoted Anglo-French discord. Leader of the French Socialist Party, the Section française de l'internationale ouvrière (SFIO), Léon Blum was a passionate advocate of disarmament. Over the winter of 1930–1 alone, he wrote twenty-six articles devoted to the subject in his beloved Party newspaper, *Le Populaire*. After the final collapse of the Disarmament Conference in April 1934, Blum disparaged suggestions of a preventive war against Germany. Infused with the tradition of socialist internationalism, Blum insisted that renewed efforts be made to achieve a multilateral arms limitation accord.[32] Ironically, the withdrawal of Socialist Party backing for Edouard Herriot's centre–left coalition in December 1932 – six weeks before Hitler took office in Germany – ushered in a series of short-lived ministries less able to formulate a viable approach to the Geneva disarmament talks. Although the independent socialist, Joseph Paul-Boncour, dominated the Quai d'Orsay in 1933, and the great elder statesman, Louis Barthou, did so in 1934, French parliamentary politics was increasingly fractious.[33] More significant from the standpoint of entente relations, the Foreign Office identified Paul-Boncour with backstairs French diplomacy at Geneva.

Similarly, Barthou's determined quest for an eastern security pact caused alarm within Ramsay MacDonald's Cabinet. Like Paul-Boncour, Barthou was impossible to whip into line.

During the disarmament talks the onus was on France to offer a compromise formula reconciling French security requirements with Germany's claim to equal treatment among the Conference powers. Hence, it was always likely that France would be blamed for any failure of negotiations. This was unfair. Between 1932 and 1934, politicians as dissimilar as Paul-Boncour and the right-wing theorist, André Tardieu, offered ingenious and significant concessions in an effort to secure German acceptance of an arms limitation convention. In December 1932, the French had admitted the critical principle of equality of rights.[34] In consequence, the German delegation returned to the Conference talks in February 1933, having walked out three months earlier. Insurmountable problems remained. Already embarked upon their expansionist drive into mainland China, the Japanese did not conceal their contempt for disarmament. The German delegation manipulated whatever proposals Britain or France put forward, deliberately sowing entente division in the process. The British refused to contemplate a more solid guarantee of French security.[35] The diplomats of the Quai d'Orsay were increasingly adamant that such a guarantee was essential to offset the risk inherent in a disarmament pact which lacked watertight provision for control and inspection of German arms production. In hindsight, it seems that British readiness to blame France exclusively for the collapse of the Disarmament Conference was deeply unjust.[36]

The failure of the Disarmament Conference confirmed Barthou's intention to revert to the containment of Germany rather than waste time in an abortive appeasement effort. In October 1934 Barthou was assassinated in Marseilles during the state visit of the Yugoslav King Alexander. His death ensured that he would be remembered as the leading protagonist of an Eastern Pact, a defensive agreement designed to afford security to Germany's eastern neighbours on a basis of guarantees comparable to those provided by Locarno in the west. In fact, the idea of a multilateral eastern alliance linking Poland and the Soviet Union for the first time was originally discussed between Paul-Boncour and Soviet Foreign Minister Maxim Litvinov in October 1933. French Air Minister, and future Popular Front member, Pierre Cot, had alerted the French government to Soviet interest in such an agreement following an earlier visit to Moscow. Negotiations over a pact limped on into 1935. Barthou's successor, Pierre Laval, then abandoned the project, opting instead for the less ambitious, and ultimately hollow, Franco-Soviet Pact.[37]

In July 1934 Barthou had discussed his plans for an Eastern Pact with his opposite number, Sir John Simon, in London. The Foreign Office gave cautious support to Barthou's project. This was not because Simon or his advisers favoured an eastern alliance against Germany. Rather, the Foreign Office agreed to back the pact in exchange for additional French concessions over disarmament.[38] It was hoped that this would encourage Germany to reopen talks over arms limitation or, more precisely, the legalization of limited German rearmament. The British attempt to mould the Eastern Pact negotiations into a strategy of appeasement was hidden by the unbending German and Polish opposition to Barthou's diplomacy. The German government was never willing to sign a binding multilateral treaty covering eastern Europe. The Polish authorities were committed to the policy of equilibrium between Germany and the Soviet Union which was born of a diminishing faith in the effectiveness of the existing Franco-Polish alliance.[39]

While Barthou had pursued an Eastern Pact in 1934, the politics of the French left had altered dramatically. On 6 February 1934 infamous and bloody clashes took place outside the Assemblée Nationale between ultra-right members of the extra-parliamentary Leagues and demonstrators from the Parti Communiste Français (PCF). Fourteen demonstrators and one policeman were killed. Apart from precipitating the fall of Edouard Daladier's ten-day-old government, this incident encouraged a groundswell of support for unity among the rank and file of the French socialist and communist parties. Hitherto, the principal obstacle to any such left-wing coalition had been the PCF's adherence to the Comintern strategy which pitted 'class against class': proletarian communism against bourgeois parliamentary socialism. Between February and June 1934, pressure from the PCF membership and dissension within the Party's Central Committee – identified above all with the rogue figure of Jacques Doriot – was instrumental in persuading the Comintern leadership in Moscow to advocate a policy of united action against fascism. This was the core idea of Popular Frontism. By mid-June 1934 the SFIO had begun talks with their former PCF rivals. These discussions produced an agreement on 27 July. On the initiative of Party leader, Maurice Thorez, the communists were also willing to contemplate an electoral alliance with the Radical Party, a quite remarkable *volte face*.[40] Although second-ballot agreements among the left-wing parties produced impressive victories in the French municipal elections in May 1935, it was almost a full year before this collaboration bore fruit in a Popular Front government.[41] After the death of Barthou and the fall of Gaston Doumergue's ministry in November 1934, the intervening period of French foreign policy came to be identified with the figure of Pierre Laval.

# V

In 1935 several issues added to the resentments which marred Anglo-French relations. Firstly, the acrimony generated by the failure of disarmament in the previous year was fuelled by Britain's readiness to negotiate bilateral arms limitation agreements with Germany in response to Hitler's contravention of Part V of the Versailles Treaty. Having failed to make headway with an air limitation agreement over the spring, in June 1935, Britain signed a naval agreement with Germany. This accord conferred no immediate strategic benefit but it implicitly forgave Hitler's earlier abrogation of the Versailles disarmament restrictions. The second problem was Pierre Laval's worsening reputation within the British government. As French Foreign Minister, and later Premier, Laval appeared to object to Britain's bilateral advances to Germany more out of jealousy than moral indignation. As such, Laval was himself an obstacle to Anglo-French understanding. Few within the British Cabinet or the Foreign Office found a kind word to say of him. Many adopted a snobbish attitude to his humble origins and provincial manner. But none doubted his ingenuity.[42]

This brings us to the third point. In 1935, Laval's first diplomatic triumph was to secure a series of agreements with Mussolini while visiting Rome in January 1935. Although Britain and Italy were co-signatories of the Stresa accords in April 1935, the Cabinet feared that closer Franco-Italian relations would adversely affect the prospects for Anglo-German negotiations. The Stresa Front was a diplomatic paper-tiger. The supposed common front against German expansionism disintegrated within twelve months. But the development of Franco-Italian military co-operation promised real security gains for France. Germany was bound to object. Moreover, while the French War and Air Ministries looked upon Franco-Italian collaboration as an end in itself, Laval saw it as a means to open doors in Berlin.[43] In this sense, like his British counterparts, Laval favoured bilateral diplomacy.

The fourth element behind the Anglo-French *mésentente* in 1935 was, of course, the Italo-Ethiopian war. Historians have exhaustively studied the diplomatic consequences of this conflict, from its exposure of League of Nations inadequacy to the improvement in Italo-German relations which followed it. There is a consensus that the Abyssinian war damaged entente relations, and enhanced Neville Chamberlain's status as a British politician prepared to take unsavoury decisions in the teeth of French opposition.[44] While Chamberlain was decisive in bringing League sanctions upon Italy to an end in June 1936, British policy in the previous twelve months was ill-judged.

On 24 September 1935 Churchill's confidant, Leo Amery, summarized the problems of British policy towards the impending Abyssinian war. Amery recorded his impressions of a private chat with Foreign Secretary, Sir Samuel Hoare, who, on 11 September, had made a widely misunderstood speech at Geneva regarding the necessity of a collective League response to unprovoked aggression,

> His [Hoare's] whole line was that it was far too late to change the policy when he took office, that we have got to see through the attempt to make the Covenant work, that we might get out by the failure of others to support us, or alternatively, that Mussolini might find his difficulties too great for him, and under economic pressure come to reasonable terms soon after his war started, if not before. He refused to admit that ineffective economic sanctions must create the demand for effective ones and that these would bring us to the verge of war. Altogether his view struck me as dangerously fatalistic. We were committed to the current and perhaps there might not be a Niagara![45]

In the event, when Britain's sanctions policy tumbled over Niagara, France was accused of giving it the final push. Laval's ability to land Britain with primary responsibility for sanctions was never forgiven in London. Laval acted upon a continuous stream of advice from the French Ambassador in Rome, Charles de Chambrun, and his Chargé d'affaires, Jules Blondel. Both men insisted that a Franco-Italian détente could and should survive the Abyssinian emergency. The assurance of continued Italian goodwill would be hugely beneficial to French defensive planning.[46] Ironically, it was equally important to the British Chiefs of Staff to avoid antagonizing Italy needlessly. Although British victory in a bilateral Anglo-Italian conflict was not in doubt, the complications arising from possible German or Japanese involvement in any such war were profoundly shocking. From the perspective of the British service ministries, Britain's obligations to the League, and France's self-seeking behaviour during the Abyssinian crisis, had made the three power threat all too real.[47] As during the Disarmament Conference, British soldiers and diplomats tended to blame France for the intransigence of the dictators. It was against this background of Anglo-French discord that Hitler resolved to send troops into the Rhineland.

# Notes

1. David French, *British Strategy and War Aims, 1914–1916*, London, 1986, pp. 245–7; David Stevenson, *French War Aims against Germany, 1914–1919*, Oxford, 1982, pp. 37–49.
2. Regarding the mutinies, see Leonard V. Smith, '"War and Politics": The French Army Mutinies of 1917', *War in History*, 2, 1995, pp. 180–201.
3. Martin Horn, 'External Finance in Anglo-French Relations in the First World War, 1914–1917', *IHR*, 17, 1, 1995, pp. 56–68.
4. Eden was awarded the Military Cross for valour but lost two brothers in the war, the youngest, Nicholas, aged only 16, see David Carlton, *Anthony Eden: A Biography*, London, 1981, pp. 12–13; Victor Rothwell, *Anthony Eden: A Political Biography 1931–57*, Manchester, 1992, p. 8; Halifax served with the King's Own Yorkshire Dragoons, see Andrew Roberts, *The 'Holy Fox': A Biography of Lord Halifax*, London, 1991, p. 11; Elisabeth du Réau, *Edouard Daladier 1884–1970*, Paris, 1993, pp. 28–33.
5. For surveys of British and French pacifism, see Martin Caedel, *Pacifism in Britain, 1914–1945: The Defining of a Faith*, Oxford, 1980; Norman Ingram, *The Politics of Dissent: Pacifism in France 1919–1939*, Oxford, 1991.
6. Keith A. Hamilton, 'A Question of Status: British Diplomats and the Uses and Abuses of French', *Historical Research*, LX, 1987, p. 125.
7. Erik Goldstein, *Winning the Peace: British Diplomatic Strategy, Peace Planning and the Paris Peace Conference, 1916–1920*, Oxford, 1991, pp. 280–3; Georges-Henri Soutou, 'L'Allemagne et la France en 1919', in Jacques Bariéty *et al.*, *La France et l'Allemagne entre deux guerres mondiales*, Nancy, 1987, pp. 9–10.
8. Bruce Kent, *The Spoils of War: The Politics, Economics and Diplomacy of Reparations, 1918–1932*, Oxford, 1989, p. 373. Regarding reparations, see Alan Sharp, *The Versailles Settlement: Peacemaking in Paris, 1919*, London, 1991, pp. 78–84.
9. Anne Orde, 'Britain and European Reconstruction after the Great War', in Peter Catterall and C.J. Morris (eds), *Britain and the Threat to Stability in Europe, 1918–1945*, Leicester, 1993, pp. 8–9.
10. Paul Guinn, 'On Throwing Ballast in Foreign Policy: Poincaré, the Entente and the Ruhr Occupation', *EHQ*, 18, 1988, pp. 427–37; Walter A. McDougall, *France's Rhineland Diplomacy, 1914–1924. The Last Bid for a Balance of Power in Europe*, Princeton, 1978, pp. 140–4, 183–90.
11. SAEF, carton B.32057/Dossier Tchécoslovaquie, Direction du Trésor, no. 2281, Quai Relations Commerciales memo, 'Participation du

capital étranger dans les établissements de crédit Tchécoslovaque',
26 July 1929.

12. Arthur Turner, 'Anglo-French Financial Relations in the 1920s',
*EHQ*, 26, 1996, pp. 31–56. See also Kenneth Mouré, 'The Limits
to Central Bank Co-operation, 1916–36', *CEH*, I, 1992, pp. 267–73.

13. Kenneth Mouré, *Managing the Franc Poincaré: Economic Understanding and Political Constraint in French Monetary Policy,
1928–1936*, Cambridge, 1991, pp. 4–7, 49–53.

14. PRO, Sir Richard Hopkins papers, T175/55, Leith-Ross note of
interview with Rueff, 2 Dec. 1931.

15. PRO, Treasury finance division files, T160/860/F14923/1, draft
Treasury report to IIC, 6 April 1936.

16. Christopher M. Andrew and A.S. Kanya-Forstner, *France Overseas: The Great War and the Climax of French Imperial Expansion*,
London, 1981, pp. 205–8, 223–6; G.H. Bennett, 'Britain's Relations
with France after Versailles: The Problem of Tangier, 1919–23',
*EHQ*, 24, 1994, pp. 53–84; E.P. Fitzgerald, 'France's Middle Eastern Ambitions, the Sykes–Picot Negotiations, and the Oil Fields of
Mosul, 1915–1918', *JMH*, 66, 1994, pp. 697–725.

17. SHAT, 7N2812/AM, assistant military attaché, Colonel Cuny,
memo, 'Le Réarmement de l'Armée Britannique en 1936', 15 Jan.
1937.

18. MAE, série Z, Europe 1930–1940, file Tchécoslovaquie 148, 'Note
sur la Petite Entente', 29 June 1935; Piotr Wandycz, 'The Little
Entente: Sixty Years Later', *Slavonic and East European Review*,
59, 1981, pp. 552–6.

19. Neither the 1926 Franco-Romanian treaty nor the 1927 Franco-
Yugoslav treaty contained military conventions. For comprehensive
treatments of French alliance diplomacy in the 1920s, see Nicole
Jordan, *The Popular Front and Central Europe: The Dilemmas of
French Impotence, 1918–1940*, Cambridge, 1992, pp. 5–17, and the
two complementary volumes by Piotr Wandycz: *France and her
Eastern Alliances, 1919–1925*, Minneapolis, 1962 and *The Twilight
of France's Eastern Alliances 1926–1936. French–Czechoslovak–
Polish Relations from Locarno to the Remilitarisation of the
Rhineland*, Princeton, 1988. For the alliance origins, see Kalervo
Hovi, *Cordon sanitaire or Barrière de l'est? The Emergence of the
New French Eastern European Alliance Policy 1917–1919*, Turku,
1975, *Alliances de revers: Stabilization of France's Alliance Pol-
icies in East Central Europe 1919–1921*, Turku, 1984.

20. George Sakwa, 'The Franco-Polish Alliance and the Remilitarization of the Rhineland', *HJ*, 16, 1973, pp. 128–9; Georges
Soutou, 'L'alliance franco-polonaise (1925–1933) ou comment s'en

débarrasser?', *Revue d'histoire diplomatique*, 2, 1981, pp. 295–348; for Weygand's comment see SHAT, carton 4N93/dossier 1, Weygand letter to unnamed researcher, 21 May 1955.

21. MAE, Pologne 318, no. 3, Laroche to Philippe Berthelot, 13 Jan. 1932; no. 31, Laval to Tardieu, 25 Jan. 1932.

22. SAEF, B.32904, Direction du Trésor, Pologne, 'Emprunt du Gouvernement Polonais', 21 Oct. 1930, note by Maxime Robert, 18 Dec. 1930.

23. Manfred J. Enssle, 'Stresemann's diplomacy fifty years after Locarno: Some recent perspectives', *HJ*, 20, 4, 1977, p. 942.

24. Jonathan Wright, 'Stresemann and Locarno', *CEH*, 4, 2, 1995, pp. 109–31.

25. Jean-Marie d'Hoop, 'Le Problème du réarmement français jusqu'à Mars 1936', in Henri Michel (ed.), *La France et l'Allemagne 1932–1936*, Paris, 1980, p. 85.

26. SHAT, 7N2370/D1, General Riedinger report to Etat-Major de l'Armée deuxième bureau (EMA-2), 5 March 1936; Martin S. Alexander, *The Republic in Danger. General Maurice Gamelin and the Politics of French Defence, 1933–1940*, Cambridge, 1992, pp. 179–83.

27. R.A.C. Parker, *Chamberlain and Appeasement. British Policy and the Coming of the Second World War*, London, 1993, p. 9.

28. See, for example, R.P. Shay, *British Rearmament in the Thirties. Politics and Profits*, Princeton, 1977; George C. Peden, *British Rearmament and the Treasury, 1932–1939*, Edinburgh, 1979; Paul Haggie, *Britannia at Bay: The Defence of the British Empire against Japan, 1931–1941*, Oxford, 1981; Parker, *Chamberlain*; Malcolm S. Smith, 'Rearmament and Deterrence in the 1930s', *JSS*, 1, 3, 1978, pp. 313–37.

29. Quoted in d'Hoop, 'Le problème du réarmement français', p. 77.

30. Pascal Vennesson, 'Institution and Airpower: The Making of the French Air Force', *JSS*, 18, 1, 1995, pp. 45–6.

31. Uri Bialer, 'Elite Opinion and Defence Policy: Air Power Advocacy and British Rearmament during the 1930s', *British Journal of International Studies*, 6, 1980, pp. 32–51.

32. Jacques Bariéty, 'Léon Blum et l'Allemagne 1930–1938', in F.G. Dreyfus (ed.), *Les Relations Franco-Allemandes 1933–1939*, Paris, 1976, pp. 34–40.

33. Jacques Bariéty, 'Les Partisans français de l'entente franco-allemande et la "prise du pouvoir" par Hitler Avril 1932–Avril 1934', in Bariéty *et al.*, *La France et l'Allemagne entre les deux guerres mondiales*, p. 25.

34. Documents Diplomatiques Français, edited by P. Renouvin *et al.*,

Paris, Imprimerie nationale, 1963 *et seq* (hereafter DDF), 1st series, volume II, nos. 80, 81, 82, compte-rendus, Geneva conversations, 8 Dec. 1932.

35. DDF, 1, II, nos. 412, 418, compte-rendus, 15 and 16 March 1933.
36. MAE, Archives Privées, Papiers Massigli 10, 'Note pour le Ministre', 23 Jan. 1935. For a rounded defence of French actions, see Maurice Vaïsse, *Sécurité d'abord: la politique française en matière de désarmement*, Paris, 1981; Dick Richardson, 'The Geneva Disarmament Conference, 1932–34', in Dick Richardson and Glyn Stone (eds), *Decisions and Diplomacy*, London, 1994, pp. 60–82.
37. Lisanne Radice, 'The Eastern Pact, 1933–1935: A Last Attempt at European Co-operation', *Slavonic and East European Review*, 1, 1977, pp. 45–64.
38. DDF, 1, VII, Addendum, annexes i–iii, record of Anglo-French discussions, 9–10 July 1934.
39. Radice, 'The Eastern Pact', pp. 50–1; Jean-Baptiste Duroselle, *La Décadence 1932–1939*, Paris, 1979, pp. 107–10; Nicholas Rostow, *Anglo-French Relations, 1934–36*, London, 1984, pp. 21–8, 58.
40. For PCF influence upon the Comintern, see Jonathan Haslam, 'The Comintern and the Origins of the Popular Front 1934–1935', *HJ*, 22, 3, 1979, pp. 678–82; John Santore, 'The Comintern's United Front Initiative of May 1934: French or Soviet Inspiration?', *Canadian Journal of History*, 16, 1981, pp. 413–21; Julian Jackson, *The Popular Front in France: Defending Democracy, 1934–38*, Cambridge, 1988, pp. 22–36.
41. Jackson, *Popular Front*, p. 39.
42. PRO, Foreign Office Private Papers – Sir Samuel Hoare correspondence, FO 800/275, Hoare letter to Ralph Wigram, 14 Sept. 1935.
43. MAE, Papiers Joseph Avenol, vol. 29, 'Le rapprochement franco-italien et le voyage de M. Laval', 22 Nov. 1934.
44. Geoffrey Warner, *Pierre Laval and the Eclipse of France*, London, 1968, pp. 93–131; R.A.C. Parker, 'Great Britain, France and the Ethiopian Crisis, 1935–1936', *EHR*, 89, 1974, pp. 269–97; Rostow, *Anglo-French Relations*, pp. 214–32; Jean-Paul Cointet, *Pierre Laval*, Paris, 1989, pp. 190–7.
45. John Barnes and David Nicholson (eds), *The Empire at Bay. The Leo Amery Diaries 1929–1945*, London, 1988, p. 398.
46. As examples, see MAE, Italie 302, no. 3, Blondel to Laval, 10 Jan. 1936; no. 17, Blondel to Laval, 20 Jan. 1936; Robert J. Young, 'French Military Intelligence and the Franco-Italian Alliance, 1933–1939', *HJ*, 28, 1, 1985, pp. 150–63.
47. PRO, Admiralty Mediterranean Station files, ADM 116/3476, History of the Italo-Abyssinian Emergency, 20 Dec. 1937.

# –2–

# Anglo-French Relations in the Aftermath of the Rhineland Crisis, March–May 1936

From its demilitarization under articles 42 and 43 of the Treaty of Versailles, throughout the inter-war years the Rhineland zone was a focal point not only of Franco-German, but also of Anglo-French tension.[1] Conventional wisdom within the Whitehall service ministries held that France was apt to exaggerate the security afforded by the existence of a narrow buffer zone on the Franco-German border which could be easily traversed by motorized columns, and swiftly overflown by any reconstituted German air force. This assertion in turn led the French to complain at British perfidy. If, as Britain suggested, a demilitarized Rhineland contributed so little to western European security, the operation of the 1925 Locarno Treaty, by which Britain was obliged to defend France against unprovoked German attack, should be made automatic – the better to guarantee France's Rhine frontier. Recrimination of this kind was pointless. In January 1935 René Massigli, Assistant Director of the Quai d'Orsay's direction des affaires politiques, warned Foreign Minister, Pierre Laval, not to press the British in this manner. Massigli was well aware of the inconsistencies within Britain's Locarno guarantee. It had committed the British to defend both the French eastern, and the German western, frontiers. But the guarantee had not specified exactly how this was to be done. Massigli noted, 'There is no place for surprise over these gaps: the English dislike any precision and, besides, the bilateral character of Britain's Rhine guarantee in 1925 obliged us to content ourselves with a generalistic formula.'[2]

In January 1936, Pierre Laval resigned from office. His efforts to find a basis for bilateral discussions with Berlin had failed. The Franco-Italian détente built up over 1935 was being pushed to breaking point by the stresses of the Abyssinian crisis. This directed Albert Sarraut's caretaker administration to the imperative of a western European defensive alliance to replace the weaker bonds of the entente. This was brought into sharper relief by Germany's reoccupation of the Rhineland bridgeheads on 7 March.

One might be forgiven for thinking that the Rhineland remilitarization would increase British concern for French security. French territorial integrity was a vital British interest. But a military obligation, involving the dispatch of an expeditionary force to north-west Europe, ran contrary to Britain's self-appointed mediatory position in European affairs. During the 1930s the National Governments worked to a simple three-stage calculation. Alliance with France would preclude meaningful negotiation with Germany. Alliance would also compound French inflexibility, increasing the likelihood of Nazi aggression. Finally, an Anglo-French alliance would give British sanction to a French security policy considered fundamentally defective. Britain would become the agent of an encirclement strategy lacking the necessary strategic coherence to work as an effective deterrent to German expansionism. Superficially, the prospects for an improvement in Anglo-French relations did not look good.

# I

On 19 March, twelve days after the Rhineland remilitarization, Stanley Baldwin's government reiterated Britain's formal commitment to the defence of French and Belgian territory against unprovoked aggression. This signalled that, while Germany's actions had made a mockery of the Versailles and Locarno provisions, the British government was none the less determined to uphold the security arrangements of the latter at least. Though the British pledge added nothing new to Britain's existing engagements, it was ostensibly reinforced by the acceptance of Franco-Belgian requests for staff conversations. These were held in London in mid-April.

The chiefs of staff sub-committee of the Committee of Imperial Defence (CID), the executive arm of civil–military relations within Whitehall, recognized the permanence of this concession. Talks would breed talks, albeit with a tightly confined agenda. The British service chiefs were bound to refer technical questions for consideration by a plethora of sub-committees.[3] In February, General Robert Voruz, French Military Attaché in London, informed the War Ministry's intelligence section, the deuxième bureau, of the CID's liking for sub-committees and meetings. He pointed out that the CID in all its sub-committee guises had held 880 meetings since 1931.[4] The French service establishment saw the opportunity to widen the net of Anglo-French technical exchanges by stealth rather than by means of a formal agreement.

On the surface, the first Anglo-French discussions were anodyne. The April conversations were strictly limited to exchanges of information regarding forces available to repel a German offensive in the west. This was supplemented by a cursory survey of the facilities required to implement co-operation, something of a short-term irrelevance a full month after Germany's first incursion into the Rhineland zone.[5] The most tangible result of the naval discussions, for instance, was an agreement to extend existing exchanges of technical information on Mediterranean deployments to cover forces deployed in the western Atlantic.[6] As the CID Secretary, Sir Maurice Hankey, commented, 'The military "Conversations" were merely a makeweight thrown in to ease matters for the French.'[7]

The talks also eased matters for London by appearing to meet French Foreign Minister, Pierre-Étienne Flandin, on the most pressing of his short-term demands.[8] Staffs conversations had taken place, but Hitler had not been needlessly alienated. By limiting the scope of Anglo-French discussion, the service chiefs had overcome Baldwin's complaint to the Cabinet on 11 March that French insistence on joint action would expose the actual inadequacy of British armaments. If Britain's military weakness were revealed, then the Cabinet's reluctance to consider military sanctions against Germany would be read as a measure of frailty and nothing more. The Cabinet had wanted British passivity to be seen in Germany as proof of Britain's steadfast goodwill.[9] Foreign Secretary Anthony Eden's summary of the French position had alarmed Baldwin. On 8 March, Eden reported that between the alternatives of a forcible eviction of German forces or the renewal of dialogue with Berlin, Sarraut's ministers were likely to opt for 'a policy of sulking and passive obstruction'. It was the British government's task to dissuade them from this.[10]

Eden's line illustrated that the British reaction to a likely Rhineland remilitarization had been determined well in advance of 7 March 1936. At the funeral ceremony for King George V in late January, Eden had let slip to Soviet Foreign Minister Maxim Litvinov that Britain was not capable of a decisive military intervention to safeguard the Rhineland.[11] On 24 February, the Foreign Secretary derided Flandin's insistence that remilitarization should be treated as a *casus foederis*. Instead, Eden recommended to the newly established Cabinet committee on Germany that the Foreign Office be allowed to take up Sir Samuel Hoare's earlier plans for an international enquiry into the terms of trade in raw materials. This might provide a means to initiate bilateral discussions with Berlin.[12] To involve France would diminish Britain's room for manœuvre, and inevitably lead to press leakage. Furthermore, in his first meeting as Foreign Minister with Eden and Chamberlain in January 1936, Flandin conceded that Sarraut's interim administration could not risk an approach to Hitler until the French deficit was brought under control, and the French rearmament position improved.[13]

The Cabinet agreed on 5 March that Britain would not take a rigid view of any violation of Locarno. Nor would it demand that Mussolini shoulder a military obligation to assist France commensurate with Italy's place as co-guarantor of the 1925 treaty.[14] This circumvented Flandin's efforts to trade a fresh British commitment to the defence of the Rhineland in return for French compliance with an oil sanction upon Italy. Much to British discomfort, this proposal was repeatedly considered by both the League of Nations' Assembly and Council as the war in Abyssinia neared its dénouement.[15]

To pre-empt a German seizure, the British Cabinet preferred a little trading of their own – the Rhineland should be bartered 'for what it will fetch', perhaps a western European air pact restricting the construction of heavy bombers.[16] This proposal built upon discussions in mid-February between Ralph Wigram, head of the Foreign Office central department, and the German embassy Counsellor, Prince Bismarck. By 15 February, the German Foreign Minister, Constantin Freiherr von Neurath, was confident that the British would lead France into negotiation over the Rhineland in return for the elusive air-limitation agreement with Germany.[17]

Since the abortive Anglo-French talks in London in February 1935, an air pact was seen by the British government as the most promising route into more general negotiations with Hitler.[18] Yet on 2 March, the Foreign Office and the Air Ministry independently advised the Cabinet committee on Germany that a multilateral air limitation agreement had become unattainable. This was blamed on France. In November 1935, the inter-service Haut Comité Militaire (HCM) had agreed that all discussion of an air pact should be shunned until the Laval government's temporary 'pause' in its release of rearmament funding had been nullified by the approval of military budgets in the new year.[19] In 1935 the HCM was more interested in a different sort of air pact: a mutual assistance agreement with Italy under which French and Italian bomber squadrons would operate from one another's territory and the burdens of fighter defence would be shared.[20]

## II

Clearly the British government was not well disposed to France on the eve of the Rhineland crisis. Flandin was accused of horse trading over sanctions at Geneva. His guilt was presumed because of Laval's dallying with the Italians over the previous year.[21] On the other hand, Flandin drew upon Ambassador Charles Corbin's advice that the inexperienced Eden was anxious to take the moral high ground. According to Corbin, Eden worked closely with his 'young entourage' – a reference to his

Private Secretary, Oliver Harvey, and the Under-Secretary of State, Lord Cranborne. In Corbin's view, these were advisers 'imbued with theories but lacking practical knowledge'.[22]

In British eyes, the vagaries of the French deficit had forced the French high command into an unreasonable reluctance to contemplate a resumption of talks for an air pact. This was irritating. But it was not the potential disaster that seemed inherent in the Sarraut government's determination to put forward the May 1935 Franco-Soviet pact for ratification by the Chamber of Deputies. Seen from London, French ratification of the Soviet pact would offer Hitler an ideal pretext to reject Britain's diplomatic sweeteners before staging his Rhineland coup. There was also a measure of British sympathy for the German Foreign Ministry's argument that ratification of the Franco-Soviet pact would necessarily mean that Russian air strength should be included in any future calculations of air-force disarmament. This was bound to increase Germany's preferred upper limit for bomber construction. In December 1935, exploiting British Air Ministry unease, Hitler had offered a bilateral exchange of secret information on air-force strengths with London, provided that all information thus revealed be strictly withheld from Paris.[23] Unfortunately from the British viewpoint, another bilateral disarmament agreement, hot on the heels of the June 1935 Anglo-German naval agreement, was impermissible. But this consideration did not prevent another surge of resentment against France within the British service ministries and the meeting rooms of the CID sub-committees.[24]

British anxiety over the impending ratification of the Franco-Soviet accord was shared in Paris by the chief of general staff, General Maurice Gamelin, and chief of army staff, General Louis Colson. Both men unsuccessfully lobbied Flandin's Quai d'Orsay in an effort to secure a referral of the French right to ratify the pact to the International Court of the Hague or to the League of Nations Council. This was less to obtain judgement than to delay ratification by judicial pretext.[25]

Having intended to use the Rhineland zone as the prize by which to draw Hitler into talks, the British government was keen to pursue the German proposals that accompanied remilitarization. The surprisingly rapid conclusion of the naval agreement in June 1935 added to the attractions of direct dialogue, preferably outside the restrictive framework of the League covenant. Unlike the naval agreement, this time any talks would have to be conducted with prior French consent. The effort to win this consent made Sarraut's government the focus of British attention. Flandin exploited this situation adroitly. The French Foreign Minister held a key advantage over his predecessor, Laval. In addition to laying Versailles to rest, Hitler had now openly violated Locarno, a freely signed treaty. To expect French acquiescence in a dialogue with

Berlin merited a substantial *quid pro quo*. Even the unflappable Foreign Office central department appeared star-struck by Hitler's sudden readiness to talk after months of ominous German silence since the beginning of the Ethiopian war in October. Corbin surmised that all the policy options under review in Whitehall after 7 March posited continued talks with Berlin.[26]

Flandin also capitalized upon British indecision over the most urgent short-term issue in the week following 7 March – a possible temporary withdrawal of German and Franco-Belgian forces from both sides of the Rhineland zone.[27] On 10 March, the three western Locarno powers held their first meeting since the remilitarization. Flandin, backed by the Belgian Foreign Minister Paul-Henri Spaak, duped Eden and his temporary associate, Lord Halifax, then Lord Privy Seal, into believing that the French Cabinet were still contemplating a military riposte to evict German forces. Flandin was not inclined to be friendly. He was convinced that Baldwin had issued Eden with precise instructions to obstruct any French proposals.[28] Neither Eden nor Halifax saw through the sham of apparent Franco-Belgian unity. Yet there were strong indications that Paris and Brussels did not see eye to eye. On 27 February the Belgian Chamber of Deputies rejected the so-called Devèze project, named after the Minister of Defence in Paul van Zeeland's government. In order to secure the passage of Albert Devèze's proposed modifications to the recruitment and terms of service of the Belgian militia, the van Zeeland government felt bound to offer proofs that Belgian military planning was not beholden to France. This meant the sacrifice of the 1920 Franco-Belgian military accord, the basis for the common planning of French 'forward defence' against Germany. Although eventually passed, the Devèze project only covered an interim period pending the conclusion of a new army statute, itself under scrutiny by a parliamentary commission. The seeds of Belgium's disastrous declaration of neutrality in October 1936 were already in bud in the spring.[29]

The Sarraut government could not risk military sanctions against Germany. Anticipating German resistance, the French army lacked the mobile forces immediately capable of mounting a counter-offensive in order to regain the Rhineland. By contrast, the War Ministry was particularly struck by Germany's equipment of three armoured divisions and the quality of its new field artillery. Though the HCM was determined to meet this challenge, notably through the re-equipment of the army's General Reserve with a minimum of fifteen tank battalions, it was in no position to do so in early 1936.[30] Gamelin and Colonel Maurice Gauché, head of the deuxième bureau, were painfully aware of French military shortcomings. They were inclined to exaggerate German strength by tallying units in the process of formation as if on the active list. Air Ministry intelligence also tended to exaggerate German strength, notably with regard to the productive capacity of the Reich's key aircraft manufacturers.[31] On balance though, the French government possessed sound information on the escalation of rearmament, the trends in German military planning, and the numerous indications of a formal occupation of the zone. This came from several sources: from the War and Air Ministry intelligence services, from General Georges Renondeau, Military Attaché in Berlin, and from several French consuls in western Germany and Switzerland.[32]

None the less, it took Flandin several pleading letters, sent at Sarraut's behest, to cajole the service chiefs into providing technical briefs on France's immediate military options.[33] The significance of this should not be exaggerated. War Minister General Louis Maurin, though deeply unenthusiastic about a riposte, had not been inactive. He did evaluate the military alternatives of a reoccupation of the left bank of the Rhine or a pre-emptive seizure of Luxembourg. These options were presented to him by Gamelin's deputy, General Alphonse Georges.[34] There were powerful inducements for Maurin to confirm his military colleagues' rejection of any recourse to force. Among these were the inevitable sluggishness of France's five-stage mobilization programme, Plan D-bis, in which the role of the armée de l'air remained undecided, the high estimates of German troop strength and the problems inherent in a violation of Luxembourg's sovereignty.[35]

Historical debate on the true French military position in March 1936 has understandably focused on the War Ministry and the army.[36] A sideways glance at the Ministry of Marine and the Air Ministry reveals a similar picture. The German high seas fleet was still relatively small. Yet the Ministry of Marine's deuxième bureau warned that Germany posed a pressing naval threat. Their best evidence of this was that *Kriegsmarine* ratings were being scrupulously trained in offensive tactics.[37] On 12 March, the Etat-Major de la Marine (EMM) operations section advised that, beyond the seizure of merchant shipping in French ports, no naval sanctions against Germany were viable without couverture-stage mobilization of France's Atlantic coastal defences. This alone would necessitate the call-up of 30,000 reservists. It would still leave the marine without offensive options. Germany's twenty active submarines, its bomber strength and its well-defended estuarine ports allegedly precluded a French first strike.[38]

Within the French Air Ministry in the Boulevard Victor, on 10 March, General Paul Dumanois, Inspector General of metropolitan air defence, requested full information from all home-based squadrons regarding the aircraft ready for service. Of a theoretical medium bomber strike force of 205 aircraft, only 95 were immediately available. Insufficient reserves and spare parts shortages ruled out the repeated use of even these planes. Casting their eyes over the March 1936 position, the Boulevard Victor's deuxième bureau concluded in May 1936 that, had the French bomber 'fleet' been called into action, less than half of the first-line bombers could have been employed. Almost all of these could only be used in night raids as inadequacies of speed or armament precluded daylight sorties.[39]

If the service ministries reached similarly pessimistic conclusions regarding French prospects for action, Flandin received a more varied cocktail of advice within the Quai d'Orsay. As was so often to be the case, the views of the Secretary General, Alexis Léger, and his close associate, René Massigli, stood out. Léger initially suggested firmness. He cited the widespread rumour that Hitler had ignored his War Minister, General von Blomberg's reservations over the planned timing of the reoccupation.[40] Massigli was more cautious than Léger. Pre-occupied with the strategic ramifications of the loss of the demilitarized zone upon the effective operation of the French eastern alliance system, Massigli was convinced that remilitarization confirmed the importance of a clearer British military commitment to France.[41]

Neither Léger nor Massigli could hope to co-ordinate the vast array of incoming material from embassies and attachés. Despite the hierarchical restructuring of the Quai's services généraux by a decree of June 1934, incoming information from embassies was not first summarized by the ambassador in question. This was the British practice, and it was fundamental to the efficiency of the Foreign Office's regional departments.[42] The Quai had consciously copied the British model in reorganizing its services extérieurs into geo-political zones akin to Foreign Office departments. Yet Flandin still received reports from ambassadors acting more as individuals than as the representatives of a coherent embassy structure. The Foreign Ministry's information and press service (service d'information et de presse) did co-ordinate incoming material and provide summative reports. But the service d'information lacked influence. Nor did it have the regional focus of the Quai's political affairs departments (directions des affaires politiques). Unlike the Ministry of Colonies, whose direction des affaires politiques provided quarterly reports on the condition of the French Empire as a whole, the Quai did not, as a matter of course, prepare regular memoranda on events across a particular region, eastern Europe for example. In short, while the Foreign Ministry had a mass of information about the European reaction to the Rhineland reoccupation, it did not have the means to refine it quickly into policy advice.[43]

In the event, declarations of support for France from Moscow,

Warsaw and the capitals of both the Little and Balkan Entente states were not immediately acknowledged. Given the signs of Polish, Yugoslav and Romanian governmental division regarding the degree to which a firm French response should be supported, the Quai's tardy reaction is unsurprising. Massigli was clearly aware that ill-judged replies might strengthen the hand of the francophobic elements in the allied capitals.[44] It is fair to assume that Flandin too saw little reason for haste, given the nature of the diplomatic game he was playing with the British.

Maurin's War Ministry offered the eastern allies a more immediate clarification of the French view. A week after the German action, Gamelin invited the Military Attachés of the Little Entente and Poland to the rue Saint Dominique. He warned them quite candidly that the erection of German fortifications in the Rhineland zone would constitute as much of a threat to eastern Europe as to France. Remilitarization was bound to impede the development of inter-allied operations based upon a French move into the Rhineland. Indeed, Germany's action added to the importance of a resolution of Polish–Czechoslovak differences in order that the two states could construct a more viable eastern defensive front.[45] The Czechs were subsequently given precise information regarding the French army's deployments to meet the Rhineland crisis. This was preparatory to Franco-Czech staff conversations in mid-April.[46] These military talks did little to make up for the enormous strategic reverse inherent in the German reoccupation of the Rhineland zone.

Although in the days following 7 March Gamelin was more forthcoming than Flandin with the eastern allies, it would be wrong to suggest that the Quai d'Orsay was deliberately inactive. Prior to the remilitarization, the Foreign Minister had discussed possible courses of action in several exchanges with his Polish counterpart, Colonel Jósef Beck, and with the Polish Ambassador to Paris, Alfred Chlapowski. On 17 February Flandin attempted unsuccessfully to coerce the Poles into an unequivocal pledge to mobilize alongside France, should remilitarization take place. Beck was aware of Flandin's overriding preoccupation with the likely British attitude. His conditional support for France on 7 March was only to be expected. Beck informed the French Ambassador, Léon Noël, that while Poland would stand by its alliance obligation to France, it did not consider the reoccupation of the Rhineland a *casus foederis* justifying a military riposte. The Polish press, above all the quasi-official *Gazeta Polska*, had, after all, been uniformly hostile to the French ratification of the Franco-Soviet pact. Once it was clear that France would not in fact march, the Polish Foreign Minister assured Léon Noël that Poland was prepared to do so.[47]

Beck's unusual solicitude was largely explained by the tempting prospect of French war material being supplied to the Polish forces. After the chief of general staff, General Waclaw Stachiewicz, put forward the initial Polish request in October 1935, this idea had been canvassed by Flandin and the rue Saint Dominique.[48] General Charles d'Arbonneau, the Warsaw Military Attaché, discussed the matter further in early 1936 with Stachiewicz and General Kazimierz Sosnkowski, the army Inspector General. On 4 March General Maurin advised him that the French government was ready to proceed with negotiations for a rearmament credit and a separate Polish defence loan. D'Arbonneau had suggested that Warsaw was likely to request up to 500 million francs.[49] Hardly surprising then that Beck seized upon the remilitarization to stress Polish fidelity to France. This was itself a means to induce the Sarraut Cabinet to revise the Franco-Polish alliance, making the provision of mutual assistance automatic once an act of aggression occurred.[50] Beck's flamboyant loyalism was also designed to weaken French insistence upon a linkage between financial support for Polish rearmament and an improvement in Polish–Czech relations.

Whatever the suggestions that France should remain firm, there is little doubt that neither Flandin nor Sarraut wished either to dispute service ministry advice or to act contrary to the majority sentiment in the Conseil des Ministres. In Conseil discussions, only the Minister of Communications, Georges Mandel, and the Minister of State, Joseph Paul-Boncour, appear to have favoured the use of force. On 27 February the Conseil effectively precluded unilateral military action anyway.[51] With Britain refusing to take a lead, there is little doubt that this decision remained in effect once the remilitarization got underway. Lacking a French Cabinet Secretariat and hence Conseil minutes, historians have been left to weigh up the inconsistencies of the various memoirs available.

As Stephen Schuker has pointed out, the summary provided by Air Minister, Marcel Déat, stands alone in having been written before the war. Despite Déat's later controversial actions as a member of the Milice under Vichy, his recollections as a junior minister in 1936 are well balanced. According to Schuker, Déat portrayed a government conscious of forthcoming elections, understandably reluctant to risk general war and determined that France should not act alone. In consequence, the French Cabinet succumbed to virtual inertia.[52] Ironically, this promoted a genuine ministerial consensus that Flandin should concentrate upon extracting fresh guarantees from Britain. This added to the Foreign Minister's determination to make the best of Britain's need for French co-operation. France's economic weakness also set limits to its foreign policy. Passage of the budget for 1936 on 1 January had been secured by a sweeping 7 billion franc cut in expenditure and the creation of a separate extraordinary budget to meet the Treasury's short-term deficit.[53] The Bank of France had lost some 5.7 billion francs in gold since the Chamber of Deputies finance commission savaged Prime Minister Laval's economy measures in November 1935. As Kenneth Mouré has shown, by 1 May 1936 the gold reserve at the Bank of France had fallen by 20 billion francs over the preceding year. Prior to the remilitarization, the Sarraut government finalized terms for a British £40 million loan. The funds were raised cheaply on the London market, and were intended to tide over the caretaker administration's capital outlay in the months before the May election.[54] The British sterling loan was quickly exhausted. But it had served a purpose. The loan had guaranteed interim funding to Sarraut's caretaker government before Sarraut passed on France's enormous financial problems to his successor.

On 30 January Flandin had raised the question of a loan with the Chancellor of the Exchequer, Neville Chamberlain. The loan issue was subsequently approved without condition, despite the Admiralty's efforts to link British largesse to French signature of the second London naval treaty.[55] Chamberlain considered that the loan levelled the playing-field after French provision of loan capital to the National Government in September 1931 at the height of the sterling crisis. Ironically, in late January, Gamelin had urged Flandin to bargain acceptance of the naval treaty for a firm pledge of British support should Germany reoccupy the Rhineland. The Sarraut government enjoyed a brief access of confidence once the loan appeared secure in February. The Bank of France discount rate was lowered from 4 to 3.5 per cent. Two state loans covering the postal and railway services were issued, though with limited success. In the eyes of the British Treasury, on the eve of the Rhineland crisis French financial circles, though hardly optimistic, at least had one or two crumbs of comfort.[56]

Remilitarization provoked a severe run on the franc which all but nullified the beneficial effects of the British loan. This prompted Wilfrid Baumgartner, the Finance Ministry's Directeur du Mouvement Général des Fonds, to a significant *volte-face*. This normally conservative adviser reported that Laval's November rearmament 'pause' could no longer be adhered to. Acting on Baumgartner's analysis, though dismissing his concomitant advice, the government obtained Chamber approval on 20 March for an increase in the ceiling on exceptional borrowing through Treasury bonds from 15 to 22.8 billion francs. In return for its consent to a further 6 billion increase in the 'fonds d'armement' attached to the budget, the Chamber was given free rein to repeal Laval's earlier decree laws.[57] The inflationary pressure generated by this abrupt expansion of public spending made devaluation unavoidable in the autumn. But during the Rhineland crisis, the Sarraut Cabinet did just enough to survive the financial storm for a few weeks longer. Again, Stephen Schuker's argument on this score seems convincing. Gamelin estimated that initial mobilization would have cost some 30 million francs each day.[58] If implemented, this would have denied the government its tenuous financial lifeline.

## III

During his discussions with British ministers during March and April, Flandin exploited the German refusal to make interim concessions over the strength of forces stationed in the Rhineland as a stick with which to cajole the British into some security 'compensation'. The Foreign Minister took up several causes – submission to the Hague Court of the question of compatibility between the Franco-Soviet pact and Locarno (as Gamelin and Colson had earlier suggested), the need for at least a symbolic German troop withdrawal backed by an undertaking not to construct fixed fortifications within the zone and, lastly, the demand that French border security be guaranteed afresh. He left Corbin and Massigli to argue the case for the involvement of France's eastern allies in any multilateral exchanges with Berlin.[59]

Eden and Halifax, who continued to act as a negotiating partnership throughout the crisis, could not dismiss French demands outright. The Cabinet had insisted that France should be mollified in order to leave the door ajar to future talks with Hitler. On 11 March, still reeling from the Paris discussions with Flandin and Spaak, Eden warned the Cabinet that the French appeared serious about joint military sanctions.[60] This had little impact on Baldwin. He saw no reason to summon the Cabinet between 12 to 16 March, preferring to leave matters to Eden, Halifax and Chamberlain. When the full Cabinet reconvened, Eden reiterated that Hitler's 7 March proposals should be accepted in good faith as the basis upon which to initiate talks between the Locarno powers. The first objective would be to secure non-aggression pacts by which to guarantee the permanence of Germany's western frontiers. Despite Germany's rumbling disagreement with Belgium over the disputed Belgian territories of Eupen and Malmedy, this would signify little more than a formal affirmation of the western status quo. After remilitarization, frontier guarantees were simply the obvious route by which to get to the nub of talks – a mutual assistance treaty to replace Locarno. A new Locarno would, in turn, open the way to a complementary treaty covering Germany's eastern frontiers. To ice the cake, both a German return to the League, and the limitation of air armaments, would also be pursued.[61] This sequential negotiation, somewhat reordered to take account of the destruction of Locarno, set the government back on an even keel in its efforts to achieve the 'general settlement' with Germany. The Foreign Office central department had been consistently working on plans for this since the London declaration of February 1935.

The entire superstructure of planned agreements rested on an elusive and intangible element, the restoration of a 'favourable atmosphere'. This lay at the heart of Anglo-French differences over the coming year. If France insisted upon a rigid interpretation of its treaty rights, Hitler would remain evasive. In this scenario, the first stage of talks on arms limitation would not get off the ground. The more important matter of Germany's eastern frontiers would never be reached. France would still have to defend eastern allies, but from a much weakened strategic position. The British government let it be inferred that, were negotiations to fail in this way, France would be portrayed as intransigent. Britain would be even less disposed to assist in any reconstruction of a ring of defensive alliances.

To begin the process of reconciling Paris to British plans, the Foreign Office urged the government to reaffirm its Locarno obligation to France, opening limited staff conversations into the bargain. The Cabinet was reticent until Chamberlain's decisive intervention, made after a tête-à-tête with Flandin on 15 March. During their conversation, Chamberlain developed Flandin's idea of an interim German promise not to fortify the Rhineland by adding his own suggestion for an international peace-keeping force to monitor the zone. In return, France was to agree to talks on the basis of Germany's new proposals.[62]

It was as much Chamberlain's impatience with the Foreign Office's slow progress as it was Flandin's ability to dig his heels in that produced the joint agreement of 19 March. This opened the way for negotiation with Germany on a new Locarno, and for British staff talks with France and Belgium. If Germany rejected negotiation – now speciously refashioned as the 'effort of conciliation' in order to emphasize Britain's mediatory role – the British military was to begin detailed joint defensive planning with France and Belgium. How, when and exactly why was not specified. In effect, the 19 March proposals signalled an acceptance of the Rhineland reoccupation, if not of its precise terms. The first and decisive stage of the crisis was over.[63]

Unfortunately, Hitler's pretence of wounded indignation at the condemnation of German action which prefaced the offer of talks proved decidedly troublesome. On 20 March the Berlin Ambassador, Sir Eric Phipps, informed London that the German general staff were trying to persuade the Führer to begin negotiations. But Hitler was refusing to enter any direct talks with the French. On 21 March Ralph Wigram got word from Hans Dieckhoff, State Secretary at the Reich Foreign Ministry on Berlin's Wilhelmstrasse, that Germany could not negotiate on the basis of an inflexible *diktat*.[64] The renewed British guarantee to France and Belgium, originally accepted by the Cabinet as a necessary palliative in order to keep talks alive, thus became the element of lasting importance in the 19 March plan. Until the *Anschluss*, the Foreign Office was charged with keeping the effort of conciliation at least nominally in progress. A semblance of negotiation, or even of preparations for negotiation, ensured that the western alliance implicit as a last resort in the 19 March guarantee never came to fruition.[65]

Theoretically, Flandin had coaxed Britain into a firmer commitment to France. In fact, the Rhineland crisis had not shaken the fundamental tenets of Whitehall appeasement policy. Flandin had been most successful in winning a few limited concessions by highlighting Anglo-French disagreements, raising the spectre of the complete breakdown of the entente. At the Foreign Office, Lord Cranborne unwittingly confirmed Massigli's conclusion that the British government did not understand the French linkage of western and eastern European security – the so-called 'indivisibility of peace'. On 17 March Cranborne advised Eden that Britain shared with France a mutual interest in the European territorial status quo, but not the French obligation to uphold it.[66] Speaking in June 1936, Wigram was more precise: 'Indivisibility of peace is excellent for Russia, but if war is not avoided, it means the indivisibility of war with the chance that we, as the keystone of any European coalition and with the development of the air weapon now perhaps its most vulnerable element, will be singled out for the first attack.'[67]

The lack of common entente purpose was apparent in the dismissive British attitude to the outgoing French ministers which followed fruitless discussions in London with Reich representative and Ambassador-in-waiting, Joachim von Ribbentrop. The lack of Anglo-French unity also surfaced in the launch of the British Questionnaire to the German government in mid-April. Apart from regaining the diplomatic initiative from Hitler, the British needed to re-establish a certain distance from France. An inexperienced Front populaire administration, by now widely expected in London, promised to be more pliable in British hands. During March and April, Léon Blum's socialist mouthpiece, *Le Populaire*, backed immediate negotiation with Germany.[68]

Eden was infuriated by the latest in Flandin's tricks: an insistence that the 19 March proposals were in the nature of a 'final offer' to Germany. The Foreign Secretary chastised France's permanent League representative, the wily Paul-Boncour, for his temerity in suggesting the inevitability of war unless Germany were immediately contained. Eden's response was curt. European peace rested 'on the wisdom and unity of those chiefly concerned in its preservation'.[69] The Foreign Secretary had missed the point. On this occasion, Sarraut's ministers were actuated by the fear that the British might yet be tempted to abandon them in favour of direct talks with Berlin.

The legacy of Anglo-French bitterness built up over 1935 played a crucial role here. The British were suspicious of Laval's evasiveness over the contents of the January 1935 Rome agreements with Mussolini, and over the army and air staff exchanges that followed them. The French resented Britain's precipitate conclusion of the naval agreement with Germany in June 1935 – on Waterloo Day no less. But, above all, the British government was exasperated at being out-foxed by France's equivocation regarding Italy and the League during the Abyssinian crisis. This had undermined British efforts to act with comparable ambivalence. All of these elements compounded the British tendency to blame France whenever approaches to Germany fell flat.[70]

On 31 March the German Foreign Ministry's new proposals for talks brought the British face to face with Hitler's rejection of the 19 March scheme. The British response, the so-called 'Questionnaire' formulated in early April, marked a change of tack. To offset French requests for a new Locarno power meeting to formulate a reply to the German plan, Eden latched on to Flandin's statement that he was prepared to meet Hitler in conference once outstanding anomalies in the German attitude to negotiation were removed.[71] Hence the Questionnaire. Its purpose was ostensibly simple. The Führer should specify German grievances, and his preferred solutions. Had the Questionnaire been answered in earnest it would have made the most interesting diplomatic reading of the decade. But it was not to be. It was precisely by retaining the option to increase their demands over time that Hitler and his underlings kept the negotiating initiative. The Foreign Office and the Quai d'Orsay were keenly aware of this. Unfortunately, so was Hitler.

## IV

By April 1936 the three principal players all favoured negotiation for reasons other than the merits of the proposals under discussion: the British to win time, the Germans to guarantee general acquiescence in their Rhineland *fait accompli*, and the French in order to prove German insincerity and the consequent merits of a Franco-British alliance. Within the Chamber of Deputies, Sarraut was pressed by the left wing of his own party – the Radicals – for a firmer stand over the 19 March proposals.[72]

On 8 April the French delivered their response to the Questionnaire

– a 'peace plan' of their own. This was sub-divided into a *mémorandum* and a *déclaration*, the two amounting to a comprehensive refutation of Germany's excuses for the remilitarization. The underlying intention was to prove to London that the effort of conciliation had failed, and that the British guarantee to France should be brought into effect with immediate staff conversations.[73] The *mémorandum* was not as uncompromising as the Conseil des Ministres made out. The demand that the Locarno powers 'study' the possibility of sanctions against Germany was certainly not a request to apply them. Gamelin warned ministers on 4 April that military sanctions would require full mobilization. Once Germany completed the construction of fortifications capable of withstanding artillery bombardment, the likely outcome would be a military stalemate. He reiterated this view in a further meeting on 23 April.[74] Sure that the British would keep trying to entice Hitler into talks, the French Cabinet shifted the blame for the diplomatic impasse onto Britain while overtly making a firm pre-electoral stand. There was a further advantage in such tactics. Corbin and Flandin still regarded Eden as a loose cannon at Geneva.[75] British reluctance to contemplate sanctions against Germany was the ideal means to kill off any further League discussion of additional punitive measures against Italy in respect of Abyssinia.

The British quickly exacted revenge for this French duplicity. First Sea Lord, Admiral Ernle Chatfield, still smarting like his fellow officers at France's limited co-operation in the naval policing of sanctions in the Mediterranean, successfully advised the Cabinet to use the vacuous Anglo-French naval conversations of the previous autumn as a useful precedent for the London staff exchanges in the coming week.[76] The Admiralty gleefully anticipated the snub that could thus be inflicted on Admirals Durand-Viel and Decoux, both of whom had been reticent over co-operation with Britain's Mediterranean fleet during the Abyssinian war.[77]

Only Eden and the Foreign Office Permanent Under-Secretary, Sir Robert Vansittart, raised any note of protest at the Admiralty's pettymindedness. Like the naval chiefs, the Treasury had been antagonized by the French suggestion that 'mild economic sanctions' against Germany might begin with the suspension of the 1934 Anglo-German payments agreement.[78] Chamberlain's impatience with the lack of any substantive talks led him to disturb the hornet's nest of German colonial claims in a parliamentary speech on 6 April. During his remarks, he refused to preclude the possibility of restoring territory to Reich control.[79] On 10 April Eden, Halifax and the head of the Foreign Office League of Nations section, William Strang, engaged in some shrewd damage limitation through a joint Locarno power communiqué which shelved the French peace plan by referring it to the League council.

Eden had commended this idea to Paris via Corbin.[80] The Questionnaire would be dispatched to Berlin instead, though, in itself, this was a futile exercise. The Foreign Office had framed the Questionnaire's contents carefully. The questions asked begged an equivocal German reply. The British document skirted sensitive issues, such as Hitler's exact plans for eastern Europe. It passed over the matter of the fortifications being erected in the Rhineland. Commenting on this obfuscation, on 20 April Hankey remarked, 'I wish I saw a real policy emerging, but frankly I don't.'[81] When the German government duly replied to the Questionnaire, the only clear point was Hitler's ludicrous insistence that all negotiation for a replacement Locarno be completed within four months or not at all. In sum, the Questionnaire was useless, except in allowing the British government to avoid the consequences of the March guarantee to France.

Calculated British equivocation also characterized the Anglo-French-Belgian staff conversations held between 15 and 16 April. Deputy chief of army staff, General Victor-Henri Schweisguth, leader of the French delegation, had prepared his ground well with a preliminary visit to London from 17 to 23 March. But his appreciation of the limited influence of the War Office on British governmental policy left little ground for optimism.[82] To conclude that, from the British perspective, the talks were a success because they covered very little and avoided a commitment to joint military planning is as insufficient as the suggestion that, for the French, they were a failure for precisely the same reasons. Such an approach overlooks two points. Firstly, the conversations had a lasting symbolic importance. In time of continental crisis, Britain's first military response was consultation with its entente partner. Secondly, the French negotiators geared their tactics to the presentation of such a volume of mundane questions that closer co-ordination would develop by default.[83]

The British delegation undermined this French plan of work by a series of technical questions of its own. Since the provision of answers would require referral to Paris and Brussels, talks would be relegated to the level of service Attachés who could relay the replies at leisure. Only Schweisguth's readiness to provide a preliminary verbal reply to the British questions prevented the abrupt end to conversations evidently foreseen by the chief of imperial general staff, Field Marshal Sir Cyril Deverell, and General Sir John Dill, head of the War Office military operations directorate.[84] The French army delegation enjoyed more success in its suggestion that Britain's meagre two-division Field Force should confine its operations to Belgium. This was the continental force that Dill envisaged as being ready for service within a fortnight of the outbreak of war.[85] The French proposal was offered as reassurance to the

Belgians because British support was unlikely to drag Brussels into war. Conversely, it highlighted the overwhelming predominance of French military manpower, a factor which the British clearly did not intend to challenge.[86] Put together, this amounted to an indirect warning of the danger inherent in the Belgian government's 11 March abrogation of the 1920 military accord with France, a strategic reverse which perhaps should have alarmed the War Office rather more than it did.

In the event, only the disclosure of British plans to dispatch the two-division Field Force relieved the dullness of the other talks. The British air staff rejected General Mouchard's request for equally precise information regarding planned RAF deployments.[87] In late April, the British service chiefs also spurned the French suggestion that the Field Force should occupy a particular sector between the French and Belgian armies. This measure was seen as a roundabout way to deny the British both the freedom of manoeuvre they craved, and the chance to keep British motorized columns in reserve behind the Belgian army.[88]

While the staff conversations did not add up to much, the French and Belgians kept the British to their word by continuing technical discussion through their service Attachés. Unambitious co-operation such as this, combined with the generally good impression left by Schweisguth's delegation, did much to blunt the outright hostility with which the British military establishment had greeted the prospect of discussions.[89] Still, the French army staff was thwarted in its attempt to make best use of the promise of British mechanized forces in order to revitalize prospects for a limited allied offensive through Belgian territory.

It has been suggested that, in the wake of the Rhineland crisis, Britain was relegated to a limited role in French military planning.[90] The meagre British land forces on offer in April 1936 might seem to confirm this. But, in fact, this was not the case. A small mechanized Field Force would add strategic options, even if its role had not been settled in the London staff talks. More importantly, all French strategic appreciations still rested on the expectation of a *guerre de longue durée* in which the support of all the British service arms would be vital. Britain was simply too powerful a nation to be lightly ruled out of French strategic planning. If its land forces did not add up to much in the spring of 1936, there was still little doubt that Britain would rearm effectively. The Poles and Czechs certainly had more divisions immediately available. But, in war, they would not have the luxury of equipping larger forces over time. By dint of the Channel and the defensive capacity of the French army, the British were better placed to rearm extensively once a war with Germany had begun. Moreover, the inescapable fact was that French security, like that of Belgium and Holland, was a vital British interest. For all their arguments, there was little prospect of complete British disinterest in the fate of France.

## V

The fall-out from the Rhineland crisis underlined that, as in 1934 and 1935, the fascist powers still determined the issues over which the entente powers divided. By late April the Abyssinian crisis had once more become the principal focus of dispute between London and Paris. This confirmed the limited impact of Germany's strategic advance into the demilitarized zone upon the British attitude to France.

As the Cabinet did not meet over the Easter period from 9 to 22 April, the Foreign Office was left in charge of British policy at League of Nations' sessions in mid-April. Here, Eden undermined Paul-Boncour's efforts to secure League approval for direct Italo-Ethiopian talks. The French government was attempting to eliminate Geneva from a role in the final settlement of the war to Italian benefit. Encouraged by the Rome Ambassador, Charles de Chambrun, Paul-Boncour hoped to extract a renewed declaration of Italian opposition to *Anschluss* in return. After all, Italy's strategic importance to the French eastern alliance system was increased by the prospect of Rhineland fortification.[91]

The British government continued to underestimate the strategic importance the French attached to Italy. For Britain, with the threat to the Mediterranean fleet subsiding, turning a blind eye to Italian actions in east Africa damaged imperial security and prestige, but was ultimately containable. For France, the niceties of image were far outweighed by Italy's possible role as either an opponent of German irredentism and a land bridge to south-central Europe, or as a troublemaker for France in the Mediterranean and North Africa.[92] Throughout 1935, Laval's War Minister, Jean Fabry, laid emphasis on Italy's ability to lend immediate military support to France far in excess of Britain's Field Force.[93]

The Foreign Office misread the impact of the Rhineland remilitarization upon French attitudes to Mussolini. Far from diminishing French hopes of Italian aid as Eden thought, the crisis added to the hankering of the French military for a return to the halcyon days of the January 1935 Rome accords, and the Franco-Italian collaboration which followed in the spring and summer of 1935. This was amplified by Ambassador de Chambrun and his Chargé d'affaires, Jean Blondel, in Rome. Both diplomats insisted right up to the conclusion of the Rome–Berlin Axis in November that Mussolini and Marshal Pietro Badoglio were as anxious as the French War Ministry to resurrect their previous co-operation.[94] In the fortnight prior to the Rhineland crisis, when the League's committee of eighteen briefly considered an extension of sanctions, Mussolini frequently repeated his commitment to the Rome agreements. 'Anything was possible' provided that France prevented the imposition of an oil embargo. When the Ethiopian forces collapsed in May, Chambrun reminded Flandin that Badoglio remained 'a sincere advocate of Franco-Italian entente'.[95]

Although Flandin was increasingly sceptical of enduring Italian goodwill, he was convinced of two things. Firstly, Mussolini had to be made to appreciate the extent of French sacrifices on Italy's behalf during the Abyssinian war, not least with respect to Anglo-French relations. It was particularly galling to imagine the loss of Italian friendship given that Laval, Flandin and the service ministries had always understood that Britain's pro-sanctions policy was a sham. Secondly, Flandin was certain that the Italian victory did not affect the community of Franco-Italian interest in the prevention of *Anschluss*.[96] In his last few days in office in May 1936, the Foreign Minister considered Quai d'Orsay suggestions that a rapid French recognition of Italy's Ethiopian conquest might be bartered for the implementation of Italian concessions over Morocco and Tunisia, originally envisaged in the January 1935 accords. Between 11 and 15 May, the Italian government made four separate approaches to members of the French embassy. These all suggested that an agreement be wrapped up immediately. In each case, the embassy officials justified their inability to respond by reference to the adverse impact of a Franco-Italian dialogue upon Franco-British relations.[97]

Regardless of the viability of schemes to integrate Italy within the operation of the Little Entente, Italian friendship would immediately release seventeen divisions from the Franco-Italian and Tunisian–Libyan frontiers for service on the border with Germany.[98] In August 1935 Fabry had summed up the position in his diary,

> Italy's friendly attitude has coincided with German rearmament and our ability to use our Alpine army [against Germany] and the certainty of safe transports from North Africa to France has allowed us to maintain an equilibrium with the German military effort on the north-east frontier.
> Should Italy adopt a different attitude these factors would disappear from our hand.[99]

Generals Gamelin and Georges agreed with their Minister. In October the War Ministry criticized Massigli and Joseph Avenol, the League of Nations Secretary General, for their simpering attitude to Britain. Kowtowing to the British presumed that Italy could easily be abandoned. Even without the added incentive of the eastern alliances, to the French general staff Italian co-operation was an end in itself.[100] In 1936 the

Franco-Italian military planning of the previous June was still very much alive. On 30 April Gamelin notified the general staff that the Italian War Ministry intelligence service had confirmed the presence of seven Italian divisions on the Austrian frontier.[101] The Italians looked forward to the arrival of a French division to assist them should a rumoured Nazi-inspired coup in Vienna take place. The eventual French rift with Italy may have been implicit in the limited adoption of sanctions. But, encouraged by the military, Sarraut's Cabinet had kept the way open for an enthusiastic French government to improve relations with Mussolini. In this respect, the ideological sentiments of the Popular Front would prove decisive to the breakdown of Franco-Italian understanding.

## VI

Sarraut and Flandin left office three weeks after the confirmation of the Popular Front's electoral victory in the second ballot on 3 May. By this time, the caretaker government had made plain through its Rhineland diplomacy that the first objective of French European policy was to extract new commitments from Britain. Flandin's attempt to corner the British into an acceptance of alliance had faltered by April. This was because the Baldwin Cabinet's view of Germany was not fundamentally altered by the reoccupation of the zone, an event long expected. Nor was the British government much affected by French arguments in the weeks that followed. In the short term, the Quai d'Orsay took limited comfort from the renewed British guarantee of 19 March and the anticipated results of British rearmament. The latter was typified by Britain's ambitious naval construction programme for 1936 – a long planned Admiralty celebration of its release from the limitations of the first London naval treaty – and by the addition to the Cabinet of Sir Thomas Inskip as Minister for Co-ordination of Defence. Meanwhile, British appeasement policy did not address the fact that Germany was entrenched in the Rhineland and had shown no sincere wish to negotiate.[102] To acknowledge this would have marked an acceptance of the French logic of an alliance combination. In April 1936, the hard evidence of German expansionism was concealed by the spate of Anglo-French argument over the best methods of approach towards Berlin and Rome. This was exemplified by disputes over the Questionnaire, and by disagreement regarding the settlement of the Abyssinian war.

If the British had accepted their Locarno obligation to France, and had turned to serious consideration of an alliance, the Cabinet would not have been free to exploit any increase in the influence of the 'moderates' within the German government. The key practitioner of such 'moderation' appeared to be the Economics Minister and Reichsbank president, the colonial enthusiast Hjalmar Schacht. He was now set to take centre-stage in the continuing effort of conciliation. Yet over the coming months the hard evidence of Nazi disregard for international law would also give the new French coalition ample opportunity to draw Britain more irrevocably into European affairs.

# Notes

1. For France's Rhineland policy in the 1920s, see McDougall, *France's Rhineland Diplomacy* and Stephen A. Schuker, *The End of French Predominance in Europe: The Financial Crisis of 1924 and the Adoption of the Dawes Plan*, Chapel Hill, 1976. Regarding British policy, see David G. Williamson, *The British in Germany, 1918–1930: The Reluctant Occupiers*, Oxford, 1991, part IV; Kent, *The Spoils of War*, pp. 191–242.
2. MAE, Papiers Massigli 10, 'Note pour le Ministre', 23 Jan. 1935, Note 'Amélioration possible du pacte Rhenan', 26 Jan. 1935.
3. PRO, Cabinet memoranda, CAB 24/C.P.105(36), COS sub-committee memo, 3 April 1936.
4. Ministère des Affaires Etrangères, CADN, Londres carton 285, tel. 120, General Voruz to EMA-2, 20 Feb. 1936.
5. PRO, CAB 24/C.P.105(36), 3 April 1936.
6. PRO, ADM 116/3379, naval intelligence directorate minutes, 27 Nov. 1936.
7. PRO, Papers of Sir Maurice Hankey, CAB 63/51, Magnum Opus files, M.O.(36)4. n.d.
8. PRO, CAB 24/C.P.73(36), FO memo, 8 March 1936.
9. PRO, Cabinet minutes and conclusions, CAB 23/Cabinet 18(36), 11 March 1936.
10. PRO, CAB 24/C.P.73(36), 8 March 1936.
11. CADN, Londres 267, tel. 153, Corbin to Flandin, 30 Jan. 1936.
12. PRO, Foreign Office general correspondence, FO 371/19884, C763/4/18, Clerk conversation with Flandin, 7 Feb. 1936; FO 371/19885, C62/1/17, Ralph Wigram minute, 10 Jan. 1936; C1028/4/18, 'Policy suggestions to the Cabinet committee on Germany', 24 Feb. 1936; Cabinet sub-committee files, CAB 27/599, G(36)1, 17 Feb. 1936.
13. PRO, CAB 23/Cabinet 3(36), 29 Jan. 1936.

14. PRO, CAB 23/Cabinet 15(36), 5 March 1936.
15. CADN, Rome 496, 'Rapport au sujet des effectifs de l'armée italienne', 3 March 1936; Massigli 'Notes prises au cours d'une conversation franco-britannique, Geneva', 2 March 1936.
16. PRO, FO 371/19884, C585/4/18, William Strang minute, 31 Jan. 1936.
17. Parker, *Chamberlain*, p. 58; regarding von Neurath's views, see DGFP (edited by M. Baumont *et al.*,) series C, 1933–7, 7 volumes, (London, HMSO, 1957–83), C, IV, pp. 1136–9 and 1147–9, cited in John L. Heineman, *Hitler's first Foreign Minister. Constantin Freiherr von Neurath, Diplomat and Statesman*, Berkeley, 1979, p. 287, note 78.
18. By the London Declaration of 3 February 1935 the British government reiterated its interest in guarantees of Austrian independence and arms limitation agreements. The Declaration called for a freely negotiated general settlement. This was to be composed of defence pacts ensuring western and eastern European security. In central Europe the *procès verbal* of the January Rome Agreements would be taken as the model for settlement. The military limitations imposed under Part V of the Versailles treaty would be dropped and Germany would rejoin the League.
19. PRO, FO 371/19887, C1352/4/18, 'Prospects for an Air Limitation agreement', 2 March 1936; also C1353/4/18-G(36)5, Air Ministry memo, 2 March 1936. Regarding the HCM, see SHAA, carton 1B1/HCM, séance du HCM, 22 Nov. 1935. All three service ministry archives hold records of the HCM's proceedings.
20. SHAT, 2N19/D3, 'Note pour M. le Général chef de l'Etat-Major de l'Armée', 4 May 1935.
21. PRO, CAB 23/Cabinet 15(36), 5 March 1936; for a penetrating assessment of the French view on the Laval era, see Young, *In Command*, pp. 99–117.
22. MAE, Italie 302, tel. 164, Corbin to Flandin, 6 March 1936.
23. Churchill College Archive, University of Cambridge, Papers of Sir Eric Phipps, File 2/17, Phipps letter to Van, 14 Dec. 1935, fos. 204–7.
24. PRO, CID memoranda, B Papers, CAB 4/24, CID 1221B, COS sub-committee memo, 17 March 1936.
25. Maurice C. Gamelin, *Servir*, vol. II, *Le Prologue du Drame*, Paris, 1946, p. 198; Young, *In Command*, p. 119.
26. PRO, CAB 24/C.P.42(36), 11 Feb. 1936, p. 6; DDF, 2, I, no. 317, Flandin to Corbin, 8 March 1936.
27. PRO, CAB 24/C.P.73(36), FO memo, 8 March 1936.
28. PRO, CAB 23/Cabinet 18(36), 11 March 1936. SHM, sous série

1BB2, c. 91/EMG-2, Bulletin des Renseignements 1, 4–17 March 1936; Young, *In Command*, pp. 123–4.

29. Alexander, *Republic*, pp. 187–90. Also Martin S. Alexander, 'In Lieu of Alliance: The French General Staff's Secret Co-operation with Neutral Belgium, 1936–1940', *JSS*, 14, 4, Dec. 1991, pp. 413–15; SHAT, 7N2370/D1, no. 641, Riedinger to Maurin, 10 March 1936.

30. SHAT, 2N19/D3, EMA-2 note, 'L'Effort militaire allemand', 3 Jan. 1936, EMA-3 'Note concernant l'emploi des chars modernes', 8 Jan. 1936; Alexander, *Republic*, pp. 75–7.

31. Stephen A. Schuker, 'France and the Remilitarization of the Rhineland, 1936', *FHS*, 14, 3, 1986, p. 317; General Maurice-Henri Gauché, *Le Deuxième Bureau au travail (1935–1940)*, Paris, 1953, pp. 46–7. Regarding the Air Ministry deuxième bureau, see Peter Jackson, 'La Perception de la puissance aérienne allemande et son influence sur la politique extérieure française pendant les crises internationales de 1938 à 1939', *RHA*, 197, 4, 1994, pp. 77–80.

32. It is now well proven that French military intelligence was well informed of the nature and pace of German rearmament. See Sakwa, 'Franco-Polish Alliance', p. 128, and Schuker, 'France and the Remilitarization', pp. 317–18. For more detailed treatments of French military intelligence, see Patrice Buffotot, 'La Perception du réarmement allemand par les organismes de renseignement français de 1936 à 1939', *RHA*, 3, 1979, pp. 173–84; P. Buffotot, 'Le Réarmement aérien allemand et l'approche de la guerre vus par le IIᵉ bureau air français (1936–1939)', in *Deutschland und Frankreich 1936–1939*, K. Hildebrand and K.F. Werner (eds), Munich, 1981, pp. 249–89; Martin S. Alexander, 'Did the Deuxième Bureau Work? The Role of Intelligence in French Defence Policy and Strategy, 1919–1939', *INS*, 6, 2, 1991, pp. 293–333; Peter Jackson, 'French Military Intelligence and Czechoslovakia, 1938', *Diplomacy and Statecraft*, 5, 1, March 1994, pp. 81–106.

33. DDF, 2, I, nos. 390, 391, 392 and 425: Flandin's instructions for the London meetings, 11 March 1936; André Reussner, *Les Conversations Franco-Britanniques d'Etat-Major, 1935–1939*, Vincennes, 1969, p. 3.

34. Charles Serre, *Rapport fait au nom de la commission chargée d'enquêter sur les événements survenus en France de 1933 à 1945*, Paris, 1947, vol. I, piece 1, Maurin report, 11 March 1936; Young, *In Command*, pp. 121–3.

35. SHAA, c. 2B21, doc. 89, 3R EMG, EMAA-3, Déat to Maurin, 5 Feb. 1936. For an analysis of successive plans, see Henri Dutailly,

*Les Problèmes de l'armée de terre française (1935–1939)*, Paris, 1980.

36. Alexander, *Republic*, presents the most comprehensive picture of the three services. The most thorough French surveys are Robert Frankenstein, *Le Prix du réarmement français, 1935–1939*, Paris, 1982 and articles by the Vincennes historians Henri Dutailly, Philippe Masson and Charles Christienne in *Deutschland und Frankreich*, note 32. See also Anthony Adamthwaite, *France and the Coming of the Second World War, 1936–1939*, London, 1977, p. 39.

37. SHM, 1BB2, c. 94/EMG-2, 'Activité de la flotte allemande', n.d. March 1936.

38. SHM, 1BB2, c. 182/EMG-3, doc. 225, 'Des mesures de coercition maritimes', 12 March 1936.

39. SHAA, c. 2B8, doc. D/25 EMAA-2, 'Rapport de Général Inspecteur de l'Aviation de la Défense Métropolitaine', n.d. May 1936, pp. 2–3.

40. DDF, 2, I, no. 392, Flandin's instructions for the London meetings, 11 March 1936; Schuker, *France*, pp. 314–16 and 328–9.

41. Flandin agreed with Massigli, see Sakwa, 'Franco-Polish Alliance', p. 129.

42. Maurice Vaïsse, 'L'Adaptation du Quai d'Orsay aux nouvelles conditions diplomatiques (1919–1939)', *RHMC*, 32, 1985, pp. 159–60; Elisabeth du Réau, 'L'information du "décideur" et l'élaboration de la décision diplomatique française dans les dernières années de la IIIᵉ République', *Relations internationales*, 32, 1982, pp. 525–41.

43. Vaïsse, 'L'adaptation', pp. 152–3; ANCOM, c. 2538/D1, affaires politiques, politique coloniale étrangère, no. 315, André Maginot to overseas Governors, 20 July 1929.

44. Jordan, *Popular Front*, pp. 85–8.

45. SHAT, 7N3096/EMA-2, no. 343, Maurin to Faucher, Prague, 13 March 1936; 7N3000/AM, no. 33/S, General d'Arbonneau to EMA-2, 1 April 1936.

46. SHAT, 2B97/Tchécoslovaquie, no. 395, procès verbal, 16–18 April 1936; 7N3096/EMA-2, no. 316, Maurin to Faucher, 9 March 1936; regarding Faucher, see Jackson, 'French Military Intelligence'.

47. SHAT, 7N3000/AM, d'Arbonneau rapport no. 25/S, 4 March 1936; Sakwa, 'Franco-Polish Alliance', pp. 134–5 and 139; see also George Sakwa's earlier article, 'The "Renewal" of the Franco-Polish Alliance in 1936 and the Rambouillet Agreement', *Polish Review*, 16, 2, 1971, p. 50, note 17; Waclaw Jedrzejewicz (ed.),

*Diplomat in Paris 1936–1939. Papers and Memoirs of Juliusz Lukasiewicz*, New York, 1970, pp. 3–6.

48. Jordan, *Popular Front*, pp. 85–7 and 149; Sakwa, 'Franco-Polish Alliance', pp. 127–8.
49. SHAT, 7N3012/EMA-2, General Colson to Warsaw, 4 March 1936.
50. Jedrzejewicz, *Diplomat*, pp. 4–5.
51. It remains difficult to piece together the French Cabinet discussions during the crisis though Robert Young and Stephen Schuker have certainly produced convincing records of events, see Young, *In Command*, pp. 121–2, and Schuker, *France*, pp. 328–30. Among the divergent memoir records available, see Joseph Paul-Boncour, *Entre Deux Guerres*, Paris, 1946, vol. III, pp. 34–6; Georges Bonnet, *Le Quai d'Orsay sous trois Républiques*, Paris, 1961, pp. 152–55; and *Vingt ans de vie politique, 1918–1938. De Clemenceau à Daladier*, Paris, 1969, pp. 241–7; Gamelin, *Servir*, vol. II, pp. 208–11.
52. Schuker, *France*, p. 328.
53. PRO, FO 371/19861, C412/9/17, Ashton-Gwatkin minute, 17 Jan. 1936.
54. PRO, FO 371/19861, C67/9/17, Rowe-Dutton memo, 3 Jan. 1936. Regarding the French deficit position, see Schuker, *France*, pp. 331–5. Schuker argues that the Sarraut government did not experience any immediate financial relief in the aftermath of the Rhineland crisis owing principally to the huge losses of gold and savings which followed it. See also Mouré, *Managing the franc Poincaré*, pp. 183–90.
55. SAEF, B12.619/D2, no. 66.269, Emmanuel Monick to Direction du Mouvement Général des Fonds, 4 Feb. 1936; PRO, FO 371/19861, C673/9/17, Ronald Fergusson to Wigram, 30 Jan. 1936.
56. PRO, T160/860/F14923/1, IIC, Reports on France, 1936–1939, Sir Edward Bridges memo, 4 April 1936; FO 371/19861, C675/9/17, Allen minute, 4 Feb. 1936; C739/9/17, C951/9/17 and C1195/9/17, all Clerk to FO, 6, 14 and 25 Feb. 1936; SAEF, B12.619/D2, no. 66.279, Monick to Wilfred Baumgartner, 5 Feb. 1936.
57. PRO, FO 371/19861, C2156/9/17, Clerk to FO, 20 March 1936; Frankenstein, *Le Prix*, pp. 126–9; Schuker, *France*, pp. 331–3.
58. Schuker, *France*, p. 330.
59. DBFP, 1919–1939 (edited by W.N. Meddlicott *et al.*, London, 1977, 2nd series, vols XVI–XIX, 1936–1938), 2, XVI, nos. 78, 82, 88, 91, 98.
60. PRO, CAB 23/Cabinet 18(36), 11 March 1936; Parker, *Chamberlain*, pp. 63–4.
61. PRO, CAB 24/C.P.79(36), 15 March 1936; CAB 23/Cabinet 20(36), 16 March 1936.

62. DBFP, 2, XVI, no. 115, record of Chamberlain–Flandin conversation, 15 March 1936.
63. PRO, CAB 23/Cabinet 21(36), 18 March 1936; DBFP, 2, XVI, no. 144, text of Anglo-French proposals, 19 March 1936; Young, *In Command*, p. 124.
64. DBFP, 2, XVI, nos. 148 and 155, Phipps to Eden, 20 March; record of Wigram-Dieckhoff conversation, 21 March 1936.
65. Parker, *Chamberlain*, p. 68.
66. DDF, 2, I, no. 407, Massigli note, 12 March 1936; DBFP, 2, XVI, no. 122, Cranborne minute, 17 March 1936.
67. PRO, FO 800/292, Wigram papers, 'The European Situation', 3 June 1936.
68. PRO, FO 371/19855, C2495/1/17, Clerk to FO. Throughout the crisis *Le Populaire* showed some enthusiasm for talks with Germany.
69. DDF, 2, I, no. 489, Flandin to Corbin, 23 March 1936; PRO, FO 371/19896, C2256/4/18, Flandin press statement, 24 March 1936; DBFP, 2, XVI, no. 166, Eden to Clerk, 25 March 1936.
70. MAE, Massigli 17, dossier 'Accords de Rome 7 Jan. 1935'; University of Cambridge Library, Templewood Papers, box VIII, section 1, Sir Robert Craigie paper, 'Effect on France of the Anglo-German Naval Agreement', n.d. June 1935. Jean-Baptiste Duroselle, *La Décadence, 1932–1939, Politique Etrangère de la France*, Paris, 1979, pp. 123–52; Cointet, *Pierre Laval*, pp. 171–6 and 190–5.
71. PRO, CAB 23/Cabinet 25(36), 1 April 1936, DBFP, 2, XVI, no. 184, meeting of ministers, 30 March 1936.
72. PRO, FO 371/19894, C2048/4/18, Clerk to FO, 18 March 1936.
73. DDF, 2, II, nos. 30 and 33, Arnal to Flandin, 6 and 7 April 1936; DBFP, 2, XVI, no. 236, minutes.
74. DDF, 2, II, nos. 23 and 113, Quai d'Orsay compte-rendus, 4 and 23 April 1936.
75. MAE, Italie 302, no. 164, Corbin to Flandin, 6 March 1936; CADN, Rome 496, no. 316, Corbin to Flandin, 18 May 1936.
76. PRO, CAB 24/C.P.105(36) COS memo, 3 April 1936.
77. For more background on Admiralty opinion, see PRO, ADM 116/3398, Captain Hammill, Naval Attaché, Paris, report, 8 Nov. 1935; ADM 116/3476, Sir Dudley Pound report, 20 Dec. 1937.
78. PRO, FO 371/19900, C2702/4/18, Vansittart to Eden, 31 March 1936; FO 371/19917, C2669/8/18, S.D. Waley to Ashton-Gwatkin, 1 April 1936.
79. DBFP, 2, XVI, no. 214, Phipps to FO, 7 April 1936.
80. DBFP, 2, XVI, no. 231, Edmond (Geneva) to FO, 10 April 1936.
81. PRO, CAB 63/M.O.(36)4, Hankey letter to Major R. Casey, 20 April 1936.

82. Alexander, *Republic*, pp. 193–4.
83. DDF, 2, II, no. 4, Flandin to Piétri, 1 April 1936.
84. SHM. 1BB2, EMG/SE-1, c. 182, d. 1, Schweisguth, 'Rapport sur les conversations d'Etat-Majors', 16 April 1936, fo. 1. The final version is DDF, 2, II, no. 97.
85. PRO, FO 371/19896, C2203/4/18, meeting with Gamelin and Colonel J. Petibon, 21 March 1936.
86. Several historians have seen the significance of the French emphasis on Belgium: Alexander, *Republic*, p. 194; and 'In Lieu of Alliance', pp. 416–17; Jordan, *Popular Front*, pp. 76–7 and 79; Young, *In Command*, p. 127.
87. PRO, Air Ministry deputy director of plans archive, AIR 9/74, file II/A/1/61/11, record of April 1936 staff conversations, 1st meeting, 15 April 1936.
88. Brian Bond, *British Military Policy between the Two World Wars*, Oxford, 1980, pp. 231 and 235. For the later COS recommendations regarding the use of the Field Force motorized column, see PRO, joint planning committee files, CAB 55/8, COS 155th meeting, 26 Oct. 1936.
89. CADN, Londres 96, record of de Margerie–Wigram conversation, 12 June 1936. Wigram admitted that Schweisguth's tact changed the nature of the April talks.
90. Jordan, *Popular Front*, ch. 2.
91. DBFP, 2, XVI, no. 250, Edmond to FO, 18 April 1936; PRO, FO 371/20419, R2233/614/22, Drummond to FO, 18 April 1936; DDF, 2, II, no. 138, 'Réunion des Chefs d'Etat-Major Général', 30 April 1936.
92. Robert Young and William Shorrock are the ground-breakers in their work on Franco-Italian relations in the mid-1930s. See Young, *In Command*, and his two articles on the subject, 'Soldiers and Diplomats: the French embassy in Franco-Italian Relations, 1935–1936', *JSS*, 7, 1984, pp. 74–91, and 'French Military Intelligence and the Franco-Italian Alliance, 1933–1939', *HJ*, 28, 1, 1985, pp. 143–68. Also William I. Shorrock, *From Ally to Enemy: The Enigma of Fascist Italy in French Diplomacy, 1920–1940*, Kent, Ohio, 1988. See also the HCM files at Vincennes, SHAT, 2N19/D3, HCM p.v./notes préparatives 1935.
93. SHAT, 5N581/D2, 'Journal de marche, 7-6-35- 25-1-36', and D2 annex, note for Fabry, 10 Jan. 1936.
94. MAE, Italie 302, nos. 42, 67, 84 and 431, Chambrun to Flandin, Blondel to Flandin, all Jan.–March 1936; Italie 308, Chambrun to Flandin, nos. 349 and 445, 27 March and 17 April 1936.
95. MAE, Italie 270, Chambrun to Flandin, 27 Feb. and 27 May 1936.

96. As early evidence of French knowledge of the Italian dilemma, see SHAT, 5N579/D3, EMA-2, 'Note envisageant les répercussions possibles du conflit italo-ethiopien', 9 Sept. 1935; MAE, Italie 270, tel. 160, Flandin to Chambrun, 1 March 1936.

97. SHAT, 5N579/D1, EMG-EAN, Section d'Etude des armements navals note, 12 June 1936; MAE, Massigli 17, 'Tendances de la politique italienne', 4 June 1936.

98. SHAT, 2N19/D3, EMA-2, 'Note pour le HCM', 18 Jan. 1936. Historians have noted this potential release of French military manpower and the genuine enthusiasm of Pierre Laval and Jean Fabry for Italian co-operation, see Alexander, *Republic*, pp. 51–5, Young, 'Soldiers and Diplomats', pp. 81–3, Duroselle, *La Décadence*, pp. 138–9; Nicole Jordan, 'Maurice Gamelin, Italy and the Eastern Alliances', *JSS*, 14, 4, 1991, pp. 428–41.

99. SHAT, 5N581/D2 annex, Fabry, 'Journal de marche', entry for 28 Aug. 1935.

100. SHAT, 5N579/D3, CSG, no. 2604, Gamelin to Fabry, 29 June 1935.

101. DDF, 2, II, no. 138, Réunion des Chefs d'Etat-Major Général, 30 April 1936.

102. DBFP, 2, XVI, appendix 1, Cabinet minutes, 29–30 April 1936.

# −3−

# The Election of the Front Populaire and Entente Planning for Talks with Germany, May–December 1936

The Front populaire coalition, dominated by a tripartite parliamentary alliance of the SFIO, the Radical-Socialist Party and the PCF, was elected in May 1936 on a sweeping programme of social and political reform. It was avowedly opposed to the spread of fascism, and was notionally tied to the principles of collective security espoused within the League covenant.[1] The new government was certainly anxious to consolidate the entente with Britain. The Socialist Party leader, Léon Blum, directed the coalition but experienced Radical Party figures held the key portfolios of foreign affairs and the three service ministries. This helped conceal the Radicals' disappointing electoral performance. Conversely, this poor showing vindicated Edouard Daladier's efforts to fashion a clearer ideological identity for the party.[2] As Edouard Herriot refused the offer of a Cabinet post, Daladier was the most senior among the crop of Radical ministers. Aside from being Deputy Premier and Minister of War, he took on a newly created post – Minister of National Defence. This gave him, and a select group of senior army staff personnel, a co-ordinatory responsibility for the re-equipment of all three service arms. After the announcement of the Popular Front four-year rearmament programme in September, Daladier slowly acquired a more supervisory role.[3]

The new government faced unprecedented hostility from the democratic and extra-parliamentary right. Almost as intimidating were the awesome expectations of the coalition's supporters. The equivocal backing of Maurice Thorez's Communists, who had rejected the discipline of posts within the Conseil, was a foretaste of the PCF sniping to come. This was directed from the floor of the Chamber of Deputies primarily against former SFIO rivals.[4] Other thorns in Blum's flesh were the highly vocal *Bataille Socialiste* and *Gauche Révolutionnaire* wings of the SFIO. In modern parlance a 'hard left', under the direction of Jean Zyromski, the *Bataille Socialiste* remained faithful to the Marxist prescriptions of the early French socialist, Jules Guesde. Meanwhile, Marceau Pivert's *Gauche Révolutionnaire* advocated policies closer to Trotskyism. Advocates of class war, both Zyromski and Pivert were suspicious of any joint venture with bourgeois radicalism. Their factions were none the less anxious to see the government implement sweeping change immediately.[5]

Relative to the precision of its planning in economic, industrial and constitutional terms, the Popular Front's electoral programme was vague about its intentions in foreign affairs. Blum had appointed a relatively inexperienced Foreign Minister, Yvon Delbos, who had been Minister of Justice and Deputy Premier in Sarraut's Cabinet. Delbos had not previously held office at the Quai d'Orsay. He was best known as titular leader of the Radical deputies in the Chamber. On 23 June, Delbos and Blum made foreign-policy statements before the two Houses of the Assemblée. Both referred to their expectation of 'the unconditional support of the great English democracy' in the French effort to restructure collective security.[6] This would involve squaring a circle by reconciling Blum's pan-European vision of collective security with the British government's more limited western European horizons. It was soon apparent that the bedrock of Popular Front diplomacy would be the continued effort to draw Britain further into continental affairs, not by challenging British appeasement policy, but by appropriating it.

# I

The British reaction to the May elections was relatively sanguine, dictated above all by the financial consequences anticipated. On 11 May Charles Corbin reported that the City of London welcomed the end of 'anti-social' deflationary polices, while all shades of parliamentary opinion saw some merit in an anti-fascist coalition.[7] From Paris, Ambassador Sir George Clerk reported speeches by Paul Faure, the SFIO General Secretary, and Roger Salengro, the Socialist Interior Minister, both threatening a resort to extra-legal measures to achieve revolutionary change. The Foreign Office central department wisely treated these statements with disdain.[8] In fact, the incoming reports from Paris were frequently off-beam. Clerk had been confident that the new Foreign Minister would be either Edouard Herriot (who refused the post) or Joseph Paul-Boncour. In London, the central department soon recognized that the appointment of Delbos would facilitate personal interventions by Blum and Daladier in foreign affairs matters.[9]

Baldwin's Cabinet was deeply averse to any talk of socialist transformation, whether rhetorical or not. But in the short term, the clearest complaints against the new French government came from Chamberlain and the President of the Board of Trade, Walter Runciman. They were afraid that Blum's repeated promises to avoid devaluation heralded the imposition of unacceptable import restrictions. As the French Assistant Financial Attaché, Félix le Norcy, recognized, this was simply a recapitulation of the rumours circulating in the City of London.[10]

Meanwhile, after its initial hiccups, the Foreign Office grew confident that the new French leadership would not significantly alter course in foreign policy. Before Blum had even moved into the Hôtel Matignon, Clerk had foreseen the Front populaire dilemma:

> The Left, whose foreign policy is generally sound and far-seeing, have still to prove that they can carry out a firm policy within the country and, above all, that they can successfully order the country's finances. It is not irrelevant in this regard once more to quote M. André Siegfried's dictum that Left Governments are always faced by the same dilemma, namely, that 'if they govern they cease to be true to their principles, and if they adhere to their principles they cannot govern.'

Developing Clerk's comments, the Foreign Office news section noted on 11 May that 'the keynote of French policy at the moment is their keen anxiety for the fullest and most public co-operation with us.'[11]

This was underscored by the ready French acquiescence in the British resolve to put an end to sanctions on Italy. On 12 June Corbin hinted to Vansittart that the French shared the British longing to see sanctions lifted. Blum had even met Flandin to confer over Eden's remarks to them on the subject. French policy would be tailored accordingly. On 10 June Chamberlain made the decisive public acknowledgement that sanctions were the 'very mid-summer of madness'. This was a mercy killing which brought the sanctions policy to an end a week later. In the weeks that followed, Eden developed a keener appreciation of the eagerness to please Britain that was as evident among Blum's government as it was within Paul van Zeeland's second Belgian administration, formed in June.[12] In the early weeks of the Blum ministry, there was also a residual enthusiasm for the conciliation of Italy. Flandin had taken fright at Mussolini's new appointee, Foreign Minister Count Galeazzo Ciano, whose hostility to the francophile Italian Ambassador in Paris, Cerruti, presaged a wholesale reorientation of fascist diplomacy. Delbos's predecessor was anxious lest a final opportunity to achieve a measure of détente with Mussolini be missed before Ciano established himself in office.[13]

The French Ministry of Marine also shared the British Admiralty's concern about unchecked Italian naval power. Much like the First Sea Lord, Chatfield, the dominant figure within the CID, Vice-Admiral Jean-

François Darlan, though still officially deputy to the soon-to-retire Vice-Admiral Georges Durand-Viel, was able to dominate naval policy following Blum's appointment of the colourless Alphonse Gasnier-Duparc as Minister.[14] In addition to serving on the EMM, Darlan acted as Gasnier-Duparc's *chef de cabinet*. Darlan was the moving force behind sweeping alterations to the French naval high command. By December 1937, every serving Admiral on the naval staff had changed post. Apart from surrounding himself with intensely loyal senior officers, Darlan's principal objective was to achieve a thoroughly integrated command system capable of more rapid decision-making.[15] The greater decisiveness of the naval command under Darlan was foreshadowed in the EMM's dismissal of a Quai d'Orsay proposal for a Mediterranean security pact on 9 June 1936. To the diplomats, this plan presented a means to reassert France's European prestige in the eyes of its browbeaten eastern allies. To the French marine, however, it was deeply unwelcome. To explain this one needs a little background information.

French naval chiefs did not want to discuss arms limitation with the Italians. This would undermine what the French navy regarded as the main achievement of the second London naval treaty: the discrediting of quantitative limitation. Since the conclusion of the first London naval treaty in 1930, the French naval staff had effectively formalized the 'opt-out' clause it had then secured regarding a five-year extension of the 1922 Washington treaty restrictions on capital shipbuilding.[16] Despite this, French naval construction had been insufficient to maintain the long-term goal of a two-power standard based on the combined fleets of Italy and Germany. In these circumstances, the probable renewal of Italy's claim for parity with France was especially unwelcome. A theoretical naval equivalence with Italy was enshrined in the naval force ratios determined by the Washington naval treaty in 1922. But, after the passage of the 1922 French naval statute, inter-war Ministry of Marine planning rested on the maintenance of a capital-ship strength equal to that of the *Regia Marina* and the *Kriegsmarine*.[17]

During the conversations preparatory to the London treaty in 1930, the Minister of Marine, Jacques-Louis Dumesnil, rejected a string of British appeals for minor symbolic concessions to the Italians. René Massigli and Sir Robert Craigie, respectively the chief French and British Foreign Ministry negotiators at the naval talks, were unable to temper the Ministry of Marine's inflexibility. By May 1931, the British Admiralty was totally exasperated with French hostility to the notion of parity with the Italian navy in any class of vessel. So much so that the First Lord, A. V. Alexander, suggested that France be threatened with the prospect of a tripartite naval agreement between Britain, Italy and Germany.[18] The Ministry of Marine was unmoved. Once the Geneva

Disarmament Conference got under way in 1932, the parity issue became the principal impediment to cordial Franco-Italian relations.[19] This added to the Ministry of Marine's sharp sense of being 'odd one out' after the beginning of Franco-Italian military and air-staff talks in June 1935. In the same week that these military exchanges began, the Minister of Marine, François Piétri, pestered Eden for a formal British recognition of the French right to capital-ship superiority over the Italian fleet.[20]

Years of rivalry with their Italian counterparts had brought little reward. During the 1920s, the marine followed a long-term construction programme capably supervised by Georges Leygues. But in the early 1930s, French naval estimates were pared down. The Conseil Supérieur de la Marine warned in November 1935 that France needed to increase its tonnage construction ceiling from 630,000 to 750,000 tons in order to hold the existing position relative to the Italian and German navies. Quite apart from issues of funding, this was a production target beyond the existing capacities of the *arsenaux* and *chantiers* of St Nazaire, Brest and Toulon. Of a total of twenty-eight working shipyards in 1936, nine of which were administered by the Ministry of Marine, only Brest and Lorient could produce capital ships. As it was, the Toulon and Cherbourg *arsenaux* were behindhand with destroyer and submarine orders.[21]

In the naval programme for 1936, the construction of two *Dunkerque* battleships was accelerated. This was in response to Germany's construction of *Deutschland*-class vessels, and the Italian decision to build two 42,000-ton *Vittorio Veneto* battleships.[22] In the confined space of the Mediterranean, Italian submarine and aircraft strength added to the French general staff's anxiety regarding the safety of army reinforcement from North Africa in time of war. Toulon and Marseilles were within easy striking distance of Italy's northern airfields. Algiers, Oran and Bizerta could be raided by aircraft from southern Italy and Libya. On 9 June 1936 Durand-Viel issued a clear warning to his naval staff colleagues: 'France has no interest in assisting the construction of an anti-Italian coalition . . . as, without a doubt, the logical consequence of this would be the quest for close agreement between Rome and Berlin, an agreement which would put us, on sea as on land, in a dangerous position.'[23] Although neither Durand-Viel nor Darlan favoured a Mediterranean pact, each saw good reason for the conciliation of Italy.

## II

Once the sanctions albatross had been cast off, the first substantive test of Anglo-French collaboration came in the troubled evolution of plans for the appeasement of Germany through colonial concessions in Africa.

Before discussing this, however, it is worth looking eastwards to an abiding French preoccupation in 1936 – relations with Poland.

The Warsaw government still hankered after a French commitment to automatic assistance in the event of a German attack. Encouraged by the prospect of French financial and material help in the re-equipment of the Polish military, in April 1936 Colonel Beck suggested a reversion of the Franco-Polish mutual assistance arrangements to the model of the 1921 treaty between the two states. This had specified the requirement for immediate French assistance. In early May Alexis Léger rejected Beck's proposal. Instead, Léger insisted that any financial support should be conditional upon an improvement in Polish–Czechoslovak relations.[24] Apparently smarting from this, on 5 May Beck warned Ambassador Léon Noël that the new French government should not enter negotiations for a replacement Locarno which ignored Polish interests. This chimed in with German offers to supply war material to Poland, in return for transit rights across the Polish corridor, and the cancellation of Reich debts in Warsaw. According to the British Military Attaché in Paris, Colonel Beaumont-Nesbitt, this idea was tempting the Polish Finance Ministry.[25] The Quai d'Orsay's diplomatic quarrel with Beck rumbled on into June. But Gamelin, the War Ministry deuxième bureau and Marshal Pilsudski's putative heir, commander-in-chief, General Edouard Rydz-Smigly, were more concerned with the elaboration of a French arms supply agreement. Gamelin conspicuously favoured the Poles above the other eastern allies for sound reasons of demography and strategic location.[26] The army staff also regarded a strengthened Poland as a means to undermine the advocates of closer military ties with the Soviet Union. Léon Noël proved a willing collaborator in War Ministry efforts to sew up arrangements with the Poles before Blum took office. This is an important home truth because, as Nicole Jordan has shown, historians have tended to accept the Warsaw Ambassador's critical accounts of Franco-Polish relations in 1936.[27]

In fact, Rydz-Smigly deliberately slowed the pace of the early exchanges. He was understandably reluctant to negotiate any supply agreement until a new French government was firmly in place. Rydz-Smigly, Beck and the new Paris Ambassador, Juliusz Lukasiewicz, also resented Quai-inspired efforts to foment dissension within the Polish government.[28] Both the army supremo and his Foreign Minister viewed Poland as an aspiring great power. Both were devout disciples of Pilsudski, whose foreign policy had been driven by a quest for greater Polish prestige. This outlook presupposed territorial disputes with Czechoslovakia and the Soviet Union; causes of friction which the French government with its overarching alliance arrangements was anxious to remove.[29]

In late June, the Warsaw Military Attaché, General Charles d'Arbonneau, informed Daladier that the Polish government waited 'with impatience' for confirmation of French assent to rearmament credits and a loan. In response, Daladier wrote to Delbos on 1 July, warning of the likelihood of a limited Polish–German rapprochement should France prove incapable of meeting Poland's defence requirements.[30] So the famous Gamelin–Rydz-Smigly exchanges preparatory to the 6 September Rambouillet agreement took place with the full consent of the Blum administration. The purpose here is to note that the Popular Front was faced with an agreement virtually *in situ*, in part arising from the French military establishment's misguided alarmism over the prosovietism of the French left.[31]

Léger's imprint upon the Foreign Ministry's Polish policy provides one indication that Yvon Delbos had not asserted his authority within the Quai. In his early actions as Foreign Minister, Delbos made plain that the new government would not immediately challenge the conventional wisdom of the military or the Quai d'Orsay's professional staff. Delbos's initial malleability was a welcome relief to London after Flandin's trickiness during the Rhineland crisis. But Sir Eric Phipps warned Eden that the Front populaire's electoral victory had increased Hitler's unwillingness to contemplate negotiations for a new Locarno. The advent of the Blum government threatened a situation in which the Wilhelmstrasse would judge the merits of all proposals for talks on the basis of their contribution to a bilateral Anglo-German understanding.[32] On 29 May Joachim von Ribbentrop said as much to Sir Samuel Hoare. Germany would forget 'trifles' like its threat to build cruisers beyond the limit of the 1935 Anglo-German naval agreement if Britain consented to conversations *à deux*. Sir Orme Sargent, a leading light of Wigram's central department, immediately reiterated Phipps's warning: 'If Hitler's policy appears obscure I think it is only because we are inclined to lose sight of his sole and ultimate objective . . . as soon as we recognise that the isolation of France is the one and only thing he is working for, all his manoeuvres become clear.'[33]

German intractability was especially annoying because, in Foreign Office eyes, the French government had not stepped out of line. Following the meeting of the Little Entente permanent council at Bucharest on 7 June, President Benes called for the negotiation of a comprehensive eastern mutual assistance pact. This was rejected by the French Foreign Ministry later in the month despite Romanian Foreign Minister Nicolae Titulescu's energetic lobbying of Delbos and Massigli at Geneva.[34] On 13 May Titulescu had confided to Eden that the Romanian government, while faithful to its alliances, would ultimately defer to Britain rather than France. A month later, Titulescu said precisely the reverse to the

French Minister in Bucharest, André d'Ormesson.[35]

Titulescu's flattery of Eden did reveal a basic truth. In the wake of the French ratification of the Franco-Soviet pact in February 1936, the Rhineland reoccupation in March and the Italian victory in Abyssinia in May, the politics of France's eastern allies were rapidly diverging in response to their differing fears of the Soviet Union, Germany and Italy. By the same token, intermittent Soviet efforts to foster détente with Germany by reviving bilateral trade and credit negotiations at various points during 1935 and 1936 indicate that France's most powerful formal ally was not unequivocally committed to a collective security strategy.[36] The common denominator among all these eastern states was a loss of faith in France.

In 1935 Dr Milan Stojadinović's Yugoslav government refused to follow its Little Entente partners in the cultivation of improved relations with Moscow after the joint Czech–Romanian recognition of the Soviet government in January 1934.[37] The Yugoslavs were staunchly anti-communist. Yugoslavia was also a member of another south-eastern European alliance bloc, the Balkan Entente. As such, Belgrade identified with the anti-Sovietism of fellow Balkan Entente states, Turkey and Greece. Once Titulescu was dismissed from the Bucharest Foreign Ministry in August 1936, Romania – like Yugoslavia, a member of both the eastern ententes – also edged closer to its Balkan Entente clients at the direct expense of the Czechs and the Soviets. This came as little surprise. The substantive reason for Titulescu's fall from grace lay in his over-zealous pursuit of a Romanian–Soviet mutual assistance pact. The French were dismayed by the increased cohesion of the Balkan Entente at the expense of the Little Entente grouping of Czechoslovakia, Yugoslavia, and Romania. Dating from 9 February 1934, the Balkan Entente was in no way attached to France, and was primarily directed against Bulgarian and Italian revisionism. The agreement was at odds with French interest in Italian military collaboration. It undercut French military hopes of joint Franco-Italian–Yugoslav operations against Germany.[38]

Alone among the Little Entente states in their central European strategic outlook, the Czechs were further isolated by Germany's timely conclusion of a friendship agreement with Austria on 11 July. This nullified tentative French efforts to revive a central European combination uniting the western powers, Italy and the Little Entente in common hostility to German penetration into central-eastern Europe. In fact, prior to the establishment of the Rome–Berlin Axis in November, the point of convergence in the German and Italian outlook on central Europe was a shared aversion to any multilateral mutual assistance treaty uniting Danubian states with a western power.[39]

Czechoslovakia's increasingly exclusive reliance on France was indirectly encouraged by the British Ambassador to Prague, Sir Joseph Addison. The Ambassador was consistently pejorative about the Czech government. Addison's six-year tenure of the Prague Embassy ended in late 1936. His disparaging attitude towards the Czech state, Czech foreign policy and Czech treatment of the country's Sudeten German minority helped determine the Foreign Office and British Cabinet attitude towards the Benes government. This only became fully apparent as the Czech crisis gathered momentum in 1938. But in 1936, Addison's reports added to Foreign Office hostility to the proposals for a France–Little Entente pact which were canvassed by Titulescu and Yugoslavia's League delegate, Bojidar Pouritch, during the summer.[40]

The respect accorded to Addison's opinions in Whitehall was part of a wider problem – the inadequacy of Little Entente representation in London. During 1935 and 1936, the inexperienced new Yugoslav Ambassador, Slavko Grouitch, was the sole representative of the Little Entente states regularly in the capital. His Czech colleague, Jan Masaryk, was frequently in Prague, the more so as the health of his illustrious father gave out. Romania had no ministerial representation at all, a shortfall only partially covered by a Chargé, and Titulescu's frequent stop-overs. In December 1936 the French government at last came to grips with the incipient collapse of the eastern alliance system by accepting revised Czech plans for a France–Little Entente pact. But from January 1937, the Foreign Office supported the views of the Prague Chargé, Charles Bentinck. Like his mentor Addison, Bentinck had concluded that Czechoslovakia could not be saved by France, the Soviet Union or its Little Entente partners. According to Bentinck, the Czechs' only hope was to secure a bilateral deal with Germany.[41]

## III

If France's connections to eastern Europe remained problematic, Eden's optimism about Popular Front foreign policy was partially realized in the development of colonial appeasement. On 27 April, the day after the first ballot of the French elections, Eden reiterated Baldwin's earlier claim that the British government was not considering the cession of mandated territory to any power. In fact, because Hitler's 7 March proposals referred in passing to Germany's interest in its former imperial territories, on 9 March the Cabinet had established an investigative committee chaired by Lord Plymouth to report on the feasibility of colonial concessions.[42]

Britain, France, Japan, South Africa and Australia had shared the principal spoils of the redistribution of the German Empire at Versailles.

The British and South Africans secured the major prizes of Tanganyika and German South-West Africa. Clemenceau contented himself with territory in west Africa. From the outset, successive French governments made plain their distaste for the Mandate system, despite the fact that France secured exclusive rights to conscript native levies in time of war.[43] The Plymouth committee raked over these Versailles coals in its assessment of the wisdom of any transfer of Mandates to German control.

Lord Plymouth's work was facilitated by the prior existence of an inter-departmental committee, established at Treasury behest, to investigate international trading access to colonial raw materials.[44] By March 1936, both this committee and Chamberlain's inner circle of Treasury officials had thus spent several months deliberating the economics of colonial concessions. Within the Treasury a broad two-way split had emerged. The two senior Treasury Secretaries, Sir Frederick Phillips and Sir Richard Hopkins, were persuaded by the arguments of the Principal Assistant Secretary, S. D. Waley. He stressed that colonies offered no solution to German economic difficulties; difficulties which were substantially of Hitler's own making anyway. It would be more beneficial to Germany for Britain to continue its efforts to reduce protectionist barriers between European states.[45]

This view was supported by the Colonial Office, whose representative on the raw materials committee, G.L.M. Clauson, pointedly remarked that all the ex-German colonies carried heavy public debts. Tanganyika's deficit alone was in excess of £8 million. Although Chamberlain remained aloof from Treasury discussions of the colonial question in early 1936, his later advocacy of transfers was reflected in the arguments in favour of such action put to Phillips and Hopkins by Sir Horace Wilson, and the joint head of the Foreign Office economic section, Frank Ashton-Gwatkin.[46] Both men saw in colonial economic concessions a means to foster genuine Anglo-German détente, and to strengthen the efforts of Economics Minister, Hjalmar Schacht, to restore orderly finance to Germany. The British government was gradually seduced by the simplicity of this view. Even if colonial concessions were in themselves trifling, they might exert a disproportionate influence upon the economic – and hence the military and political – direction of German foreign policy.

Lord Plymouth's committee submitted its findings to the Cabinet on 9 June. The Plymouth report became the yardstick for the next two years of British governmental debate on the merits of colonial appeasement. It rested on three premises. The first was unequivocal: the importance of colonies to Germany was more psychological than practical. The second was equally forthright. Tanganyika could not be ceded owing to its strategic location on the Cape Town-to-Cairo communications route, the steady influx of British settlement to it and the adverse reaction to transfer across the rest of British Africa. Finally, the report insisted that the 'colonial problem' could not be successfully regulated through the League, although Germany's former colonies were all held under League Mandate.[47]

The Plymouth report was succinct, sensible and abundantly clear. It was a pipe-dream to imagine that Germany would become a peaceful partner in Europe out of gratitude for colonial concessions. In essence, Plymouth's conclusions echoed a 1933 Colonial Office assessment of the viability of Mandate transfers. This had produced two conclusions. Firstly, if a single tract of territory were returned to Germany, the entire Mandate system would collapse because the notion of holding territories 'in trust' would be destroyed. Secondly, the British Cameroons and Togoland, the west African Mandates of least strategic and material concern to Britain, would be an inconsequential offering unless surrendered alongside the much larger French Cameroons. This the Colonial Office dismissed as 'extremely improbable'.[48]

Unfortunately, as chairman of an advisory committee, Lord Plymouth had not been required to recommend a policy. While his committee's conclusions were rarely challenged in Cabinet, and were warmly accepted by both the Foreign and Colonial Offices, their implied conclusion that colonial appeasement would be a waste of time was overlooked. Instead, the Cabinet focused upon the committee's admission that, should concessions be pursued regardless, they were best confined to west Africa. This coalesced into a policy that could be put another way. France was to be encouraged to bear the lion's share of any loss of territory. Corbin warned Delbos of this growing British interest in 'buying European peace by throwing a few African scraps to the Prussian eagle'.[49]

Throughout the rest of June, Baldwin blocked the referral of the Plymouth report to the CID whence it would be put forward for Cabinet scrutiny. He was thus able to reassure Parliament that no colonial transfers were under government discussion. Slowly recuperating from his virtual breakdown earlier in the year, Baldwin was generally ineffectual in foreign-policy matters. To Chamberlain he confided his relief that the League Assembly session scheduled for July had been put back until September. This postponement would allow the Cabinet to avoid unpleasant policy decisions for a further month.[50] This sort of indecisiveness, and the Chancellor's exasperation with it, was at the root of Chamberlain's dynamic interest in European diplomacy.

As in the case of the withdrawal of sanctions, so with colonies it fell to Chamberlain to grasp the nettle. On 9 July the Cabinet agreed to his proposal that the ministerial committee on foreign policy – successor to the Cabinet committee on Germany – should study Plymouth's report. Given Baldwin's fragile health and his disdain for foreign affairs, any recourse to the foreign-policy committee carried with it the implication that 'Neville would sort it out'. Backed by the Home Secretary, Sir John Simon, the newly rehabilitated First Lord of the Admiralty, Sir Samuel Hoare, the Air Minister, Lord Swinton, and Sir Maurice Hankey, Chamberlain ensured that this committee met regularly over the summer recess under his chairmanship.[51] On 21 and 27 July the foreign-policy committee discussed Lord Plymouth's conclusions. On both occasions the senior trio of Chamberlain, Halifax and Hoare clashed with the junior partnership of Eden and the Colonial Secretary, William Ormsby-Gore.[52] The result was that the entire issue was shelved. Formal proposals were not immediately put to the Cabinet. But Chamberlain's obvious irritation at the lack of progress suggested that this was only a temporary postponement.

Quite how temporary, not even Chamberlain could foresee. An issue hitherto discussed without tremendous urgency, the notion of colonial concessions gathered momentum in August 1936 owing to Blum's unexpectedly candid discussions with Schacht in Paris.[53] Never a part of Hitler's inner circle, the Economics Minister was frequently at pains to emphasize his own authority within the German establishment. Schacht's affirmation that he had the Führer's approval for the pursuit of colonial concessions echoed his earlier insistence to Soviet negotiators in 1935 that Hitler favoured a progressive expansion of trading agreements with the Soviet Union. In Berlin, the French Financial Attaché, Berthelot, was convinced that Schacht's authority was being eroded by Goering, Robert Ley and the Führer's personal economic adviser, Wilhelm Keppler. Despite the enthusiastic support of the Finance Minister, Count Schwerin von Krosigk, and increasing evidence of concerted colonial campaigns across Germany throughout 1936, there were other indications that Schacht's proposals cut against the grain of German foreign policy. Even the mild-mannered Foreign Minister, von Neurath, had forced the resignation of Schacht's predecessor as Economics Minister, the nationalist leader Alfred Hugenberg, when Hugenberg had publicly demanded the restoration of Germany's former colonies in 1933.[54]

The only striking evidence in Schacht's favour was the success of his tour of Balkan capitals in June 1936 during which he finalized several raw-material supply agreements. The rapid conclusion of a number of contracts with the Belgrade government was particularly hard for Paris to swallow. The French had been unable to complete a similar arms-for-primary products arrangement in which the French armament firms Brandt and Hotchkiss supposedly enjoyed the full backing of the Quai d'Orsay, the Finance Ministry and the Belgrade Military Attaché.[55] Schacht exploited the inability of south-east European states to balance their clearing accounts with Germany through payments in currency. His success caused alarm in Paris and London. As Emmanuel Monick, Financial Attaché in London, pointed out, Schacht was suspending Reichsmark payments for raw material imports. This forced Balkan states to accelerate the export of such commodities in order to cover their outstanding debts to Germany.[56]

## IV

Despite the enormous problems inherent in colonial concessions to the Nazi regime, the idea was made more attractive to London by Hitler's refusal to negotiate a western security pact on the basis of his 7 March proposals. The Blum–Schacht meeting on 27 August took place only a fortnight after the French, British and Belgian Foreign Ministers met in London in an unsuccessful attempt to devise a strategy to entice Germany and Italy into talks for a new Locarno. Not, as one might expect, an occasion where the three western partners agreed that German behaviour had been unreasonable, the London meeting underlined the residual British distrust of French diplomacy. On 17 July Vansittart warned Corbin that Anglo-French relations would suffer if British opinion were led to believe that the prospects for negotiation with Berlin had been undermined by undue French insistence on past German misdeeds. The clear implication was that the British public would be so informed by official leaks. Delbos was warned not to use a Locarno power meeting in order to demand the immediate invocation of Britain's April guarantee, an option that Massigli in particular was anxious to pursue.[57]

Vansittart's threat was explicable in the light of the events in Cabinet eleven days earlier. On 6 July Eden had a bruising encounter with his more senior ministerial colleagues when he challenged the Cabinet's reluctance to allow him to attend any talks with French ministers which had not first been explained to Berlin. The result was a carefully limited agenda for the London meeting, and perhaps the most illuminating National Government discussion of the tenets of British foreign policy before the Czech crisis in 1938. Eden opened the session by suggesting that Britain should resolve upon a definite European policy. He had several reasons to do so. The Foreign Secretary had just returned from a League Council session which he considered 'the most exacting and depressing yet' owing to its admission of defeat over sanctions. He came to Cabinet primed with Industrial Intelligence Centre (IIC) information that Germany could already equip three armoured divisions. He also bore alarming news of renewed pro-German disturbances in the free city of Danzig.[58]

The 6 July Cabinet meeting produced a renewed commitment to work for a replacement Locarno in an effort to salvage some continental security for the western powers while, of course, avoiding formal alliance with France. The Cabinet reiterated both its interest in a further restriction of the League's coercive powers and its refusal to contemplate any formal commitment to eastern Europe.[59] This added to the British enthusiasm for further consideration of colonial concessions to Germany. None of this was new. But the corollary of these appeasement stratagems was – namely, that the French government should be tied more closely to Britain in a strictly subsidiary role. Only then could the Cabinet's plans for the preservation of western European security bear fruit.

Ironically, on 9 July the French chiefs of staff submitted a memorandum to the Quai d'Orsay which revealed a similar division between those western European nations – Britain and Belgium – which, if attacked, could anticipate direct assistance from France, and the eastern allies which the army, now denied the Italian land-bridge, could only support by a direct attack on Germany. Such an operation could only be mounted if British support were assured.[60] Again, this was hardly new, except that the EMG's intention was to counter growing Foreign Ministry reluctance to contemplate a fresh approach to Rome. The chiefs of staff justified their actual desire for a restitution of Franco-Italian military co-operation by dressing up the idea as a means to revitalize the eastern alliance network.

Meanwhile, within the Foreign Office central department, Orme Sargent and Ralph Wigram expected Hitler and Ribbentrop to insist on the abrogation of France's eastern alliances as the prerequisite to Germany's signature of a new Locarno. The Wilhelmstrasse was unlikely to exercise a restraining influence. Von Neurath's position had weakened following the deaths in the first four months of 1936 of the Ambassadors to London and Paris, Leopold von Hoesch and Roland Köster, and the enforced retirement of von Neurath's closest advisers, the part Jewish Minister-Directors, Köpke and Meyer. Dismissing the Foreign Office prognosis on the eastern alliances, Léger later remarked to Eden that the electoral basis of Front populaire support would prevent the repudiation of France's overseas commitments, even if the Conseil des Ministres could be brought to accept it.[61]

Sargent and Wigram worked closely together throughout 1936. They began the year by presenting the Cabinet with the definitive exposition of central department thinking on the prospects for a general settlement.[62] After the stalemate in the months following the Rhineland crisis, the central department was resigned to the pursuit of western pact talks as the best hope of revealing Nazi duplicity. At this early stage in Chamberlain's appeasement effort, Foreign Office scepticism still chimed with his own. Chamberlain told Lord Lothian on 10 June that he suspected that Germany was 'merely playing for time'. But Chamberlain judged it imperative to pursue all avenues for settlement.[63]

For Chamberlain and the Foreign Office, French pliability had been successfully tested by the Quai's grudging acceptance of the anodyne terms for the London conference in July. By August the Foreign Office was at work on possible revisions to the Franco-Soviet pact which might overcome German objections to it.[64] Delbos evidently accepted the British government's interpretation of the post-Rhineland negotiation effort as stalled rather than stillborn. This was the spring-board for British planning of colonial appeasement once the Foreign Office got precise word of the contents of the Blum–Schacht conversations. The colonial issue was also given added weight by the dismal progress of preparatory discussions on the replacement Locarno treaty during the autumn.

On 25 August the foreign-policy committee agreed that Britain should agree to a western pact even if it were not directly linked to a resumption of talks with Germany over eastern Europe. The British concentration on western Europe flew in the face of the London conference where all delegates had affirmed that the crucial task in any negotiations was to secure binding German guarantees to the successor states. This about-turn only slipped by unnoticed because the German government ignored the London conference altogether. Hitler preferred to exploit the French governmental *crise de conscience* over Franco's rebellion in Spain, and its *crise de crédit* as domestic and Anglo-American pressure for a devaluation of the franc mounted.[65] The British government was trapped by the contradiction inherent in its approach to a western agreement. Unable to admit its actual disinterest in eastern Europe, the Cabinet portrayed the conclusion of a replacement Locarno pact as integral to a wider European settlement. Yet ministers had also agreed that France should not be allowed to wreck the prospects for the more limited western pact by petitioning on behalf of its eastern client states.[66] The Cabinet accepted that France was legally entitled to assist her allies. But the British were irritated that the separate issue of air limitation was bound to collapse once Hitler complained at the injustice of the French alliance system, the Franco-Soviet pact above all. On 19 August Eden advised his Cabinet colleagues to approve definite proposals for a new Locarno power meeting in order that the French and Belgian governments should not do so first, stealing the initiative from London in the process.[67]

Blum had been coy over the details of his discussions with Schacht. This was easily explained. He had been coaxed into a virtual promise that France would surrender its portion of the Cameroons and Togoland, provided that Britain would also part with its west African Mandates.[68] To compound this indiscretion, in early September, following Interior Minister Roger Salengro's announcement that the Front populaire would strive for an arms limitation accord, Blum proposed that the Geneva Disarmament talks be reconvened. As Corbin put it, 'the British believe that the French government, with the best will in the world, has embarked upon projects for which it has perhaps not had time to weigh up all the consequences.'[69]

British policy was no less confused. On 2 September the Cabinet approved conflicting Foreign Office and CID memoranda on future western-pact negotiations. Ministers first of all accepted the Foreign Office interpretation that talks with Berlin should be postponed. Any signature of a western pact was likely to prompt German crowing at the settlement of all outstanding Anglo-German differences, bar colonies. Hence, negotiation of a new Locarno would be a diplomatic cul-de-sac liable to bring Britain face to face with the colonial question. Yet within a week, the British government acted upon the CID's imploring call for talks by suggesting to the other Locarno signatories that five-power discussions resume in London in October. As was so often the case, British policy was determined by German demands. Von Neurath insisted that Germany could not agree to a conference until it first received a prospectus detailing the current proposals of all the Locarno powers. This relegated any such meeting to the distant future.[70]

On 17 September the French government submitted its proposals for the planned western-pact conference. This also militated against any movement in the short term. As Vansittart noted, the French had addressed German objections – but too bluntly. Léger and Massigli comprehensively refuted Germany's criticisms of France's right to assist her allies under the terms of any revised western treaty.[71] With no immediate prospect of western pact talks, British interest in a colonial settlement increased. Furthermore, by October 1936, French foreign policy was far more prone to British influence. This stemmed from three principal causes: the outbreak of the Spanish civil war in July, the circumstances of the devaluation of the franc in September and Belgium's declaration of neutrality in October. The first of these will be analysed in detail in chapter 4. It is worth recording here that the Quai d'Orsay considered that the British government had saved France from diplomatic crisis and governmental upheaval by its sponsorship of the August Non-Intervention agreement which theoretically precluded foreign support for the warring parties in Spain. This helps explain Delbos's long fuse in the face of the Foreign Office's sometimes hectoring tone over the subsequent year.

The terms of the long-awaited depreciation of the franc also owed much to British action. Alongside France and the United States, Britain was the third signatory to the Tripartite agreement of 28 September. This accord regulated the devaluation. It established a *franc élastique* with no fixed parity, but with an agreed range of fluctuation. This amounted to a currency depreciation of between 25 to 35 per cent.

The Tripartite agreement originated in Emmanuel Monick's earlier spate of shuttle diplomacy between Paris, London and Washington.[72] As Alfred Sauvy has pointed out, the Popular Front's efforts to stem the flight of capital from France should logically have resulted in exchange controls to counteract those who 'trouvaient la patrie trop petite'.[73] But Blum's initial lip-service to the opponents of devaluation belies his early approval of Monick's exploratory visits to Washington and London. In Blum's first government, the French Finance Ministry was directed by the former president of the Chamber finance commission, a veteran of numerous Franco-American war debt talks, the Socialist, Vincent Auriol. He hoped that Monick would secure Anglo-Saxon acceptance of a treaty formalizing the exchange relationship between France, Britain and the United States. This was always unlikely given the French infatuation with a gold standard, and its leadership of the European 'gold-block' nations. Even the new Governor of the Bank of France, Emile Labeyrie, conceded that France's large stock of gold, if left unregulated, and thus prey to unlimited withdrawals by private investors, would destabilize the economy. Rather than the broad treaty that Auriol favoured, Chamberlain and the Treasury Permanent Secretary, Sir Frederick Phillips, encouraged the American Treasury Secretary, Henry Morgenthau, to agree to a pre-determined range for the parity of sterling, the dollar and the franc. Chamberlain told Blum on 11 July that he could not 'limit his power of independent action by a formal agreement'.[74]

The circumstances of the French devaluation owed much to an alarming resurgence of industrial unrest, and pressure from Radical Party ministers. Still, the Tripartite agreement was among the first tentative efforts to re-establish the international monetary co-operation destroyed by the 1929 crash. It also tied Blum's government more closely to Britain. The French acquired a vested interest in the stability of sterling, and Vincent Auriol chose to defend the devaluation – something he had long resisted – in terms of its contribution to European peace. Rather than the sober currency adjustment that Chamberlain preferred, Vincent Auriol proclaimed a 'free-trading front'.

This may have made devaluation more palatable to some, but it undermined the efforts of the French Financial Attachés in London to win Treasury respect for Finance Ministry policy. On 29 September Sir Frederick Phillips noted that Vincent Auriol's ill-judged remarks were bound to encourage smaller nations in financial difficulties to seek British assistance. The Treasury could hardly admit that the phrasing of the Tripartite agreement had been devised purely to help the French Finance Ministry overcome its domestic critics. Treasury irritation increased in October. The French government then suggested that Britain might take the lead in any further reductions of trade tariffs. As Monick's deputy, Félix le Norcy, put it, it fell to the Finance Ministry 'to moderate itself' in order for France to achieve a role as financial mediator between London and Washington.[75]

Although the Tripartite Agreement might have been better exploited, this accord and the Non-Intervention Agreement, made a joint Anglo-French pursuit of colonial appeasement more likely. Furthermore, these agreements were complemented by a major strategic reverse: Belgium's declaration of neutrality. On 14 October King Leopold made the neutrality declaration in the presence of the Belgian Cabinet. This confirmed that the Brussels government felt that its policy of independence remained compromised by the vestiges of the moribund 1920 Franco-Belgian military agreement. The 1920 arrangement, which theoretically provided for military co-operation and regular staff contacts, had been abrogated by Brussels on the eve of the Rhineland remilitarization.[76] The October declaration amplified a shift in Belgian policy long presaged in the divisions between the broadly neutralist Flemish and the more francophile Walloon political parties. The planning of French 'forward defence' in Belgian territory, which the 1920 agreement was designed to permit, had to be re-designed anyway in the wake of the German seizure of the Rhineland.[77]

The October declaration was still crucial. It killed off the residual hope within the Quai d'Orsay that Paul van Zeeland's second ministry, eager as it was to avoid offending any of Belgium's major neighbours, might stop short of outright neutrality. Léger was outraged. He lambasted the luckless Belgian Ambassador, Comte de Kerchove, for daring to presume that Belgium's security might be improved by cutting the umbilical cord to Paris:

> In fact, the situation will remain the following: Germany will still be free to violate Belgium's borders when and where it pleases, with all the consequent risks for us. By contrast, France will not be allowed to enter Belgium, except after a German attack when she will no longer be able to make use of the usual communications towards the German frontier.[78]

Belgian intransigence facilitated German prevarication over the western pact. But in London, reactions to King Leopold's announcement were mixed.[79] The CID's chiefs of staff sub-committee believed that Germany would respect Belgian independence. Hitler knew that in the eyes of the world little Belgium had freed itself from association with the inequities of French foreign policy. Belgian neutrality ought to discourage Germany from westward expansion certain to bring Britain into war. Moreover, if France were now denied the possibility of constructing fixed defences on the Belgian–German frontier, French governments would be less inclined to pursue hopeless interventions on behalf of the eastern allies. In a speech on 28 October the Belgian Foreign Minister, Paul Henri Spaak, maintained that in no circumstances would the Belgian government permit the use of its territory as a platform for aggression against another state. Though the Quai insisted that Spaak was referring solely to German aggression, his statement was a clear warning against a limited French offensive, based upon a march into Belgium, in defence of any eastern ally that might fall victim to Germany's *drang nach Osten*.[80]

In contrast to the British service chiefs, since March the Foreign Office had been sympathetic to the French predicament. Their mood turned to frustration in October as it became apparent that the Quai d'Orsay was reluctant to accept that the Belgian declaration was irrevocable. The French tried to circumvent the Belgian decision by insisting that Belgium act as a guarantor as well as a guaranteed state under a new western pact. This would commit Belgium to the planning of mutual assistance arrangements with France.[81] Acting at the request of van Zeeland and Spaak, by the end of the month, the British had stifled this French idea. To keep Delbos reasonably sweet, the Foreign Office agreed to use van Zeeland's next scheduled visit to London in late November to seek clarification of the exact Belgian position regarding staff contacts, defensive obligations, and, above all, transit rights for British and French troops and aircraft.[82] Meanwhile the British and French Ambassadors to Brussels, Sir Esmonde Ovey and Jules Laroche, arrived at the same conclusion. A watertight British guarantee of Belgian independence, combined with a well-publicized divorce from France, offered Belgium the best hope of keeping out of war.[83] Daladier's War Ministry continued to postulate the deployment of a strategic reserve inside Belgium. Gamelin pursued limited planning on that basis with the Belgian general staff.[84] Although Franco-Belgian military co-ordination subsisted, it was inevitably restrained. One effect of this was to promote closer Anglo-French co-operation, first evident in the discussion of Schacht's initiatives.

# V

Immediately after his infamous 27 August meeting, Blum caused the British government considerable embarrassment by advising Schacht to consult London, should he wish to pursue colonial questions in greater detail. On 20 September Eden replied to Blum's proposal to take up discussions with Schacht. The Foreign Secretary was non-committal. The German government should include any formal colonial demands within its suggestions for the agenda of the next Locarno power conference. It should be aware that Britain adhered to the principles of Eden's 27 July parliamentary statement precluding transfers of territory. This bland reiteration of British policy was well received by Delbos and Léger, though its negative tone caused irritation within the French Cabinet.[85]

The Foreign Office had yet to penetrate the French smoke-screen which lingered over the finer points of Schacht's August visit. During a League Assembly session on 23 September, Eden and Lord Halifax discussed the matter with Delbos and the Minister of National Economy, Charles Spinasse. The British ministers learnt little. As Wigram commented, it was alarming enough to surmise that Blum had given the German government the impression that the western powers were ready to begin colonial conversations, let alone that the French would discuss precise concessions, but for British reluctance. The effort to induce Blum to 'come clean' heralded a long interlude before Schacht sought fresh talks.[86]

By 9 October, when Blum met Eden personally to discuss the question, his indiscretion had lost its short-term significance. Blum noted that German reluctance to reply to British suggestions for a five-power conference would increase if the western powers appeared unduly eager for a response. Eden agreed that it was pointless to rush matters. It was difficult to overcome German objections to any League involvement in the talks. It was equally difficult to justify German opposition to the planned 'exceptions' clauses in a new Locarno. These clauses were designed to enable France to fulfil its mutual assistance obligations should an ally be attacked.[87]

But to give up on western pact talks would mean that the French could legitimately invoke the 1 April letter of guarantee committing Britain to begin preparations for a military alliance once the effort of conciliation had failed. To prevent this, on 18 October Eden gave the central department the thankless task of seeking out any points of agreement between the views of all the Locarno signatories. Reporting to Delbos on the lack of progress, Corbin summoned an image of a British government squirming at the realization that a replacement Locarno was more unlikely than ever.[88]

Blum had more urgent matters to worry about. The devaluation had little beneficial effect upon French investor confidence. Bank of France interventions remained essential to hold the franc's new parity, and the Radical Party congress loomed. It was widely speculated that the Radical rank-and-file would use the conference, scheduled for Biarritz in late October, to insist upon an end to coalition ties with the PCF. On 18 October Blum made clear that any ministerial defection from the Cabinet would precipitate the government's resignation. Even the Minister of State, Camille Chautemps, and the Washington Ambassador, Georges Bonnet, the most restive of Blum's Radical backers, were unwilling to shoulder such responsibility at so early a stage in the Popular Front experiment, particularly while Daladier remained committed to the coalition. Blum knew several days before the Biarritz congress that Chautemps, the most credible alternative leader, would support continued participation in the coalition. In the week before the conference, Chautemps made a speech at Angers calling for Radical support for the government. This had been written in consultation with Blum.[89]

Redolent of the Atlantic winds outside the hall, the Biarritz congress was remembered for its unruliness, and for the vociferous rank-and-file criticism of the Communists. But British embassy officials in Paris judged the conference an anti-climax because the Radical leadership had remained placid. There were resounding statements in favour of participationism by Daladier, the *grand chef* Edouard Herriot and a somewhat chastened Chautemps. Only the Foreign Office economic section remained unimpressed. The Radical leadership might rally to Blum, but the party's *classes moyennes* supporters were not reinvesting their savings through the Bourse. Capital investment was inhibited by fear of another devaluation. High unit wage costs were exacerbated by rigid adherence to the newly established forty-hour week. Persistent employer hostility was soon illustrated by the refusal of the Confédération du Patronat Français to renegotiate collective employee contracts in a revised Matignon agreement. Indeed, it was several weeks after the September devaluation before several of the key elements of the original June accord came into force when the principal components of the Matignon *loi cadre* were finally enacted by decree.[90]

Given the mounting evidence of impending French financial crisis, it was unsurprising that Schacht re-entered the fray on 1 October by proclaiming his wish to participate in any extension of the Tripartite agreement. Having sown Anglo-French discord with mention of colonies, he now did so by reference to differences over trading policy.[91] Chamberlain, already irritated by the amateurism of the first Blum–Schacht discussions, was prompted to intervene by the prospect of the German minister dangling fresh bait before the Paris government. The

Chancellor, Sir Frederick Phillips, and the chief economic adviser to the Treasury, Sir Frederick Leith-Ross, were adamant that Britain should act alone in pursuing Schacht's interest in trade talks. Leith-Ross was well qualified to give tactical advice. Since 1934 he had discussed Anglo-German clearing arrangements and the convertibility of the Reichsmark on numerous occasions with both Schacht and his advisers, Hülse and Blessing, themselves both Reichsbank directors.[92]

Leith-Ross's abiding concern was that, unless corrected, a worsening deficit position and a non-convertible currency would add to Nazi extremism. Schacht had confirmed this in earlier conversations with the French Financial Attaché Berthelot. When pressed, he conceded that the Reichsbank's financial difficulties were entirely generated by the pressure of rearmament.[93] As the Tripartite agreement contained no provision for accession by other states, Chamberlain and Leith-Ross considered that the German Economics Ministry should first clarify its position in direct discussion with the Treasury. Approaching Schacht in this fashion reflected the wider Treasury interest in pragmatic face-to-face discussion with senior German ministers over Germany's trading policy.[94]

On 4 November the Cabinet accepted Chamberlain's proposal for a joint Treasury and Foreign Office investigation into possible economic concessions to Germany. The intention was to increase German export potential. As Corbin noted, the Cabinet calculated that Schacht's colonial demands were a gambit being used to extract more significant financial concessions.[95] Why then did the Cabinet rebuff Schacht's attempts to secure an invitation to London for preliminary talks in December? The fact was that the government remained frightened by Blum's suggestions that Britain might accede to the surrender of colonial territory in west Africa. Schacht might nominally come to Britain to discuss Anglo-German economic co-operation, but he was likely to turn the conversation round to colonies. This would be putting the cart before the horse. Any transfer of colonial territory could only be justified as the ultimate concession within a general settlement. It was not open for discussion from the outset of talks.[96] Sir Charles Pinsent, the British Financial Attaché to Berlin, was adamant that British monetary intervention would not affect Germany's economic position. To offer capital support to an already burgeoning industrial sector was bound to hit Europe's more inefficient industrial producers – France foremost among them – especially hard. This would result in a reinforcement of tariff barriers.[97]

This was cold comfort to the Treasury. Having achieved a £32 million balance of payments surplus by December 1935, twelve months later this had turned into a £18 million deficit. Not a large figure in itself,

Chamberlain saw this as firm evidence of the brief recession that would dog the economy during 1937. One way to close the deficit gap was to provide greater stimulus to recent upturns in commodity prices. This would enable British export customers in commodity-dependent economies to increase their orders for British manufactures. A British loan to Germany would be a practical means to go about this. It would give Schacht limited foreign exchange purchasing power with which to buy raw materials on the open market from these same commodity producers, adding to their economic recovery, and hence their eventual interest in British goods. For Chamberlain and Leith-Ross in particular, economic assistance to Germany provided a means to initiate negotiations, and made sound financial sense.[98]

The Cabinet had not yet formally sanctioned such economic appeasement. During November and December, however, the disintegration of plans for a western pact conference, combined with the rapidity of progress in bilateral talks with Italy over a Mediterranean Gentlemen's agreement, added to the appeal of a bold approach to Berlin. In late October 1936 the British had gathered a compendium of western pact proposals from the Locarno powers. Within the French proposals was the suggestion that not only metropolitan France, but also its Empire, be guaranteed under a new Locarno. The Italians meanwhile had insisted that only the original 1925 guarantees between France, Belgium and Germany would be acceptable. The French stipulation was easily brushed aside. It was little more than a Quai d'Orsay effort to backpeddle over the possibility of colonial concessions. Yet the Italian view of guarantees, supported by Hitler, would prevent Britain from receiving a German non-aggression pledge.[99]

For its part, the German government was working to undermine any British objections to a western pact without an eastern sequel by trying to entice the Czech government into a non-aggression pact analogous to the January 1934 German–Polish agreement. The French Ambassador to Berlin, André François-Poncet, and his fellow Ambassador in Prague, Victor de Lacroix, had predicted that the Germans would approach François-Poncet's Czech colleague, Vojtěch Mastny. Although von Neurath duly obliged on 17 August, Hitler only authorized Albrecht Haushofer, sponsor of the irredentist lobby, the *Verein für das Deutschtum im Ausland* (*VDA*), to initiate talks in Prague in November on the basis of Haushofer's own draft pact.[100] A bilateral non-aggression deal, backed by the July accord with Austria, and German fidelity to the 1934 pact with Poland, would allow Hitler to claim that he had negotiated the major paper contributions to European peace. He might then agree to a western pact as the definitive settlement of Anglo-German differences — not the start of general negotiations, but rather their last stage.

Hitler's ploy was clearly intended to isolate France. The British Cabinet indirectly abetted it by agreeing on 28 October that the agenda for western pact discussions should be flexible, 'to avoid putting so much prominence on the Eastern settlement as to block the way to a settlement in Western Europe'.[101] The Foreign Office tried to limit the damage by reaffirming the British right to expect a non-aggression guarantee, and the French right to demand an exceptions clause allowing it to aid its allies. It was made clear at the Bratislava conference of the Little Entente council six weeks earlier that French signature of a western pact without exceptions clauses would destroy its alliance network.[102] For Britain to allow German hegemony in east–central Europe would be to acquiesce in France's relegation to the status of second-class power. This would deny Britain a continuing role as a continental mediator, a position heavily dependent upon the assurance of French support.

At a specially convened ministerial meeting on 13 November, Eden convinced his colleagues that a western pact had to be compatible with France's eastern alliance obligations. He also insisted upon Britain's right to a guarantee by stressing the need to appear firm in the eyes of the electorate and the Dominion governments.[103] This was a hollow plea. But it had the desired effect because it secured Baldwin's enthusiastic support. Nevertheless, the Foreign Office was instructed to redraft that part of Sargent's memorandum which stated that a western pact was 'intended to lead' to a general settlement. In the resultant British memorandum communicated to the Locarno powers on 19 November, this west–east connection was left for the recipients to infer or ignore, whichever suited them better.[104]

The French were not so tricky. Blum's government wanted to avoid interminable conversations, and insisted on linking a western pact to a general settlement. Blum and Delbos were not simply resting their hopes upon the promised British guarantee should the appeasement talks fail. Given the British interest in discussing colonies, and the alarmingly poor rate of French air rearmament, the central department considered pursuing Corbin's repeated suggestions that Blum be invited to talk over matters in London. Eden was enthusiastic about this. He was coming round to the French view of matters.[105] But, in November, the first evidence of the new Rome–Berlin Axis appeared in the concerted Germano-Italian refusal to reply to the British proposals for a Locarno power conference. Faced with this, Blum's visit was shelved.

## VI

Six months of western pact discussion had produced nothing. The only silver lining was the progress made in the same period in improving

Anglo-French relations. Vansittart feared that the Cabinet might undermine this by blaming the Blum government for the diplomatic stalemate. The beleaguered Foreign Office chief could do little. He was keenly aware of his own isolation within the Whitehall establishment as Eden tried to shunt him out to the Paris embassy.[106] Vansittart was surely unsurprised at the comments in a Christmas Day letter he received from Chatfield. According to the First Sea Lord, if Germany intended to dominate south-eastern Europe, Britain should not resist it. 'Europe must work out its own salvation in that quarter. It would not only be quixotic, but wrong to spread the conflict to a general European war. We should so inform France confidentially.'[107]

Chatfield was no defeatist. He spoke on behalf of those who saw appeasement as a strategic imperative given the diffuse threats to the British Empire from Germany, Japan and Italy. His CID colleague, Maurice Hankey, agreed. According to him, past French actions, such as their withdrawal from the Disarmament Conference in April 1934, made Paris culpable for Britain's failure to reach agreement with Germany at a much cheaper price than was presently contemplated. Close association with Paris implied collusion in the encirclement of Germany. Neither the British public nor the Dominions would tolerate this. The notion of alliance with France could never be considered while the French government stood by its obligations in eastern Europe.[108] Hankey's views were prejudiced, jaundiced and, for such a senior figure, highly naïve. As to his comments regarding the disarmament talks, French logic in 1934 – 'tout vaut mieux que désarmer quand l'Allemagne réarme' – was harder still to dispute in 1936.[109]

Compared with Hankey's vitriol, the record of Blum's 2 December interview with Philip Jordan of the *News Chronicle* reads like a breath of fresh air. Blum pointed out that the effort to convene a five-power conference had been a means to keep the diplomatic initiative, and to demonstrate French loyalty to Britain. He reiterated that the Franco-Soviet pact would not be allowed 'to grow teeth' by the addition of a military convention. The French government's growing sympathy for the high command's dismissive view of Soviet military potential was indicative of this.[110] In June the Quai d'Orsay approved the continuation of arms supply contracts negotiated in 1934 between the Soviet government and the artillery manufacturers, Schneider and Hotchkiss, covering the provision of naval and field guns and armour plate. Yet by the time Robert Coulondre took up his post as Moscow Ambassador in November, the Foreign Ministry was working alongside the service ministries in an effort to justify the indefinite postponement of these arms deliveries.[111]

Blum's remarks regarding the pact with Moscow made light of his government's exposure to the political cross-fire between the coalition's Communist-led left wing, which demanded consolidation of the Soviet alliance, and the broad spectrum of right-wing opinion, which was increasingly hostile to the entire alliance network. As the appeasement effort moved into 1937, the British government exploited French governmental goodwill more fully as the Popular Front's domestic problems gradually overwhelmed it.

## Notes

1. As Robert Frank noted, the quantity of secondary writing on the Popular Front was for long matched by its partisanship, see Frank's, 'Le Front populaire a-t-il perdu la guerre?', *L'Histoire*, 58, 1983, pp. 58–66. Partisan views also pervade the plethora of memoirs and diaries, among which the four-volume *L'Œuvre de Léon Blum*, Paris, 1955/1964–5 has been heavily used. With increasing access to archives, since the early 1980s historians have written more empirical studies of the Front populaire experience: Georges Lefranc, *Histoire du Front populaire*, Paris, 1974; Jean Lacouture, *Léon Blum*, Paris, 1977; Jean-Pierre Cuvallier, *Vincent Auriol et les Finances Publiques du Front Populaire*, Toulouse, 1978; Jacques Kergoat, *La France du Front Populaire*, Paris, 1986. Useful translations of general French works include Philippe Bernard and Henri Dubief, *The Decline of the Third Republic, 1914–1938*, Cambridge, 1985; Maurice Agulhon, *The French Republic, 1870–1990*, Oxford, 1993. Two indispensable edited collections are Helen Graham and Paul Preston (eds), *The Popular Front in Europe*, London, 1987; Martin S. Alexander and Helen Graham, *The French and Spanish Popular Fronts*, Cambridge, 1989. Nothing has completely superseded Joel Colton, *Léon Blum, Humanist in Politics*, Cambridge, Mass., 1966. There is now, though, a standard work: Julian Jackson, *The Popular Front in France: Defending Democracy, 1934–38*, Cambridge, 1988. Jackson's preface provides an informative survey of French writing on the Popular Front, pp. ix–xiv.

2. Serge Bernstein, *Histoire du Parti Radical*, II, *Crise du radicalisme, 1926–1939*, Paris, 1982; John E. Dreifort, *Yvon Delbos at the Quai d'Orsay. French Foreign Policy during the Popular Front, 1936–1938*, Lawrence, 1973, pp. 21–9; M. Schlesinger, 'The Development

of the Radical Party in the Third Republic: The New Radical Movement, 1926–1932', *JMH*, 46, 1974, pp. 480–4 and 496.

3. Daladier's power was limited by his extensive party responsibilities, and the absence of clear executive authority over the other service ministries, see Alexander, *Republic*, pp. 83 and 89–93.
4. Zeev Sternhell, *Ni droite ni gauche. L'idéologie Fasciste en France*, Paris, 1983; Pierre Milza, 'L'ultra droite des années trente', in Michael Winock (ed.), *Histoire de l'extrême droite en France*, Paris, 1993, pp. 157–90. Regarding the extreme left see Irwin M. Wall, *French Communism in the Era of Stalin*, London, 1983. The best overall treatment is again Jackson, *Popular Front*, especially pp. 234–58.
5. Jackson, pp. 95–6, 226–8; Colton, *Léon Blum*, pp. 132, 136.
6. PRO, FO 371/19856, C3589/1/17, Clerk memo, 'French Internal Situation', 11 May 1936. Regarding the PF programme, see Davis A.L. Levy, 'The French Popular Front, 1936–1937', in Graham and Preston, *The Popular Front in Europe*, pp. 64–7; Adrian Rossiter, 'Popular Front Economic Policy and the Matignon Negotiations', *HJ*, 30, 3, 1987, pp. 663–84.
7. CADN, Londres 13, no. 292, Corbin to Paris, 11 May 1936.
8. PRO, FO 371/19858, C5010/1/17 and C5324/1/17, Clerk to FO, 9 and 19 July 1936.
9. PRO, FO 371/19856, C3156/1/17, Wigram minute, 25 April 1936; C3467/1/17, Clerk to FO, 7 May 1936; C3927/1/17, Allen minute, 28 May 1936; FO 371/19857, C4238/1/17, Vansittart minute, 10 June 1936; FO 371/19858, C5617/1/17, Lloyd-Thomas letter to Vansittart, 29 July 1936.
10. PRO, CAB 23/Cabinet 41(36), 10 June 1936; SAEF, B12.619/D2, nos. 66.526 and 66.539, Le Norcy to Direction du Mouvement Général des Fonds, 4 and 6 May 1936; B12.636/D1, Emmanual Monick memo, 'Les élections françaises et l'opinion britannique', 4 May 1936.
11. BDFA, part II, series F, vol. 22, no. 35, Clerk to Eden, 15 April 1936; PRO, FO 371/19907, C4408/4/18, news section minute, 19 June 1936.
12. DBFP, 2, XVI, no. 403, record of Eden–van Zeeland conversation, 3 July 1936.
13. DBFP, 2, XVI, no. 337, Eden to Lloyd-Thomas, 25 May 1936; no. 364, record of Vansittart–Corbin conversation, 12 June 1936. MAE, Italie 270, no. 176, Blondel to Flandin, 18 June 1936.
14. Jules Moch, *Rencontres avec Darlan et Eisenhower*, I: *Souvenirs sur l'amiral de la flotte française, Darlan*, Paris, 1968, pp. 24–7.
15. PRO, ADM 1/9583, Admiralty minutes, 7 Feb. 1938; Hervé Coutau-

Bégarie and Claude Huan, *Lettres et notes de l'Amiral Darlan*, Paris, 1992, docs. 18 and 19; Ronald Chalmers Hood III, *Royal Republicans. The French Naval Dynasties Between the World Wars*, Baton Rouge, 1985, p. 159.

16. SHM, 1BB2, c. 208, Dossiers de Darlan 14, file 2 EMG/EAN, 'La situation navale en Juin 1936', fo. 15, 9 June 1936; PRO, ADM 116/3624, C.P.64(31), A.V. Alexander memo, n.d. 1931.

17. SHM, 1BB2, c. 208, Darlan 14, 2 EMG/EAN, fo. 15, 9 June 1936. Regarding the Franco-Italian parity issue see Joel Blatt, 'The Parity that Meant Superiority: French Naval Policy towards Italy at the Washington Conference, 1921–1922, and Interwar French Foreign Policy', *FHS*, 12, 2, 1981, pp. 223–48; Brian R. Sullivan, 'Italian Naval Power and the Washington Conference of 1921–1922', *Diplomacy and Statecraft*, 4, 3, 1993, pp. 220–48; Ronald Chalmers Hood III, 'The French Navy and Parliament between the Wars', *IHR*, 6, 3, 1984, pp. 386–403.

18. PRO, ADM 116/3264, conversations with Italian Minister of Marine, Sirianni, 4 Sept. 1930; Admiralty to Captain Bellairs, Geneva, 16 Sept. 1930; Alexander to MacDonald, 7 Nov. 1930.

19. PRO, ADM 116/3291, 1347/68/17/32, Paris Naval Attaché to Admiralty NID, 1 Oct. 1932; 1652/105/36/32, record of Mussolini–Sir Ronald Graham conversation, Paris, 15 Dec. 1932.

20. MAE, Massigli 17, dossier 'Accords de Rome', 7 Jan. 1935 and Laval to Piétri, 27 July 1935.

21. SHM, 1BB2, c. 208/D2, fo. 20, 9 June 1936; PRO, T160/860, ICF/470, IIC draft, 'France-General survey', 17 Feb. 1936. The IIC stressed the decline in French shipbuilding output: notably, an inter-war low figure of 16,000 tons launched in 1934. Although production had since increased, much *arsenaux* skilled labour had moved into other industries during the Doumergue and Laval eras leaving a serious personnel shortage in the shipyards by 1936.

22. SHM, 1BB2 c. 208/D14, file 1, EMG-SEG, 'Renseignements numériques sur les armements navals français, 1922–1943', 15 May 1938; Reynolds M. Salerno, 'Multilateral Strategy and Diplomacy: The Anglo-German Naval Agreement and the Mediterranean Crisis, 1935–1936', *JSS*, 17, 1994, p. 59.

23. SHM, 1BB2, c. 208/D14, file 2, fo. 26, Durand-Viel notes, 9 June 1936.

24. Jordan, *Popular Front*, pp. 16–17, 154–8 and 179; Sakwa, 'The "Renewal"', pp. 45–7; SHAT, 7N3012/D1, no. 613, Léger to Maurin, EMA-2, 28 Feb. 1936.

25. PRO, FO 371/19859, C6285/1/17, Beaumont-Nesbitt memo, 3 Sept. 1936; Jordan, *Popular Front*, p. 158; Sakwa, 'The "Renewal"', p. 53.

26. Alexander, *Republic*, pp. 285–6; Jedrzejewicz, *Diplomat*, pp. 13–21.
27. Jordan, *Popular Front*, pp. 146–51. Léon Noël's account has a particular importance since the Warsaw embassy files were destroyed in 1939.
28. Léon Noël, *L'Agression allemande contre la Pologne*, Paris, 1947, p. 3; Jedrzejewicz, *Diplomat*, pp. 10–12; SHAT, 7N3000/AM, d'Arbonneau rapport 37/S, 9 April 1936.
29. MAE, Pologne 375, no. 626, Pierre Bressy, Warsaw Chargé, to Laval, 17 Jan. 1935; CADN, Londres 136, François-Poncet to Delbos, 18 June 1936.
30. DDF, 2, II, no. 238, Léon Noël to Flandin, 24 May 1936, no. 364, Léon Noël to Delbos, 27 June 1936; Jordan, *Popular Front*, pp. 152–3; SHAT, 7N3012/Départs, no. 934, Daladier to Delbos, 1 July 1936.
31. Jordan, *Popular Front*, pp. 182–7; Patrice Buffotot, 'The French High Command and the Franco-Soviet Alliance 1933–1939', *JSS*, 5, 4, 1982, pp. 547–51.
32. Phipps papers, file 1/16, fo. 62, Phipps to Eden, 26 May 1936.
33. PRO, FO 371/19911, C5680/4/18, Phipps to FO, 3 Aug. 1936; FO 371/19906, C3879/4/18, Sargent minute, 28 May 1936.
34. Paul-Boncour, *Entre deux guerres*, vol. III, p. 62; Jordan, *Popular Front*, pp. 190–2.
35. PRO, CAB 24/C.P.140(36), Eden memo, 16 May 1936; MAE, Tchécoslovaquie 149, d'Ormesson, Bucharest, to Paris, 15 June 1936.
36. Geoffrey Roberts, 'A Soviet Bid for Coexistence with Nazi Germany, 1935–1937: The Kandelaki Affair', *IHR*, 16, 3, 1994, pp. 441–60.
37. MAE, Tchécoslovaquie 148, no. 244, Payart, Moscow, to Paris, 10 June 1934; PRO, FO 371/21201, R1496/1496/92, Annual Report on Yugoslavia 1936, 26 Feb. 1937.
38. CADN, Londres 13, no. 320, Flandin to Corbin, 12 Feb. 1936; MAE, Papiers d'agents, Joseph Avenol 36, Marcel Hoden to Avenol, 22 July 1936; Jordan, *Popular Front*, pp. 189–99; Mustafa Türkes, 'The Balkan Pact and its Immediate Implications for the Balkan States, 1930–34', *Middle Eastern Studies*, 30, 1, 1994, pp. 135–6.
39. MAE, Massigli 15, no. 630, Blondel to Massigli, 6 June 1936; CADN, Londres 136, no. 1230, François-Poncet to Delbos, 5 Aug. 1936 and no. 1384, A. Lamarle, Berlin Chargé, to Delbos, 10 Sept. 1936.
40. Mark Cornwall, 'The Rise and Fall of a "Special Relationship"? Britain and Czechoslovakia, 1930–1948', in Brain Brivati and

Harriet Jones (eds), *What Difference Did the War Make?*, Leicester, 1993, pp. 132–8; MAE, Massigli 15, note, 'Sécurité française', 8 July 1936.

41. CADN, Londres 267, sous dossier 'Relations avec la Yougoslavie, 1935–1939', nos. 373 and 781, Corbin to Laval, 11 April and 10 Sept. 1935; PRO FO 371/21125, R133/133/12, Bentinck to FO, 5 Jan. 1937.

42. Parker, *Chamberlain*, p. 70; DBFP, 2, XVI, appendix III, Plymouth committee report, 9 June 1936.

43. Andrew and Kanya-Forstner, *France Overseas*, pp. 182–6; Andrew J. Crozier, 'The Establishment of the Mandates System 1919–1925: Some Problems Created by the Paris Peace Conference', *JCH*, 14, 1979, pp. 492–6.

44. PRO, T160/856/F14545/1, note by G.L.M. Clauson, 15 Feb. 1936; Andrew J. Crozier, *Appeasement and Germany's Last Bid for Colonies*, London, 1988, pp. 118–21.

45. PRO, T160/856/14545/2, S.D. Waley to Barlow, 20 April 1936 and note by Waley, n.d. May 1936; T160/856/F14545/3, Bottomley minute, 9 July 1936.

46. PRO, T160/856/F14545/1, note by G.L.M. Clauson, 15 Feb. 1936; Ashton-Gwatkin memo, 31 Jan. 1936.

47. For the fullest analysis of the Plymouth report see Crozier, *Appeasement*, pp. 142–9.

48. PRO, Colonial Office Private Office papers, CO 967/108, Colonial Office Under-Secretaries joint memo, 22–8 March 1933.

49. CADN, Londres 267, no. 481, Corbin to Delbos, 20 July 1936; the Ministry of Marine agreed that a return of west African mandates would bring no reward, see SHM, 1BB2, c. 180/EMG-SE-1, section d'études memo, 'La situation des anciennes colonies en 1913 et en 1937', 1–2, n.d. 1937.

50. DBFP, 2, XVI, no. 378, Ashton-Gwatkin memo, 23 June 1936; University of Birmingham, Neville Chamberlain papers (hereafter Chamberlain papers), Diaries 1936, NC/2/23A, entry for 11 July 1936.

51. PRO, CAB 23/Cabinet 51(36), 9 July 1936; Chamberlain papers, Misc. correspondence 1936, NC7/11/29/2, Baldwin to Chamberlain, 19 Aug. 1936.

52. PRO, Cabinet committee on foreign policy proceedings, CAB 27/622, F.P.(36) 3rd and 4th meetings, 21 and 27 July 1936; Crozier, *Appeasement*, pp. 150–1.

53. Crozier, *Appeasement*, pp. 175–80.

54. Roberts, 'A Soviet Bid', p. 472, note 3; regarding Ley and Keppler see CADN, Berlin 372, no. 1814, Berthelot notes, 9 April 1936;

MAE, Allemagne 800, no. 30, Gabriel Richard, Consul Koenigs-burg, to Flandin, 6 March 1936, no. 814, François-Poncet to Flandin, 16 May 1936; Crozier, *Appeasement*, pp. 55–8.

55. MAE, Yougoslavie 149, Direction Politique 'Analyse de matériel de guerre', 8 Jan. 1935, no. 65, de Dampierre to Flandin, 6 Feb. 1936.

56. CADN, Berlin 372, no. 1925, Berthelot to Directeur du Mouvement Général des Fonds, 10 June 1936; Londres c. 136, Monick memo, 15 June 1936; Jordan, *Popular Front*, pp. 108–10; DDF, 2, II, no. 418.

57. DDF, 2, II, no. 468, Corbin to Delbos, 17 July 1936; DDF, 2, II, no. 8, Massigli, 'Note de la direction politique', 21 July 1936.

58. PRO, CAB 23/Cabinet 50(36), 6 July 1936, p. 8; Inskip papers, CAB 64/14, Deverell to Inskip, 16 June 1936; regarding the IIC see Wesley K. Wark, *The Ultimate Enemy: British Intelligence and Nazi Germany, 1933–1939*, Ithaca, NY, 1985, pp. 155–87.

59. PRO, CAB 23/Cabinet 50(36), 6 July 1936.

60. DDF, 2, II, no. 419, 'Note de l'EMA', 9 July 1936.

61. PRO, FO 371/19909, C5290/4/18, Wigram and Vansittart minutes, 2 and 27 July 1936, FO 371/19912, C6223/4/18, notes on COS report C.P.218(36), C6259/4/18, FO minutes, 11 Sept. 1936; regarding Köpke and Meyer, see Heineman, *von Neurath*, pp. 139–41; regarding Léger's comments see FO 371/19912, C6528/4/18, Vansittart notes, 17 Sept. 1936.

62. Crozier, *Appeasement*, p. 126; PRO, FO 371/19883, C454/4/18, FO memo, 17 Jan. 1936. Ralph Wigram died in December 1936.

63. Chamberlain papers, NC7/7/5, correspondence with Lord Lothian 1936–7, Chamberlain letter to Lord Lothian, 10 June 1936.

64. PRO, CAB 27/626, FO memo, 19 Aug. 1936, also as DBFP, 2, XVII, no. 114.

65. PRO, CAB 27/622, F.P.(36) 5th meeting, 25 Aug. 1936; DBFP, 2, XVII, no. 87, Phipps to FO, 13 Aug. 1936; FO 371/19908, C4986/4/18, record of Newton–von Neurath conversation, 7 July 1936.

66. PRO, CAB 27/622, F.P.(36) 5th meeting; FO 371/19912, C5871/4/18, Phipps to FO, 13 Aug. 1936; DBFP, 2, XVII, no. 36, note 7, 29 July 1936: Baldwin admitted that were Germany to move eastwards 'it wouldn't break the Prime Minister's heart'.

67. PRO, CAB 23/Cabinet 56(36), 2 Sept. 1936; CAB 27/626, F.P.(36)9, FO memo, 19 Aug. 1936.

68. PRO, T160/856/F14545/3, Waley report on Blum–Schacht conversations, 16 Sept. 1936; DBFP, 2, XVII, nos. 145 and 210, Clerk to Eden, 28 Aug. 1936, Clerk to FO, 20 Sept. 1936.

69. PRO, Lord Avon papers, FO 954/8A, France 1936, Fr/36/29, Eden to FO, 2 Oct. 1936; DDF, 2, III, no. 349, Corbin letter to Léger, 14 Oct. 1936.

70. PRO, CAB 23/Cabinet 56(36), 2 Sept. 1936, 2; FO 371/19912, C6430/4/18, Vansittart minute, 10 Sept. 1936, C6431/4/18, record of Vansittart–Prince Bismarck conversation, 11 Sept. 1936.

71. PRO, FO 371/19912, C6523/4/18, record of Vansittart–Corbin conversation, 17 Sept. 1936.

72. Bernard and Dubief, *Decline*, p. 32; René Girault, 'Léon Blum, la dévaluation de 1936 et la conduite de la politique extérieure de la France', *Relations Internationales*, 13, 1978, pp. 97–9; Mouré, *Managing the franc*, pp. 247–52.

73. Preface by Alfred Sauvy to Cuvallier, *Vincent Auriol*, p. viii; Mouré, *Managing the franc*, pp. 237–42.

74. S.V.O. Clarke, *Exchange-Rate Stabilisation in the mid-1930s. Negotiating the Tripartite Agreement*, Princeton, 1977, p. 37; Vincent Auriol, *Hier-Demain*, I, Paris, 1945, p. 39; regarding Labeyire's views see Mouré, *Managing the franc*, p. 255; DDF, 2, III, no. 288, copy of Tripartite declaration, 25 Sept. 1936.

75. PRO, Treasury papers of Sir Frederick Phillips, T177/31, minute for Sir Richard Hopkins, 29 Sept. 1936; T177/32, Hopkins to Phillips, 5 Oct. 1936; SAEF, B12.619/D3, no. 66.830, Le Norcy to Direction du Mouvement Général des Fonds, 27 Sept. 1936.

76. DDB, vol. III, Période 1931–1936, no. 173, Comte de Kerchove to Foreign Ministry, 27 Feb. 1936; Alexander, 'In Lieu of Alliance', pp. 413–15. Regarding the 1920 accord see Jonathan Helmreich, 'The Negotiation of the Franco-Belgian Military Accord of 1920', *FHS*, 3, 3, 1964, pp. 360–78.

77. DDF, 2, III, no. 300, Quai d'Orsay, 'Note du Département', annex III, 30 Sept. 1936; SHAT, 7N2370/D1, no. 242, General Riedinger to EMA-2, 15 Oct. 1936.

78. DDB, vol. IV, no. 138, Comte de Kerchove to Spaak, 16 Oct. 1936; MAE, Grande Bretagne 314, no. 2449, 'Pacte Occidentale', 24 Dec. 1936.

79. MAE, Grande Bretagne 314, no. 1842, François-Poncet to Delbos, 17 Dec. 1936.

80. PRO, CAB 4/25, CID 1260B, COS sub-committee memo, 10 Sept. 1936; DDF, 2, III, no. 463, Laroche to Delbos, 10 Nov. 1936, no. 477, Corbin to Delbos, 13 Nov. 1936, no. 508, Riedinger to Daladier, 18 Nov. 1936.

81. PRO, FO 371/19913, C7180/4/18, Sargent minute, 13 Oct. 1936, C7206/4/18, record of Vansittart–Corbin conversation, 13 Oct. 1936, C7232/4/18, Ovey to FO, 13 Oct. 1936.

82. DDF, 2, IV, no. 5, Corbin to Delbos, 20 Nov. 1936; PRO, CAB 24/ C.P.308(36), Eden memo, 11 Nov. 1936; FO 371/19915, C8323/4/ 18, final draft, 20 Nov. 1936.

83. DDF, 2, IV, no. 84, Laroche to Delbos, 3 Dec. 1936; DDB, IV, no. 153, record of conversation between Baron van Zuylen, General van den Bergen and Ovey, 22 Oct. 1936.

84. Jordan, *Popular Front*, pp. 76–80; Alexander, 'In Lieu of Alliance', pp. 413–27.

85. DBFP, 2. XVII, nos. 211 and 214, Clerk to FO and Eden to FO, 20 and 21 Sept. 1936; PRO, FO 954/8A, Fr/36/29, Eden to FO, 2 Oct. 1936. Van Zeeland made plain his opposition to any discussion of the Belgian Congo territories within colonial talks, MAE, Allemagne 800, no. 215, Laroche to Flandin, 27 Feb. 1936.

86. DBFP, 2, XVII, no. 223, Eden to Vansittart and minutes, 23 Sept. 1936

87. DBFP, 2, XVII, no. 282, record of Eden–Blum conversation, 10 Oct. 1936; PRO, FO 371/19913, C7128/4/18, Clerk to FO, 9 Oct. 1936; CAB 23/Cabinet 57(36), 14 Oct. 1936.

88. PRO, FO 371/19913, C7247/4/18, German memo, 14 Oct. 1936; CADN, Londres 263, no. 2177, Corbin to Delbos, 7 Nov. 1936.

89. PRO, FO 371/19859, C7191/1/17, Clerk memo, 13 Oct. 1936; FO 371/19860, C7348/1/17, Lloyd-Thomas to Eden, 18 Oct. 1936, C7983/1/17, Lloyd-Thomas to Vansittart, 14 Nov. 1936; Jackson, *Popular Front*, pp. 231–2; Dreifort, *Yvon Delbos*, p. 118.

90. PRO, FO 371/19860, C7602/1/17, Lloyd-Thomas report on Radical congress, 24 Oct. 1936, C7436/1/17, Rowe-Dutton memo, 14 Oct. 1936; regarding the congress and the *classes moyennes* see Jackson, *Popular Front*, pp. 230–3; regarding the *patronat* see Rossiter, 'Popular Front Economic Policy', pp. 678–83.

91. DBFP, 2, XVII, no. 256, Schacht letter to Leith-Ross, 1 Oct. 1936.

92. PRO, T177/32, Sir Richard Hopkins letter to Phillips, 5 Oct. 1936, Leith-Ross letter to W.B. Brown, 13 Oct. 1936; DBFP, 2, XVII, no. 296, Leith-Ross letter to Schacht, 15 Oct. 1936; Gustav Schmidt, *The Politics and Economics of Appeasement. British Foreign Policy in the 1930s*, Leamington Spa, 1986, p. 37.

93. CADN, Berlin 372, nos. 2003 and 2071, Berthelot to Directeur du Mouvement Général, 27 Aug. and 8 Oct. 1936.

94. DBFP, 2, XVII, no. 296, Leith-Ross letter to Schacht, 15 Oct. 1936.

95. PRO, CAB 23/Cabinet 62(36), 4 Nov. 1936, 8; CADN, Londres 96, no. 2141, Corbin to Delbos, 4 Nov. 1936.

96. DBFP, 2, XVII, no. 512, Vansittart letter to Leith-Ross, 24 Dec. 1936, no. 519, Leith-Ross reply to Vansittart, 28 Dec. 1936.

97. Phipps papers, 5/6, fos. 26–31, Pinsent memo, 6 Nov. 1936; PRO, CAB 24/C.P.341(36), economic advisory council survey, 18 Dec. 1936.

98. C.A. MacDonald, 'Economic Appeasement and the German "Moderates", 1937–1939', *Past and Present*, 56, 1972, p. 108; Parker, *Chamberlain*, pp. 71–3; Peden, *British Rearmament*, pp. 75–81.

99. PRO, FO 371/19913, C7247/4/18, minutes on German reply to conference proposals, 14–18 Oct. 1936, C7384/4/18, Italian reply, 20 Oct. 1936; FO 371/19914, C7599/4/18, French *aide-mémoire*, 24 Oct. 1936.

100. DDF, 2, III, nos. 442 and 475; Ronald M. Smelser, *The Sudeten Problem, 1933–1938. Volkstumspolitik and the Formulation of Nazi Foreign Policy*, Folkestone, 1975, p. 249. The *VDA* was led by Dr Hans Steinacher, and publicly backed by the Haushofer family.

101. PRO, CAB 23/Cabinet 60(36), 28 Oct. 1936, 2; FO 371/19913, C7712/4/18, Vansittart minute, 29 Oct. 1936.

102. PRO, CAB 24/C.P.278(36), Eden memo, 23 Oct. 1936; DDF, 2, III, no. 260, de Lacroix to Delbos, 17 Sept. 1936.

103. PRO, FO 371/19915, C8048/4/18, Wigram's comments on COS 522, 9 Nov. 1936; CAB 23, Cabinets 64(36) and 65(36).

104. PRO, CAB 23/Cabinet 65(36), 13 Nov. 1936, and FO 371/19915, Vansittart minutes on Cabinet 65 conclusions, 14 Nov. 1936.

105. PRO, FO 371/19914, C7740/4/18, record of Eden–Corbin conversation and minutes, all 3 Nov. 1936.

106. Ibid., Vansittart minute, 3 Nov. 1936; University of Cambridge Library, Stanley Baldwin papers (hereafter Baldwin papers), Baldwin 171, Letters 1936, fo. 326, Vansittart letter to Baldwin, 30 Dec. 1936; Norman Rose, *Vansittart, Study of a Diplomat*, London, 1978, pp. 199–214.

107. PRO, FO 800/394, Ge/36/6, Chatfield letter to Vansittart, 25 Dec. 1936.

108. PRO, CAB 63/51, M.O.(36)10, Hankey's remarks on Vansittart's 'World Situation and Rearmament', n.d.

109. SHAT, 2N19/D3, CSG, 'Note avant la réunion du conseil de défense nationale pour le désarmement', 8 March 1934.

110. PRO, FO 371/19860, C8781/1/17, Clerk to Eden, 3 Dec. 1936. Several historians have emphasized the French Cabinet's acceptance of deputy chief of staff, General Victor-Henri Schweisguth's critical report of the Soviet manoeuvres he attended in September 1936 as a good indication of the prevailing mood regarding the pact: Alexander, *Republic*, pp. 292–301; Young, *In Command*, pp. 145–9; Jordan, *Popular Front*, pp. 206–9; Adamthwaite, *France*, p. 49; Dreifort, *Yvon Delbos*, p. 110.

111. MAE, URSS 931, Z610/2, 'Fourniture éventuelle de matériel d'armement à l'URSS', 16 June 1936, no. 358, Coulondre to Delbos, 16 Nov. 1936.

# 4

# The Anglo-French Response to the Spanish Civil War and Talks with Italy, July 1936–January 1937

The issue uppermost in Anglo-French relations in late 1936 was the conciliation of Germany. It is, however, impossible to assess the course of appeasement policy in 1937, heralded as it was by an informal Mediterranean agreement between Britain and Italy, without first studying the impact of General Francisco Franco's rebellion upon the entente powers. Until comparatively recently, the foreign policy of Blum's first government was more readily identified with events in Spain than with the appeasement process.[1] The precise origins of the August 1936 Non-Intervention Agreement, the official Anglo-French response to the outbreak of the civil war in July, have attracted exhaustive historical interest among British, French and Spanish scholars.[2] The controversy over non-intervention, though now played out, has occasionally superseded analysis of the long-term impact of the Spanish conflict upon Britain's relations with the Popular Front government.[3]

Blum and Delbos were frequently preoccupied with Spanish concerns because the civil war threatened to destroy the unity of the governing coalition. It proved impossible to reconcile the entire Rassemblement populaire behind a single policy. This resulted in a public adherence to non-intervention, combined with the occasional surreptitious provision of small quantities of arms and equipment to the Republican government. This 'relaxed non-intervention' was largely a sop to the PCF. It also tempered the guilty consciences of many within the SFIO, the Premier and his *chef de cabinet*, André Blumel, among them. French military assistance to the Republican forces had no real strategic impact upon the civil war.

## I

The Popular Front did not unite around a single policy towards Spain. The fear of governmental and national division stimulated the Quai d'Orsay's initial decision to pioneer a neutrality policy. The architects of this were the Secretary-General, Alexis Léger, the Assistant Political Director, René Massigli, and his former colleague as Joint Director, Moscow Ambassador Robert Coulondre. The urgency within French Foreign Ministry planning was not echoed within the Foreign Office. There, the head of the western department, the uninspiring Sir George Mounsey, first recommended only 'cautious support' for the non-intervention idea. In stark contrast to Mounsey's lassitude, Charles Corbin was deluged with daily communications from Delbos on the need to promote a neutrality policy. Corbin lobbied Eden, and numerous officials within the central and southern departments, in order to secure a prompt British reply to the non-intervention scheme.[4]

During the first fortnight of the rebellion the French government received more detailed reports than its British counterparts on the course of events in Spain. Precise intelligence from French Morocco on the *Africanista* preparations across the border in the Spanish zone was distributed between the Quai d'Orsay, Marius Moutet's Ministry of Colonies and all three service ministries. The Ministry of Colonies and the service departments also maintained direct communication with force commanders in French North Africa via an Etat-Major Section d'Outre-Mer.[5] The fear that the rebellion might encourage Muslim sedition within French Morocco added to the weight of intelligence material transmitted to the Ministry of Colonies. Since mid-June, the French Moroccan Residency in Rabat had warned of a copy-cat strike wave across Morocco inspired by the famous sit-down strikes then sweeping France.[6] Intelligence from Morocco was also analysed by the secretariat of the inter-departmental Haut Comité Méditerranéen. This committee was established by Flandin in February 1935. From its inception, the committee's agenda was determined by the French Premier's office at the Hôtel Matignon. Clearly then, Morocco was very much in the mind of the French imperial establishment by the time Franco's rebellion got underway. Information on events was channelled upwards to Blum's Private Office.[7]

Although the French Ambassador, Jean Herbette, and the service attachés in Madrid found it difficult to gather information from the provinces most affected by the uprising, they all agreed that, unless the capital fell before the winter, the civil war was likely to be a long one. Herbette was hostile to the Republican government. He considered the Republican forces a subversive, communist-influenced rabble. But the Military Attaché, Lieutenant-Colonel Morel, developed a grudging admiration for the militias. On 31 July Morel noted, 'If one measures the forces in the field, the rebels should win: but they must win quickly. Delay would not mean defeat. It would mark a diminution of their chances. On paper, they will continue to hold more advantages than the government, but they must bring about the fall of Madrid.'[8]

The 1935 Franco-Spanish commercial treaty generated additional news and intelligence from Spain. It was by dint of this agreement that the outgoing Spanish Ambassador, Juan de Cárdenas, pleaded for French arms on 20 July. The request threatened to precipitate a Cabinet rift between the majority of the Conseil on the one hand, and Blum, Vincent Auriol and the Air Minister, Pierre Cot, on the other. As is well known, this trio was sympathetic to the Republican plea.[9] Delbos and Minister of State Camille Chautemps led the advocates of a policy of strict neutrality. Initially, they fought a rearguard action in which they stressed the juridical implications of arms supply. But Delbos was offered a credible, made-to-measure policy once Léger finalized the Quai d'Orsay's non-intervention proposals. The Foreign Ministry also made good use of Sir George Clerk's forthright warning on 7 August that intervention might compromise the integrity of the entente with Britain.[10]

This added to the existing indications of British hostility regarding any French military assistance to the Spanish Republic. Evidence of the British view derived less from Eden's informal plea to Blum on 23 July to tread warily regarding Spain, than from the Admiralty's cold reception to Admiral Darlan's impromptu mission to London in early August.[11] Darlan received short shrift when he suggested that military support to the Republic made strategic sense in the light of persistent rumours of Italian designs on the Balearic islands. Hankey and the First Lord, Sir Samuel Hoare, refused an audience to the Admiral. Both men disguised their aversion to what amounted to informal staff talks by emphasizing the irregularity of Darlan's visit. Hence the comic picture, gossiped about within Whitehall, of two rather flustered and secretive Frenchmen – Admirals Darlan and Decoux – who had arrived at the Admiralty in plain clothes, without any formal introduction, to seek talks with Britain's naval chiefs.[12] Hoare and Chatfield shied away from Darlan because of their overriding concern to avoid placing the Mediterranean fleet back on a war footing so soon after the end of the Abyssinian conflict. Fleet readiness had only been relaxed on 9 July. The prospect of maintaining ships on alert in the Mediterranean in collaboration with the French naval staff was odious.[13]

Darlan's mission revealed that the Ministry of Marine had taken fright at the size of the German and Italian naval contingents sent to Spanish waters – ostensibly for the protection of their nationals. The French naval staff feared a joint plot to sever French imperial communications with North Africa. Throughout August, the War Ministry maintained that it would not risk troop transports across the Mediterranean unless the naval position improved. This encouraged Darlan to utilize an alleged threat to French security as a lever to secure immediate staff conversations with Britain. The French marine was also acutely aware of its short-term weakness. Effectives for 1936 were below the required intake, especially for officers and junior ratings. French tonnage comparisons with the Italian and German fleets made dismal reading.[14]

Although his surreptitious visit to London perhaps suggested otherwise, Darlan differed from chief of naval staff Durand-Viel and Minister of Marine, Gasnier-Duparc, in craving greater naval independence from Britain. Darlan estimated that Italian air and submarine attacks could preclude Britain's use of its Mediterranean command centres at Malta and Alexandria. If the Royal Navy found itself engaged against Japan in the Far East, Darlan was sceptical that it could lend much assistance in a Mediterranean war. The Admiralty rebuff meted out to him in August helped turn these reasonable strategic assumptions into the rationale for his nascent Anglophobia.[15]

Ironically, the Admiralty took the lead in preparing the first strategical appreciation of the wider consequences of the Spanish civil war, Hankey and Chatfield having drafted the most recent CID review in early July. Taking up the theme of the CID, Hoare warned Halifax on 5 August, 'On no account must we do anything to bolster up Communism in Spain, particularly when it is remembered that Communism in Portugal, to which it would probably spread and particularly in Lisbon, would be a grave danger to the British Empire.'[16] The Cabinet only discussed the civil war in two meetings before 2 September. The rebellion had started less than a fortnight before the summer recess. This apparent lack of concern was actually an indication of the Whitehall consensus over Franco's revolt. Two sessions of the foreign policy committee on 21 and 27 July were entirely devoted to the London conference and the Plymouth report. Spain was only referred to in passing.[17]

Those historians who have seen in British policy an overarching fear of communist revolution across the Iberian peninsula, have naturally relied more heavily on Foreign Office reportage during the recess period. There is no doubt that the British Cabinet had uniformly disliked the Madrid government since its election in February. The British government also disapproved of embattled Prime Minister José Giral's decision to arm the first Republican militias. Yet the British ministers' supposed fear of bolshevism was not reflected in any spate of unusual Whitehall activity comparable to the frenetic response generated within the Quai d'Orsay and the French service ministries by the news of the uprising.[18] The Foreign Office came under the caretaker management of Lord Halifax, and Deputy Under-Secretary, Sir Alexander Cadogan, in the first two weeks of August. Sir George Mounsey's western department, theoretically in charge of incoming reports from Spain, was in terminal decline. The central and southern departments had been encroaching steadily upon the western department's Mediterranean jurisdiction. In February 1936 Frank Ashton-Gwatkin had proposed the abolition of Mounsey's office, suggesting that its duties be redistributed between the remaining regional departments. This would have made it possible for Ashton-Gwatkin's economic section to acquire full departmental status in Mounsey's place. As it was, Vansittart's central department clique dominated foreign policy formulation over Spain. This alone was proof that the conflict was usually subordinated to the requirements of appeasing Germany.[19]

Certainly, in the months preceding the war, the British diplomats in the field, from Madrid Ambassador, Sir Henry Chilton, to his subordinate consuls in the Republican industrial cities from Catalonia to Asturias, painted an alarming picture of creeping Sovietization. But, as was the case with the French elections in May, the 'Whitehall response', in so far as it appeared homogeneous, was primarily a Treasury one. What would be the impact of the war upon British commercial and trading interests in Spain? How best could they be safeguarded? These interests were substantial. As Enrique Moradiellos has shown, British investments composed over 40 per cent of the total foreign capital invested in Spain. The British-owned Rio Tinto mining conglomerate was the industrial giant among Spain's primary producers.[20] Clearly then, the British had much to lose. Nevertheless, the 'official line' on Spain was more sanguine than has been widely supposed. The government's decision to underwrite non-intervention, and the *de facto* complicity in Franco's advance that this implied, was driven by a policy of diplomatic damage limitation. Put crudely, the Spanish situation, though worrying, especially to the specialists in the field, did not matter as much as the replacement Locarno talks.[21]

This assumption was reinforced by the expectation that Franco's well-trained regulars would force the collapse of Madrid, and win the war within a matter of months rather than years. There were thus two cardinal objectives within Britain's Spanish policy. Firstly, non-intervention was intended to contain the international frictions caused between France and the Soviet Union on the one hand, and Portugal and the fascist powers on the other. Whether non-intervention was practised nominally as originally intended, or with some naval muscle as eventually occurred, did not especially matter, except in so far as it affected British naval power in other regions of the globe. Secondly, British policy was intended to preserve reasonable political and trading relations with the eventual victor in Spain. If one follows these objectives,

British policy was fairly successful, if morally questionable, regarding the first, but a wholesale failure regarding the second.

## II

Success in containing the diplomatic damage wrought by the civil war was easily measured. British policy did not prevent the consolidation of détente with Italy, despite Mussolini's increasingly flagrant provision of arms, equipment and men to Franco's forces. Nor was Hitler able to condemn Anglo-French policies in Spain in a manner akin to his vilification of Soviet actions. Unable to avoid this unpleasant and unforeseen Spanish complication to the appeasement process, the British government grafted its policy towards Spain onto that process. Official British reaction to the Spanish civil war provides another instance of the appeasement of the fascist powers in action.

This was something in which the French government was more often to be found conspiring than complaining, even if the bulk of the SFIO rank and file shared the disgust of the PCF leadership at an allegedly craven submission to British interests.[22] In a speech at Luna Park in Paris on 6 September, Blum made a well-publicized defence of non-intervention. Within a week, the government resumed its covert supply of obsolete aircraft to Spain – the practice ambiguously labelled 'relaxed non-intervention'.[23] Still, the French government shared the British wish to keep the non-intervention accord in place. Perhaps the cardinal difference between London and Paris was that several of Blum's ministers were genuinely troubled by the hypocrisy involved. Moreover, for France the policy was not only one of appeasement abroad, but also of appeasement at home. The fragile cohesion of the governing coalition would have crumbled had anything more than the Air Ministry's *non-intervention relachée* been attempted.[24] Blum was also persuaded by the Republican envoys, Fernando de los Ríos and Ximenes de Asua, that the Front populaire could best assist their Spanish brethren by remaining in office to work for real non-intervention by the fascist powers. By conspicuously failing to repudiate the rumours that Britain had cajoled them into non-intervention, the French government also found an additional means to blunt the arrows of its left-wing critics.[25]

Neither France nor the Soviet Union could match the scale of Italo-German arms supply without seriously denuding their own rearmament. The few French aircraft initially sent to Spain were not intended for the armée de l'air. They were purchased on the open market in Paris. The Quai d'Orsay also remained a restraining influence. On 28 September, Léger warned Cot's *chef de cabinet*, Puget, that he had contacted the Ministry of Interior to clarify whether American export licences issued for the French purchase of nine transport aircraft prohibited their onward sale to Spain. Perhaps aware that Puget had already set about finding suitable pilots for these planes, Léger warned that the American government had plainly insisted upon this precondition.[26]

Based at the Hôtel Matignon, Jules Moch, the head of Blum's General Secretariat, also worked for the occasional release of aircraft to the Spanish Republic. So too did the Finance Minister, Vincent Auriol, and a leading light of his *cabinet*, the head of customs, Gaston Cusin. This Rue de Rivoli assistance was essentially passive. Cusin did not follow Léger in placing barriers in the way of supply. Cot's thinly veiled provision of aircraft has attracted disproportionate historical interest. Two Dewoitine 510 fighters and one Bloch 210 bomber were the only 1936-type planes ever sent to Spain. The other obsolete French aircraft delivered to Spain, including Loiré and Potez models, in addition to those mentioned above, were all designed for high-altitude flying. This made them unsuitable for the tasks of tactical support to which they were usually allocated by the Republican forces. In December 1936 the EMA deuxième bureau dismissed these aircraft as insignificant relative to the first deliveries of Soviet Kaliouska planes. Cot was also careful to ensure that any aircraft flown into or out of Spain landed at civil airstrips. This enabled him to distance the Air Ministry from the resultant controversy.[27]

The romance of these cloak-and-dagger activities is more alluring than their material importance. There were certainly French volunteer airmen in Republican Spain, paid a monthly fee and substantial bonuses for every Nationalist aircraft shot down. Unlike the Soviet pilots who superseded them, these men were largely from civilian backgrounds. They were not beholden to the French Air Ministry. While this is interesting, the argument over Front populaire involvement has been spiced by the enduring controversy over Cot's pro-sovietism. Furthermore, during 1937, war *matériel* earmarked for Spain was occasionally sabotaged by members of the right-wing extremist Cagoulards.[28]

Among the most telling indications of the limited impact of relaxed non-intervention is General Jean-Henri Jauneaud's account of his support for Cot's policy. An ardent advocate of a Soviet military alliance, Jauneaud was Cot's closest collaborator within the Air Ministry in his capacity as the minister's *chef de cabinet militaire*. In his unpublished memoirs, Jauneaud recorded his efforts to win Conseil sympathy for cooperation with the Soviet government in the deployment of aircraft in eastern Europe and Spain. Blum, Delbos and Daladier all rejected his arguments outright. As Jauneaud put it, he was 'completely isolated' within the French military establishment.[29]

André Blumel stated that 'Non-intervention was essentially an attempt to prevent others from doing what we were incapable of accomplishing.'[30] Furthermore, after popular relief at the conclusion of the Matignon agreements subsided, Radical ministers were less chary in asserting their views. They no longer left it to Edouard Herriot and Jules Jeanneney, the Radical Party leaders in the two Chambers, to take the lead in opposing involvement in Spain. The Radicals tapped the vein of anti-communism stirred up by the right-wing press. It was clear that popular indignation at PCF subservience to Moscow was widespread. Daladier, Chautemps, Delbos, Herriot and Jeanneney were a formidable combination to be opposed by a collection of more junior Socialist Ministers, Under-Secretaries and the renegade Radical, Pierre Cot.[31]

Both the SFIO and the PCF operated within the legal confines of a constitutional system in which there was no possibility to fulfil their declared maximum programmes. But the Socialists could not admit this without risking a loss of support to their more extreme, and less resolutely parliamentary, left-wing rivals. This fear of losing out to the PCF was evident in Blum's Spanish policy. The SFIO leadership was caught between a belief in the Republican cause, and a recognition that open support for it was inimical to the government's survival.[32] On 9 September Sir George Clerk reported that Blum could not contain PCF demands for intervention. The Premier had held a fruitless meeting with Maurice Thorez at the Hôtel Matignon on the previous day. If Franco's troops capitalized on their recent victory at Irun, almost within earshot of the French border, Clerk expected the renascent strike wave in France to become more politicized.[33] Thorez did not withhold PCF parliamentary support from the coalition. But once the Soviet government followed up its temporary withdrawal from the non-intervention committee (NIC) in October by increasing its supplies to the Spanish Republic, the French Communists pilloried Blum's timidity once more. By this time, British opposition to any French resumption of intervention was only a secondary determinant of French policy over Spain. But playing the British card remained critical as a means to secure Socialist and Communist acquiescence in Quai d'Orsay policy.[34]

On 20 August Eden warned of a realignment of European powers built upon divisions over Spain. The Foreign Secretary used this argument to press for greater British support for Blum. In effect, this was a call for the Cabinet foreign policy committee to agree that the proposed non-intervention committee should sit in London; the British, by extension, taking the lead in the policing of the scheme. Although the foreign policy committee approved this course of action, it referred the consideration of ways and means to make the policy effective to an interdepartmental sub-committee. When it reported in early September, the sub-committee dodged a decision. Only Eden's proposal that the cumbersome NIC be divided into malleable sub-committees gave real impetus to the operation of non-intervention.[35]

Ralph Wigram was quick to point out the threat to British strategic interests inherent in the sponsorship of non-intervention. Britain would be blamed for getting in the way, imposing a neutrality policy upon combatants and their supplying nations. All of the parties directly engaged in Spain were, to varying degrees, hostile to the non-intervention idea. In a rare identification with the CID and Admiralty view, Wigram suggested that the non-intervention policy Eden proposed might add to the number of Britain's enemies. In fact, the British were trapped. The Italian Ambassador, Dino Grandi, warned repeatedly that his government would only sit in conference with the French under British supervision. Ambassador Ribbentrop was also adept at hinting at the possibility of a genuine fascist alliance nurtured by a common outlook over Spain. Germano-Italian pressure such as this left the British government with no alternative but to accept a leading role in the NIC. If it did not do so, non-intervention would collapse. This would leave France more dangerously exposed. Léger agreed with Wigram's conclusion that the German and Soviet governments were using the civil war to foment discord and stunt the development of the western pact.[36]

In contrast to these machinations, the British and French governments only disagreed strongly over Italy. Prior to the unilateral British approaches to Mussolini in November, these differences were evident in the Quai d'Orsay's tendency to revive the idea of a multilateral Mediterranean pact whenever a détente between London and Rome appeared likely. In November, the British government precluded any regional arms limitation scheme liable to impede Britain's ability to reinforce the Mediterranean fleet at will. Two weeks earlier, the Cabinet had postponed NIC consideration of alleged Italian intervention in Spain for fear of cutting across foreign-policy committee plans to convene a Locarno power conference.[37]

It was soon apparent that the NIC would never succeed in its avowed purpose. Within a fortnight of its inaugural meeting the committee was deadlocked. NIC proceedings were only livened up by the trading of insults between Dino Grandi, German embassy Counsellor, Prince Bismarck, and the Soviet Ambassador, Ivan Maisky.[38] By mid-October, British preparations for a western-pact conference had been thwarted by the niggling objections from Berlin and Rome. This made an approach to Italy the short-term focus of British appeasement policy. The formulation of an attractive package of colonial concessions to Germany remained, as yet, incomplete.

Faced with the prospect of bilateral Anglo-Italian exchanges, the French government took a new tack in its opposition to the British détente with Rome. The Quai d'Orsay began by recalling its suggestion in April that France's 'possessions and dependencies' should be included in any western pact guarantee. Léger stressed that the Spanish situation had added to the importance of this request for the Locarno powers to underwrite French imperial security. The EMG expected that, were Italy to enter a war alongside Germany, Mussolini's opening gambit would be an attempt to disrupt French maritime communications with the three French *maghreb* territories.[39] Roger Cambon, the Chargé d'affaires in London, told Sargent that the French government did not expect a blanket guarantee of the French Empire. The Quai simply hoped that a sympathetic British response would be sufficient to deter Mussolini from encroaching upon the Balearic islands or Spanish Morocco as a preliminary to challenging French supremacy in the western Mediterranean.[40] The Foreign Office saw through this. As with the Mediterranean pact, this French proposal was transparently impractical. Léger and Delbos were trying to throw a spanner into the works of Anglo-Italian diplomacy.

The British and French reactions to the announcement of the Rome–Berlin Axis in November are explicable in view of these divisions over an approach to Rome. The Cabinet's cool response was designed to pre-empt any French requests for immediate military discussions. By the same token, official French alarm was intended to support the Quai's argument for the immediate abandonment of British plans to discuss matters *à deux* with the Italians.[41] Meanwhile, the French embassy in Rome was striving to overcome the prevailing Italophobia of the Quai d'Orsay. Charles de Chambrun even suggested that the Axis might be little more than a means by which Mussolini could reintroduce the idea of a four-power pact to France and Britain. In this scenario, the Axis was simply the latest twist to Mussolini's opportunistic foreign policy. Germany posed 'the only real danger' to Italian security. De Chambrun also had assurances from the Italian Ministry of Marine that, contrary to rumour, it had no interest in base facilities in Majorca.[42]

Chamberlain shared the French Ambassador's optimism. He was confident that the German government remained anxious for an agreement with Britain. The announcement of the Axis was not necessarily prejudicial to this. It simply illustrated Hitler's anxiety to improve his bargaining position. Nor did the Cabinet regard the Axis as evidence of Mussolini's definitive recognition of German supremacy in central Europe. In short, the rationale behind an Anglo-Italian agreement was not much affected. An Anglo-Italian deal would add to Hitler's envy of an accord with the British. It would fortify Italian resolve over Austria, itself an additional means to coax Germany towards the conference table.

Even the Foreign Office drew some comfort from the evidence of increasing Germano-Italian collusion in Spain. The Italian Ambassador in Berlin, Attolico, claimed that the Axis was '51 per cent' attributable to Spanish events. Mussolini had long been feeding Rome Ambassador, Sir Eric Drummond, with assurances along similar lines. The logic behind this was simple. An Axis built upon anti-communism need not necessarily pose a threat to western power interests. As part of the 'October Protocols' signed by Hitler and Ciano at Berchtesgaden, both men agreed to co-operate in a propaganda offensive against communism, and to recognize Franco's government jointly. Hitler confirmed his intention not to interfere in the Mediterranean, confident that events in Spain would perpetuate the Franco-Italian suspicion created by the Abyssinian conflict.[43] It was far easier for the more hawkish ministers in Chamberlain's coterie to forgive an agreement based on the sound principles of anti-bolshevism than to believe the pessimistic arguments of a left-wing French administration which seemed to be preaching nothing except strategic doom and gloom regarding Italy in particular.

In late December, the French Chargé d'affaires in Rome, Jules Blondel, advised Delbos that the Italians considered that the ideological make-up of the Paris government placed France 'outside the circuit' of international diplomacy. Equally, the French were not about to recognize Italy's conquest of Ethiopia.[44] If there was no sign of any thaw in Franco-Italian relations, there were more serious obstacles to bilateral Franco-German negotiations. The mere suggestion of such exchanges would put several nails in the coffin of the eastern alliance network. Although the alliances were in terminal decline, the Popular Front was none the less committed to uphold them. There was one way forward. Were France to agree to tripartite conversations in which London took the leading role in appeasing Berlin or Rome, then French involvement could be justified with the eastern allies, and the alliance network ostensibly maintained in full vigour.

This desire to make London the focal point for policies as much authored in Paris had governed the establishment of the NIC. In 1937 the same attitude coloured the French response to Germany's colonial demands. But, in as much as certain individuals in the Paris diplomatic establishment wanted a stake in the appeasement of Italy, the policy was a singular failure. This was because Blum was prepared to give so little ground.[45]

The Spanish civil war destroyed the residual hopes of the French army and air staffs that the removal of sanctions would permit a renewal of collaboration with Italy. Soon after sanctions were lifted in June, Ciano confided to de Chambrun that 'the flame of Franco-Italian friendship could easily be re-kindled within two or three months.'[46] On 18 July, the day after the *Africanista* rebellion, the EMAA asked Cot to authorize an informal approach to the Italian air staff suggesting a resumption of the contacts stipulated under the Rome agreements. Delbos vetoed the proposal on 28 July.[47] The EMG expected that the Front populaire's ideological hostility to Italy might prejudice the swift re-establishment of a Franco-Italian military détente. In the event, the generals saw their hopes dashed by events in Spain. Whereas there was some hope of tempering the impact of the former, there was little that the French military could do about the latter.

## III

Negotiation of the Gentlemen's agreement with Italy proved how hollow British governmental interest in the fate of Spain really was. Responding to a typically ebullient speech by Mussolini at Milan on 1 November, the Foreign Office suggested that Britain should impress upon the Italian government that Germany was not the only friend available to them.[48] An agreement would integrate Italy into the London naval treaty system. This would meet chiefs-of-staff complaints that poor relations with the Italians saddled Britain with an otherwise avoidable commitment. The service chiefs were less concerned at the potential for confrontation in the naval policing of non-intervention than at Italian disruption – actual and potential – in the eastern Mediterranean. The fascist government transmitted anti-British propaganda to the Arab world from radio stations at Bari, and in Libya. This became more of a headache after the outbreak of civil disorder in Palestine during the summer of 1936. The CID was also diverted by the spectre of an Italian pincer movement against Egypt or Sudan directed from Libya and Abyssinia.[49]

The first British feelers to Rome were put out in October, just as the German–Italian contacts prior to the announcement of the Axis reached a peak. On 10 November the heads of the Foreign Office European departments agreed that Britain should cultivate better relations with Italy. They advised the government to steer a middle course intended to convince Mussolini that while Britain was anxious to avoid confront-ation, it was in no way desperate for agreement.[50] In Rome, Drummond proved as gullible as Charles de Chambrun. The British Ambassador had welcomed Ciano's visit to Berlin as an opportunity for a genuine Locarno enthusiast to parley with Hitler. In an exchange of letters with members of the southern department, Drummond enthused about the forthcoming discussions with Mussolini. Neither Drummond nor the southern department head, Owen O'Malley, was much of a friend to France. O'Malley's experience of the Abyssinian and Rhineland crises had convinced him that the French would fight for nothing except their own soil.[51]

By November Eden was convinced that the Italians intended to annex Majorca when opportunity arose. Still, he ruled out any Anglo-French military demonstration by way of deterrent, claiming that such intervention would provoke a French governmental crisis.[52] The French suggestion of a joint naval action was intended to allay the Ministry of Marine's anxiety regarding the likely British response to the establishment of Italian air bases on Majorca. Italian aircraft would then be capable of sustained bombardment of Malta. When debating the importance of the Balearics, the EMM concluded that the Italian naval presence in the western Mediterranean was sufficiently superior to their own to justify the preparation of plans for the dispersal of the main fleet from Toulon. Understandably alarmed, on 21 November the Ministry of Marine tentatively suggested a renewal of exploratory talks over Mediterranean security to the Admiralty. This was done with Léger's approval.[53] Jules Blondel warned Delbos that the Italians were determined to win the contest with France for naval superiority in the western Mediterranean. They had already won the battle regarding first-line air strength. Despite the Quai d'Orsay's pessimism, the War Ministry remained doubtful that Franco would cede control of territory in return for Italian military aid. In a series of reports conveyed via General Georges to the EMA, Madrid Military Attaché Morel disparaged the notion of a community of interest between the Spanish army and the Italian government.[54]

In London, the Admiralty responded favourably, if cautiously, to the Ministry of Marine's requests for discussions. The French naval staff had made a substantial concession by stipulating that any contacts should be based upon the model of the limited 1935 conversations. While the war in Spain continued, the Admiralty had little choice but to talk matters over with its French counterpart. French naval co-operation was essential to the implementation of the most recent NIC monitoring scheme. This had established a zonal grid of naval patrols off Spain's principal ports. On 21 October the French government had confirmed the marine's participation in this.[55] But the British chiefs of staff were still remarkably placid about the possibility of Italian use of Majorca. Disparaging the likelihood of successful air attacks on a Malta fleet, the CID concluded in August that no vital British interests would be affected. This conclusion was not reversed in the months that followed.[56]

The chiefs of staff had an ulterior motive for their benign assessment of the Italian connection with Spain. To the COS it was preferable to assist the appeasement process by stressing the inoffensive nature of the British naval role within non-intervention than to risk military confrontation in defence of a Republican cause with which the Admiralty had no sympathy. Conversations with the French naval staff in no way altered the Admiralty's preference for a withdrawal of the fleet at the first available opportunity, ideally as part of a regional agreement involving the Italians.[57]

It was no surprise that First Sea Lord, Sir Samuel Hoare, was the most outspoken advocate of an immediate grant of belligerent rights to Franco. This was tantamount to a full recognition of the Nationalist cause. The Cabinet rejected this on 18 November, accepting that such a concession could only be made if Madrid were to fall. With a lengthy siege of the capital becoming more probable, Hoare renewed his suggestion in the following week. He was armed with information from the Naval Intelligence Division warning of possible incidents arising from the Nationalist effort to prevent any resupply of the Republican forces by sea.[58] This tallied with the latest information in the hands of Colonel Gauché, head of French military intelligence. From Madrid, Morel advised that the Republican militias were capable of a sustained defence, even if they were insufficiently trained to grasp the strategic initiative. In order to win quickly, the Nationalists would have to strangle sources of Republican supply more effectively.[59]

On 22 November a special meeting of ministers reconsidered British policy over belligerent rights. The Admiralty was disappointed at the committee's recommendation of more stringent legislation to control the carriage of war *matériel*. Hoare then suggested discussion of belligerent rights in forthcoming trade talks with the competing Spanish authorities. Again his proposal was rejected, this time on the grounds that the NIC had devised a more effective system of maritime supervision. This was little consolation to the Admiralty. Increased naval patrolling threatened to expose Britain's actual strategic vulnerability in the Mediterranean. The CID joint planning staff had decided in July that Far Eastern convoy traffic could not use Suez in the event of Italian hostility.[60]

The British government was losing confidence that the Spanish situation could be subordinated to the appeasement of Italy. If the Admiralty and CID view was clear, the Foreign Office was sending out mixed messages. Its original recommendation of an Anglo-Italian declaration of friendship, the negotiation of which was to proceed while the fleet maintained a high-profile presence in the Mediterranean, marked an uneasy compromise between two schools of thought. The division within the Foreign Office was easy to trace. Most Foreign Office advisers favoured an agreement at the cost of a little humble pie if need be.[61] But Eden and Cranborne doubted the merits of a swiftly agreed informal accord. Without genuine Italian goodwill, it would be worthless. A loose agreement with Rome would enable the CID to convince the Cabinet to reduce the British naval contribution to non-intervention. Far from convincing Mussolini of Britain's magnanimity and muscle, the agreement would simply encourage the Duce's dream of hegemony within the Mediterranean.

Although the Cabinet had not gone as far as Hoare had wanted, the majority of ministers sympathized with the CID's arguments. In mid-December Eden insisted that the chiefs of staff re-examine the strategic importance of Italian air bases on the Balearics. But he could not persuade his fellow ministers that talks with Italy were moving too quickly. Nor was the Cabinet concerned that French strategic interests were being overlooked.[62] Although the Quai d'Orsay was irritated by British policy, Delbos opted to press his case discreetly. While Corbin urged the Foreign Office to contemplate French admission to the planned exchanges with Rome, Delbos pointed out that the idea of joint declarations affirming British and Italian respect for free maritime communications derived from an idea put forward in the original French proposals for a Mediterranean pact. Delbos reminded Eden that the malaise in Italian relations with the western powers since 1935 was attributable to Anglo-French fidelity to the League. It was therefore nonsensical to exclude France from an agreement designed to reduce that friction.[63]

These mild French blandishments were counter-productive. In effect, they confirmed that the Foreign Ministry saw little prospect of an improvement in Franco-Italian relations. Mussolini was not interested. Nor was Blum. Furthermore, in November, the French withdrew de Chambrun from Rome. This left only the Chargé d'affaires, Jean Blondel, to represent French interests. This remained the position until October 1938. The German government was delighted at the prospect of a second British abandonment of France (after the 1935 naval agreement) in order to secure a quick agreement with a fascist power. The Gentlemen's agreement would not weaken the Axis. Quite the reverse — the accord weakened the entente. The French government dismissed the specious Foreign Office argument that an informal bilateral arrangement with Italy might pave the way to a rapprochement between Paris and Rome. Confronted with this, on 19 November Eden admitted to Corbin that Mussolini would have no truck with the Blum administration.[64] By the end of November Eden had given in to the Cabinet's wish for a quick solution. He agreed to drop 'delicate' questions from the exchanges with Rome, the understanding being that Italian intervention in Spain was best side-stepped. Reference was carefully avoided to possible French involvement in any future Anglo-Italian discussions. Policy over Spain was not even referred to within the final joint declarations, but was covered by a separate exchange of notes on 2 January 1937.[65]

**IV**

Non-intervention had remained nominally in force while Britain's Mediterranean policy turned to the appeasement of Italy in late 1936. On 25 November the Cabinet approved the first comprehensive NIC scheme based upon naval patrolling, and the establishment of an international Control Commission on Spanish soil. But most ministers were still uncomfortable regarding Britain's pre-eminent role within any such policy. Only the Royal Navy was expected to be scrupulously neutral in its monitoring of the coasts. On 16 December, in typically business-like fashion, Chamberlain told the Cabinet that, short of coercive measures, the only way to prevent intervention was to secure the direct agreement of the culprits to cease their misbehaviour.[66] At the Chancellor's request, the Cabinet authorized Eden to make a further direct plea to the notorious supplier nations offering to abandon the control scheme as soon as supplies dried up. This pious appeal was bound to fail. It did serve to justify the continuation of non-intervention which, in reality, the Cabinet knew to be vital to the stability of French foreign and domestic policy. Defence of the Popular Front was certainly not Chamberlain's primary purpose. PCF abstention in a vote of confidence on government foreign policy on 4 December none the less illustrated the fragility of French official support for non-intervention.[67]

Since the object of the non-intervention initiative was more to avoid the escalation of civil war into international crisis than to prevent supply, the NIC was a highly worthwhile organization. The NIC chairman, Lord Plymouth, agreed with the Foreign Office diagnosis that dispatch of a Control Commission was essential to keep non-intervention alive. Any practical effect would be a bonus.[68] On 16 December the Cabinet decided to ask participating states to give plenipotentiary powers to their delegates on the NIC. This would enable the committee to function without the constant referral of decisions back to individual governments. Eden, Chamberlain and Baldwin canvassed this idea within the Cabinet, and it was these three who also proposed a further initiative: an attempt to prohibit the entry of volunteers to Spain.[69]

Hence, as one non-intervention scheme was finalized, implemented and flouted, another was in preparation. The most serious aspect of the 'volunteer' question did not turn on volunteers at all. It was primarily an effort to secure an end to the dispatch of Italian army and fascist militia units to Spain. The new British initiative was one policy affecting Italy that Paris could whole-heartedly support. On 24 December the entente powers issued a joint proposal for the cessation of traffic in volunteers. An NIC sub-committee formulated proposals prohibiting the recruitment and transportation of volunteer groups. The British stressed that the plan would wipe the slate clean; there would be no indictments regarding volunteers already in Spain.[70] On 22 December the Soviet government withheld its backing for the scheme until the Control Commission was in operation. This ruled out any immediate progress through the NIC. Still, the Anglo-French proposal regarding volunteer forces marked a return to direct dialogue with the interested powers over Spain.[71]

The prospects for this were not encouraging. The Italians complicated matters by maintaining their linkage of volunteer withdrawal with the prohibition of all other forms of indirect aid, notably arms and financial support. On 5 January 1937, three days after the conclusion of the Gentlemen's agreement, some 5,000 Italian troops disembarked at Cadiz. Over 15,000 Italian personnel had been sent to Spain over the Christmas period. Eden knew that Italy was the central obstacle to the success of the plan. But he was encouraged by reports of German opposition to flagrant intervention, and by Ciano's apparent readiness to consider volunteer withdrawal.[72] Still, Foreign Office opinion was hardening. On 6 January Eden warned the Cabinet, 'The character of the future Government of Spain has now become less important to the peace of Europe than that the Dictators should not be victorious in that country.' The corollary of this view was that the volunteer initiative should be presented as a last-ditch effort to reach a viable international agreement over the civil war. Believing Mussolini's support for intervention to be fundamentally opportunistic, the diplomats were quite prepared to bend over backwards to find a workable formula for withdrawal.[73]

The volunteer initiative was qualitatively different from previous NIC schemes in that the content was as important as the form. This led Hoare to dismiss it, Baldwin to reconsider his initial enthusiasm for the idea and Halifax to disparage Foreign Office influence upon Britain's Spanish policy. On 9 January the volunteer project only scraped through at the second meeting of the Cabinet's situation in Spain committee because Chamberlain backed it. Eden also stressed the number of favourable replies received from interventionist governments.[74]

Events had turned full circle since July 1936. Aside from PCF criticism, Blum's ministers were at least no longer outwardly divided over Spain. By contrast, the British Cabinet was finding adjustment to its role of leading advocate of non-intervention more painful than expected. Admiralty bitterness over non-intervention was nourished by the evident willingness of the Foreign Office to add to British commitments without thought for the burden placed on the fleet. Lord Halifax took up the CID mantle in the Cabinet on 13 January, warning that Britain's current intimacy with France had led the government to view the Spanish conflict 'through French spectacles'.[75] Hankey was less circumspect in his criticisms than Halifax had been. Hankey's disdain for the Popular Front continued to colour his judgement: 'she [France] is inoculated with the virus of communism, which is at present rotting the body politic, delaying much needed rearmament and causing acute internal dissension.' In a private letter to Vansittart, Chatfield seconded his CID colleague's opinion, 'France, our only real support, is . . . unreliable both politically and militarily, especially the former.'[76]

## V

The alarm over the new NIC scheme was a little premature. In January, the Cabinet approved the principle of naval monitoring of Spanish ports. But implementation of the plan was delayed for a further three months, chiefly because of Portuguese and Italian objections to the exact terms of control. Ironically, by the time this naval policing became operational in mid-April, Franco's blockade of the Basque ports made it a more explosive task than anticipated.[77] In the interim, the opponents of closer entente with France among the British military cut their teeth on a brief French war scare during the second week of January 1937. The focus of French concern was the Morocco protectorate. For several weeks the Quai d'Orsay had been feeding the Foreign Office with intelligence on heightened German involvement in Spanish Morocco. The Spanish were not permitted to build fortifications or strategic works outside the ports within their sector of the Moroccan coastline. This was stipulated under the terms of the 1912 extension to the original 1906 Act of Algeciras, by which Spain began 'sub-letting' the Spanish zone from France. Furthermore, the Spanish were expressly forbidden to cede control of their sphere of influence to any third power.[78]

Within the Foreign and Colonial Ministries in Paris it was feared that Spanish rights and territories in Morocco might yet figure in a final pay-off to Germany. Since the German battlecruiser *Deutschland* first anchored off Ceuta two weeks after the outbreak of hostilities, rumours abounded in the Quai of a sequel to the pre-1914 Moroccan crises and a 're-édition d'Agadir'. Reich interest in Moroccan iron-ore deposits compounded this alarm. The former Moroccan Resident-General, Marcel Peyrouton, suggested that the Germans be warned off. In fact, the only measures taken were defensive, largely confined to a reinforcement of the land frontier with the Spanish zone.[79] Corbin noted that the Germans were violating the 1912 treaty with impunity. On 22 December the British consul at Tetouan reported unusual German troop landings and a build-up of equipment.[80]

The war scare was ignited on 6 January 1937. Peyrouton's replacement, General Charles-Auguste Noguès, warned that a large contingent of German 'volunteers' was imminently expected in the Spanish zone. Barracks to accommodate several thousand troops had been hastily erected on the instructions of Colonel Juan Beigbeder, the Nationalist High Commissioner in Tetouan.[81] French forces in Morocco were placed on full alert. On 9 January the Paris press reported that Daladier was to make a tour of the country in the following week. Minister of Marine, Gasnier-Duparc, was to visit neighbouring Algeria and Tunisia. The annual January manoeuvres of the French Mediterranean squadron off the Moroccan and west African coasts were given an unusually high profile.[82]

Over the subsequent week, the British chiefs of staff dismissed the French suggestion that a joint naval watch be mounted off Ceuta. By 10 January, both the German Admiralty and Colonel Beigbeder had issued unequivocal assurances that nothing untoward was planned. The British considered the whole episode a manufactured crisis, designed in part to disguise French governmental opposition to a binding commitment to prevent volunteers from reaching Spain.[83] On the one hand, this view seemed correct. On 12 January Delbos dropped the Quai d'Orsay's allegations once Foreign Minister von Neurath issued a formal *démenti*. But, on the other hand, Blum publicized his instructions to the Minister of Colonies, Marius Moutet, to improve French defences in Morocco. On 13 January Léger informed the Italian Ambassador Cerruti that the Premier was determined to resist any *coup de force* whether in Czechoslovakia or North Africa.[84]

In Whitehall, only Eden was impressed by this French bluster. On 28 January Corbin reported that a British naval delegation sent to investigate the alleged German activities at Ceuta and Melilla had found nothing. The only Reich nationals in the ports were a handful of representatives of the Hissma organization promoting German bilateral trade with the Nationalist authorities.[85] In fact, if anyone was considering a transfer of Spanish Morocco, it was the Republican government. In late January Léger studiously ignored hints from the Spanish Foreign Ministry suggesting that the zone might be ceded to France in return for additional French material aid.[86] Putting Eden's endorsement of Blum's policy to one side, the general British distrust of the French claims regarding German activities in Morocco reflected a deeper truth. Anything which pushed the Spanish problem to the forefront of European diplomacy was intrinsically unwelcome. The British government was committed to its policy of damage limitation in which the prospects for appeasement were always valued more highly than the requirements of Spain.

## VI

By October 1936 London was established as the clearing-house for the non-intervention regime. The Foreign Office effectively controlled NIC agenda. The Quai d'Orsay, having devised the idea, was determined to remain in Britain's slip-stream thereafter. The course of events in Spain did not disturb this arrangement. By contrast, the British pursuit of talks with Italy damaged Anglo-French cordiality. It marked the first real set-back to the rapid improvement in entente relations achieved over the preceding six months. Strategically, the Gentlemen's agreement made little appreciable difference to the dangerous stand-off in the western Mediterranean. As the pace of the Nationalist advance slowed, so Franco's need for Italian assistance increased.

Unfortunately, Britain's signature of a second bilateral arrangement with a fascist power again advertised France's diplomatic and strategic insecurity. Clear evidence of this emerged during 1937 in the renewed interest among France's traditional eastern European and Balkan clients in closer ties with Britain. In his reaction to the Gentlemen's agreement, the Turkish Foreign Minister, Rustu Aras, epitomized the trend. In February 1936 Aras assured Flandin that Turkish policy 'will always be a Franco-British policy in execution'. Yet on 5 January 1937 Aras confessed his eagerness for a Turkish–Italian détente to the British Ambassador, Sir Percy Loraine: 'If now a *friendly* Italy took France's place as second string that would suit Turkey equally well.'[87]

The thaw in Anglo-Italian relations made the Spanish conflict more exasperating because it complicated the negotiation effort, and stretched Admiralty resources afresh. The conflict in Spain unnerved the Blum administration since it raised the possibility – albeit a distant one – of a war on three fronts. More serious in the short term, the civil war threatened to undo the Popular Front's domestic achievements by destroying the unity of the coalition. Though London and Paris disagreed on several fine points of non-intervention policy, there remained a shared belief that containment of the civil war was the only means to sustain entente unity and keep the appeasement process alive.

# Notes

1. Works which stress British pressure on Paris include Dante Puzzo, *Spain and the Great Powers, 1936–1941*, New York, reprint, 1972, p. 120; M.D. Gallagher, 'Léon Blum and the Spanish Civil War', *JCH*, 6, 1971, pp. 56–64; Dreifort, *Yvon Delbos*, pp. 31–54; Jill Edwards, *The British Government and the Spanish Civil War, 1936–1939*, Oxford, 1979, pp. 1–43. Others emphasize the French designation of non-intervention, see Colton, *Léon Blum*, ch. VIII; Carlton, *Anthony Eden*, pp. 89–92; Parker, *Chamberlain*, ch. 5; Glyn A. Stone, 'The European Great Powers and the Spanish Civil War, 1936–1939', in Robert Boyce and Esmonde M. Robertson (eds), *Paths to War: New Essays on the Origins of the Second World War*, London, 1989, pp. 199–232; Stone, 'Britain, France and the Spanish Problem', in Richardson and Stone, *Decisions and Diplomacy*, pp. 129–52.

2. See n. 1, and Enrique Moradiellos, 'The Origins of British Non-Intervention in the Spanish Civil War: Anglo-Spanish Relations in Early 1936', *EHQ*, 21, 1991, pp. 339–64, 'British Political Strategy in the Face of the Military Rising of 1936 in Spain', *CEH*, 1, 2, 1992, pp. 123–37, and 'Appeasement and Non-Intervention: British Policy during the Spanish Civil War', in Catterall and Morris, *Britain and the Threat to Stability in Europe*, pp. 94–104; Douglas Little, *Malevolent Neutrality: The United States, Great Britain and the Origins of the Spanish Civil War*, Ithaca, NY, 1985, and 'Red Scare, 1936: Anti-Bolshevism and the Origins of British Non-Intervention in the Spanish Civil War', *JCH*, 23, 1988, pp. 291–311; H. Haywood Hunt, 'The French Radicals, Spain and the emergence of appeasement', in Alexander and Graham, *French and Spanish Popular Fronts*, pp. 38–49.

3. See references to Glyn A. Stone in n. 1.

4. Lacouture, *Léon Blum*, p. 322; PRO, FO 371/20526, W7504/62/41, Mounsey to Halifax, 2 Aug. 1936; MAE, Massigli 14, Delbos note, 'Exportation d'armes', 1 Aug. 1936.

5. ANCOM, Affaires Politiques, c. 920/D1, Haut Comité Méditerranéen, rapport no. 1, 15 Feb. 1937; SHAT, 7N3890/D1, EMA-3, 'Instruction générale pour la défense de l'Afrique du Nord', 3 Jan. 1936.

6. ANCOM, aff. pol., c. 901/D4, 'Situation politique et économique', 1–15 June 1936.

7. ANCOM, aff. pol., c. 920/D1, H.C.Med. rapport, 15 Feb. 1937. Regarding Franco's preparations in Spanish Morocco see Paul Preston, *Franco: A Biography*, London, 1993, pp. 137–59.

8. Jackson, *Popular Front*, p. 153; SHAT, 7N2754/D3, EMA-2, no. 317, Morel to Daladier, 31 July 1936.

9. The 1935 Franco-Spanish commercial agreement permitted arms sales to the value of 20 million francs, the exact total requested by Giral's envoys on 21 July; Colton, *Léon Blum*, p. 236. Regarding French divisions see Colton, *Léon Blum*, pp. 242–7; Jackson, *Popular Front*, pp. 202–9.

10. PRO, FO 371/20524, W6960/62/41, Clerk to FO, 25 July 1936; DDF, 2, III, no. 108, 'Note de la Sous-Direction d'Europe', 8 Aug. 1936. Clerk spoke 'sans ambages', i.e. without beating about the bush, see Carlton, *Anthony Eden*, pp. 92–3.

11. Some historians place greater emphasis on Darlan's mission. See Edwards, *British Government*, pp. 23–4; Carlton, 'Eden, Blum and the Origins of Non-Intervention', pp. 48–9; Little, 'Red Scare', p. 300.

12. DBFP, 2, XVII, no. 56, annex, note by Hoare, 5 Aug. 1936. For the Ministry of Marine report on Darlan's mission, see SHM, 1BB2, c. 203, Contre-amiral Decoux, compte-rendu, 6 Aug. 1936.

13. PRO, CAB 64/14, JPC 158, Strategical Review, 3 July 1936; CAB 24/C.P.233(36), FO memo, 31 Aug. 1936.

14. DDF, 2, IV, no. 10, 'Note de l'EMM', 20 Nov. 1936; SHM, 1BB2, c. 32, EMG-1, 'Programmes navals: plans d'armement', 3 Jan. 1936 and EMG-1 note, 3 Dec. 1936.

15. SHM, 1BB2, c. 208/D14, file 2, EMG-EAN, 'La situation navale en Juin 1936', 9 June 1936; Chalmers Hood III, *Royal Republicans*, pp. 159–61.

16. PRO, CAB 64/14, JPC 158, 3 July 1936; Stone, 'The European Great Powers', p. 213; Moradiellos, 'British Political Strategy', p. 127; Little, 'Red Scare', p. 301.

17. PRO, CAB 23/Cabinet 54(36) and Cabinet 55(36), 22 and 29 July 1936; CAB 27/622, F.P.(36) 3rd and 4th meetings, 27 July 1936.

18. Douglas Little, 'Red Scare' provides the clearest exposition of the supposed Bolshevik threat.

19. The central and southern departments were themselves rivals, see Donald Boadle, 'The Formation of the Foreign Office Economic Relations Section, 1930–1937', *HJ*, 20, 4, 1977, pp. 919–36, and 'Vansittart's Administration of the Foreign Office in the 1930s', in Richard Langhorne (ed.), *Diplomacy and Intelligence during the Second World War*, Cambridge, 1985, pp. 68–84.

20. Little, 'Red Scare', pp. 294–7; Moradiellos, 'British Political Strategy', pp. 23–4; Stone, 'The European Great Powers', pp. 212–13; Charles E. Harvey, 'Politics and Pyrites during the Spanish Civil War', *Economic History Review*, 31, 1, 1978, pp. 89–104.

21. Moradiellos, 'Appeasement and Non-Intervention', pp. 94–104.

22. Stone, 'Britain, France and the Spanish Problem', pp. 145–6.

23. Renouvin, 'Les Relations Franco-Anglaises, 1935–1939' in *Les Relations Franco-Britanniques, 1935–1939*, Paris, 1975, pp. 29–31; Stone, 'Britain, France and the Spanish Problem', p. 131.

24. Haywood Hunt, 'The French Radicals, Spain and the emergence of appeasement', in Alexander and Graham, *French and Spanish Popular Fronts*, 43–9; Colton, *Léon Blum*, pp. 242–5; Dreifort, *Yvon Delbos*, pp. 38–44; Adamthwaite, *France*, pp. 42–3.

25. Moch, *Front Populaire*, p. 236; Colton, *Léon Blum*, pp. 249–50; PRO, FO 371/19858, C6126/1/17, Lloyd-Thomas letter to Sargent, 25 Aug. 1936.

26. CADN, Londres 13, Léger to Air Ministry, 28 Sept 1936.

27. SHAT, 7N4134, Afrique du Nord-SR, EMA-2, 'Synthèse des renseignements', no. 6, n.d. Dec. 1936; MAE, Espagne 183, no. 12803B, Salengro to Delbos, 19 Oct. 1936.

28. Kergoat, *France*, p. 334; Madeline Astorkia, 'Les leçons aériennes de la guerre d'Espagne', *RHA*, 2, 1977, pp. 147–9. Cagoulards translates as 'hooded ones'.

29. SHAA, Z213020/D3, Fonds Jauneaud, unpublished memoir, 'L'Affaire Jauneaud, (1920–1945)', p. 2.

30. Quoted in Lacouture, *Léon Blum*, p. 333; also cited in Jackson, *Popular Front*, p. 206.

31. Moch, *Front Populaire*, p. 232; Haywood Hunt, 'French Radicals', pp. 44–7; Dreifort, *Yvon Delbos*, pp. 48–9.

32. Colton, *Léon Blum*, pp. 177–97; Jackson, *Popular Front*, pp. 216–34.

33. PRO, FO 371/19858, C5939/1/17, Clerk to FO, 17 Aug. 1936; SHAT, 7N2754/D3, EMA-2, Morel to General Armengaud, 29 July 1936; regarding Irun and San Sebastian see Preston, *Franco*, pp. 172–3.

34. PRO, FO 371/19858, C6126/1/17, Lloyd-Thomas to Sargent, 25 Aug. 1936.

35. PRO, FO 371/19858, C5939/1/17, Eden minute, 20 Aug. 1936; Stone, 'The European Great Powers', pp. 214–15; DBFP, 2, XVII, no. 161, first meeting of the inter-departmental committee on non-intervention, 3 Sept. 1936.

36. PRO, FO 800/292, Wigram memo, 3 Oct. 1936, fo. 251; FO 371/19858, C6086/1/17, Cadogan note, 21 Aug. 1936; FO 371/19912, C6490/4/18, Wigram minute, 17 Sept. 1936.

37. DDF, 2, III, no. 276, Massigli to Léger, 22 Sept. 1936; PRO, CAB 23/Cabinet 57(36), 14 Oct. 1936, 15.

38. PRO, NIC memoranda, CAB 62/7, NIS(36)101, 103 and 105, 21, 22 and 23 Oct. 1936.

39. PRO, FO 371/19913, C6903/4/18, Quai d'Orsay memo, 2 Oct. 1936; DDF, 2, III, no. 314, Corbin to Delbos, 3 Oct. 1936.
40. PRO, FO 3721/19914, C7612/4/18, record of Sargent–Cambon conversation, 26 Oct. 1936; BDFA, II, F, 23, no. 9, Lloyd-Thomas to Eden, 14 April 1937.
41. PRO, FO 371/19914, C7824/4/18, Lloyd-Thomas to FO, 3 Nov. 1936; FO 371/19915, C8697/4/18, Phipps to FO, 2 Dec. 1936.
42. MAE, Italie 308, no. 306, Chambrun to Delbos, 30 Oct. 1936; Italie 270, no. 345, Chambrun to Delbos, 20 Nov. 1936.
43. PRO, FO 371/19915, C8701/4/18, Drummond to FO, 28 Nov. 1936; FO 371/20410, R2515/226/22, Drummond to FO, 3 May 1936.
44. MAE, Italie 308, nos. 389 and 48, Blondel to Delbos, 29 Dec. 1936 and 30 Jan. 1937.
45. Young, *In Command*, pp. 134–7; Shorrock, *From Ally to Enemy*, pp. 191–5.
46. MAE, Italie 308, no. 306, Chambrun to Delbos, 30 Oct. 1936.
47. SHAA, 2B104, EMAA-3, doc. 666/3R, General Aube note for Cot, 18 July 1936 and Puget note, 28 July 1936.
48. PRO, FO 371/20412, R6646/226/22, FO memo, 2 Nov. 1936.
49. PRO, ADM 116/3468, c-in-c. Med., 'Recent emergency in the eastern Mediterranean', 19 March 1936; C.A. MacDonald, 'Radio Bari: Italian Wireless Propaganda in the Middle East and British Counter-Measures, 1934–1938', *Middle Eastern Studies*, XIII, 1977, pp. 195–207; David Omissi, 'The Mediterranean and the Middle East', pp. 23–7, and Meir Michaelis, 'Italy's Mediterranean Strategy, 1935–1939', pp. 50–4, all in Cohen and Kolinsky, *Britain and the Middle East*.
50. PRO, FO 371/20412, R5963/226/22, Drummond to FO, 7 Oct. 1936; FO 800/296, Lord Cranborne's private correspondence, record of FO meeting, 10 Nov. 1936.
51. PRO, FO 371/20417, R3302/341/22, O'Malley minute, 11 June 1936 and R5980/341/22, Drummond to FO, 8 Oct. 1936; FO 371/20412, R6679/226/22, Drummond to FO, 9 Nov. 1926.
52. PRO, CAB 24/C.P.335(36), Eden memo, 14 Dec. 1936.
53. DDF, 2, IV, nos. 10 and 23, EMM notes, 20 and 23 Nov. 1936.
54. MAE, Italie 270, no. 365, Blondel rapport, 'L'Italie à la veille de 1937', n.d. Dec. 1936; SHAT, 7N2754/D3, no. 334/A, Morel to Daladier, 26 Sept. 1936, no. 351/A, Morel to Daladier, 26 Nov. 1936.
55. PRO, ADM 116/3379, Hammill to NID, 21 Nov. 1936; CAB 23/Cabinet 75(36), 16 Dec. 1936, 4–5; René Sabatier de Lachadenède, *La Marine française et la guerre civile d'Espagne, 1936–1939*, Paris, 1993, pp. 21–4.

56. PRO, CAB 4/25, CID/COS 509(36), draft, Aug. 1936.

57. PRO, CAB 24/C.P.211(36), COS memo, 29 July 1936.

58. PRO, CAB 23/Cabinet 66(36), 18 Nov. 1936, 6–7; Cabinet 67(36), 25 Nov. 1936, 2–3.

59. SHAT, 7N2754/D3, Morel to Gauché, 5 Oct. 1936; Morel later revised his opinion as alarm within the capital grew when Franco's forces severed land communications to Madrid, see DDF, 2 III, no. 350, Morel to Daladier, 14 Oct. 1936.

60. PRO, CAB 23/Cabinet 67(36), 25 Nov. 1936, 2–3; CAB 24/C.P.211 (36), COS memo, 29 July 1936.

61. PRO, FO 800/296, heads of department meeting, 10 Nov. 1936.

62. PRO, CAB 24/C.P.335(36), Eden memo, 14 Dec. 1936; C.P.10(37) (COS 544), COS memo, 19 Jan. 1937.

63. CADN, Londres 267, no. 2328, Corbin to Delbos, 26 Nov. 1936. Also as DDF, 2, IV, no. 41; DDF, 2, III, no. 511, Delbos to Corbin, 14 Nov. 1936.

64. DDF, 2, III, no. 511, Corbin's reply to Delbos, 19 Nov. 1936.

65. CADN, Londres 267, no. 2906, Delbos to Corbin, 18 Dec. 1936; DBFP, 2, XVII, no. 527, Sargent minute, 1 Jan. 1937.

66. PRO, CAB 23/Cabinet 67(36), 25 Nov. 1936, 6; CAB 23/Cabinet 75(36), 16 Dec. 1936, 4–5.

67. PRO, CAB 23/Cabinet 66(36), 18 Nov. 1936, and CAB 23/Cabinet 67(36), 25 Nov. 1936; FO 371/19860, C8702/1/17, Clerk to FO, 4 Dec. 1936, and C9097/1/17, Lloyd-Thomas to FO, 21 Dec. 1936.

68. DBFP, 2, XVII, no. 338, note 1, 26 Oct. 1936.

69. PRO, CAB 23/Cabinet 75(36), 16 Dec. 1936, 5–6.

70. PRO, CAB 62/16, NIS(T.A.3)(36)1, 2, 22 and 31 Dec. 1936; DBFP, 2, XVII, no. 436, Eden to Phipps, 4 Dec. 1936. Regarding Italian reinforcements see J. F. Coverdale, *Italian Intervention in the Spanish Civil War*, Princeton, 1975, pp. 113–17 and 165–71; regarding the volunteer plan see Edwards, *British Government*, pp. 142–55; Lachadenède, *La Marine française*, pp. 20–7.

71. PRO, CAB 24/C.P.6(37), Eden memo, 6 Jan. 1937.

72. Ibid., 1–3; Edwards, *British Government*, pp. 146–7; Carlton, *Anthony Eden*, pp. 93–9.

73. PRO, CAB 24/C.P.6(37), Eden memo, 6 Jan. 1937, 1; Baldwin papers, file 124, foreign affairs, series B, 1936, fos. 55–7, Eden letter to Baldwin, 27 Dec. 1936.

74. PRO, CAB 23/Situation in Spain committee, S.S.1, 1st meeting, 8 Jan. 1937, 7–12; Templewood papers, Box IX/3, undated notes on Admiralty [rearmament] progress, Jan. to April 1937.

75. PRO, CAB 23/Cabinet 1(37), 13 Jan. 1937, 3.

76. PRO, CAB 63/51, MO(36)10, Hankey's commentary on Vansittart's

'World situation and rearmament', n.d.; FO 800/394, Chatfield to Vansittart, 25 Dec. 1936.

77. PRO, CAB 23/Cabinet 14(37), 7 April 1937, 2–6, Cabinet 15(37), 11 April 1937, 15–16, and Cabinet 16(37), 14 April 1937, 11.

78. French fears of Spanish–German collusion within the Spanish zone dated back to 1918. See ANCOM, aff. pol., c. 518/D26, copy of EMA-2 memo, 'Maroc Espagnol', 15 April 1918; regarding French reports on German activity see DBFP, 2, XVII, no. 126, annex. See also William A. Hoisington jnr., *The Casablanca Connection: French Colonial Policy, 1936–1943*, Chapel Hill, 1984, pp. 137–8.

79. The phrase came from Marcel Hoden, MAE, papiers Joseph Avenol, Marcel Hoden letter to Avenol, 4 Aug. 1936; regarding iron ore and Peyrouton's views see Hoisington, *Casablanca Connection*, pp. 137–8; Robert H. Whealey, 'How Franco Financed his War – Reconsidered', *JCH*, 12, 1, 1977, pp. 134–5.

80. DBFP, 2, XVIII, nos. 35 and 38, record of Eden–Corbin conversation, 8 Jan. 1937, and FO to Keeling, Tangier, and reply.

81. DBFP, 2, XVIII, no. 35.

82. DBFP, 2, XVIII, no. 36, Clerk to Eden, 9 Jan. 1937; Lachadenède, *La Marine française*, pp. 65–6.

83. DBFP, 2, XVIII, nos. 35 and 36, Clerk to Eden, 9 Jan. 1937, no. 42, n. 2, FO minutes, 10 Jan. 1937; SHAT, 7N2812/EMA-2, Lelong to Daladier, 14 Jan. 1937.

84. DDF, 2, IV, nos. 275 and 278, both Corbin to Delbos, 11 Jan. 1937; PRO, FO 371/20705, C383/1/18, record of Sargent–Crolla conversation, 13 Jan. 1937.

85. DBFP, 2, XVIII, no. 64, Eden minute, 13 Jan. 1937; MAE, Allemagne 801, no. 68, Corbin to Delbos, 28 Jan. 1937.

86. DDF, 2, IV, no. 342, Massigli to Léger, 23 Jan. 1937.

87. CADN, Londres 13, no. 320, Flandin to Corbin, 12 Feb. 1936; PRO, FO 371/21136, R264/5/67, Loraine to FO, 12 Jan. 1937.

# 5

# Economic Appeasement and Negotiations on Colonies, January–May 1937

During the first half of 1937 the British government pursued two associated strategies of economic appeasement. These were based on a politico-economic bargain through which the ailing German economy was to be revived with the help of Anglo-French financial and commercial concessions. This assistance was only to be made available when Hitler had bound himself to a general settlement in Europe. The Anglo-French support envisaged, though subject to variation, was essentially based upon the provision of long-term loans and the arrangement of preferential trading agreements with Germany. An additional option was to return one or more of Germany's former colonies. While the British Cabinet thus responded to the 1936 stalemate in the talks over a western pact with policies bearing the hallmark of the Treasury and the Foreign Office economic section, the government's continued insistence upon the prior receipt of binding German political concessions blocked the actual practice of 'economic appeasement'.[1]

Several historians have been drawn to the Anglo-French consideration of Germany's colonial claims. But it is, at best, doubtful that Hitler much cared about the restitution of colonial territory. Indeed, in early 1937 the British government, closely directed by Chamberlain, attached greater weight to trading concessions in its analyses of possible economic assistance to the Reich. A high-profile League of Nations enquiry into the world trade in raw materials seemed to offer a vehicle for such aid in a manner acceptable to both the Dominion governments and the ardent Tory supporters of imperial preference.[2]

What may appear surprising is that the French government should have seen itself, (and should have been seen by the British) as being capable of making any economic concessions whatsoever. The essential difference between what Britain and France might contribute was determined by their commercial policies. Whereas Britain saw benefit in a general return to European free trade and, in the short term, could offer a seductive clearing agreement to Germany, France's contribution to freer trade would be essentially negative – the selective abandonment of key import quotas.[3] For the immediate future, the prospects for this were not encouraging. In December 1936 the French government was considering the introduction of legislation to ensure that the French state could lay first claim to any strategic raw materials produced within France or its Empire.[4]

# I

The western powers were generally expected to play a key role in any European trade recovery. In October 1937 the governor of the Czecho-slovakian national bank, Dr Englis, told Frank Ashton-Gwatkin of the expectations of smaller European nations. An end to British and French tariffs and quotas would be intrinsically beneficial. The resultant increase in exports to the western nations would also assist debtor countries in the settlement of their outstanding payments to London and Paris. Only then could one expect an end to the Balkan clearing agreements, exchange controls and other restrictive trade practices which Germany had exploited so adroitly through its bilateral trade arrangements with these states.[5]

Evidently encouraged by the tenacity of the Tripartite accord over French devaluation, in early December 1936 Baldwin instructed Sir Frederick Leith-Ross to prepare a report on supplementary agreements for the removal of tariffs and obstacles to trade. Leith-Ross duly obliged, his findings produced in consultation with the Board of Trade and the Department of Overseas Trade. By mid-December Leith-Ross's recommendations – and Baldwin's interest in them – were forgotten amid the controversy over the abdication crisis.[6] But the nub of Leith-Ross's argument, that Britain should seek bilateral preferential trade arrangements with key competitors, including Germany and Japan, reflected Chamberlain's thinking on the matter. The Chancellor of the Exchequer saw a measured use of the Export Credits Guarantee Department, annexed to the Treasury, as a useful tool in the conciliation of Berlin.[7]

If the Reichsmark were devalued in order to foster a recovery in German export production, Nazi exchange controls ought to become redundant. The German government might then abandon the nonsense of autarky, and regain a vested interest in a prosperous free-trading order with Britain and Germany as its principal European pillars. All rather wistful perhaps. Quite apart from the ideological and strategic impediments to such a reversal in Nazi policy, the outstanding technical difficulty was the perceived inability of the German economy to sustain public confidence in the face of a severe currency depreciation. A large sterling loan, offered with French support, might make a managed devaluation of the Reichsmark feasible. It would certainly confirm the goodwill of the western powers.[8]

These ideas built upon Schacht's many suggestions during his conversations with British and French politicians during 1936. Discussions with Schacht had stalled in October when Blum informed him of the British reluctance to pursue the points that the Economics Minister had raised in Paris on 26–7 August. Blum misrepresented the British position. The British government was bound to insist that it could not discuss economic or colonial concessions until the German government had responded properly to the April Questionnaire.[9] Yet it was obvious that this was a dead letter. What the British really wanted was a firm indication of Hitler's readiness to parley. This would enable London to resume discussions without having to frame policy as part of the 'effort of conciliation'. As we have seen, during 1936 the strict adherence to this diplomatic form was itself part of the gambit by which the British government avoided French calls for wider staff conversations or an alliance. By the end of the year, the abundant evidence of French affability allowed the British Cabinet a freer hand. This meant that a more forthright dialogue with Germany could be contemplated.

On 11 January Phipps reported that neither Schacht nor Hitler was aware of Britain's actual readiness to enter economic talks. François-Poncet had not explained the British view of the Blum–Schacht exchanges when he had been invited to see Hitler at Berchtesgaden, though Eden had earlier clarified matters in a letter to Delbos. Instead, the French Ambassador had told Schacht that the British adhered to Eden's 27 July parliamentary statement precluding colonial discussions. The Foreign Office judged Blum the culprit for this breakdown in communication.[10]

By January 1937 the possible resumption of formal contacts with Schacht revealed the confusion at the heart of British policy, a confusion sustained by the incompatibility of Treasury and Foreign Office objectives. Neither ministry could decide exactly where Schacht fitted into the German governmental hierarchy. Neither was sure what Hitler thought about colonies. Furthermore, as Corbin pointed out, all proposals for intermediate colonial concessions which stopped short of a simple transfer of ownership were notable for their technical complexity and consequent impracticality.[11] Little wonder that there was uncertainty over Berlin's understanding of the British view. In conversation with Phipps on 29 October, Schacht accused the British government of stifling French plans for the discussion of colonial concessions.[12]

On 21 December E.H. Lever, acting Chairman of the committee for German long-term debts, met Schacht in Berlin to arrange the renewal of interest funding on non-Reich loans. The German Economics

Minister enthused about a comprehensive accord to settle Germany's outstanding debts to Britain based upon a rescheduling of the interest payable on the Dawes and Young loans.[13] British insistence upon a binding German pledge to meet the service payments for these 1920s loans had hitherto prevented the implementation of the Anglo-German payments agreement. This was particularly ironic since it was Leith-Ross who had negotiated this accord in November 1934. Schacht told Lever that he recognized that any reduction in interest payments merited something in return. Again, he stated that he had felt unable to pursue this because of the hostile British reaction to his earlier talks with Blum.[14]

Leith-Ross immediately took the matter up with the Foreign Office. He was alarmed that when he had written to Schacht in October, suggesting that Germany should make the first gesture, he had apparently been unaware of Schacht's professed willingness to do so. Leith-Ross suspected that the central department had deliberately withheld information from the Treasury.[15] But Schacht had not made any official proposal, nor was he in a position to do so. Hitler had yet to express a firm view. Similarly, the British government had no precise policy beyond the precept that economic or colonial concessions justified German political guarantees covering eastern Europe. On 17 October Monick's deputy, Félix le Norcy, tried to clarify the difference of outlook between the Treasury and the Foreign Office:

> Like the Foreign Office, they [the Treasury] are not disposed to accede to the demands of Dr Schacht who, in return for devaluing, would at once demand foreign credits, colonies and facilities by which to obtain primary materials. But on financial matters alone, the Foreign Office will oppose the granting of any loans to Germany unless that power grants England [*sic*] all necessary political assurances ['tous les apaisements politiques nécessaires'].[16]

In other words, the two departments were only sharply divided over procedure. Although Chamberlain's Treasury circle shared the Foreign Office scepticism, they were willing to contemplate financial concessions as a means to restart talks. This sentiment was spiced by a certain guilt at the peremptory dismissal of Schacht's previous overtures. Leith-Ross was anxious to make amends to his German friend. The Treasury conveniently overlooked the fact that it had given short shrift to French suggestions in October that the Tripartite agreement be followed up by a relaxation of imperial tariffs. Chamberlain had then expressed his annoyance at French efforts to 'spring a policy upon us'. Leith-Ross had told Le Norcy on 13 October that it was 'outrageous' for the French to expect the British to reduce tariffs for German benefit.[17]

By January 1937 Leith-Ross had changed his tune. He planned to invite Schacht to London for a routine financial meeting intended to develop into a wide-ranging discussion. Here too, Chamberlain's hidden hand was at work. The Chancellor saw Leith-Ross's personal rapport with Schacht as a means to dispense with cumbersome diplomatic channels, thus avoiding Vansittart in particular.[18] Eden shared Vansittart's anxiety that the confusion over the exact linkage between a general settlement and economic concessions would be perpetuated unless due diplomatic process was properly re-established.[19] The Foreign Secretary arranged to talk this over with Chamberlain and Leith-Ross in early January. Eden and Vansittart feared that any discussions supposedly confined to economic questions would rapidly coalesce into German demands for colonial transfers from a banker-turned-minister who lacked either the legitimacy of a foreign affairs portfolio or the authority of a senior Nazi Party post. None the less, lacking firm evidence of Goering's stranglehold on the operation of the Four Year Plan Office – and hence of Schacht's declining economic influence – the Foreign Office was ready to speak to Schacht by default.[20]

The Treasury had always acknowledged that the colonial question was essentially political. Hence Leith-Ross's personal wish for greater Foreign Office involvement in any future talks with Schacht.[21] But Chamberlain had a more ambitious breadth of vision than Eden. The Foreign Secretary was more sensitive to the immediate diplomatic and party political ramifications of discussion over colonies. Chamberlain was prepared to accept Schacht's claim to represent Hitler. With hindsight, we know this was a mistake. But, in early 1937, it appeared to Chamberlain that Schacht held the key to a general settlement scheme. Talking to Schacht had an added advantage. By focusing on Germany's pressing economic requirements, which Britain was best placed to remedy, France would be confined to a secondary role. On 16 January Chamberlain confided to his sister Ida that he believed that Germany's precarious internal stability was its Achilles heel.[22]

The Foreign Office had no immediate alternative to Chamberlain's suggested procedure. Eden fell in with Chamberlain's plan, though he expected that Leith-Ross's meeting with Schacht on 2 February would simply clear the air. The exchange was seen as a way to tie up all the loose ends left by Blum's over-eager diplomatic intervention over the previous six months. In anticipation of Leith-Ross's meeting, the central department also prepared a fresh repudiation of Germany's colonial claims, backed by a specially groomed editorial in *The Times* prepared by Rex Leeper.[23]

# II

The French government did not demur at Britain's assertiveness in taking up the reins dropped by Blum and Schacht in August 1936. But the Blum administration doubted the wisdom of British economic appeasement strategy. It was not openly critical because it too was divided over the extent of acceptable concessions to Germany.[24] François-Poncet had gone further than Phipps in convincing his government that Schacht commanded little authority. On 10 December he submitted a meticulous dissection of the Economics Minister's latest statement on the merits of colonies; a speech at Frankfurt which, according to François-Poncet, was marked 'with the brutality and off-handedness which so often characterizes the actions of Dr Schacht'. The German minister presented himself with a 'scientific allure' as an object-ive economist free from the ideological constraints of Nazism. Yet in the same breath he produced fatuous statistics on the benefits of colonial markets, and stressed his influence with the Führer.[25]

François-Poncet had got it right. In striving for Anglo-French col-onial concessions, Schacht was also fighting for his own political survival. But even if he succeeded, it was a fantasy to believe that Hitler would see in African colonies anything more than a temporary diversion from his plans for German expansion in eastern Europe. Though he stopped short of spelling it out, François-Poncet's point was clear. Colonial appeasement was a non-starter. The Ambassador's persuasive analysis was distributed to other ministries. But the Quai d'Orsay also circulated Corbin's heartening advice that Britain respected the caution evident in French foreign policy since the Rhineland crisis. Delbos con-cluded that it would be folly to jeopardize British trust by carping over economic concessions. Daladier and Gamelin were receiving exactly the same advice from the London Military Attaché, General Albert Lelong.[26]

On 21 December 1936 Roger Cambon, Chargé d'affaires in London, told Sargent that the Minister of Colonies, Marius Moutet, was con-sidering proposals to allow Germany limited trading access to the Cameroons. This resurfaced in January as a German request to establish a joint trading company to develop the production of Cameroon produce – bananas and sugar products above all.[27] The originator of these ideas was not Schacht, but the London Financial Attaché, Emmanuel Monick. He based the scheme on the model of the Suez Canal company. On 15 January Monick suggested to Leith-Ross that the Tripartite agreement signatories should offer the Reichsbank sufficient loan capital to main-tain a long-term foreign exchange reserve. Germany could then compete openly on international raw materials markets. On 28 January Gladwyn

Jebb derided Monick's proposals as the vaguest colonial scheme yet dreamt up by a French official. Sargent and Cadogan saw evidence in Monick's ideas of a softer French line towards Germany. In the aftermath of the Anglo-Italian Gentlemen's agreement, the Quai d'Orsay was anxious to avoid giving Hitler any means to weaken the Anglo-French entente.[28]

Eden used a speech to the Commons on 19 January, and a meeting with Blum in Paris two days later, to inject a little confidence into the French government. Rehearsing the Foreign Office rather than the Cabinet line, Eden reminded the French Premier that economic appeasement remained subordinate to the prior attainment of a satisfactory political agreement with Germany. Blum was already furious that Monick had represented personal ideas as French policy. He quickly distanced his government from the errant Financial Attaché. Blum promised Eden that he would echo the Foreign Office view in a speech he was scheduled to make in Lyon on 24 January.[29] The French leader was a more congenial partner to the Foreign Office in the economic appeasement debate than Chamberlain or the Treasury.

This is not to suggest that the French government was any better at speaking with one voice over the colonial question than the British. The contours of French policy were further blurred by the actions of Marius Moutet. A distinguished Lyonnais lawyer who had worked as defence counsel to Joseph Caillaux before the French High Court in 1920, Moutet, though new to the Ministry of Colonies, had long been an influential Socialist parliamentarian. On 15 January the *Echo de Paris* published an interview with Moutet in which he ruled out any territorial adjustment to the French Empire. He added that the government realized that even theoretical consideration of German colonial demands would give Schacht's ideas unwarranted legitimacy. Moutet concluded that Germany's enthusiasm for its former colonies waxed and waned according to the requirements of its European diplomacy.[30] Like François-Poncet, Moutet had got it right. But he too was countermanded by the Quai d'Orsay which moved swiftly to reassure London that the opinions of a single minister did not necessarily represent official policy. On 20 January Massigli told Clerk that 'in France, ministers often spoke for themselves'. Undeterred, Moutet continued his campaign during February with a series of press interviews. His frankness won popular acclaim.[31]

The lack of cohesion in French policy, evident in Moutet's outspoken firmness on the one hand, and in Blum's eagerness to please Eden on the other, added to the British determination to proceed unilaterally. Returning from a League session on 2 February, Leith-Ross was able to 'drop in' on Schacht at Badenweiler. His brief from Chamberlain and Eden was simply to listen to what Schacht put forward.[32] The Badenweiler meeting transformed the broad issue of economic appeasement into the far cruder, though more problematic, colonial question. Schacht repeated what he had stated to Blum in August, adding detail as to method and Germany's precise demands. He suggested the opening of confidential exploratory talks between the signatories of the Tripartite agreement to concert a policy regarding Germany's pressing economic and financial requirements. Once this had been done, the Americans might be asked to chair a final conference to settle matters. Colonial concessions were foremost among Schacht's requests, though he only mentioned the Cameroons and Togoland specifically. These were territories which should be returned to Reich management and currency. In return, Germany would guarantee the maintenance of a colonial 'open door', and the continued demilitarization of the territories themselves.[33]

Schacht dismissed the importance of foreign loans to underpin a German devaluation, and flatly refused to approve additional German payments of standstill credits. This left the British government no room to build a package of economic concessions around anything other than colonies. On 15 March Eden warned the Cabinet that Schacht's promised concessions were nonsense. The notion that Hitler would join 'whatever sort of [European] Pact was thought best' was utterly unconvincing. Schacht had merely reeled off the appeasement catch-phrases – 'general settlement' and 'arms limitation' – hoping that Leith-Ross would not ask him to elaborate.[34] When Leith-Ross did so, Schacht revealed the sham of a politico-economic negotiation supposedly delegated by Hitler to the Reichsbank President.

According to Eden, if talks were to proceed, they should take place via the Foreign Office, Phipps and von Neurath.[35] This, of course, was an assertion of Eden's departmental jurisdiction rather than a repudiation of colonial appeasement. It failed. As in the previous year, when faced with opposition in Cabinet, Chamberlain turned to the forum of the foreign policy committee. In that committee, the Chancellor and Leith-Ross won the day by admitting the extravagance of Schacht's proposals. During 1936 Schacht claimed that the political dimension of the colonial question was secondary to the economic. In an abrupt change of tack, he now stressed the immeasurable psychological benefits of west African colonial transfers. This was swallowed by the foreign policy committee in March because its members were convinced that the German government was itself bitterly divided. Colonial cessions were presented as the means to ensure the triumph of those 'moderate' conservatives within the German hierarchy whom Schacht was supposed to represent.[36]

Schacht put the same argument to the French, though they were far less receptive. He insisted to François-Poncet that colonial concessions would not only bring commercial benefits but would also contain the aggressive energies of Nazism. This implausible justification led the French Ambassador to a crisp conclusion: 'perhaps he [Schacht] only requests the maximum in order to secure the minimum and to procure himself a bargaining chip, which he would abandon in exchange for other advantages.'[37] Another reason for scepticism was the growing economic power of Goering's Four Year Plan bureaucracy. As Goering's star rose, so Schacht's would inevitably fall. The Economics Ministry was bound to decline in importance as the drive for autarky proceeded.[38] This brought out Anglo-French differences regarding the German 'moderates'.

Neither the Quai d'Orsay, the service ministries nor the Conseil were seduced by the idea that Schacht headed an inchoate collection of senior officials, ministers and generals who might bring Hitler to reason if offered colonial concessions. In London, the principal members of the foreign policy committee, with the exception of Eden, were prepared to follow Chamberlain's hunch that a moderate party might indeed take shape. More surprisingly, Chamberlain, Halifax, Simon and Hoare, as well as Ashton-Gwatkin and Gladwyn Jebb in the Foreign Office economic section, regarded Goering as the joker in the pack; if not a moderate, then at least a figure detached from the ideological extremism of Goebbels. This assumption was flawed. Goering and Schacht were diametrically opposed. Once Goering commanded sufficient economic power to ride roughshod over Economics Ministry and Reichsbank advice, it would be impossible to consider Schacht a worthy negotiating partner.[39] Accelerated German rearmament was inextricably tied to intensified autarky under the Four Year Plan. It was an enormous task for the economic appeasers to prove that Germany could achieve certain 'legitimate' goals without either. The appeasers deluded themselves that Goering might be enlisted to persuade Hitler to abandon the autarkic plans for which Goering was himself responsible.

Immediately after the Badenweiler meeting, Leith-Ross conceded that Schacht's political survival rested upon a resolution of the colonial question. This gave added significance to Schacht's acceptance of a further term as Reichsbank President in March 1937.[40] Leith-Ross and the Foreign Office economic section suggested immediate consultation with the French over colonial talks. Yet Ashton-Gwatkin and Gladwyn Jebb were privy to the central department's intelligence from Germany which indicated that the concept of a moderate party was inaccurate. Vansittart, Sargent and Strang all concluded that Hitler merely tolerated Schacht's diplomatic game. The Führer knew that if the entente powers took Schacht's bait, London could no longer insist upon a replacement western pact built around the provisions of the Locarno treaty.[41]

It was this above all that divided Chamberlain and Leith-Ross from Eden's central department advisers. Chamberlain was convinced that the lack of diplomatic progress, and the rearmament burden it imposed, necessitated his personal intervention.[42] This conflicted with the image of British strength that the Foreign Office wished to convey by refusing to negotiate on a new basis. By March 1937 the central department had compiled numerous reports – notably through Vansittart's network of contacts in Germany – which emphasized the unity of purpose within the German establishment. According to Vansittart's informants, the *Wehrmacht* chiefs were more anxious to establish unified military authority over Germany's economic preparations for war than to oppose the direction of foreign policy. If Schacht objected to increased rearmament, the army would oppose him.[43]

## III

The French government had few illusions regarding German military support for an expansionist foreign policy. The Berlin Military Attaché, General Georges Renondeau, reported to Gauché's deuxième bureau with a clarity which contrasted with François-Poncet's tendency to ramble. On 27 January Renondeau speculated that the senior army triumvirate of Freiherr von Fritsch, Ludwig Beck and Werner von Blomberg had struck a bargain with Hitler based upon the Führer's pledge not to increase German commitments in Spain. In return, the *Wehrmacht* backed Hitler's long-term military objectives. François-Poncet agreed that the German army command was agitated about continuing raw-material shortages, and the shortfall in officer trainees. This was delaying the attainment of a 36-division front-line strength. On 16 March Renondeau reiterated to Daladier that the *Wehrmacht* was thoroughly Nazified. The zeal of the party enthusiasts among its junior ranks more than cancelled out the pockets of Junker conservatism that remained.[44] In January 1937 the French air and naval staff intelligence sections agreed that the *Luftwaffe* and the *Kriegsmarine* were fully integrated into Nazi foreign-policy planning. For instance, the onus in German fleet manoeuvres was placed upon attacks on merchant shipping, enemy bases and extended supply lines. This aggressive orientation suited the Nazi leadership and the German naval command equally well.[45]

By January 1937 the Minister of Commerce, Paul Bastid, was the only member of Blum's Cabinet receptive to economic concessions to Germany.[46] Worsening financial difficulties, soon to culminate in the February announcement of the 'pause' in Front populaire reforms, precluded serious discussion of concessions within the Finance Ministry.[47] There was no complaint from those most inclined to appease such as

Minister of State, Camille Chautemps, and Georges Bonnet, Bastid's predecessor, who was exiled as Ambassador to Washington during Blum's first term. The Front populaire's reaffirmation of the French commitment to colonial assimilation also appeared to rule out transfers of territory. During the spring of 1937 the Foreign and Interior Ministries, which together maintained the civil administration in French North Africa, assisted Daladier in the completion of a colonial defence review initiated by the CSDN in the previous December. The avowed purpose of this was to integrate the *maghreb* more fully into the defence of metropolitan France. This took no account of a possible German return to west Africa.[48] At the Ministry of Colonies, Moutet remained unrepentant over his public rejection of any territorial cessions.

The transparency of Schacht's colonial demands was highlighted by his dismissal of the League's raw-materials enquiry. On 8 March Germany was formally invited to join the League investigative committee studying the opportunities for international access to strategic raw materials. Schacht refused the offer. He alleged that the enquiry was rigged in order to disprove the economic worth of the mandated territories. Seeing one of his key justifications for a restitution of colonial territory about to be undermined in open court, Schacht was anxious to nip the League's activities in the bud.[49] François-Poncet was certain that Hitler was using Schacht as an additional mouthpiece in a series of polemical exchanges with Eden. These had started with the Foreign Secretary's speech to the House of Commons on 19 January.[50] Hitler was waiting for Chamberlain to take a firmer hold on British policy: 'I have frequently heard it said that even if Mr Eden remains at the Foreign Office, Mr Neville Chamberlain, the future Prime Minister, would pursue a policy less hostile to Germany and more detached from continental affairs.'[51]

Hitler did not have long to wait. On 1 March Ribbentrop called for the restitution of all German colonies as a spontaneous gesture of international goodwill. The following day, Eden reaffirmed that the British government was not considering any such transfer of territory. Eden later warned Ribbentrop that the colonial question might become as destructive as the Anglo-German naval rivalry which had dogged relations between the two countries before 1914.[52] Despite Eden's apparent firmness, on 18 March the foreign policy committee acted upon the outcome of the Badenweiler meeting.[53] The full Cabinet was then preoccupied with the disappointing German and Italian proposals regarding the new western pact, the imminent settlement of Belgium's neutral status and the Spanish Nationalist blockades of Vizcaya. This offered the pretext for Chamberlain to shunt the colonial question into his favoured committee domain. Chamberlain reassured his colleagues that the only territories which could be transferred were the Cameroons and Togoland. Since these were principally French mandates, Paris would have to be persuaded of the logic behind British policy. In practice, this would entail British compensation to France.[54]

Since any hope of resuming the western pact talks was rapidly fading, the prospect of restarting negotiations on the basis of French territorial concessions was doubly attractive. Even so, the foreign policy committee reasoned that Hitler was unlikely to be satiated by a return of the Cameroons and Togoland, a conclusion at variance with Chamberlain's emergent scheme. The Chancellor avoided a final decision on the matter. A communication was to be sent to Paris suggesting that France restore its tropical African mandates to German rule. Britain would make economic concessions of equivalent value, and might consider territorial compensation to France. The exact nature of these British sacrifices was not specified. The proposed surrender of French territory was justified as the final element within a general settlement, preceded by German political guarantees covering the Reich's eastern neighbours.[55]

Eden and Ormsby-Gore drew up draft communications to the French government which steered it towards a rejection of the cessions Chamberlain had insisted be put forward. Eden concentrated on the political aspect of the issue, Ormsby-Gore on the legal and moral impediments to transfer. Eden conceded that colonial discussions were central to the appeasement process. But he listed numerous justifications for British, Dominion, and Belgian refusal to cede any territory just as the Plymouth report had done in the previous year. He left it for the French to infer that these objections applied in equal measure to their possessions.[56] Ormsby-Gore was firmer still. He stressed that colonial producers had refused to accept German currency in open market transactions. Germany would only be able to exploit the raw material resources of its former west African mandates by compelling these territories to supply goods. The transfers would be a dangerous precedent. They would contravene article twenty-two of the League covenant which obliged the mandate holders to act in the best interests of the indigenous population of their territories.[57]

Chamberlain struck back successfully on 2 April, four days before a decisive session of the foreign-policy committee. He criticized Eden and Ormsby-Gore for according undue prominence to the colonial question. Chamberlain concentrated upon Schacht's suggestion that the western powers should formulate their precise demands as a prelude to talks.[58] The logic of the April 1936 Questionnaire had been turned on its head: now the western powers were to specify their requirements to Germany. Although Chamberlain intended to urge the French to make colonial concessions, he made no direct reference to this. He banked upon

resolving British policy by default, first by securing foreign-policy committee assent to the formulation of precise demands, and then by making
an immediate approach to Paris.

On 6 April the committee followed Chamberlain's lead, though even
Hoare and Halifax shared Eden's reservations about Schacht's authority.
The detail is crucial here. As Andrew Crozier has shown, only Ormsby-
Gore maintained that colonial conversations should be rejected outright.
Eden reminded the committee that it was effectively reversing declared
government policy. But in the presence of Chamberlain, the Foreign
Secretary's remarks were more conciliatory than the memoranda he had
prepared on the subject. The Foreign Office duly approved the inclusion
of colonial issues in future Anglo-German discussions, provided that
exchanges were conducted through normal diplomatic channels, and that
binding political guarantees were received before colonial concessions
were enacted.[59] Put another way, Hoare, Halifax, Eden and the Foreign
Office were prepared to link colonial concessions to an eventual general
settlement, provided that Hitler stood by the outcome of these negotiations.

Chamberlain played upon Blum's unguarded comments to Schacht of
the previous August. More precisely, he exploited Conseil and Quai
d'Orsay discomfort at the choice he confronted them with: either the
French government repudiate Blum's suggestions to Schacht, undermining the Premier's position in the process, or it make quite clear that
colonial appeasement was essentially a waste of time. There was sufficient French doubt over each option to preclude them both. To sweeten
the pill, Chamberlain pointed out that Britain might renounce its own
minority interests in the Cameroons and Togoland, or perhaps offer the
French a British west African territory.[60] The choice of the Gambia made
geographical sense because it partially bisected French Senegal. In the
foreign-policy committee, Halifax was immediately swayed by the prospect of the French shouldering the main burden. Even Ormsby-Gore's
opposition softened, though only temporarily, at the suggestion that
Britain might only have to surrender a tiny colony to a friendly power.
The committee agreed that instructions should be drafted for Hugh
Lloyd-Thomas, acting head of the Paris embassy in the interregnum
between the end of Clerk's term and Phipps's arrival as new Ambassador.[61]

Lloyd-Thomas was told to discuss Germany's colonial claims with
French ministers, using Chamberlain's 2 April memorandum as the basis
for his comments. He was to find out whether the French government
considered Schacht a suitable conduit. But he was to clarify that the
British government was prepared to recognize Schacht's diplomatic
authority regardless. As regards the formulation of Anglo-French

demands, it was assumed that these remained largely unaltered: a replacement Locarno pact in the west, conclusion of non-aggression accords between Germany and her eastern neighbours, Germany's return to the League and an arms limitation agreement.[62] Other requirements might be quietly dropped. These included the demand that the Soviet Union be included in an eventual eastern settlement, and the previous British insistence upon receipt of a German guarantee under the proposed new Locarno. In return for eventual French cession of the Cameroons and Togoland, it was now suggested that Britain would offer Germany financial assistance of an equivalent value. The calculation of this was left suitably vague.[63]

## IV

The British proposals ignored the electoral and strategic considerations that were uppermost in French official thinking. Blum's government had no precise economic appeasement plan. This was apparent in the dead-locked Franco-German commercial negotiations which had opened on 3 March. The talks hinged upon a new payments agreement intended to accelerate the liquidation of outstanding German debts. The stalemate had been broken by the time Schacht visited Paris in late May. None the less, the French government did not try to make political capital out of the section of the eventual commercial accord which dealt with Germany's trading access to French West Africa.[64] The negotiations themselves were left in the hands of the Finance Ministry's Direction du Mouvement Général des Fonds, and above all, Jacques Rueff, Monick's predecessor as London Financial Attaché, and a close friend of Leith-Ross.[65]

On 3 May Phipps put the British proposals forward officially in a meeting with Blum and Delbos. In early February, Clerk had warned that the French public was broadly hostile to any transfer of territory to German control. Neither Blum nor Delbos suggested any alternative to Phipps.[66] To understand this, it is useful to remember that by early 1937 the Popular Front's ambitious plans for the political regeneration of the French Empire lay in tatters.

In May 1936 Blum had appointed Pierre Viénot as Under-Secretary of State for Foreign Affairs with special responsibility for colonial reform in the Levant and French North Africa. Viénot had long-standing experience of the *maghreb* dating back to his service on Marshal Louis Lyautey's *cabinet civil* in Morocco in the 1920s. France's North African territories were outside the administrative jurisdiction of the Ministry of Colonies, unlike Indo-China, where French colonial mismanagement and downright oppression caused Moutet and his *chef de cabinet*,

Robert Delavignette, enormous problems.[67] Among Blum's other appointments was Minister without portfolio, Maurice Viollette, a close colleague of Paul-Boncour. Viollette had a particular remit – a series of electoral reforms for Algeria.[68] By December 1936 Viénot and Viollette had masterminded two packages of colonial reform. First was Viénot's draft treaty which provided for Syrian self-government after a three-year period. Second was the Blum–Viollette plan extending the franchise to a narrow Muslim elite in Algeria. Both schemes fell foul of Senate opposition, and the power of the French North African *colon* settler lobby.[69]

The French government was caught between a rhetorical commitment to the well-being of France's subject peoples, settler hostility to the emergence of Muslim nationalism and unprecedented service ministry insistence upon the strategic importance of a passive Empire. As colonial protests spread across French North Africa in 1937, Radical ministers reiterated their support for *l'ordre*. The entrepreneurial achievements of French settler communities and the inviolability of the Empire had to be guarded. Although eighteen of France's thirty colonial governors were replaced during Blum's first term, resistance to colonial reform was little diminished.[70] Government inertia also stemmed from the number of ministries with a direct stake in French imperial administration and from the constant shadow of the French military in the field. Although they shared a common frontier, Algeria and Tunisia were administratively further apart than, say, French West Africa and Indo-China. Whereas the latter territories were administered by the Ministry of Colonies, Algeria was under Ministry of Interior jurisdiction while its *maghreb* neighbours were ruled from the Quai d'Orsay.

The establishment of an inter-departmental advisory committee, the Haut Comité Méditerranéen et de l'Afrique du Nord, in February 1935 had done little to rectify matters. In the preface to the decree which established the committee, Flandin had emphasized the importance of centralizing information on the French Empire to ensure that the government spoke with one voice in colonial policy, particularly with regard to French North Africa.[71] In fact, the dominance of military personnel on the committee, and its primary concern for order, reflected the importance attached to control of the *maghreb* in French strategic planning.[72] In 1936 Blum established a permanent Secretariat for the Haut Comité Méditerranéen under the capable guidance of the *maghreb* expert, Charles-André Julien. Though this gave the committee a more academic and civil flavour, it did little to dilute the influence upon government of the service ministries' imperial strategists. Flandin's war minister, General Maurin, had warned that the army command would not tolerate any interference in its absolute right to use colonial troops for whatever purposes it deemed fit. This remained the War Ministry line in 1937.[73]

In short, the reassertion of the conservatism traditional in French colonial affairs did not augur well for any concessions over the west African mandates. The French had always valued the three-fifths stake in Togoland, and the control of five-sixths of Cameroon, for military reasons above all.[74] Retention of these territories was essential to the strategic coherence of French West Africa and French Equatorial Africa. Togoland facilitated access to landlocked Niger. The Cameroons were a gateway to Chad and to the interior of the French Congo. Between March and June 1937, the inter-departmental comité consultatif de défense des colonies, chaired by Moutet, formulated defence plans for all French black African territories. On 12 March General Jules-Antoine Bührer, head of the War Ministry staff responsible for troops in Indo-China, approved the reinforcement of French West Africa with soldiers previously designated for service in the Far East.[75] In mid-June the comité consultatif agreed that the Cameroons and Togoland were integral to the overall strategic plan for the defence of West Africa and Equatorial Africa. By February 1938 a comprehensive mobilization scheme covering French forces in the Cameroons was in place.[76]

The further one looks into the French military planning of Empire defence, the more unlikely it appears that any surrender of colonial territory would ever have been approved. Within the French military establishment, the Ministry of Marine had the clearest conception of France's global imperial defence requirements. This was because the ministry exercised central control over all French naval forces regardless of their location. Conversely, where troops or aircraft were permanently maintained within a black African colony they came under the authority of the Ministry of Colonies, which in turn usually delegated the resultant responsibility for the co-ordination of defence within an individual territory to the colonial administration concerned.[77] This resulted in an uneasy partnership between the Ministry of Colonies and the service ministries regarding the strategic requirements of colonial defence and the expenditure this generated.[78]

In 1929 and 1933 the Ministry of Colonies strengthened the powers of its corps du contrôle. In effect, the corps was a supervisory bureaucracy for all colonial forces. The intention was to ensure that the ministry's requirements were not being overlooked because of the greater importance attached to metropolitan defence within the service ministries. In 1900 a decree made the War Ministry theoretically responsible for 'all that which concerns the personnel, the instruction and the command' of troops within the sub-Saharan colonies. In practice, the day-to-day operations of these forces were subject to negotiation between the civil governors and the regional military commanders. This complex structure may have facilitated a more flexible response to the requirements of imperial policing, but it certainly impeded the development of a global strategic perspective within the War Ministry.[79]

During the latter half of 1937, Daladier's sweeping colonial defence review successfully overhauled the War Ministry's supervision of the African Empire.[80] On 14 February 1938 the colonial defence review was submitted as four *Plans d'ensemble de défense des colonies* covering black Africa, Indo-China, the Indian Ocean and the western Atlantic. The review confirmed the CSDN's responsibility for strategic planning in these regions. Ominously, it was further stipulated that the committee should formulate policy 'within the context of national defence'. Neither the *maghreb* nor the Levant territories had been included in the review. While this reflected their separate administrative status, it also illustrated that the army's colonial preoccupations had turned on these two areas prior to 1938.[81]

The Ministry of Marine did not share the War Ministry's limited imperial horizon. Under Darlan's impetus, the naval planners were keenly aware of the need for a coherent strategy for the preservation of the Empire. In March 1937, in one of his many articles publicizing the French marine, this time in the journal *Le Miroir du Monde*, Darlan argued that the French should be prepared to make greater sacrifices in order to conserve their country's imperial prestige. The following July, Darlan's deputy chief of naval staff, Vice-Admiral Bourragué, summed up the essential difference between the marine and the army in a letter to General Bührer, his colleague on the comité consultatif de défense des colonies:

> The defence of the French Empire has always been one of the central concerns of the French naval staff. The link between the different parts [of the Empire] is, in effect, the sea. Whatever the type of war, it will fall to the marine to defend the communications – both military and economic – between our colonies and metropolitan France and to ensure the naval security of the territories under threat of attack.[82]

During 1937 and again in January 1938, the Ministry of Marine planning section stressed the land threat to the three centres of French colonialism in Africa (French North, West and Equatorial Africa) inherent in a German return to the continent. Douala, the main port in the Cameroons, could be militarized to rival Dakar as a strategic naval base. This would double the operational range of the German fleet in the southern Atlantic.[83] The Ministry of Marine section d'études envisaged that, if the French fleet was forced to evacuate the Mediterranean because of Italian hostility, all merchant traffic to France's Indian Ocean colonies would have to take the Cape route. Goods destined for Indo-China and Madagascar alone were expected to exceed 5.4 million metric tons per year. These would be a soft target for German submarine attacks mounted from Douala. So too would be the British convoys destined for Australasia, India and Malaya which would also be forced to traverse the Cape.[84] By the same token, German ships might interrupt the flow of African conscripts to France in the Atlantic just as the Italians were expected to do in the Mediterranean. A foothold in west Africa would also enable the Germans to spread anti-French propaganda in comparable fashion to Italian transmissions to the Muslim world from the Bari radio station.[85]

The French naval command also speculated about a German land campaign mounted from Douala in order to drive into the Congo basin and facilitate the eventual seizure of Portuguese Angola. In September 1937 these suspicions increased when the EMM deuxième bureau got word of an alleged draft German–Portuguese treaty under which German settlement would be permitted in Angola as a prelude to autonomous German rule in certain regions of the country. In return, the Portuguese dictator, Antonio de Oliveira Salazar, would receive sufficient German war material to complete Portugal's rearmament programme.[86]

The contrast between the breadth of the French strategic view and the narrow-mindedness of Britain's defence planners on the CID is striking. In Chatfield's view the Cameroons was simply one of the many imperial hostages to British sea power that the entente had to cope with. Chatfield supported colonial concessions not only as a means to satisfy the Nazis but also in order to pass on an imperial burden which might limit Germany's freedom of manoeuvre. On 17 May Hankey informed the foreign-policy committee that the strategic implications of a transfer of the Gambia had not been 'recently' examined. Previous objections had been confined to moral, commercial and sentimental grounds.[87]

The French strategists were far ahead of their British counterparts. On 13 January 1938 the Ministry of Marine planning section pointed out that, if Germany regained all its former colonial territory in Africa, it would control Dar-es-Salaam, principal port of British-ruled Tanganyika. Although the British had long since ruled this out, Chamberlain's infatuation with colonial appeasement had encouraged the French service ministries to consider these scenarios anyway. This was a sensible precaution. On 23 September 1936, in a letter to Chamberlain, the Home Secretary, Sir John Simon, alluded to the flexibility inherent in the British approach to colonial appeasement: 'I would sooner they [Germany] got Tanganyika than that London was bombed and if it came to that, British opinion would agree . . . but the Germans must make an effective agreement for peace in Western Europe first and at present it is all take and no give.'[88] The Ministry of Marine was wise to consider British policy imprecise. The planning section warned that German possession of Tanganyika's ports on the Indian Ocean would encourage an Axis pincer movement against British and French African territories. From Douala and Dar-es-Salaam, German forces could strike out along the western and eastern coastlines of Africa. Italian forces might descend from east Africa, and the Japanese might encroach further westwards from the South China Sea. The French planners concluded, 'The anti-communist [pact] triangle is inscribed upon the Indian Ocean.'[89]

When, in March 1938, the French high command circulated the Ministry of Marine's findings to the CSDN, these were accompanied by a thorough refutation of Germany's claim to colonies. The high command reiterated three points already made by the Ministry of Marine during 1937. Firstly, Germany's territorial demands were seen as a coherent strategic plan to undermine Anglo-French imperial security. Secondly, the military importance of any territory Germany acquired could only be assessed in the light of Italy's support for Germany in the Mediterranean, and Japan's support in the Indian Ocean. The third point was more wistful. In view of the preceding considerations, the high command hoped that Germany's colonial demands would encourage greater Anglo-French co-operation in joint imperial defence measures.[90]

The poverty of the Cameroons and Togoland reinforced the impression that Germany harboured an ulterior military motive. It is unnecessary to reiterate here that the notion of colonial transfers as a key means to regenerate German export trade was ridiculous.[91] It is perhaps sufficient to refer to a single statistic, again provided by the Ministry of Marine. In 1913, with its Empire wholly intact, only 0.56 per cent of Germany's total exports had gone to its colonies, and German colonial imports were 0.49 per cent of the national figure.[92] By 1937, France, which had acquired its mandates almost as an afterthought to Clemenceau's preoccupations in Europe, took the broadest strategic view of the possible consequences of territorial transfers.

## V

The 3 May meeting between Blum, Delbos and Phipps left the ball in the French court. The two ministers gave provisional approval to the British schedule for future talks, subject to the receipt of François-Poncet's latest evaluation of Schacht's political influence. Past indications were that the Ambassador's views would be overlooked anyway. The British list of proposed German concessions was sufficiently familiar to be sanctioned without question. Blum's ailing government was as unenthusiastic as the British were about Soviet inclusion in an eastern pact. But Blum and Delbos rejected any unilateral cession of territory.[93]

The only valid reason to make a special case of the Cameroons and Togoland was that these were among the territories upon which the 'colonial guilt lie' had been based. When France took control of its share of these mandates, German nationals had been expelled, their property expropriated and reparations levied for damages incurred by French nationals in the 1900–14 period of alleged German maladministration. France was granted exemptions from the usual conditions attached to control of type B mandates. In practice, this meant that there was no League supervision of French activity, notably with regard to the conscription of native troops.[94] While it was at least questionable whether life for the indigenous population had greatly improved under the French tricolour, Schacht never based any of his arguments on these facts.

In a private letter to Orme Sargent, Phipps suggested that French opposition to the British scheme of mainly French concessions would allow the Foreign Office to drop it 'gracefully and even gratefully'. Vansittart preferred to duck the issue altogether. He considered it unwise to veto the transfer of colonial territory unless and until British rearmament made a more tangible impact upon the course of German policy.[95] Eden recognized that such deliberate obfuscation – or 'cunctation' as it was termed – was untenable. Colonial restitution was the cornerstone of Schacht's proposals. As Phipps had stressed, Hitler allowed Schacht to push the colonial question in order to facilitate British acquiescence in his plans for eastern Europe. It was pointless to act as if the colonial issue was either totally unimportant or the mainstay of Nazi policy.[96]

The French government carried the British hand by assenting to further conversations with Schacht. It was impossible for the French to contemplate ignoring Schacht completely during his pre-arranged visit to the Paris Exhibition on 25 May. Nevertheless, neither Blum nor the Quai d'Orsay were willing to discuss anything substantial with him. On 20 April the Conseil discussed the League's raw materials enquiry, and precluded unilateral financial concessions to Germany. An academic decision perhaps, given the government's looming financial difficulties. Still, the French government had further circumscribed the options for any future talks with Schacht. During April and May François-Poncet continued to report on Schacht's increasingly wild demands for territory without bothering to measure the prospects for the concessions proposed in return.[97]

On 11 May Blum responded to this pervasive French scepticism with a request that Leith-Ross participate in the forthcoming Paris discussion with Schacht. This would prevent a repetition of any ill-feeling akin to that caused by the August 1936 Paris talks. Eden rejected the idea, mindful of the likely publicity Leith-Ross's presence would attract. As things stood, the British Cabinet had only authorized exploratory conversations with Schacht. On 30 April Ernst Woermann, Counsellor at Ribbentrop's embassy in London, let slip that Schacht had again turned his attention to Paris because the British had been less forthcoming than expected.[98]

In fact, the French government was not likely to raise anything new during Schacht's visit to Paris. As Blum's government was unwilling to offer territory to Schacht, Foreign Office attention turned to ensuring French compliance with the British policy of delay. In mid-May, Eden remined Delbos that Anglo-French policy over the colonial question remained unresolved. It would thus be impossible to begin detailed talks. Delbos agreed, though he remained anxious for a British observer to sit in on the Paris meeting. This would leave no grounds for any British carping if Schacht's visit proved pointless.[99] In the short term, French negotiators were being used as the agents of Britain's policy of cunctation. In the longer term, British policy was unaltered. The French were still expected to bear the greater burden of colonial transfers whenever the matter was finally deemed ready for discussion.[100] Eden carefully avoided telling Delbos that the foreign-policy committee had not abandoned Chamberlain's colonial project but had merely shelved it.

Schacht visited Paris between 25 and 29 May. Immediately prior to his departure, von Neurath and Goering hinted that Schacht commanded minimal influence. Von Neurath assured François-Poncet that neither Hitler nor the Foreign Ministry regarded colonial concessions as a *sine qua non*. On 24 May Goering made the same point: colonies were merely Schacht's 'hobby'.[101] Von Neurath and Goering had obvious ulterior motives. Schacht and Ribbentrop, the other leading colonial enthusiast, had done much to undermine the authority of the Wilhelmstrasse. Conversely, Schacht's authority was being eroded by Goering's burgeoning Four Year Plan bureaucracy. Von Neurath's comments were enough to secure him an invitation to talks in London in June. Meanwhile, Chamberlain again circumvented the Foreign Office, enlisting Lord Lothian to ascertain whether Schacht should still be taken seriously. By the start of June Lothian had reported that the answer was 'no'.[102]

Schacht arrived in Paris without proposals. In talks with Vincent Auriol and Paul Bastid, he avoided political questions. His 'lamb-like' approach was contrived in order to tempt Blum to indiscretion. On 28 May, at their second meeting, Blum acknowledged Schacht as a recognized intermediary between France and Germany. Although Blum had not consulted London over this, subsequent Foreign Office complaints were rather hollow, particularly since Schacht had met Phipps alone on

27 May in order to emphasize his overriding anxiety to resume talks with Leith-Ross.[103] The Foreign Office was anxious that Schacht should not be given grounds to claim that French promises had been made on behalf of the entente. On 10 June preparations for von Neurath's arrival in London gave Eden the pretext to request that the Quai d'Orsay terminate the dialogue with Schacht.[104] Tempered by Lord Lothian's pessimistic conclusions about Schacht's position, Chamberlain raised no objection. On 12 June Delbos warned Phipps that Schacht had asked to return to Paris to sign the Franco-German commercial treaty that he and Bastid had helped iron out in late May. Delbos readily agreed that this should be nothing more than a ceremonial occasion.[105]

# VI

Schacht's efforts to initiate colonial appeasement negotiations collapsed only days before the Blum government fell. When Chamberlain resurrected the idea of French territorial concessions in November 1937, neither Schacht nor Blum was closely involved. Even at this late stage, Lord Halifax's visit to Germany still rested on the premise that Goering was, at least potentially, a German 'moderate'. The planned discussions in June with another moderate – von Neurath – collapsed, ostensibly because of unidentified attacks on German ships policing non-intervention off the Spanish coast. This was a convenient pretext for the German government, which was eager to await the outcome of the developing French ministerial crisis before beginning any new talks.[106]

On 11 June the foreign policy committee completed the circle transcribed in British economic appeasement policy in the first six months of 1937 by re-establishing the Geneva raw materials enquiry as the focal point for any British commercial concessions to Germany. Acting on the advice of Leith-Ross's inter-departmental committee on trade policy, the Cabinet agreed that Britain might lift imperial preference tariffs in its tropical African colonies, subject to a parallel relaxation of colonial quota and tariff restrictions by France and Belgium. This would permit Germany free-trading access to the Cameroons and Togoland.[107]

Closer to home, Eden was alarmed at the increasing economic division of Europe into west and east. Most of the Balkan and successor states of eastern Europe were fast becoming reliant upon their clearing and barter arrangements with Germany. The Czechoslovakian Prime Minister, Milan Hodza, had not succeeded in his efforts to stop the rot by transforming the Little Entente into a coherent trading bloc. Quite apart from Yugoslav and Romanian objections, agrarian interests within Czechoslovakia were hostile to increased agricultural purchases from their Balkan neighbours. Further east, the Soviet Union remained a natural trading partner for Germany as each craved the principal exports of the other.[108]

On 4 June Chamberlain met the principal delegates to the London imperial heads of government conference. He told them that he drew encouragement from Schacht's evident lack of political authority because this indicated that the demand for colonies was not vital to the German leadership. Chamberlain was hopeful that the colonial question could lie fallow while the British pursued a more sober discussion of financial and trading concessions to Germany.[109] Another six months of discussion between the British and French governments and Schacht had not brought the entente any closer to a politico-economic settlement with Germany. The French could at least claim to have overhauled their imperial defence requirements. Despite Blum's initial enthusiasm in 1936, there was never a sustained French investment in Schacht's initiatives. It was always a fallacy to assume that colonial appeasement could work. It was equally misguided to assume that the French government could be cajoled into one-sided concessions. The reorientation of Germany's overseas trade towards south-eastern Europe in the mid-1930s suggests that economic appeasement could never have succeeded either. Schacht's most lasting contribution to German imperialism was to place Germany well on the way to building an effective informal Empire within Europe.[110] Yet perhaps the most compelling reason for rejecting the viability of economic appeasement is also the most simple: Hitler had never been fully involved.

Britain's tortuous attempt to persuade France to give up its African Mandates was futile. François-Poncet, several members of the French Cabinet and the French military establishment realized this. But, in their eagerness to please the British, Blum and Delbos held their tongues. Hitler did not trust Schacht, nor did he believe in his minister's economic prescriptions for Germany. The Reichsbank President was, after all, the main critic of the intensity and pace of German rearmament. To imagine that Hitler would be converted to Schacht's way of thinking by the offer of a few colonial morsels was a nonsense. With this in mind, the only defence of colonial appeasement would be as an entrée to more sweeping talks for a European settlement. But the connection between colonial transfers, the restoration of German trade or German imperial prestige and the negotiation of a new frontier settlement in eastern Europe was, to say the least, marginal. Ultimately, in pursuing colonial appeasement, Chamberlain was for the first time clutching at straws. If it were ever to succeed, a general settlement had to be negotiated on the basis of reciprocal concessions within the European continent, not outside it.

# Notes

1. British economic appeasement is explored by Schmidt, *Politics*, pp. 201–25; see also MacDonald, 'Economic Appeasement', pp. 105–35.
2. The leading authority on colonial appeasement is Andrew Crozier. See his *Appeasement*, and articles: 'Prelude to Munich: British Foreign Policy and Germany, 1935–1938', *European Studies Review*, 6, 1976, pp. 357–81, 'Imperial Decline and the Colonial Question in Anglo-German Relations 1919–1939', *European Studies Review*, 11, 1981, pp. 207–42. See also Helmuth Stoecker (ed.), *German Imperialism in Africa. From its Beginnings until the Second World War*, London, 1986; A. Edho Ekoku, 'The British Attitude Towards Germany's Colonial Irredentism in Africa in the Inter-War Years', *JCH*, 14, 1979, pp. 287–307; Parker, *Chamberlain*, pp. 70–9; regarding the preference for trade concessions, see Sir Frederick Leith-Ross, *Money Talks. Fifty Years of International Finance*, London, 1968, p. 229.
3. For a wider discussion of French protectionism, see Mouré, *Defending the franc Poincaré*; Frank, *La Hantise du Déclin*, pp. 168–73; Kuisel, *Capitalism and the State*, pp. 119–25; Tom Kemp, 'The French Economy under the franc Poincaré', *Economic History Review*, 24, 1971, pp. 82–99.
4. SHAT, 2N18/D5, commission d'études de défense nationale, projet de loi relatif aux ententes industrielles et commerciales, 12 Dec. 1936.
5. PRO, FO 371/21125, R7013/77/12, Newton, Prague, to Eden, 13 Oct. 1937; regarding Germany's economic penetration of the Balkans see David E. Kaiser, *Economic Diplomacy and the Origins of the Second World War: Germany, Britain, France and Eastern Europe, 1930–1939*, Princeton, 1980; M.C. Kaser and E.A. Radice (eds), *The Economic History of Eastern Europe, 1919–1975*, Oxford, 1986, II, pp. 299–308.
6. Leith-Ross, *Money Talks*, p. 228; Schmidt, *Politics*, pp. 165–7.
7. Chamberlain took seriously the steady flow of reports on the German economic situation supplied by the IIC. The IIC's 'general survey' of the German economy for 1936–7 concluded that, because of foreign-exchange difficulties, lack of gold reserves and foodstuffs shortages, the German economy was near crisis point. See PRO, T160/846/F14141/3, ICF/286, 'General Survey of Germany for 1936–1937', circulated, 14 June 1937.
8. Ibid.; CADN, Berlin 372, no. 2071, Berthelot to Finance Ministry, 8 Oct. 1936.

9. PRO, FO 371/20718, C369/37/18, Strang minute, 15 Jan. 1937.
10. Ibid., Phipps letter to Sargent, 11 Jan. 1937; Crozier is inclined to be more sympathetic to the French over this matter, *Appeasement*, pp. 179–80.
11. MAE, Allemagne 801, Corbin memo, 11 Feb. 1937.
12. Phipps papers, file 1/17, Phipps telegram to Eden, 29 Oct. 1936, fos. 32–4.
13. PRO, FO 371/20718, C156/37/18, Leith-Ross to Vansittart, 23 Dec. 1936.
14. Schmidt, *Politics*, p. 167; Crozier, *Appeasement*, pp. 189–90.
15. PRO, FO 371/20718, C156/37/18, Leith-Ross to Vansittart, 23 Dec. 1936.
16. SAEF, B12.619, no. 66.880, Le Norcy to Direction du Mouvement Général des Fonds, 17 Oct. 1936.
17. PRO, Sir Frederick Phillips papers, T177/32, Leith-Ross letter to W.B. Brown, 13 Oct. 1936, Hopkins letter to Phillips, 5 Oct. 1936.
18. PRO, FO 371/20718, C156/37/18, Leith-Ross to Vansittart, 28 Dec. 1936.
19. Ibid.; CADN, Londres 97, no. 171, Corbin to Delbos, 21 Jan. 1937.
20. PRO, FO 371/20735, C2618/270/18, FO minutes, 5 April 1937; FO 371/20718, C369/37/18, Phipps to Sargent, 11 Jan. 1937.
21. PRO, FO 371/20705, C447/1/18, Leith-Ross to Cadogan, 16 Jan. 1937; Crozier, *Appeasement*, pp. 190–3.
22. Chamberlain papers, NC/18/1/991, letter to Ida, 16 Jan. 1937.
23. PRO, FO 371/20705, C475/1/18, record of FO meeting, 18 Jan. 1937; FO 371/20718, C207/37/18, Charles Baxter memo, 6 Jan. 1937; Crozier, *Appeasement*, p. 187.
24. PRO, FO 371/20705, C424/1/18, Phipps to FO, 18 Jan. 1937.
25. MAE, Allemagne 801, no. 1819, François-Poncet to Delbos, 10 Dec. 1936.
26. CADN, Londres 97, no. 235, Corbin to Delbos, 22 Jan. 1937; SHAT, 7N2812/EMA-2, Lelong to Daladier, 7 and 21 Jan. 1937.
27. PRO, FO 371/20718, C736/37/18, Gladwyn Jebb memo, 28 Jan. 1937, C375/37/18, record of Vansittart–Corbin conversation, 14 Jan. 1937.
28. PRO, FO 371/20718, C736/37/18, record of Leith-Ross–Monick exchanges, 15 Jan. 1937, C736/37/18, Gladwyn Jebb memo, 28 Jan. 1937; FO 371/20705, C447/1/18, Sargent and Cadogan minutes, 16 Jan. 1937.
29. PRO, Avon papers, FO 954/8 part 1, France 1937, Fr/37/2, Eden record of conversation with Blum, 21 Jan. 1937 (also as DBFP, 2, XVIII, no. 98); FO 371/20705, C447/1/18, Eden minute, 18 Jan. 1937; Crozier, *Appeasement*, p. 196.

30. PRO, FO 371/20718, C404/37/18, Clerk to FO, 15 Jan. 1937, Crozier, *Appeasement*, pp. 141 and 186.
31. PRO, FO 371/20718, C404/37/18, Lawford minute, 20 Jan. 1937; FO 371/20719, C1183/37/18, Clerk to FO, 11 Feb. 1937.
32. PRO, FO 371/20705, C475/1/18, record of FO meeting, 18 Jan. 1937; CAB 27/626, F.P.(36)18, Eden memo, 15 March 1937, 2; Leith-Ross, *Money Talks*, p. 236; Crozier, *Appeasement*, pp. 197–8.
33. PRO, CAB 27/626, F.P.(36)18, Eden memo, 15 March 1937, 2.
34. Ibid., fos. 4–5.
35. Ibid.
36. MacDonald, 'Economic Appeasement', p. 107.
37. CADN, Londres 97, no. 761, François-Poncet to Delbos, 19 May 1937; for the Ambassador's evaluation of Schacht see Dreifort, *Yvon Delbos*, p. 162.
38. R.J. Overy, *Goering: 'The Iron Man'*, London, 1984, pp. 58, 237; Schmidt, *Politics*, pp. 212–15.
39. MacDonald, 'Economic Appeasement', pp. 105–7; Hjalmar Schacht, *My First Seventy Six Years*, London, 1955, p. 372.
40. PRO, Avon papers, FO 954/10A, Germany 1937, Ge/37/4, Leith-Ross notes, 4 Feb. 1937; Schacht, *My First Seventy Six Years*, p. 364.
41. PRO, FO 371/20735, C2618/270/18, FO minutes, 5 April 1937.
42. Parker, *Chamberlain*, pp. 69–75.
43. Among Vansittart's informants, Group Captain Malcolm G. Christie is most well known. His papers rest alongside Vansittart's at Churchill College archive, Cambridge. See, for example, file 1/5, Christie correspondence. This contains records of conversations with Goering during 1937; PRO, FO 371/20709, C474/3/18, record of conversation with Jackh and Woermann, 12 Jan. 1937; FO 371/20710, C2337/3/18, Jackh to Sargent, 23 March 1937; Heineman, *Von Neurath*, pp. 144–6; Overy, *Goering*, p. 44.
44. DDF, 2, IV, no. 251, François-Poncet to Delbos, 7 Jan. 1937; no. 360, Renondeau to Daladier, 27 Jan. 1937; 2, V, no. 111, Renondeau to Daladier, 16 March 1937.
45. SHAA, c. 2B58/EMAA-2, 'Aéronautiques étrangères', EMAA-2/13/53, premier trimestre 1937, fos. 73 and 123; SHM, 1BB2, c. 94, EMG-2, 'Etude sur les idées tactiques de la Marine Allemande', n.d. Dec. 1936; 'Etude sur l'activité de la Flotte Allemande', n.d. Jan. 1937, fos. 43–7.
46. DDF, 2, IV, no. 243 annex, Lefeuvre to Bastid, 5 Jan. 1937.
47. SAEF, B12.636, no. 67.093, Le Norcy to Vincent Auriol, 22 Jan. 1937; Cuvallier, *Vincent Auriol*, pp. 28–36.
48. SHM, 1BB2, c. 182/EMG/SE-1, dossier 1/A14, 'Défense des Col-

onies 1936–1939', file 1, no. 396, Daladier letter to General Jamet, 24 May 1937 – transmits War Ministry note 'Organisation de la Défense des Colonies', fos. 1–8; SHAT, 2N22/CPDN 1937, CPDN séance, 15 Feb. 1937.

49. PRO, FO 371/20719, C1282/37/18, Strang memo, 9 Feb. 1937; FO 371/20706, C1185/1/18, Lawford minute, 15 Feb. 1937.

50. MAE, Allemagne 35/1, no. 191, François-Poncet to Delbos, 11 Feb. 1937.

51. DDF, 2, V, no. 39, François-Poncet to Delbos, 27 Feb. 1937.

52. DDF, 2, V, no. 62, François-Poncet to Delbos, 4 March 1937; PRO, FO 371/20710, C1788/3/18, Clerk to FO, 4 March 1937; FO 954/ 10A, Ge/37/6, Eden conversation with Ribbentrop, 13 March 1937; Stoecker (ed.), *German Imperialism*, pp. 359–60.

53. PRO, CAB 27/622, F.P.(36) 7th meeting, 18 March 1937, 2.

54. Ibid.

55. Ibid., 18, conclusion 1.

56. DBFP, 2, XVIII, no. 326, Eden memo, 22 March 1937; PRO, CAB 27/626, F.P.(36)22, note by Ormsby-Gore, 22 March 1937; Dominions Office correspondence, DO 35/551, 'Statements made by Dominion spokesmen regarding the Return of Former German Colonies', 21 March 1938.

57. Ibid., F.P.(36)20, 2; F.P.(36)22, 11–12.

58. DBFP, 2, XVIII, no. 366, Chamberlain memo, 2 April 1937.

59. PRO, FO 371/20735, C2619/270/18, proceedings of foreign policy committee, 6 April 1937, 3–4; DBFP, 2, XVIII, no. 379; Crozier, *Appeasement*, pp. 199–200.

60. PRO, CAB 27/622, F.P.(36) 8th meeting, 6 April 1937, 12.

61. Ibid., 11–12.

62. PRO, FO 371/20735, C2619/270/18, Strang instructions, 6 April 1937.

63. PRO, CAB 27/626, F.P.(36)27, Eden memo, 28 April 1937.

64. PRO, FO 371/20716, C1770/15/18, Clerk to FO, 4 March 1937, C3865/15/18, Phipps to FO, 28 May 1937.

65. Regarding the agreement, see M. Constant, 'L'Accord Commercial Franco-Allemand du 10 Juillet, 1937', *Revue d'Histoire Diplomatique*, 98, 1984, pp. 108–42; regarding Rueff and Leith-Ross see PRO, Leith-Ross papers, T188/287, Rueff letter to Leith-Ross, 23 Jan. 1934. Of his period as Attaché in London, Rueff wrote, 'my relations with you being the best souvenir which I keep of this period of my life.'

66. PRO, FO 371/20718, C931/37/18, Clerk to FO, 4 Feb. 1937; DBFP, 2, XVIII, no. 462, Phipps record of 3 May meeting, 4 May 1937; Crozier, *Appeasement*, p. 204.

67. ANCOM, P.A.19, Papiers Robert Delavignette. As examples, c.3–c.4, Affaires Politiques, dossier 29, Indochine.
68. ANCOM, aff. pol., c. 920/D1, H.C. Méd rapport 4, 'Les Assemblées élues en Afrique du Nord', n.d. Feb. 1937.
69. For a fuller discussion see W.B. Cohen, 'The Colonial Policy of the Popular Front', *FHS*, 7, 3, 1972, pp. 368–93; Ahmed Koulakssis, *Le Parti Socialiste et l'Afrique du Nord de Jaurès à Blum*, Paris, 1991, pp. 265–91; Hoisington, *Casablanca Connection*, pp. 52–4; Jackson, *Popular Front*, pp. 154–9.
70. Cohen, 'Colonial Policy', p. 382; Benjamin Stora, *Nationalistes algériens et révolutionnaires français au temps du Front Populaire*, Paris, 1987, pp. 85–95; regarding the replacement of governors see Irwin M. Wall, 'Socialists and Bureaucrats: The Blum Government and the French Administration, 1936–1937', *International Review of Social History*, 19, 1974, pp. 338–9. Viollette even speculated that 'the governors ruled the government' across the Empire.
71. ANCOM, aff. pol., c. 920/D1, H.C. Méd rapport 1, 'Le HCM et les organismes d'information Musulmane', 15 Feb. 1937; Cohen, 'Colonial Policy', p. 378.
72. William A. Hoisington jun., 'France and Islam. The Haut Comité Méditerranéen and French North Africa', in George Joffé (ed.), *North Africa: Nation, State and Region*, London, 1993, pp. 79–81; Jackson, *Popular Front*, pp. 154–5.
73. ANCOM, aff. pol., c. 920/D1, H.C. Méd rapport 1, 15 Feb. 1937; Hoisington, 'France and Islam', pp. 83–4.
74. Andrew and Kanya-Forstner, *France Overseas*, p. 165.
75. SHAT, 2B33/D1, Indochine, Conseil de Défense de l'Indochine rapport, 12 March 1937.
76. SHAT, 7N4194/D1, CCDC, procès verbal, 8 June 1937, rapport au CCDC, 'Plan de mobilisation du Groupe A.E.F.-Cameroun', presented to CCDC, 11 Feb. 1938.
77. SHM, 1BB2, c. 182/EMG/SE-1, Doss. 1/A14, section d'études, 'Défense des Colonies 1936–1939'.
78. ANCOM, aff. pol., c. 840/D3, Gaston Joseph, directeur des affaires politiques, 'Note pour la direction des services militaires', 10 April 1934, Maitre-Devallon, Inspector General of public works, to Ministry of Colonies, 23 Nov. 1934.
79. ANCOM, c. 840/D3, Colonies, direction du contrôle, 'Note pour la direction des services militaires', 5 April 1934.
80. Since 1935, the Ministry of Colonies had fought a lonely battle to secure a reinforcement of several French imperial garrisons with little encouragement from the War Ministry. See SHAT, 2N246/3$^e$ section, Défense des Colonies, no. 109/1, Colonies, direction des

service militaires, to Laval, 22 Jan. 1935.

81. SHM, 1BB2, c. 182/EMG/SE-1, file 2, 'Plans d'ensemble de défense des colonies', final version, 14 Feb. 1938; SHAT, 2N246/D2, Journal Officiel, instruction interministérielle, 2 July 1938; 2N246/D2, 'Note sur la Défense des Colonies', n.d. Nov. 1938.

82. Article by Darlan, 'Le rôle impérial de notre flotte' in Coutau-Bégarie and Huan, *Lettres et notes de l'Amiral Darlan*, doc. 20; SHAT, 2N246/D2, no. 718/EMG-3, Bourragué to Bührer, 20 July 1938.

83. SHM, 1BB2, c. 180/EMG/Se-1, SE1/A11, doss. 1, rapport, 'La situation des anciennes colonies Allemandes en 1913 et en 1937', fos. 1–13, n.d. Jan. 1938.

84. SHAT, 2N246/D3, Bulletin du Haut Commandement, 14 March 1938, fos. 3–4.

85. SHM, 1BB2, c.180/EMG/Se-1, doss. 1, rapport, 'Les conséquences au point de vue de la stratégie navale d'un retour au Reich des anciennes colonies', 13 Jan. 1938, fos. 25–8.

86. SHM, 1BB2, c. 180/EMG/Se-1, doss. 1, compte rendu no. 161, 'Politique coloniale du Portugal', n.d. Oct. 1937, fo. 21.

87. Papers of Admiral of the Fleet, Lord Chatfield, National Maritime Museum, Greenwich (hereafter Chatfield papers), CHT/3/1, 'Notes by the First Sea Lord', 5 Jan. 1937, fo. 194; PRO, CAB 27/626, F.P.(36)32, Hankey memo, 17 May 1937.

88. Chamberlain papers, NC/7/11/29/46, Simon letter to Chamberlain, 23 Sept. 1936.

89. SHM, 1BB2, c. 180/EMG/SE-1, doss. 1, rapport, 'Les conséquences au point de vue de la stratégie navale d'un retour au Reich des anciennes colonies', 13 Jan. 1938, fo. 26.

90. SHAT, 2N246/D3, Bulletin du Haut Commandement, 14 March 1938, 13–14.

91. Crozier, *Appeasement*, Schmidt, *Politics*, Parker, *Chamberlain*, provide convincing evidence that colonial appeasement was a lost cause by 1937.

92. SHM, 1BB2, c.180/EMG/SE-1, rapport, 'Les conséquences au point de vue de la stratégie navale d'un retour au Reich des anciennes colonies', 13 Jan. 1938, fo. 13.

93. PRO, FO 371/20735, C3362/270/18, Phipps record of meeting, 4 May 1937.

94. W.O. Henderson, *The German Colonial Empire, 1884–1919*, London, 1993, pp. 130–3; PRO, CO 967/108, memoranda by Colonial Office Under-Secretaries, 22–8 March 1933; Andrew and Kanya-Forstner, *France Overseas*, pp. 184–5; Crozier, 'The Establishment of the Mandates System', pp. 485–9.

95. PRO, FO 800/275, Sargent papers, Fr/37/3, Phipps letter to Sargent, 6 May 1937; FO 371/20735, C3362/270/18, Vansittart minute, 4 May 1937.
96. DBFP, 2, XVIII, no. 399, Phipps memo, 13 April 1937.
97. PRO, CAB 27/626, F.P.(36)31, Eden memo, 15 May 1937.
98. PRO, FO 371/20710, C3317/3/18, Jackh to FO, 30 April 1937.
99. PRO, CAB 27/626, F.P.(36)31, Eden memo, 15 May 1937.
100. MAE, Massigli 16, *aide-mémoire*, 27 Nov. 1937. It was only in the Anglo-French ministerial conversations in London in November 1937 that the French established irrevocably that Britain would have to make equivalent territorial concessions in any colonial settlement.
101. PRO, FO 371/20710, C3738/3/18, Phipps to FO, 18 May 1937; FO 371/20735, C3793/270/18, Henderson to FO, 25 May 1937.
102. DBFP, 2, XVIII, no. 527, note 2, Sargent and Cadogan minutes, 25 May 1937; PRO, CAB 32, Papers of the Imperial Conference, 1937, CAB 32/130, 1st meeting of principal delegates, E(G.C.), 4 June 1937.
103. DBFP, 2, XVIII, no. 548, Phipps to FO, 28 May 1937; PRO, FO 371/20734, C3919/237/18, Phipps to FO, 31 May 1937; Crozier, *Appeasement*, p. 204.
104. PRO, FO 371/20734, C3919/237/18, FO to Phipps, 10 June 1937.
105. PRO, FO 371/20716, C4250/15/18, Phipps to FO, 12 June 1937.
106. PRO, CAB 27/622, F.P.(36), 14th meeting, 21 June 1937.
107. PRO, CAB 27/622, F.P.(36), 12th meeting, 11 June 1937, 14–15; CAB 27/626, F.P.(36)34, 7 June 1937; Schmidt, *Politics*, pp. 159–65.
108. PRO, Records of the chief of air staff, AIR 8/225, Imperial Conference 1937, E(37)28, Eden memo, 28 May 1937; regarding the Hodza Plan see PRO, FO 371/21124, R. Hadow, 'Annual economic report, Czechoslovakia, 1936', 2 Feb. 1937; Jordan, *Popular Front*, pp. 117–31.
109. PRO, CAB 32/130, E.(G.C.), Imperial conference principal delegates, 1st meeting, 4 June 1937, fo. 5.
110. PRO, T160/846/F14141/3, ICF/286, 1 May 1937.

# —6—

# Anglo-French Rearmament and Defence Co-operation in the Popular Front Era

During the two years between May 1936 to April 1938 when France was governed by Popular Front administrations, the parameters of French and British rearmament were first set, then revised and expanded. Britain's five-year re-equipment programme had been determined during the course of 1935, but substantial additions to front-line strength in all three services were only achieved from late 1936 onwards. Naval rearmament in both countries had been constrained by the provisions of the 1930 London naval treaty which limited the construction of capital ships. The terms of the London treaty only lapsed through non-renewal at the end of 1936. Air force expansion rested upon the adoption of series production. This was in turn dependent upon the equipment of factory plant with sophisticated and costly machine tools, an adequate supply of skilled engineering labour, and the co-operation and commitment of a network of sub-contracted businesses which remained sole providers of certain specialist products from optical sights to transmission systems.[1] Only with regard to army expansion did the British and French practice rest upon precepts sufficiently different to make comparison difficult. Nevertheless, an attempt must be made. The acrimony generated by the provision of only a small British continental Field Force to serve in co-operation with the French and Belgian armies was central to entente relations until the fall of France, and indeed, beyond it.[2]

In September 1936 the Blum government approved a four-year rearmament plan costing 14 billion francs. This was an ambitious figure and an optimistic time-scale. In the event, both would be increased. Greater funding would be allocated and, while in certain sectors re-equipment was accelerated, in others it would be extended over five years and more. French defence spending impeded the funding of social reform, it added to the disquiet of French private investors and it lessened the benefits anticipated from franc devaluation. The cost of rearmament made the fulfilment of the Front populaire's reformist mandate impossible, precipitating the so-called 'pause' in the government's legislative programme in February 1937.[3]

Perhaps inevitably, the rapidity of France's defeat in May–June 1940, the vilification of the Popular Front by the Vichy state, and the criticisms made of French defensive strength by Britain and the eastern allies between 1936 and 1939 have, until comparatively recently, coloured the historical view of French defence policy.[4] In the discussion which follows, it may be useful to bear four general points in mind. Firstly, by 1936, the concept of *sécurité* upon which French foreign policy had rested for much of the post-Versailles period had been invalidated by German rearmament, the incipient collapse of France's eastern alliances, the actual collapse of the League and Britain's continued reluctance to extend its European obligations. Secondly, the French rearmament plan was unveiled at a time of deep national division. From the viewpoint of defence policy, this was most apparent in the continuation of restrictive industrial practices, employer hostility and turmoil within the French financial market. Thirdly, a larger proportion of French defence funding was raised through loan finance than in the British case. Successive French governments were deeply afraid of the inflationary consequences of this for a currency which, despite the Tripartite agreement, remained overvalued. Finally, it would be folly to overlook the often subtle, but no less lasting, effects of the Great War upon France and its people. The nation was acutely conscious of its rising demographic inferiority to Germany. Defence planners had to contend with a diminishing number of potential conscripts. In the Popular Front era, France was not neutral, pacifist or defeatist. But it was more deeply scarred by the previous war than Britain.

By the time the French rearmament plan came before the Chamber, Britain's five-year re-equipment scheme was nearing the end of its first year. The British rearmament plan was approved by National Government Cabinets in a series of meetings which straddled the November 1935 general election, and which were only completed with the presentation of a definitive defence White Paper to Parliament days before the Rhineland crisis broke in March 1936. The entire scheme had first been scrutinized by the Defence Requirements Committee and the Defence (Plans) Committee, the two executive committees set up to assess Britain's defence needs and oversee the initial implementation of rearmament.[5]

The total projected cost of British rearmament over its five-year term was initially set at £1,038.5 million. A year later in February 1937, the figure was raised to £1,500 million through the Defence Loans bill – an admission both that state borrowing would be required to meet rearmament targets, and that these targets were liable to increase still further in response to German, Japanese and Italian military expansion.[6] When the second Blum ministry fell in April 1938, total British expenditure on rearmament had indeed been further increased. A major defence review in late 1937 had also prioritized rearmament spending more clearly in favour of the RAF, fighter defences in particular.[7]

The purpose here is not to present a detailed analysis of the course of British or French rearmament, nor is it intended to judge the merits of one solely by reference to the shortcomings of the other. Rather, the aim is to assess rearmament as a feature within Anglo-French relations. Building up defences against common enemies may bring countries into closer alignment. How far was this the case here?

# I

Unlike Britain, France began its new era of rearmament while still in the trough of recession. This added to the likelihood of devaluation, and increased the French need for British financial support.[8] The nationaliz-ation of sections of France's war industries in August 1936 confirmed the Blum government's commitment to rearm. Parliamentary and mil-itary opposition to the measure was muted owing to the inefficiencies of the existing network of private arms suppliers, though the measures themselves were less sweeping than the employers had feared. The service ministries were left to decide how far to apply state control before the April 1937 deadline for any changes set by the Senate.[9] Shipbuilding, for example, was minimally affected. Other than at the state Fabrique d'Artillerie at Bourges, naval armaments were still largely supplied by private manufacturers such as Schneider, Le Creusot, and the established arsenals at Hommecourt and Nantes. Only the production of airframes for the armée de l'air became a sector dominated by state direction. This was partially due to the vulnerability to bombardment of an industry hitherto concentrated around the suburbs of Paris. The Soc-iété Nationale de Constructions des Moteurs was the only aero-engine firm nationalized, though the Air Ministry acquired a minority stake in Gnôme et Rhône and Hispano-Suiza. The War Ministry applied its powers sparingly to only seven firms.[10] The government acknowledged that a division of labour between the private sector and state-controlled businesses would bring about the most rapid improvements to pro-duction rates. Within the War Ministry, Secretary-General, Robert Jacomet, persuaded Daladier and, to a lesser extent, Gamelin, that greater state intervention was essential to the modernization of plant and the achievement of production targets.[11]

In June 1936 the newly established CPDN reported that the French defence sector would only operate at maximum capacity five months after a call to industrial mobilization. As the HCM had reported in the previous year, stocks of strategic raw materials and fuels were critically low.[12] Within Britain, the chief of general staff, Sir Cyril Deverell, hardly an enthusiast for nationalization, admitted that the French legislation made sense. He remained pessimistic about its prospects:

> Not only are [French] reserves of armament stores and aircraft still quite inadequate, but her plans of wartime manufacture appear to have broken down. Even if a remedy for this could rapidly be found, French manpower appears to be insufficient to mobilize the large national forces contemplated, and at the same time maintain the output of industry and agriculture.[13]

Deverell's scepticism appeared justified. In March 1937 the French air staff Inspector-General concluded that France could not take on a first-class power if it only intended to adopt full war production after the commencement of hostilities. In the previous month the CPDN noted that France might have to rely on RAF air cover to ensure that French armament production continued undiminished in wartime.[14]

The armée de l'air's previous re-equipment scheme, General Victor Denain's 'Plan of 1,000', remained incomplete well into Cot's tenure of the Air Ministry. (This may be seen from Annex 1 on page 176.) On 27 July Cot demanded that Denain's plan be completed by mid-October, the first of several impolitic statements which damaged his credibility with the military establishment on both sides of the Channel.[15] The weakness of the air force illustrated the need for more effective state direction and investment to unravel the complex of sub-contractors and artisanal production methods which so delayed deliveries.[16]

France possessed fewer than 400 modern aircraft among its declared first-line strength by the time Blum took office. The position was little better when Daladier's close colleague, Guy la Chambre, replaced Cot in January 1938. The new Air Minister was still beset with difficulties nine months later: 'What characterizes the air force in September 1938 is not so much that the number of aircraft it possesses is inadequate by comparison with the German air force, but above all that *it possesses scarcely any modern planes.*'[17] On 15 March 1938 at the first CPDN meeting of Blum's short-lived second ministry, la Chambre predicted a 50 per cent increase in aircraft output within the year, but since this only signified a rise from forty to sixty planes per month, the position remained desperate.[18] A fortnight later la Chambre took the Air Ministry's comité de matériel to task over the anomalies in air production. He had been told by the Air Ministry's deputy technical director, Mazer, that 300 Bloch aircraft could be supplied within a year. Yet over the same twelve-month period only 65 of the excellent Morane 406 fighters could be produced. Neither figure tallied with actual production rates.[19] French insistence on translating excellence in design into tested prototypes before the final approval of large Air Ministry orders resulted in the possession of numerous outstanding blueprints but little to show for them on the front line.[20]

This was an experience mirrored in the War Ministry. The equipment of a light mechanized division with medium tanks, sanctioned by Gamelin's predecessor, General Maxime Weygand, in 1932, did not result in tenders until 1934, nor prototype testing until 1935.[21] When Daladier arrived at the rue Saint Dominique he found little modern war material in use. There were neither anti-tank nor anti-aircraft weaponry prototypes nor an approved medium tank which had overcome fundamental design faults. The lack of manufacturing capacity was more serious than arguments over design. As Gamelin pointed out retrospectively, in the short term, the issue of credits was irrelevant because the service des fabrications (the War Ministry procurement arm) simply ordered the maximum that manufacturers could supply.[22]

The poverty of state orders during the 1920s and early 1930s had not encouraged producers to modernize or expand their factories. Arms exports were carefully regulated by decree, and the War Ministry insisted upon priority allocation to the French armed forces. Given their inability to mass produce for the shrinking domestic market, many arms houses had concentrated upon the production of expensive high-quality material. This was increasingly untenable in an era of rapid technological advance where a long-fought-over prototype might have become obsolete by the time it rolled off the production line.[23] The prohibitive cost of highly advanced equipment underscored the shift to a series of short-term procurement programmes in the early 1930s which suited the deflationary preferences of successive French governments. Daladier, Gamelin and Jacomet had to alter the industrial basis of arms manufacture.[24]

High unit costs could only be reduced by the assurance of continuity in orders which would make industrial investment worthwhile. This process had started before Blum took power. In April and May 1936, major tank contracts were awarded to Hotchkiss and Forges et Chantiers de la Méditerranée.[25] The Ministry of Marine had long since worked out preliminary plans for its first year of spending outside the London treaty restrictions. There was continuity in another respect: the Popular Front did not immediately launch an assault on military doctrine. Cot's efforts to do so were undermined by the junior status of the air force, the unity of the War Ministry and Ministry of Marine in opposing him, and the shortcomings of the French air industry which he did not manage to cure.[26] For instance, the army's instructions for its September 1937 manoeuvres at Tanville stressed the importance of methodical advance, fixed defences, the air force's tactical support of the army and the use of concentrated firepower. The government's commitment to the motoriz-ation of land forces conformed to general staff wishes.[27]

Within the Air Ministry Cot did reform both the conseil supérieur de l'air and the structure of the air staff. He ensured that all decisions regarding rearmament, recruitment and strategy fell to these bodies once he had his placemen – Philippe Féquant and Jean-Henri Jauneaud in particular – in control of them. Membership of both the CSA and the EMAA was determined by annual decree, subject to Cot's personal recommendation.[28] Measured in terms of accelerated air rearmament, the results were disappointing. The image of an efficient reorganization is misleading. The CSA met only three times between January 1936 and July 1937 with the consequence that orders were placed with minimal technical discussion. Following Cot's departure, apart from side-lining Féquant and Jauneaud, la Chambre was also quick to reorganize the CSA to restore its powers over strategic planning.[29] The upheaval at the Air Ministry illustrated that greater funding did not bring harmony to the service ministries. Nor did Daladier's co-ordinatory role as Minister of National Defence. Keen to exercise a *droit de regard* over the armée de l'air in particular, Daladier did not have the clear executive authority, nor indeed the time, to do so.[30]

Disputes over the Cot era air force re-equipment schemes, Plans II and III, remained acrimonious. Cot and Féquant eventually lost the battle, fought largely within the CPDN, for the creation of an independ-ent strategic bombing arm which Cot viewed as the cornerstone to a revitalized eastern collective security network. The fact that few such bombers had been produced by the time Plan III was proposed in February 1937 much diminished the force of his argument.[31] So too did the British Air Ministry's reluctance to contemplate detailed technical collaboration with its French counterpart. The construction of a heavy-bomber fleet thus became more readily identified with a pro-Soviet strategy.[32] This compounded the CPDN objections to it. Polish and Romanian hostility to a programme predicated upon Soviet access to their territory added to the implausibility of the idea. The air staff were also dependent upon the release of army manpower to bring air force effectives up to strength, requiring some 5,600 officers and troops to meet the 1937 recruitment target.[33] On 15 April 1937 the CPDN est-ablished a commission to investigate manpower allocation across the defence sector once mobilization took place. This enquiry was closely supervised by Daladier and the influential CPDN Secretary, General Louis Jamet. Its findings were discussed by the CPDN in November. These discussions led to the formulation of legislation during spring 1938 regarding a switch to war production once a war began.[34]

War Ministry pre-eminence was hardly remarkable. Quite apart from the premier position of the French army within the service establishment, broad War Ministry supervision of the defence sector was ingrained within the work of the direction des fabrications d'armement. This department had a co-ordinatory responsibility for the preparation of industrial mobilization.[35] Furthermore, as Daladier and Gamelin's senior Generals usually dominated the proceedings of the CPDN, the War Ministry also exerted a controlling influence over the body established in December 1936 to co-ordinate war production, the direction générale du contrôle des matériels de guerre.[36] Consequently, it was the War Ministry which set the priorities for the munitions factories producing anti-aircraft weapons. This caused Féquant increasing concern during 1937. It was perhaps no surprise that the Air Ministry proved less co-operative than the Ministry of Marine in providing technical staff for secondment to the industrial mobilization office created by the CPDN in July 1936 to work alongside the direction des fabrications.[37] In spite of a nominal parity between the armed services, the French perception of the German threat guaranteed the dominance of the army within French strategic planning and the allocation of resources.

## II

Effectives increases offer some guide to the gradual additions to the 14 billion francs originally allocated to rearmament. On 8 December 1936 Gasnier-Duparc approved the CSM proposal for increases in reservist recruitment and in naval officer intake to the Ecole Navale and the Ecole des Ingénieurs et Mécaniciens. This required additional funding because the credits allocated to the marine hitherto had been disbursed.[38] The French navy's defence budget for 1937, approved by the Senate on 3 January, only related to the costs of naval administration, maintenance and outlay on coastal defence craft. Payment for the shipbuilding and new works programme, though passed simultaneously, was made separately through a special Treasury account, the compte des investissements. Furthermore, this package was merely a stop-gap before Gasnier-Duparc presented a six-year supplementary construction programme in late April. In theory, the full allocation of the entire naval budget for 1937 was designed to achieve an 18 per cent expansion in the strength of the marine.[39]

The net increase in marine spending over 1936 was thus 922 million francs, a sum in excess of that envisaged only three months before. The government's refusal to contemplate a reversal of its earlier legislation introducing a rigid forty-hour week made matters worse. Adherence to the forty-hour week in the French armament industry added substantially to production costs. Since ships took many months to build, this financial burden was most severely felt within the Ministry of Marine. One direct effect of the Popular Front's industrial legislation was a 20 per cent increase in the workforce of the naval *arsenaux*. Even so, the naval munitions industry still had a shortfall of 6,520 skilled employees in January 1937. French shipbuilders thus faced a shortage of skilled labour, and were legally prevented from adopting a flexible system of overtime to make up for their lack of manpower.[40]

The complexity of the marine budget was not untypical. During 1936 the War Ministry had spent some 2.3 billion francs in supplementary capital funding through fonds d'armement separate from the ordinary defence budget. Placing new tank orders in 1937, before those sanctioned in 1935 had been completed, increased the financial burden as production costs escalated over time.[41] The army had only established an experimental heavy tank unit in November 1936, so it was as yet uncertain of the total costs this would involve if adopted. In field tests held at Sissone in April 1937, the army tried out several tanks, assessing their optimum employment as a strategic force or as a tactical support. During Blum's first term, Daladier and Gamelin approved the formation of a second and third light mechanized division to be followed by the creation of the heavy-tank division and a further motorization of infantry units.[42] Strongly backed by Gamelin, the French army had taken the cause of mechanization to heart. But most of these additions to France's mechanized strength were put in place after the Popular Front coalition had dissolved.

If, by 1937, the army was committed to a doctrine of modern warfare which it did not yet have the means to fulfil, so too was the armée de l'air. Despite the increased money it received, the Air Ministry was unable to fulfil its avowed intention to increase its long-range bomber squadrons from eight to ten and its fighter squadrons from ten to fifteen by May 1937.[43] On 5 February the Senate authorized the payment of the initial 1.2 billion franc tranche of Plan II funding. An additional half billion was annexed to the budget through the compte des investissements. In fact, this 500 million was the only money spent on Plan II during 1937.[44] The expenditure to cover the 1,500 first-line strength laid down in the plan was seriously behind-hand by January 1938 when a further 1.6 billion tranche of funding became due. A reckoning of the Air Ministry's undisclosed production rates for 1937 indicates that average production never exceeded a monthly total of forty-two aircraft at any point in the year. To set this in perspective, in January 1938 the Air Ministry deuxième bureau estimated that Germany was already producing 350 aircraft per month for the *Luftwaffe*.[45]

Cot altered his defence of the Air Ministry's performance in March 1937 as it became evident that much of the armée de l'air budget could not be usefully spent, given the absence of available modern equipment.

On 5 April he assured Daladier that the air industry would make up for the 1937 production shortfall by increases in 1938 and 1939. Once the CPDN had rejected the strategic precepts of Plan III in February 1937, Cot also turned his attention to direct lobbying of the Finance Ministry in the hope that the knowledge of further cash injections to come would galvanize aircraft manufacturers into a more rapid completion of the existing Plan II.[46]

The picture of French rearmament in 1936 and 1937 is hard to summarize. The army was making the most rapid advances in the provision of new equipment, and it received the major share of funds. Unlike Britain, which had no peace-time military service, the French army naturally had enormous personnel costs which had to be balanced against the equipment budget.[47] Although its numerical and technical superiority over the *Wehrmacht* was diminishing, Gamelin's army still considered itself the most powerful European land force in 1937. While the debate continues as to whether Charles de Gaulle's preferred solution of a mechanized assault force was wrongly neglected by the general staff, there can be no doubt that French defence planners were wholly committed to mechanization.[48] The painful slowness of much French arms production was rooted in the structural neglect of the defence industry prior to the advent of the Popular Front and the Gamelin era of general staff planning.

The marine was pursuing a coherent, if limited, long-term construction programme. Many of the tenets of this dated back to the French Naval Statute passed in response to the Washington Naval Conference in 1922. Thereafter, important foundations for future marine expansion were laid by the long-serving Minister of Marine, Georges Leygues. He carefully shepherded naval expenditure through the Assemblée in many of the years that followed. But in the Popular Front era, notional increases in naval strength were undermined by the time taken to lay down and complete individual vessels, primarily modern cruisers and the *Dunkerque* class 26,500-ton battleships. The fleet, though being steadily modernized, was not increasing its relative power. The Ministry of Marine was keenly aware that the *Kriegsmarine* and the *Regia Marina* were narrowing the tenuous French superiority in tonnage with an even larger proportion of modern vessels. Between 1937 to 1941 the marine was due to scrap 139,067 tons of obsolete shipping which, unless replaced, threatened to concede tonnage superiority to the Italians.[49] On 29 July 1936 Durand-Viel warned the CPDN of the danger in overlooking the navy's multiple requirements:

The war of tomorrow poses the marine with a much more complicated problem than that faced by the army. For, in total, it is enough for the War Ministry to know if Germany and Italy or only one of these two powers are together against us.

The marine needs to know if *all* the powers will be with us or against us – Japan, Turkey, etc.[50]

Despite the Admiral's bold claim, the Air Ministry actually had the most ambitious programme. It also had the poorest production record. Italian air strength, for example, far exceeded French air power by January 1937. Mussolini's *Aeronautica* had by then attained a 156-squadron metropolitan first-line complement, including 57 bomber squadrons. In early 1937 the Air Ministry intelligence section estimated Italian production at 165 airframes and 120 aero-engines per month.[51] By contrast, all three French services only saw pronounced additions to their equipment strength from late 1937 onwards.

## III

It was the weakness of the French air force which caused the British government greatest concern between 1936 and 1938. Yet there was remarkably little British impact upon the direction of French rearmament before the *Anschluss*. Plans II and III rested on the assumption that Britain would neutralize the Italian air force, while the marine's policing of the western Mediterranean also required Royal Naval co-operation, particularly as the Spanish conflict wore on. Still, a genuine Anglo-French defence co-ordination was not achieved.

The reasons behind this were to be found in London, not Paris. British rearmament was not pursued as part of an inter-allied strategy. French and Belgian territorial integrity were vital overseas interests but the principal British contribution to the defence of western Europe was to be made by the RAF and by the navy's blockade of Germany. Just as Britain's construction of a deterrent bomber fleet had been judged intrinsically beneficial to French security, so the switch of priorities towards fighters under the 1937 Inskip review could be defended as offering potential air cover to France as well as Britain.[52] The ships to be assigned to blockade the North Sea and Baltic approaches would come from the Home Fleet operating from bases in the northern British Isles. Superficially, it was possible to argue that Britain was contributing to French defence without need of more written commitments. It had been made plain during the Abyssinian crisis that the French navy would be given expanded duties in the Mediterranean in the event of war with Italy and Germany. The division of policing responsibilities in monitoring non-intervention along the Spanish coast underscored this point. Although from July 1937 Japanese expansion in China added to the importance of French naval co-operation to the British Admiralty, the contemplation of a possible temporary withdrawal from the Mediterranean, and hence the abandonment of the Suez route, lessened the need for extensive naval staff conversations.[53]

As more information came to light during the winter of 1936 regarding the obsolescence of much of the armée de l'air, strategic air talks became still less of a priority. The idea had never appealed to Lord Swinton or to Sir Cyril Newall, chief of air staff from 1937. Unlike Denain's scheme, which had been adopted in 1934, the RAF's Scheme F was only approved in late 1935. This had the effect of increasing the technological gap between the two air forces. Swinton was less weighed down with outdated aircraft still in service than Cot. He was also less inclined to meet his French colleague, anticipating that Cot would request British air cover for metropolitan France while the armée de l'air pursued its eastern European ventures.[54] Oddly enough, the French air staff was similarly unimpressed with Swinton's performance as British Air Minister. In 1937 the EMAA intelligence section noted that Britain's much-vaunted emphasis upon the creation of a 'shadow arms industry' – a network of engineering suppliers capable of converting to defence production at short notice – had not yet produced impressive additions to RAF first-line strength.[55] In the event, from late 1937 the route to Anglo-French air force collaboration was via exchanges of information on precisely these British production techniques, rather than by way of a common strategic outlook.

The reserve plant set aside as a shadow arms industry enabled Britain to achieve far greater aircraft production than France managed before the outbreak of the war. Negotiated over the preceding two years, in July 1938 the McLintock agreement between Swinton's Air Ministry and the Society of British Aircraft Constructors established a framework for RAF orders. Government contracts with manufacturers included 'capital clauses' designed to ensure that firms would not lose out by adding to their plant.[56] Despite the comparable familial structure of the British and French aircraft companies, British manufacturers were more receptive to the need to adopt mass production techniques. Cot did not respond to industry fears about an unwarranted expansion of capacity by guaranteeing the profitability of investment in new plant. Instead, he sought additional Finance Ministry funding in an effort to dispel manufacturers' suspicions.[57] By contrast, the 'lessons' of British air rearmament were willingly learnt by la Chambre. In his defence, it must be admitted that proper instruction was never really offered to Pierre Cot.

In 1936, only the provision of the Field Force required more detailed entente co-ordination. That force did not yet exist as an organized unit. The regular troops that were to provide its backbone were spread across the British Empire, and were hard-pressed to meet expanded commitments in Egypt and Palestine. Indeed, in the early stages of the Palestinian revolt over the summer of 1936, the army commander, General Sir John Dill, relied heavily upon naval manpower to police the mandate. Perhaps more importantly, in the April 1936 staff talks, General Schweisguth's delegation made plain that the French high command was prepared to accept a two-division force provided that it was mechanized.[58]

Having pioneered the concept of independent motorized columns years earlier, British tank production in 1936 was no more advanced than the French. The recruitment position was far worse. By 1936 the triumvirate of outstanding British tank designers, F.R. Smith, George Buchan and Sir John Carden, were all dead.[59] In October 1936, the Secretary of State for War, Alfred Duff Cooper, reported that there were only 209 modern light tanks in service. Two-thirds of these were 1931–5 models whose casings could be penetrated by armour-piercing rifle bullets. Deliveries of the excellent 1936 replacement model would not be completed before 1938. There were no medium tanks in service of the kind the French favoured for the Field Force.[60] Of the existing 166 vehicles, 164 were judged obsolete. A heavy 'infantry' tank was still at the prototype stage. The benefit of shadow arms industry re-equipment was yet to be felt in tank production.[61] Two and a half years later in March 1939, the deputy chief of staff issued a stark warning. Germany's progress in the design of tanks and anti-tank weapons meant that, unless another wave of tank development got under way, the vehicles that had at last come into service would be incapable of tackling German opponents, and 'instead of being assets are more death traps'.[62]

If the Admiralty and the Air Ministry showed the least enthusiasm for co-operation with their French counterparts, the War Office had the best excuses to avoid it. The Treasury Secretary, Sir Warren Fisher, was anxious to rule out discussion with Paris regarding the continental commitment of a Field Force until the upper limit to British army re-equipment had been determined by the Cabinet.[63] Although the dispute over the role of the continental army was increasingly acrimonious, when revised defence estimates came before the Cabinet in January 1937, the service chiefs, Hankey and Sir Thomas Inskip all supported Duff Cooper's plea for increased credits. Between November 1936 and July 1937 the Treasury inter-service committee debated some £12 million of proposed additions to the army's mechanization programme.[64] The committee justified its refusal to reach a firm decision by reference to the Cabinet's continued discussion over the proposed role of the army as a whole. In the meantime, Field Force mechanization made little headway.[65]

On 8 January 1937 Vansittart disparaged the notion of the strictly limited continental commitment represented by the Field Force. He equated 'limited liability' with a dishonourable quasi-isolationism. Vansittart's power was waning. He was not in Cabinet, nor did his opinions automatically carry weight.[66] Still, he was right. Strategically, a predetermined and carefully limited contribution of ground forces to the western European theatre was difficult to justify. Sustained aerial bombardment remained unproven as a decisive weapon of war. The RAF was not yet equipped to deliver a crushing blow sufficient to replace an *effort du sang* by the regular army. The Royal Navy could do nothing to protect the French frontier. Corbin summarized the French view: 'however complete the centuries of British domination of the seas, neither La Houghe, nor Trafalgar nor the battle of Jutland would have sufficed to break the power of Louis XIV, Napoleon and the Hohenzollerns without the victories of Marlborough or Wellington or the tenacity of the English [*sic*] armies on the western front.'[67] The technological development of the bomber remained far behind the strategic role assigned to it in Britain, France and Germany. Chamberlain was taking a considerable risk in attaching the utmost priority to a decisive contribution from the RAF.[68]

Ironically, Blum's Cabinet was highly supportive of Chamberlain's air deterrent strategy. This worried the French army staff. In April 1937 the EMA disparaged Conseil suggestions of a fresh effort to win a guarantee of British aerial assistance for fear that this would encourage the British to renege on a sizeable land contribution.[69] By March 1938 the British were committed to a five-division Field Force backed by three further contingents of Territorial Army reinforcements together comprising a further twelve divisions.[70] It had taken two years of inter-departmental dispute to reach this point.

This brings us to the heart of the limitations in Anglo-French defensive co-operation. Rising British military hostility to entente defence co-ordination was one part of the equation. But the most fundamental reason for the lack of collaboration was British political opposition to it. Chamberlain did not deny the validity of the French requests for British military assistance. Nor was he in any way dilatory over defence policy. As Chancellor and Prime Minister Chamberlain was a reluctant rearmer, but he was also a committed one. He did not see the RAF as replacing all need for a Field Force. But he was certain that an effective bomber and fighter force offered the best deterrent and the key protection against German aggression. If undertaken in addition to RAF re-equipment, the equipment of a Field Force, and twelve divisions of reserves to reinforce it, threatened to undermine Britain's balance of payments.[71] Any damage to the Treasury's financial strength was a blow to Britain's 'fourth arm of defence'. It was imperative that the British economy should remain strong enough to outlast the German over the course of a protracted conflict. The Treasury and civil service head, Sir Warren Fisher agreed:

> I am as anxious as my military colleagues to make this country safe against foreign gangsters, but we are running a danger of smashing ourselves. It is essential to remove the illusion that our resources are inexhaustible: we need to concentrate on essentials; and to get agreement as to what these are, we must bring home the fact that economic and financial strength is the foundation on which alone all our other preparations can be successfully achieved.[72]

To beat Germany in a long war, Britain had to be confident that the Reich economy would crack before Britain expended its own resources. Provided that Hitler waged the war that Britain's defence planners expected him to, these arguments had a certain logic.

Furthermore, in the Popular Front era Chamberlain's rearmament, though equipping the nation for war, was built upon the assumption that peace would be maintained. Rearmament, though expensive and long term, was none the less abnormal. Defence spending was framed with an eye to a distant future where it would no longer be necessary. In this scenario, the preservation of Britain's status as a leading trading nation would again be seen as the vital determinant of continued world power. The Treasury helmsman during Britain's emergence from depression, Chamberlain was determined not to be the originator of a British slide into financial ruin. Of all those charged with the formulation of defence policy in Britain and France, Chamberlain was among the most single-minded.[73]

The EMA did not place a large influx of British military manpower at the core of its military planning, though Gamelin remained anxious to draw a more substantial commitment from Britain. Equally, Darlan and Cot recognized that dependence upon British naval or air support would damage their own case for a stronger French navy or air force. In November 1937 Darlan justified calls for increased expenditure on the marine by reference to British irritation at France's slow construction rates.[74] On 21 January 1937 Delbos confirmed that the general staff expected the Field Force to be 'a small but powerful and highly mechanized force'. This had also emerged from talks at the War Office in December between the French Military Attaché, General Lelong, and General Robert Haining, head of the directorate of military operations and intelligence. In Paris, Beaumont-Nesbitt had been approached by a clutch of 'senior French officers to the same effect'.[75] On 23 December 1936 Lelong wrote a pessimistic evaluation of British regular army expansion to General Louis Colson, who supervised much of the daily progress of French army rearmament. British Regular troops, still following the Cardwell system governing periods of active service in India, could not furnish the desired mechanized divisions before 1939. Lelong doubted that the Territorials were up to the task of providing a second wave of mechanized support.[76]

The War Office disparaged the French enthusiasm for British army mechanization. Undue concentration upon tank construction would slow the programme of infantry re-equipment and so undermine the army's imperial policing capability. Although the Foreign Office argued that the French requests for British tank divisions did not signify an acceptance that no infantry divisions need be forthcoming, Eden and Chamberlain chose to interpret matters in that light.[77] This undercut Duff Cooper's effort to secure funding for additional expenditure on infantry equipment. While the British government was prepared to equip a mechanized two-division Field Force, the fact that this remained a distant prospect added to its hostility to staff talks in the short term.

On 16 November 1936 the War Office reported to the defence policy and requirements committee that the maximum force that the army could dispatch overseas at brief notice would consist of two infantry divisions, including a substantial proportion of non-divisional troops. Without any tanks to support it, this force was judged unfit for war with a first-class power. Since the Rhineland crisis, General Voruz, his successor as Military Attaché, Lelong, and their deputy, Lieutenant-Colonel Cuny, had often reported the same conclusion to the War Ministry. In January 1937 Cuny warned that it would be at least four years before the Regulars would be capable of continental warfare.[78] Inskip added to the Treasury's rising criticism of the War Office with a series of damning reports on army rearmament during 1937. Vickers-Armstrong, the company almost exclusively relied upon for tank manufacture, was still beset with preliminary problems of manufacture and design. The diffuse nature of the army's specialist requirements made its re-equipment especially costly, and the War Office was variously accused of mismanaging its defence spending and its strategic planning.[79]

## IV

Arguments over the Field Force intensified during February 1937 just as the French government plunged into a renewed financial crisis. The monetary pressure was briefly eased by the announcement of the reform 'pause' on 13 February and the launch of a national defence loan in

March. This was no cure. Financial difficulties brought down Blum's administration in mid-June. By the end of January the French exchange stabilization fund had expended its entire 10 billion franc gold reserve in its effort to maintain the franc at the Tripartite agreement parity. The Bank of France released 3 billion francs to the fund but this failed to prevent a severe currency depreciation on the Bourse over the subsequent week. By this stage the British Treasury had rejected Vincent Auriol's impromptu request for the right to raise a 90 million sterling loan on the London market.[80]

At Blum's insistence, on 27 January the Finance Minister reduced the proposed sum to 50 million, backed by a French state guarantee of repayment. The figure was soon cut to 40 million. This met Chamberlain's conditions for what became the largest loan raised in London during Blum's first term. The issue did more harm than good. It merely confirmed the government's urgent need for liquid funds, a fact already indicated by an increase in the French bank rate from 2 to 4 per cent.[81] The British Treasury feared that the Tripartite agreement would collapse, particularly after Henry Morgenthau ruled out additional American support for the ailing French economy. Blum was determined to abide by the Tripartite agreement, even though his personal preference remained for the reimposition of exchange controls, an option which Chamberlain was convinced would produce an unprecedented flight of private capital from France. Chamberlain made his preferences known, recalling Financial Attaché, Rowe-Dutton, from Paris for talks, and publicly insisting that the French government should stem its Treasury's gold losses.[82]

The Front populaire was in an impossible position. War debts and reconstruction payments were still a drain on the French budget, and there had never been a resurgence of private-investor confidence. The government had appropriated an extra 3 billion francs to meet the costs of reintroducing two-year military service and recruiting men for motorized divisions. In the face of this, the only advice tendered by London and Washington was that a further devaluation was unavoidable. Within the Treasury, Chamberlain, Phillips, Fisher and Hopkins agreed that the French government was deluding itself in arguing that international speculation against the franc was a cause rather than a symptom of French financial weakness.[83] Only long-term cuts in French domestic spending could reverse the decline.

In late February and early March the Blum government took several steps that the British approved of. The reform pause was announced and expenditure cuts were made, notably in public works and railway development. Three dependable figures, Charles Rist, Paul Baudouin and Jacques Rueff, were appointed to administer the exchange equalization fund and to control Bank of France indulgence towards Vincent Auriol. Above all, defence spending was protected by the launch of a public subscription national defence loan intended to raise 10 billion francs.[84] To generate what amounted to some £100 million, the Minister of National Economy, Charles Spinasse, Minister of Agriculture, Georges Monnet, Governor Labeyrie and Jacques Rueff all lobbied for British assent to a currency convertibility option attached to the loan. Subscribers would then enjoy the right to have their investment repaid in sterling. Only with this guarantee were the funds likely to be raised.[85]

Chamberlain was furious. The French Treasury was effectively seeking British financial support without formally requesting it, through a measure bound to increase financial speculation as the strength of the franc wavered. The French suggestions came only days after the launch of the Defence Loans Bill at Westminster. This legislation, intended to raise up to £400 million over five years, caused an immediate depreciation in British government stock.[86] The British Treasury remained unreconciled to dependence upon loan-finance to meet defence expenditure. Sir Richard Hopkins was horrified to learn that an additional borrowing bill was contemplated for the acquisition of foodstuff reserves.[87] The French would have to raise their money without additional British support.

Chamberlain's firmness throughout the February financial crisis was decisive. On 13 March he congratulated himself in a letter to his sister, Hilda: 'I am inclined to think that they [the French government] really did not appreciate that they were causing me any difficulty and I must say that Blum and his advisers were very ingenious in adopting the suggestions I had made to them, which amounted to a reversal of their previous policy, without involving Vincent Auriol in resignation.'[88] Flushed with success, in mid-March Chamberlain even conceded the sterling repayment option after the French defence loan had been launched – an abrupt reversal of *his* position.

The British Defence Loans Bill was not an unqualified financial success, but it did at least make a political impact in Berlin. The German government was taken aback by the evident British commitment to achieve its rearmament targets. It was less impressed with French resolve, although the Front populaire sacrifice had been considerably greater.[89] Blum had assured the survival of the rearmament programme but the price was worsening financial crisis. This diminished the government's ability to improve defence production in the immediate future. By the time French rearmament took off in 1938, the Front populaire had broken up and renewed devaluations had been enacted.

During 1937 the international situation deteriorated too. As the Spanish problem grew more intractable so it became more divisive. The

German threat to Austria and Czechoslovakia increased steadily, without much glimmer of a western pact conference or a colonial settlement to assuage it. Meanwhile, the resumption of open Sino-Japanese warfare after the July 1937 Marco Polo bridge incident challenged British efforts to redirect the greater part of its defence effort towards European threats. Anglo-French mutual dependence grew in consequence.

The Admiralty estimates for 1937 were swelled by the first injection from the consolidated fund created by the Defence Loans Act. The estimates remained insufficient to counter the combined strength of the Japanese, German and Italian fleets. On 29 April, Hoare informed the defence (plans) committee that full approval of the Admiralty's ambitious New Standard Fleet programme would still leave the navy unable to meet the three-power threat for several years to come.[90] The scheme was built upon the replacement or upgrade of unmodernized capital ships, six of which still remained in service. In March the service chiefs had proposed the seventy-day 'period before relief', defined as the time that the Singapore base would have to hold out before main-fleet reinforcement, travelling via the Cape, secured it. As this implied, sending the cream of the navy, including eight capital ships, to the Far East precluded a concurrent defence of the Mediterranean against Italy. The optimistic seventy-day relief scheme was approved by the CID in March 1938.[91]

By this stage, the deteriorating Far Eastern situation compelled the Admiralty plans division to reconsider the idea of French naval conversations, if only to admit the extent to which the marine might be left alone in Atlantic waters upon the outbreak of war with Japan. If the main fleet was sent eastwards the French would be required to use the *Dunkerque* and at least four 8-inch cruisers to contain Germany's *Deutschland*-class vessels and the *Scharnhorst*-class battle cruisers. This was an extremely tall order, requiring a more rapid completion of France's newest battleship, *Strasbourg*. Since the Admiralty doubted the French capacity to mount effective anti-submarine operations, the offer of the use of the Gibraltar naval base could hardly disguise the fact that Britain's Singapore strategy left the French marine far up a dangerous creek.[92]

In the final year of Popular Front government, Britain's naval planners formulated strategy on the assumption that the bulk of the French marine would remain in home waters in order to keep the Gibraltar Straits secure for the Royal Navy's eventual return to the Mediterranean. Having sustained Franco-Italian naval rivalry through its short-sighted support of the London conference proposals in 1930, the Admiralty blithely assumed that France would now accept the task of Italian containment. Britain's home fleet was likely to be further north containing the German threat within the Baltic.[93] Though Darlan did not care to advertise the marine's dependence on Royal Naval co-operation, he did not share the arrogant British assumption that such co-operation would take care of itself. In February 1938 the British chiefs of staff recognized that the failure to take detailed stock of the French naval position had come home to roost. In a report to the CID the service chiefs concluded: 'Between January 1939 and the end of 1940 it is at least doubtful, from a mere comparison of paper strengths, whether France can deal unassisted with the Italian navy in the Mediterranean, much less safeguard our interests, as well as her own in that sea.'[94]

On 26 April 1937 the Admiralty's New Standard Fleet proposals admitted that, prior to the programme's completion, it would be impossible to safeguard the Far Eastern Empire if Britain was also at war with Germany. The CID had advised in February that neither Japan nor Italy would attack the Empire unless war with Germany had started. This made a European, anti-German deterrent paramount. In the long run this was fatal to the British and French position in South-East Asia. If Singapore was in an exposed position, Indo-China was in an indefensible one. The French high command had no hope of protecting it without British or American assistance.[95]

Until the end of 1937, then, neither the War Office nor the Admiralty co-ordinated strategy at general staff level with their French equivalents. Each department had an *entrée* to co-operation: the War Office via the Field Force, the Admiralty via the joint policing of non-intervention and the requirements of the Singapore strategy. But political and emotional objections to staff conversations held sway. Low-level Anglo-French naval contacts had continued after the Abyssinian crisis, largely because of the continued Italian threat in the Mediterranean. Paris Naval Attaché Hammill dismissed these as 'desultory', although the exchange of information was extended to cover the North Atlantic after the Rhineland crisis. An Anglo-French liaison group, known as 'Section 3', was maintained by the Admiralty naval intelligence division to report on the Mediterranean position. But, by the time of Munich its staff of three officers was hopelessly overburdened and frequently ignored.[96]

Naval talks, including a discussion of the implications for France of the Singapore strategy, were finally approved by the Cabinet on 29 April 1938. Arguments between the Foreign Office and the Admiralty planners continued into May over the permissible scope of the discussions. On 30 May Darlan warned Gamelin that the Admiralty had not changed its 'traditional attitude of extreme reserve'.[97] The upshot was that no precise naval war plan for conflict with the German fleet was put forward for discussion at the talks in June. Even Duff Cooper, Hoare's replacement as First Lord, could see no objection to such planning. Furthermore, by late April the French had formulated plans much like those eventually adopted in 1939.[98] The disappointment expressed by France's eastern allies at the superficiality of the first major Anglo-French staff conversations since April 1936 was an apt commentary on the talks themselves.[99]

Despite Swinton's lack of enthusiasm for discussions, and Cot's idiosyncratic, self-appointed mission as collective security advocate, in many respects exchanges between the Air Ministries made most sense of all. Relations between the two Ministries remained uneasy. British uncertainty at the actual first-line strength of the armée de l'air turned to alarm during the course of 1937. Yet co-operation between the two sides was technically easier to arrange than between the other services. Although the British and French air forces shared imperial respon-sibilities, distribution of squadrons was, by this stage, overwhelmingly metropolitan. British and French air rearmament turned on the optimum means to counter *Luftwaffe* aggression, whether by deterrence, offensive bombardment or fighter defence. Moreover, the bulk of the RAF and armée de l'air units on imperial duty were stretched from North Africa through to the Middle East, all points within striking distance of Italian targets.[100]

From mid-February 1937 the British Air Ministry pooled air intelli-gence with the French, via Air Attaché Douglas Colyer. This enabled the British to exploit the French early-warning system. By December the EMAA had successfully widened the scope of these discussions to the point that detailed plans could be formulated regarding joint bombing offensives against Germany and Italy. Initial targeting was confined to the enemies' 'permanent organizations essential to their action', a euphemism for airfields, fuel and munitions installations, and transport junctions, primarily within the Rhineland. These EMAA schemes were rejected, not by the British, but by the French army staff.[101]

Gamelin considered that the scheme had been developed without due consideration for the army's requirements, particularly in the first stages of mobilization and manoeuvre. On 22 January 1938 Gamelin warned the air staff: 'Without taking sides regarding the opportunity and the effectiveness of an initial armée de l'air offensive within the Rhineland, one may ask if it is not preferable to remain ready to act, not only in the Rhineland, but in other regions, dependent upon the various possibilities of [army] manoeuvre.'[102] The plans eventually passed to the British Air Ministry reflected the triumph of War Ministry opinion in the immediate aftermath of Cot's departure from the Boulevard Victor. If, as expected, the *Wehrmacht* launched a major assault through the Low Countries, the armée de l'air was to concentrate its fire upon German forces along the three strategic waterways of the Rhine, the Meuse and the Belgian canal network.[103]

During 1937 Colyer did not gather a harvest of detailed information. On 14 May he met Baron de la Grange, member of the Senate air commission and president of the influential French Aero-Club. De la Grange's depressing prognosis regarding French air power, rather than any information relayed directly by Cot or Féquant, led to renewed Foreign Office and Air Ministry concern in London. Cot had admitted under cross-examination by the air commission that the monthly output of aircraft had fallen approximately 50 per cent since nationalization. Even Denain's old 'Plan of 1,000' was at best three-quarters complete. Still further behind was Plan II, intended to increase first-line strength to 1,500 by 1939 whilst also undertaking a wholesale modernization of material within a five-year schedule. In April 1937 Blum's government reinforced the forty-hour week, contrary to Spinasse's efforts to introduce a 45-hour maximum. This did not bode well for future productivity increases.[104]

British interest in the air exchanges shifted in consequence. The principal intelligence sought no longer related to Germany but to the French themselves. After a series of Foreign Office enquiries in late May, on 7 July the air council reported that Colyer had been unable to acquire precise information regarding French air strength. Cot's statements were considered wholly unreliable. Colyer also submitted a highly critical report on the armée de l'air's role in joint manoeuvres with army units held in mid-September.[105]

It fell to the industrial intelligence centre to provide a detailed report which comprehensively destroyed French claims to have overcome production difficulties. Without any allowances for industrial stoppages, optimum French production was reckoned at 110 aircraft per month by 1938. Lack of modern plant prevented the immediate use of several newly commissioned factories, a problem worsened by France's historic reliance upon German engineering firms for a significant proportion of its machine-tool requirements. Skilled labour shortages and administrative disorganization at government and industry level were also picked out, especially in the production of airframes. In June 1937 there was a groan of disappointment around Whitehall when Chautemps bowed to Blum's wishes and kept Cot *in situ*. Even so, an IIC survey admitted that a change of senior personnel would only affect production over the longer term.[106]

In September 1937 Colyer submitted a more upbeat report. The nationalizations had been essential to the modernization of factory production, even if the scale of the task had been underestimated by Cot and Jauneaud. Modern prototypes, such as the new generation of Morane fighters and high-quality engines from Gnôme et Rhône and Hispano-Suiza, were excellent. The situation was not irretrievable. Ironically, although Colyer was impressed by the newest French aero-engines, Cot had taken to criticizing them. The Air Minister condemned Gnôme et Rhône for sticking to under-powered designs. The company owner, Paul Louis Weiller, angrily dismissed this as political point-scoring on behalf of the nationalized airframe sector at the expense of the still privately owned aero-engine manufacturers. Seen from Britain, it was additional proof of the urgent need to establish the real position of the armée de l'air.[107] In November Chamberlain, Inskip and Eden raised the condition of the French air force in discussion with Chautemps and Delbos in London. The Prime Minister's offer of comprehensive information on British air production cornered his guests into a reciprocal arrangement which stopped well short of full staff conversations. As soon as Chautemps returned to Paris, the unfortunate Cot pleaded that the poor results in French air rearmament were entirely due to lack of funding rather than to any failure of conception or organization. To strengthen his case, Cot pointed to the lower costs of French fighter production compared with those of Britain. He skipped over the poor French construction rate which had yet to derive marked benefit from renewed state investment in series production in September 1937.[108] Cot's arguments were immaterial. The era of air missions shuttling across the Channel in both directions was inaugurated. But Chamberlain had limited the scope of discussions to the achievement of more efficient rearmament, not the development of joint strategy.

During 1938 the British government developed a high regard for Guy la Chambre – largely by drawing favourable comparisons with Cot. During the spring of 1939, genuine Anglo-French strategic air co-operation got underway as detailed planning proceeded for the establishment of an RAF Advanced Air Striking Force within France. This posited a network of British squadrons stationed at French airfields. These were intended to pose a forward-based threat of RAF bombardment of German strategic targets. In the first instance though, the need for this advanced deterrent force stemmed from France's inability to cover its own air defence.[109]

With hindsight, the British government's continued refusal to compromise its appeasement endeavours through comprehensive staff talks appears more unfortunate because by late 1937 French strategic planning was impelled by the same concerns as those in Whitehall. During November the French service ministries responded to a request put by Daladier through the CPDN to assess the probable conduct of French military operations in light of the international situation as it stood.[110] All the replies stressed the three-power threat to the entente powers. All expected Germany, Italy or Japan to exploit an attack mounted in one theatre by launching an assault in another. The French service ministers agreed that an early effort should be made to knock Italy out of the war, so securing the Mediterranean. In short, the French assessments read much like British CID reports in translation. Given the emphasis upon an initial contest in the Mediterranean – the very theatre where the British would rely most upon French naval and air support – London's cold-shoulder to talks was doubly unwise. The Minister of Marine, the Corsican Radical, César Campinchi, was quite unequivocal: survival rested upon an Anglo-French military alliance rather than the British-directed entente which remained 'more or less active according to the hour or the subject'.[111]

## VI

This survey of entente rearmament has tried to show that the impressive rate of arms production achieved by both countries by 1939 originated in the preparatory planning and spending undertaken in the Popular Front era. British rearmament was better planned and more efficiently executed. But the Blum and Chautemps administrations faced financial and industrial difficulties far beyond the British experience. This alone makes it impossible to dismiss Popular Front defence policy as in any way perfunctory.

Only between the British and French Air Ministries did technical discussions develop into an exchange of intelligence sufficient to begin planning a common bombing strategy. Even here, co-operation was stunted by Cot's refusal to acknowledge the weakness of the armée de l'air, and by the French army's intention to set air force planning within the context of combined operations. Paradoxically, an abiding belief in the strength of the French army nourished the British Cabinet's reluctance to prepare a large continental Field Force to support it. In July 1937, the War Office reckoned that France could mobilize sixty-two divisions in the first three months of war. In September a British military mission, headed by the CIGS, Deverell, came away from attendance at the French and German annual manoeuvres favourably impressed by the former.[112]

Belief in the French army was also a reflection of British attitudes towards the individuals involved. Daladier and Gamelin were known and respected, Gasnier-Duparc and Darlan were neither. Every senior Admiral within the EMM had changed post at least once during 1937. The British verdict on Cot, Féquant and Jauneaud was harsher still. Even the Foreign Office joined in the chorus suggesting that the French Air Ministry was not to be trusted. Vansittart was more amenable to confidences regarding German air strength from Goering's *Luftwaffe* deputy, General Erhard Milch, than to reassurances about the armée de l'air from Cot or the London Air Attaché, Lieutenant-Colonel Fournier.[113]

Where the Cabinet felt it mattered most – in the Royal Navy and the RAF – the benefits of the shadow arms industry were apparent in increased production by mid-1937. It was easy to assume that this was intrinsically beneficial to France. Between 1936 and 1938 closer Anglo-French relations derived more from the foreign policies each pursued than from the development of shared military responses to common strategic threats.

# Notes

1. S. Roskill, *Naval Policy Between the Wars, II: The Period of Reluctant Rearmament, 1930–1939*, London, 1974, pp. 318–25; regarding French air production see Alexander, *Republic*, pp. 154–7; Charles Christienne, 'L'Armée de l'Air', pp. 216–18; Herrick Chapman, *State Capitalism and Working-Class Radicalism in the French Aircraft Industry*, Berkeley, 1991, pp. 139–43; regarding French air-force funding see Dominique Boussard, *Un problème de défense nationale: L'Aéronautique militaire au parlement (1928–1940)*, Paris, 1983.

2. Michael E. Howard, *The Continental Commitment: The Dilemma of British Defence Policy in the Era of the Two World Wars*, London, 1972, and 'British Military Preparations for the Second World War', in David N. Dilks (ed.), *Retreat from Power. Studies in Britain's Foreign Policy in the Twentieth Century*, London, 1981, pp. 102–17; Brian Bond, *British Military Policy between the Two World Wars*, Oxford, 1980, pp. 244–77. Regarding the fall of France see Martin S. Alexander, 'The Fall of France, 1940', *JSS*, 13, 1, 1990, pp. 10–44. Finally, see SHAA, Fonds Vuillemin, Z20012/D2, Vuillemin draft memoirs (sent to SHAA in 1965), p. 2.

3. The definitive study of French re-equipment remains R. Frank [enstein], *Le Prix du Réarmement Français (1935–1939)*, Paris, 1982; 'A propos des aspects financières du réarmement français (1935–1939)', *RHDGM*, 102, 1976, pp. 1–20.

4. In English, the first balanced assessments of France's preparations for war were Adamthwaite, *France and the Coming of the Second World War*; Young, *In Command*.

5. Bond, *British Military Policy*, pp. 214–26; Peden, *British Rearmament*, pp. 68–71; Shay, *British Rearmament in the Thirties*, pp. 54–84.

6. Peden, *British Rearmament*, pp. 9–10; Shay, *British Rearmament*, pp. 144–57.
7. Bond, *British Military Policy*, pp. 247–51, 257–9; Shay, *British Rearmament*, pp. 164–73, 183–93; Peden, *British Rearmament*, pp. 128–34; Malcolm Smith, *British Air Strategy Between the Wars*, Oxford, 1984, pp. 173–98. Regarding Inskip see Sean Greenwood, '"Caligula's Horse" Revisited: Sir Thomas Inskip as Minister for the Co-ordination of Defence, 1936–1939', *JSS*, 17, 2, 1994, pp. 26–33.
8. R. Frank[enstein], 'The Decline of France and French Appeasement Policies, 1936–1939', in L. Kettenacker and W. Mommsen (eds), *The Fascist Challenge and the Policy of Appeasement*, London, 1983, p. 237.
9. J.J. Clarke, 'The Nationalisation of War Industries in France, 1936–1937: A Case Study', *JMH*, 49, 1977, pp. 411–30; Alexander, *Republic*, pp. 111–16; Chapman, *State Capitalism*, pp. 105–6.
10. Clarke, 'Nationalisation'; Alexander, *Republic*, pp. 113–14; Chapman, *State Capitalism*, pp. 104–11.
11. Alexander, *Republic*, pp. 111–12.
12. DDF, 2, II, no. 369, CPDN, procès verbal, 26 June 1936; SHAA, 1B1, HCM, procès verbal, 21 Nov. 1935, fos. 1–2.
13. PRO, Sir Thomas Inskip papers, CAB 64/14, Deverell note, 16 June 1936.
14. SHAA, 1B1/D3C, 'Conférence faite à l'Ecole Supérieure de Guerre Aérienne', n.d. March 1937, fos. 13–16; 2B1, CPDN, procès verbal, 15 Feb. 1937.
15. SHAA, 2B1, file 2B/EMAA-1, no. 784, note pour le Ministre, 27 Aug. 1936.
16. PRO, CAB 4/24, CID 1247B, 1 July 1936.
17. Ibid.; SHAA, Z12930, la Chambre memo, 'Situation avant le Plan V', n.d. 1938 (emphasis in original).
18. SHAT, 2N25, CPDN, procès verbal, 15 March 1938; Young, *In Command*, pp. 197–8; Alexander, *Republic*, pp. 163–4; regarding the increases la Chambre was working to achieve in 1939, see Jackson, 'La perception de la puissance aérienne allemande', pp. 83–5.
19. SHAA, 1B6/D1, no. 274, comité de matériel, procès verbal, 25 March 1938.
20. Air-force problems were worsened by the French liking for impractical multi-purpose aircraft which had dominated production plans in the Denain era, see Robert J. Young, 'The Strategic Dream: French Air Doctrine in the Inter-War Period, 1919–1939', *JCH*, 9, 1974, pp. 67–73.
21. Tank production is analysed in R.H.S. Stolfi, 'Equipment for Victory in France in 1940', *History*, 55, 1970, pp. 1–20.

22. Pierre Cot, *Le Procès de la République*, New York, 1944, II, p. 27; Maurice Gamelin, *Servir*, Paris, 1946, II, p. 271; PRO, FO 371/19857, C4248/1/17, enclosure II, 11 June 1936.
23. Alexander, *Republic*, pp. 56–79; PRO, T175/48, Hopkins minutes on CID 1195B, 14 Oct. 1935.
24. DDF, 2, II, no. 375, commission de l'armée de terre, compte rendu, 1 July 1936.
25. Stolfi, 'Equipment for Victory', p. 5.
26. Young, *In Command*, pp. 166–72; 'Strategic Dream', pp. 69–72; Alexander, *Republic*, pp. 89–93, 147–59.
27. SHAA, 2B115, 'Manoeuvres à l'Ouest, Septembre 1937 – Directives Tactiques', fo. 6.; PRO, FO 371/19859, C6327/1/17, Clerk to FO, 7 Sept. 1936.
28. SHAA, 1B2/CSA, file 66, 'Note concernant l'Armée de l'Air Française', n.d. Jan. 1938.
29. SHAA, Z12930, la Chambre memo, 'Plan V son origine-son élaboration-son exécution', n.d.
30. Alexander, *Republic*, pp. 91–2.
31. SHAA, 1B1, 'Rapport au CPDN', EMAA 1091-3R, 23 Dec. 1936; CSA 'Note sur le Plan II', 24 Nov. 1936; CPDN, doss. B32, no. 105, memo for CPDN, 15 Feb. 1937.
32. Jordan, *Popular Front*, pp. 263–6.
33. SHAA, 2B1, Daladier to Cot, 4 Dec. 1936.
34. SHAT, 2N22/CPDN 1937, 'Main d'œuvre travaillant pour la défense nationale', n.d. April 1937; 2N24, Ministère du Travail 2ᵉ bur. to Jamet, 16 Jan. 1938; 2N25/D1, 'Programme d'ensemble de défense nationale', n.d. Jan. 1938; Young, *In Command*, pp. 23–4.
35. SHAT, 2N56/D2, Direction fabrication d'armement, conclusions de la commission d'études, 11 May 1936; 'Œuvre accomplie par la direction des fabrications', n.d. April 1937.
36. SHAT, 2N19/Décrets, direction générale du contrôle, 10 Dec. 1936.
37. SHAA, 2B1, EMA-Cabinet, no. 134, Daladier to Cot, 4 Feb. 1937; SHAT, 2N56/D2, no. 1078, Gasnier-Duparc to Daladier, 13 Nov. 1936; no. 46/DNI, Jamet to Daladier and Cot, 14 Jan. 1937, no. 470, Cot to Daladier, 3 July 1937.
38. SHM, 1BB2/D32, EMG-1, Durand-Viel report to Gasnier-Duparc, 14 Dec. 1937.
39. PRO, FO 371/20693, C263/122/17, Hammill report, 1937, 11 Jan. 1937; DDF, 2, V, no. 353, Gasnier-Duparc to Daladier, 27 April 1937; Coutau-Bégarie and Huan, *Lettres et notes de l'Amiral Darlan*, doc. 25.
40. PRO, FO 371/20693, C263/122/17, Hammill report, 1937, 11 Jan. 1937; SHM, 1BB2/D32, EMG-1, 'Plan d'Armement, 1936 –

Officiers', 23 Jan. 1937.
41. PRO, FO 371/20693, C261/122/17, Beaumont-Nesbitt report, 11 Jan. 1937; Gamelin, *Servir*, I, p. 263.
42. Brian Bond and Martin S. Alexander, 'Liddell-Hart and De Gaulle: The Doctrines of Limited Liability and Mobile Defence', in P. Paret, G. A. Craig and F. Gilbert (eds), *Makers of Modern Strategy from Machiavelli to the Nuclear Age*, Princeton, 1986, p. 615; PRO, FO 371/20693, C1597/122/17, Clerk to FO, 24 Feb. 1937.
43. PRO, AIR 9/76, 'Comparison of the air strength of G.B. with that of certain other nations', 30 Nov. 1936.
44. SHAA, 2B1, no. B130, EMAA-1, 'Histoire des plans d'accroisse-ment', 3 March 1938.
45. SHAA, 2B1, EMAA-1, 'Note sur l'accroissement éventuel de l'Armée de l'Air', n.d. March 1938; Jackson, 'La perception de la puissance aérienne allemande', p. 80. The estimate of 350 aircraft was certainly exaggerated.
46. SHAA, 2B1, EMAA-1, no. 284, Cot to Daladier, 5 April 1937; SHAT, 2N22, CPDN, séance, 15 Feb. 1937.
47. SAEF, B12.619/D3, le Norcy memo, 14 Nov. 1936.
48. See Bond and Alexander, 'Liddell-Hart and De Gaulle', pp. 610–15; Alexander, *Republic*, pp. 37–42, 119–20; Gilbert Bodinier, 'Gamelin, les fortifications et les chars à travers les rapports de l'E.M.A. (1935–1939)', *RHA*, 4, 1979, pp. 140–4.
49. DDF, 2, V, no. 353, Gasnier-Duparc to Daladier, 27 April 1937; Philippe Masson, 'Réarmement et Marine Française', *Revue Internationale d'Histoire Militaire*, 73, 1991, pp. 73–5; Chalmers Hood III, 'French Navy and Parliament', p. 398.
50. SHAT, 2N20/D3, CPDN, procès verbal, 29 July 1936.
51. MAE, Italie 270, no. 365, Blondel report, n.d. Dec. 1936; SHAT, 2B58/D1, EMAA-2, bulletin 53, 2ᵉ trimestre 1937.
52. Smith, 'Rearmament and Deterrence', pp. 325–33. See also Uri Bialer, 'Elite Opinion and Defence Policy', pp. 32–51.
53. Arthur J. Marder, 'The Royal Navy and the Ethiopian Crisis of 1935–1936', *American Historical Review*, 75, 3, 1970, pp. 1327–56; R.A.C. Parker, 'Great Britain, France and the Ethiopian Crisis', pp. 293–332; Lachadenède, *La Marine française*, pp. 20–7; Steven Morewood, 'Protecting the Jugular Vein of Empire: The Suez Canal in British Defence Strategy, 1919–1941', *War and Society*, 10, 1, 1992, pp. 86–90; Omissi, 'The Mediterranean and the Middle East', pp. 11–16.
54. PRO, CAB 64/6, Swinton memo, 'Comparison of Air Strengths', 1 March 1937; Smith, *British Air Strategy*, pp. 159–65; Charles Christienne, 'L'Armée de l'Air Française de Mars 1936 à Sept-

embre 1939', in Hildebrand and Werner (eds), *Deutschland und Frankreich*, pp. 216–17.

55. SHAA, 2B58/EMAA-2, bulletin de renseignements sur les aéronautiques étrangères – 2ᵉ trimestre 1937, fos. 185–6.

56. J.A. Cross, *Lord Swinton*, Oxford, 1982, pp. 169–71; Shay, *British Rearmament*, pp. 120–5.

57. PRO, FO 371/20693, C1748/122/17, Colyer memo, 1 March 1937.

58. PRO, WO 282/4, Samuel Hoare to Dill, 10 Oct. 1936; regarding Schweisguth's comments see Alexander, *Republic*, pp. 260–4; Young, *In Command*, p. 133.

59. PRO, WO 32/4441, Duff Cooper memo, 19 Oct. 1936; Bond, *British Military Policy*, pp. 139–60.

60. PRO, WO 32/4441, minute by Deputy Under-Secretary, 24 May 1937; WO 32/4444, report on progress in design and construction of infantry tank A12.E1, n.d.; J. P. Harris, 'British Military Intelligence and the Rise of German Mechanized Forces, 1929–1940', *INS*, 6, 2, 1991, pp. 402–7.

61. PRO, WO 32/4439, WO progress report, Nov. 1936; Bond, *British Military Policy*, pp. 176–8.

62. PRO, WO 32/4445, DCIGS report, 22 March 1939.

63. PRO, T273/275, Fisher memo, 23 Oct. 1936; Peden, *British Rearmament*, pp. 122–8.

64. Bond, *British Military Policy*, p. 239; PRO, WO 32/4441, TISC 140th meeting, 4 May 1938.

65. PRO, WO 32/4441, E.G. Compton to F.C. Bovenschen, 26 Feb. 1937; WO 33/1472, 4th interim report of Field Force committee, n.d. July 1937.

66. PRO, FO 371/20701, C205/205/62, Vansittart minute, 8 Jan. 1937; also cited in Alexander, *Republic*, p. 267.

67. CADN, Londres 285, no. 759, Corbin to Delbos, 24 Nov. 1936.

68. Richard J. Overy, 'Air Power and the Origins of Deterrence Theory before 1939', *JSS*, 15, 1, 1992, pp. 73–101.

69. DDF, 2, V, no. 274, 'Note de l'EMA', 14 April 1937.

70. PRO, WO 33/1490, Western Plan, Composition of the Field Force, 17 March 1938.

71. PRO, CAB 24/C.P.334(36), Chamberlain memo, 11 Dec. 1936.

72. PRO, Sir Edward Bridges papers, T273/275, Fisher to Simon, 14 Oct. 1937; regarding Treasury views by this stage see Peden, *British Rearmament*, pp. 136–9.

73. Parker, *Chamberlain*, pp. 273–9; G.C. Peden, 'Sir Warren Fisher and British Rearmament against Germany', *EHR*, 94, 370, 1979, pp. 29–47.

74. Alexander, *Republic*, pp. 264–78; SHM, 1BB2, carton 208, Darlan

dossiers, 'Politique navale en générale', 16 July 1937; additional notes by Darlan, 15 Nov. 1937.

75. PRO, FO 954/8, Fr/37/3, Eden record of conversation with Delbos and Viénot, 22 Jan. 1937; DBFP, 2, XVIII, no. 126, Baxter minute, 29 Jan. 1937.

76. SHAT, 7N2811/EMA-2, Lelong to Colson, 23 Dec. 1936; regarding the Cardwell system see Bond, *British Military Policy*, pp. 98–121.

77. DBFP, 2, XVIII, no. 126, FO minutes, 29 Jan. 1937; no, 103, note 3, 1 Feb. 1937; PRO, FO 371/20705, C563/1/18, Eden minute, 31 Jan. 1937; CAB 23/Cabinet 5(37), 3 Feb. 1937, concls.

78. PRO, DPR papers, CAB 16/141, vol. IV, DPR 145, WO memo, 16 Nov. 1936; CADN, Londres 285, no. 241, Voruz to EMA-2, 11 March 1936, no. 556, Cuny to EMA-2, 2 July 1936, Cuny rapport no. 38, 15 Jan. 1937.

79. PRO, CAB 24/C.P.(40)37, Inskip memo, 1 Feb. 1937; CAB 23/Cabinet 5(37), 3 Feb. 1937, 15; Bond, *British Military Policy*, p. 176.

80. M. Wolfe, *The French Franc between the Wars, 1919–1939*, New York, 1951, p. 152; PRO, FO 371/20688, C523/53/17, FO minutes, 20 Jan. 1937.

81. PRO, FO 371/20688, C572/53/17, Clerk report, 20 Jan. 1937; FO 371/20689, C1601/53/17, Rowe-Dutton memo, 25 Feb. 1937.

82. PRO, FO 371/20688, C1143/53/17, Chamberlain to Morgenthau, 10 Feb. 1937; DBFP, 2, XVIII, no. 202, Morgenthau to Chamberlain, 11 Feb. 1937; DDF, 2, IV, no. 437, Treasury to French government, 11 Feb. 1937; PRO, T177/34, Chamberlain to Sir Robert Lindsay, 5 March 1937; R. Girault, 'The impact of the economic situation on the foreign policy of France, 1936–1939', in Kettenacker and Mommsen, *Fascist Challenge*, p. 219.

83. DDF, 2, IV, no. 458, 'Note du Gouvernement Français au Chancélier', 17 Feb. 1937; PRO, FO 371/20688, C1363/53/17, Phillips to Strang, 16 Feb. 1937.

84. PRO, FO 371/20689, C1790/53/17, Record of Phillips–le Norcy conversation, 4 March 1937; C1810/53/17, Clerk to FO, 5 March 1937; FO 371/20685, C3206/18/17, Phipps report, 28 April 1937.

85. PRO, FO 371/20689, C1877/53/17, Phillips to Strang, 7 March 1937; C1888/53/17, Strang minute, 9 March 1937.

86. PRO, FO 371/20689, C1848/53/17, Vansittart to Clerk, 8 March 1937; G. Peden, 'Keynes, the Economics of Rearmament and Appeasement', in Kettenacker and Mommsen, p. 143; CADN, Londres 285, no 67.131, le Norcy to Vincent Auriol, 11 Feb. 1937.

87. PRO, T175/96, Treasury memo, n.d. Feb. 1937; Hopkins to Fisher, 4 Feb. 1937.

88. Chamberlain papers, NC 18/1/998, Chamberlain to sister Hilda, 13 March 1937.
89. Peden, *British Rearmament*, pp. 87–9; DDF. 2, IV, no. 450, François-Poncet to Delbos, 16 Feb. 1937; DBFP, 2, XVIII, no. 399, Phipps final review from Berlin, 13 April 1937; SHM, 1BB7, carton 39/EMM-2, Du Tour report, 'Le réarmement britannique et l'emprunt de défense nationale', 18 Feb. 1937.
90. PRO, CAB 16/182, D.P.(P)3, 26 April 1937; Roskill, *Naval Policy*, II, pp. 325–7.
91. Arthur J. Marder, *Old Friends, New Enemies. The Royal Navy and the Imperial Japanese Navy: Strategic Illusions, 1936–1941*, Oxford, 1981, p. 37.
92. PRO, ADM 116/3379, Admiralty plans division memo, 23 Dec. 1937; CAB 32/128, Principal delegates 7th meeting, 26 May 1937.
93. PRO, WO 33/1507, COS 691, 21 Feb. 1938; PRO, Admiralty papers and cases, ADM 178/137, NID report, 28 Aug. 1936.
94. PRO, First Sea Lord's papers, ADM 205/57, COS 683, 11 Feb. 1938.
95. PRO, CAB 4/25, CID 1305B, 25 Feb. 1937; MAE, Papiers Emile Naggiar, vol. 4, no. 377, report on Far Eastern forces/Shanghai, 18 Dec. 1937.
96. PRO, ADM 116/3379, Hammill to Admiralty, 21 Nov. 1936; Admiralty naval intelligence papers, ADM 223/488, 'Report on Activities of Section 3', 22 Oct. 1942.
97. PRO, ADM 116/3379, directorate of plans minutes, 22 April and 6 May 1938; SHAT, 2N227/D2, no. 93, Darlan to Gamelin, 30 May 1938.
98. PRO, ADM 116/3379, Duff Cooper minute, 9 May 1938; SHAT, 2N224/D2, 'Note sur le collaboration militaire franco-britannique', 24 April 1938.
99. CADN, Londres, 263, no. 446, Léon Noël to Bonnet, no. 214, Belgrade Chargé to Bonnet, no. 366, Coulondre to Bonnet, 2, 3 and 7 May 1938.
100. Martin Thomas, 'Plans and Problems of the Armée de l'Air in the Defence of French North Africa before the Fall of France', *French History*, 7, 4, 1993, pp. 484–5.
101. Young, *In Command*, p. 161; SHAA, 2B104/EMAA-3, 'Plans de Recherche', Nov.–Dec. 1937; 'Plan de Renseignement', 6 Jan. 1938.
102. SHAA, 2B104/EMAA-3, Gamelin memo, 22 Jan. 1938.
103. PRO, AIR 9/20, 'Note on the initial employment of the French Air Force in a hypothetical war with Germany', n.d. 1938.
104. PRO, FO 371/20694, C3571/122/17, Colyer memo, 14 May 1937;

BDFA, II, F, no. 16, Colyer memo, 23 Sept. 1937; A. Sauvy, preface to Cuvallier, *Vincent Auriol*, p. viii.

105. PRO, FO 371/20694, C3571/122/17, FO minutes, 24–5 May 1937; C4989/122/17, Air Ministry note, 7 July 1937; BDFA, II, F, 23, no. 18, Colyer to Phipps, 24 Sept. 1937.
106. PRO, FO 371/20694, C5215/122/17, IIC report, 26 June 1937.
107. PRO, FO 371/20694, C6436/122/17, Colyer report, 6 Sept. 1937; FO 371/21593, C 54/36/17, Colyer memo, 22 Dec. 1937.
108. SHAA, Z12930, Cot letter to Chautemps, 6 Dec. 1937; Jean Jardel note for Vincent Auriol, 8 Oct. 1937; Chapman, *State Capitalism*, pp. 161–6.
109. SHAA, 1B2/CSA, EMAA to General Georges, 26 Nov. 1936.
110. SHAT, 2N24, CPDN procès verbal, 8 Dec. 1937.
111. SHAT, 2N24, no. 2507/EMAA, 'Note relative aux répercussions de la situation générale', 29 Nov. 1937; no. 149/EMG-SE, Campinchi to Daladier, 24 Nov. 1937.
112. PRO, FO 371/20694, C5048/122/17, Beaumont-Nesbitt report, 9 July 1937; CADN, Londres 97, no. 881, Corbin to Delbos, 5 Nov. 1937; BDFA, II, F, 23, no. 20, Beaumont-Nesbitt report, 8 Oct. 1937.
113. PRO, ADM 1/9583, Admiralty note, 7 Feb. 1938; CADN, Londres 97, no. 2430, Massigli to Corbin, 18 Oct. 1937.

## Annex 1: French Air Force Rearmament

The table below, compiled on 7 October 1938, shows the composition and completion rates of the Armée de l'Air's re-equipment Plans I–IV between 1934 and 1938.

| | Type | Order Date | Completion Date | Order time |
|---|---|---|---|---|
| Plan I | Bloch 200 | Sept. 1934 | Nov. 1934 | 2 months |
| and Plan II | Bloch 210 | Oct. 1935 | Dec. 1936 | 14 months |
| | Amiot 143 | Nov. 1933 | Sept. 1935 | 22 months |
| | Potez 540 | Dec. 1934 | May 1935 | 5.5 months |
| | Farman 221 | Oct. 1934 | Dec. 1936 | 26 months |
| | Dewoitine 500 | Dec. 1933 | June 1935 | 18 months |
| | Dewoitine 510 | May 1936 | Nov. 1936 | 5 months |
| | Liore 46 | Jan. 1936 | Oct. 1936 | 10 months |
| | Spad 510 | Sept. 1935 | May 1937 | 20 months |
| | Dewoitine 371 | April 1935 | April 1937 | 24 months |
| Cot's additions to Plan II | Bloch 131 | April 1936 | Sept. 1938 | 29 months |
| | Morane 406 | Nov. 1936 | July 1938 | 20 months |
| | Morane 406 | April 1937 | Nov. 1938* | 18 months |
| | Potez 630 | Dec. 1937 | Aug. 1938 | 9 months |
| Additions under Plans IV | Bloch 150 | April 1938 | Jan. 1939* | 8 months |
| and V | Bréguet 690 | May 1938 | Feb. 1939* | 9 months |
| 1st tranche | Liore 45 | April 1937 | April 1938* | 12 months |
| | Amiot 350 | May 1938 | Jan. 1939* | 8 months |
| | Morane 406 | April 1938 | Mar. 1939* | 11 months |
| | Morane 406 | April 1938 | Jan. 1939* | 9 months |

\* Anticipated completion date. Note also that Morane orders were placed with different company factories: hence the appearance of dual orders for the Morane 406.
*Source*: SHAA, Archive Guy la Chambre, Z12930.

# The Failure of the Western Pact and French Eastern Diplomacy in 1937

Just as Britain and France had not yet taken great strides towards joint strategic planning, by January 1937 the entente powers had yet to agree a concerted approach to the German government. The western pact negotiations had been at a standstill since November when the Foreign Office had circulated its most recent proposals for a five-power conference. Despite this delay, a resumption of talks was generally anticipated across Whitehall, albeit at a cost of additional concessions from Britain and France. Eden confided to Baldwin on 27 December 1936 that he doubted whether Germany could withstand a further winter of privation akin to that currently being endured. The autarky drive had resulted in severe foodstuff shortages. Popular discontent might push Hitler to reconsider the prospect of talks.[1]

Renascent confidence in Paris was of a different calibre. It was remarkable that so diverse a governing coalition had survived to win parliamentary acceptance of Vincent Auriol's budget. The funds voted in early January sustained the massive rearmament programme, but the Assemblée had not yet insisted upon a reversal of the government's industrial reforms.[2] Yet both the Conseil and the Quai d'Orsay were harsher in their assessments of France's diplomatic standing than they had been when Blum took office. Although the French government shared the British belief that an agreement with Hitler was still obtainable, observers in Paris were less inclined to regard the Rome–Berlin Axis as divisible. Nor did the Quai d'Orsay consider Germany's economic distress sufficient to incline the Führer towards moderation.[3]

## I

Blum's vision of a general settlement was qualitatively different from the British model. For the French leader, a comprehensive non-aggression pact covering Germany's western and eastern frontiers would only assume real meaning when and if Hitler enacted the disarmament clauses that it should contain. Despite the German refusal to enter a conference with the other Locarno powers, Blum still cherished hopes of a tiered disarmament plan linked to the territorial arrangements the British intended to put to Berlin. Blum's arms limitation scheme hinged upon an initial acceptance by the five Locarno powers of the publication of their annual defence expenditure, reinforced by government supervision of the armaments sector.[4] During the spring of 1937 French proposals were forwarded to the League's disarmament conference bureau on this basis. Blum and Cot, the one service minister with any enthusiasm for the Premier's ideas, still attached real importance to the concept of arms producers as 'merchants of death' whose business required close regulation.[5] Only when the principal powers subjected their defence sectors to public and international scrutiny could progress be made on a preliminary arms limitation agreement: the air pact that the British and French had sponsored intermittently since the London meetings in February 1935.

The Foreign Office disliked Blum's emphasis upon disarmament. This became evident in January when François-Poncet fleshed out Blum's plans with a proposal for future general settlement talks beginning with a discussion of arms levels. The Berlin Ambassador had admitted to Blum and Delbos that his suggestions would mark the *de facto* abandonment of France's eastern allies. France could not credibly claim adherence to a collective security strategy based on mutual assistance when it was also prepared to take the initiative in reducing its own armaments.[6] In return for agreeing to arms limitation, Germany was to be offered financial and trading concessions. A prerequisite would be a more effective multilateral agreement to curtail foreign intervention in Spain. In late January Vansittart compiled a list of Foreign Office objections to François-Poncet's ideas in order to kill off the project forthwith.[7]

There were striking omissions from the French scheme. Germany was not required to make a specific commitment to the territorial status quo, nor to reorganize the Reich economy on a free-trading basis. Czechoslovakia was not mentioned at all. In Paris, Massigli shared the Foreign Office alarm. The French government's eagerness to entice Germany to the negotiating table threatened to make a mockery of the concurrent effort to revitalize France's links with the Little Entente.[8] Blum remained confused about the purpose and timing of economic concessions to Germany. Speaking at Lyon on 24 January, he at first ruled out such concessions, but then indicated that they might form part of a trade-off for arms limitation. Equally, his endorsement of the eastern alliances was, at least in part, driven by the fear that Poland and the Little Entente states would be tempted to conclude bilateral non-aggression accords with Berlin.[9]

Within weeks the François-Poncet scheme had been quietly abandoned. Though Blum still entertained hopes of renewed disarmament
talks, the French government returned to the fold.[10] London again took
control of the formulation of a viable western pact. Although the Foreign
Office had chastised the French for their imprecision, British policy-
makers did not speak with one voice. On 17 March Samuel Hoare, now
well established as First Lord of the Admiralty, alleged that the Foreign
Office was so biased against the dictators that it deliberately exaggerated
the importance of good relations with France in order to undermine Germany's quest for equitable treatment.[11] Hoare's remarks recapitulated
vituperative outbursts from Hankey and Chatfield in January. According
to them, concessions to the Axis powers were a logical response to
French unreliability and Soviet communism.[12] Chatfield preferred the
risk of a German realization that Britain's continental interests were
strictly confined to France and Flanders to the continued underfunding
of Britain's Far Eastern defences that resulted from defence preparations
against Japan, Germany and Italy. He remained an unashamed supporter
of the Anglo-German naval agreement, the more so as the Foreign Office
was reluctant to defend it in the face of French allegations that the deal
had condemned France to a naval race with the *Kriegsmarine*.[13]

Chamberlain's rising irritation with the Foreign Office had long-
term origins but a short-term trigger. Fundamental to Chamberlain's
annoyance was his belief that the Foreign Office had fudged earlier
appeasement efforts because of a misplaced respect for the French view
of European security. In consequence France had pulled the wool over
British eyes, preventing the achievement of an accord with Germany
prior to the collapse of the Disarmament conference in 1934. More
immediately, Chamberlain feared that in refuting Germany's grievances,
the Foreign Office would undercut the Leith-Ross–Schacht discussions.
Leith-Ross warned Sargent on 26 January that although the François-
Poncet scheme was 'wishy-washy', British opposition to it added to the
impression that London had 'beefed up' French policy towards Germany.[14]

On 23 January Massigli met the Foreign Office legal adviser, Sir
William Malkin, and the new central department chief, William Strang.
Massigli sought to clarify the French position regarding a western pact.
He maintained French demands for an 'exceptions clause' and pro-
visions for independent arbitration within any non-aggression
arrangement. This would enable France to fulfil its eastern mutual
assistance obligations in the event of a German attack on Poland or
Czechoslovakia. According to Massigli, Germany could not legitimately
object to this by pretending that France was out to make the Franco-
Soviet pact in some way an offensive treaty.[15] On 28 January Ciano

admitted that the Franco-Soviet pact was an irrelevance. In his view, the real obstacle to a resumption of Locarno power talks was the Spanish conflict. This was not encouraging. In May, when it was clear that the western pact talks were dead, Ciano admitted that there was no logical linkage between a replacement Locarno and the Spanish situation.[16] The German government was less concerned about Spain than about the French effort to negotiate a new multilateral treaty with the Little Entente. This meant that both the Axis powers had powerful induce-ments to avoid a western pact conference for the foreseeable future. In a speech before the Reichstag on 30 January Hitler made an unsolicited offer of a non-aggression guarantee to the Low Countries. Although of little value, this proposal diminished the likelihood that the Van Zeeland government would in any way compromise Belgium's neutrality to French benefit. With all these obstacles to a resumption of the western pact talks it is unsurprising that there was no full British Cabinet dis-cussion of the prospects for a new Locarno between February and late April 1937.[17]

## II

Hitler's Reichstag speech focused Anglo-French attention upon Bel-gium. On 12 February, the Belgian government replied officially to Britain's November 1936 proposals for a five-power conference. In an eloquent defence of its 'independence' policy, the Belgian government claimed that receipt of Locarno power guarantees combined with the continuation of the Belgian rearmament programme, would add to west-ern European security. This was soon backed up by a 24 per cent net increase in the Belgian defence budget to 1,146 million French francs.[18] On 2 March Foreign Minister Spaak confirmed that any violation of Belgian airspace would be treated as a *casus belli*. Commenting on the Belgian proposals, Brussels Ambassador Ovey warned that one element in Belgian thinking was unalterable: 'The Belgian government had been scared by [the] obvious intention of France to attack the Ruhr through Belgium in case of necessity.'[19] Despite Ovey's sympathies for the Belgian predicament, the Foreign Office was hostile to a western pact devoted solely to Belgium. On 18 March Eden reminded the Ambassador:

> from the British point of view these [Franco-Belgian] securities are merely different aspects of one whole . . . Once we abandon this identity between French and Belgian security we run the risk of getting into all sorts of dif-ficulties, among others the possibility of our having to negotiate a direct Anglo-French Treaty of guarantee in addition to, and as distinct from our Treaty guaranteeing Belgium. We do not like making this distinction.[20]

Understandably, the French government viewed the settlement of Belgium's international status from a strategic perspective. In this respect, Daladier's War Ministry was more successful in developing its surreptitious relationship with the Belgian general staff than the Foreign Ministry had been in convincing the Brussels government of Belgium's identity of interests with France. Although it needed no encouragement, on 20 May Delbos advised the War Ministry's deuxième bureau to continue low-profile contacts in absolute secrecy.[21] The Quai d'Orsay cannot be blamed for its failure to modify Belgian foreign policy. Considerations of national unity and parliamentary survival had long since determined the attitude of Van Zeeland's Cabinet and, in spite of Eden's opinion, the British government continued to subordinate European strategic considerations to the continuation of dialogue with Berlin.[22]

Chamberlain shared Eden's dislike of a western pact modelled on Belgium's requirements. His objection was simple. A joint entente guarantee of Belgium would force Britain to concede full staff conversations with France. On 8 March Eden suggested a way out. Instead of a formal non-aggression pact, each Locarno power might unilaterally declare Belgian independence to be a vital interest. This would avoid any new treaty obligation. It would also prevent Van Zeeland's denunciation of the 19 March 1936 agreement whereby Belgium maintained a theoretical commitment to the League covenant. Finally, it would preclude French staff talks. Until it was obvious that there was no hope of a replacement Locarno, Eden's suggestion would be strictly withheld from Brussels and Paris.[23]

On 10 March Chamberlain and Halifax suggested to the foreign policy committee that Britain should work for the abrogation of the Franco-Soviet pact. This might satisfy Hitler's objections to the new Locarno and so facilitate the conclusion of non-aggression pacts between Germany and its eastern neighbours. This was the very antithesis of French policy. Eden stressed the need to settle the Belgian issue first in order to prevent the committee adopting Chamberlain's proposals. The Foreign Office expected the official German and Italian replies to the British western pact proposals to arrive within days. Since these replies were bound to criticize the Franco-Soviet pact, it would be folly to concede on this issue beforehand without getting anything in return.[24]

Germany's reply arrived on 12 March. It ended any prospects for a western power settlement based around the provisions of the Locarno pact. The only aspect of the 1925 treaty which the German government proposed to retain was the co-guarantor system. Here the similarities with Locarno ended. Berlin insisted that the League should be excluded from any consultative role regarding the operation of the treaty. All the non-aggression guarantees were to be absolute. This precluded French exceptions in favour of Poland and the Little Entente unless some other 'impartial' body could be found to adjudicate on the matter. Berlin wished Britain and Italy as co-guarantors to take on this role. Since Hitler also demanded that all distinction between 'flagrant' and 'non-flagrant' aggression be abolished, he was effectively insisting that in no circumstances could France respond immediately to an ally's cry for help without the prior assent of Britain and Italy. Legally, British aid to France following the outbreak of a Franco-German war would thus be dependent on Italian agreement to it.[25] In all but name, Germany was demanding an eastern free hand.

The German memorandum turned the principle of collective action against aggression on its head. It would restrict France's right to assist her eastern allies and the entente powers' right to aid one another. Belgium would be recognized as completely neutral, so precluding discussion of common military problems between London, Paris and Brussels. Even the limited benefits of the 19 March 1936 agreement and the April 1936 staff talks would be lost. The Italian reply, clearly concerted with the German, reiterated the same arguments. The German government had done the minimum required to kill the western pact short of a diplomatic rupture with Britain.[26]

This had a less dramatic impact than one might think. Since the new year it had been apparent that diplomatic stalemate suited Hitler well. The Spanish situation continued to precipitate international division, the French government had not overcome its financial difficulties, the Soviet purges were gathering pace and Italy was drawing Yugoslavia out of the Little Entente orbit. Furthermore, Chamberlain appeared set to take a firmer grip in London. Conversely, French interest in a western pact had also diminished. As matters stood, France gained more tangible benefit from the arrangements made in the immediate aftermath of the Rhineland crisis. These at least held out the prospect of an Anglo-French alliance once an appeasement impasse was reached. Eden's speeches over the winter of 1936 had made this quite explicit.[27] The French were also looking eastwards. Blum, Delbos and Massigli had not given up hope for a new France–Little Entente treaty, something to which we shall return later in this chapter.

The absence of settlement might even suit Britain. The entente relationship was more stable than at any point in the 1930s. It was largely directed by London. Quiet British acquiescence in the collapse of western pact exchanges might provide a dignified means to let it become known that the Cabinet had abandoned any pretence of commitment to eastern Europe. There was still some hope placed in the Schacht conversations. If the diplomatic status quo were accepted, the only immediate loser would be Belgium. This could be remedied by a unilateral British guarantee.[28]

In the event, there was a flurry of diplomatic activity over the spring as a Belgian settlement was finalized. Initially regarded as a *pis aller* by the Blum government, French co-operation over Belgium was important to Britain. It signified that the Paris administration did not intend to invoke its right to alliance talks on the grounds that the appeasement effort had collapsed. But remaining supine with the British added to France's requirement for at least some vestige of a forward defence strategy to remain in place in Belgium.[29] On 10 April Roger Cambon informed Strang that France would insist that, unless the Belgian government continued to make defensive preparations based upon a forward defence of the Belgian–German frontier, the French general staff would have to advise against coming to Belgium's aid whatever the circumstances. This threat was backed up by Gamelin's announcement of additional construction of fortifications along the Franco-Belgian border. This attempted *fait accompli* would have contravened the guarantee that the French were about to sign.[30]

Eden immediately summoned Corbin. The British duly badgered the French government into an abandonment of these bullying tactics. An Anglo-French guarantee of Belgian independence was issued on 24 April, though two days later the Quai d'Orsay again lobbied Spaak for a continuation of staff contacts.[31] The French retained little of substance of their former military presence in Belgium. In February 1938 the Belgian government even began the symbolic construction of fortifications along the frontier with France. Equally symbolic manoeuvres were scheduled to take place near the French border during summer 1938.[32] Flemish delight at this added to the French humiliation but, while Belgian neutrality was a sad loss to France, it was not unexpected.

## III

Throughout the first half of 1937 the Blum government tried unsuccessfully to sustain a diplomatic offensive which had begun in earnest in December 1936, the purpose of which was to transform the Little Entente into an anti-German collective security network. The intention was for the Little Entente states to negotiate mutual assistance pacts between themselves before a single France–Little Entente mutual assistance treaty was overlaid upon this superstructure of new eastern alliances. The nub of the plan was that France should only contract new obligations to Yugoslavia and Romania after these states had committed themselves to the defence of Czechoslovakia against German attack.

As it stood, the Little Entente did not contain provision for joint action against a great-power aggressor. Since the alliance was technically geared to the containment of Hungarian, Austrian or Bulgarian revisionism, there was even a slight risk of France being dragged into an obscure Balkan squabble reminiscent of the events of 1914, something the British looked upon with horror.[33] The strategic goal of the France–Little Entente pact was to lay the foundations for a durable second front of a kind which lessened the requirement for Soviet involvement. This in turn would avoid the backlash that a Soviet presence in east-central Europe would produce, particularly among the Poles, Yugoslavs and Romanians themselves.[34] This was fundamentally unsound. Even if Paris could foster a genuine Yugoslav and Romanian will to defend Czechoslovakia, the intervention of these Balkan states, backed by French support in the west, was unlikely to prevent Bohemia from being overrun. In the absence of a Soviet role, France had to attract British support for the alliance project in order to afford it both diplomatic muscle and strategic credibility. This preliminary bridge was never crossed.

Indeed, both the Romanian and Yugoslav governments kept London abreast of their objections to the proposed treaties throughout 1937. On 31 December 1936 the British Ambassador to Bucharest, Sir Reginald Hoare, relayed the Romanian Foreign Minister, Victor Antonescu's opinion of the France–Little Entente pact: 'He had suggested to [the] French Government that they consult His Majesty's Government and see whether they could evolve a formula of a reassuring nature which H.M.G. could bless as giving no offence to anybody.' In a concerted action, the Yugoslav Premier, Milan Stojadinović, said exactly the same thing to Sir Ronald Campbell in Belgrade, adding that he doubted whether any such formula could be found.[35] On 6 January, Protitch, the Yugoslav Ambassador to Prague, confided to his French colleague that Stojadinović would oppose the proposed pact on the grounds that it would dissuade Italy from offering Yugoslavia a friendship treaty.[36]

This hints at another point. In addition to the missing British dimension, the French plans were undermined by what Nicole Jordan has referred to as the collapse of two 'pivots' of the French strategic position in central Europe: Italian and Soviet goodwill.[37] As French influence diminished, so Germany's power increased. On 16 March François-Poncet summarized the position: 'More and more clearly, German tactics in central and south-eastern Europe reveal their objectives: under the cover of supposedly disinterested and pacific action, to constitute a bloc of States, whose rivalries will have been ironed out, among whom Germany will be the arbiter since the influence of the western powers will have been excluded.'[38]

A final criticism of the France–Little Entente pact relates to the military capacity of the three eastern allies. It is insufficient to calculate this on the basis of the first-line strength of Czechoslovakia, Yugoslavia and Romania. All three states maintained large standing armies. But only Czechoslovakia was capable of meeting the greater part of its requirements for war material. Until the country was dismembered in 1938, both its army and air force were competently led, efficiently trained and well equipped.[39] By contrast, Czechoslovakia's Little Entente partners were increasingly dependent on French promises of equipment to enable them to contemplate war with a first-class power. In Belgrade and Bucharest unfulfilled expectations of France were central to the dismissal of the proposed alliance arrangements.

During the Rhineland crisis, Gauché's deuxième bureau characterized Yugoslavia's war material as 'archaic and disparate'. Greater French or Czechoslovakian equipment deliveries were essential. Yugoslav artillery, for example, was a curious mixture of other nations' surplus weaponry, notable for the large proportion of pre-1914 Austrian and Serb guns it contained.[40] In early March 1937, the War Minister, General Maritch, the most ardent francophile within Stojadinović's Cabinet, defended Yugoslavia's defence budget for 1938 before the Belgrade Parliament, the Skoupchtina. He began by stressing the lasting damage caused by the depression. This had forced a net 20 per cent reduction in defence spending between 1931 and 1936 relative to the money spent over the preceding five years.[41] This had retarded the development of trusting commercial relationships with overseas arms suppliers. The Yugoslav military was struggling to catch up for lost time while the France–Little Entente pact was under consideration.

In July 1938, the French War Ministry's section des armées étrangères concluded that the Yugoslav army remained 'of Balkan type', meaning that it still relied too heavily on its sixteen infantry divisions and had yet to mechanize either of its two cavalry divisions. The key to this remained the provision of French tanks.[42] The French army retained its respect for the individual prowess of the Yugoslav soldier, a view forged in particular during the Salonica campaign of the First World War. But by 1937 it was apparent that France would no longer sell the volume of war material to Belgrade that had been supplied between 1928 and 1934. Failure to supply added to the degradation of Franco-Yugoslav relations. The Belgrade government had over 100 million francs resultant from trade with France in 1936. It wished to use this money to purchase French Morane 405 and Potez 63 aircraft. Anxious to incorporate newly produced planes into French first-line strength, Cot simply did not answer Yugoslav enquiries during May and June 1937.[43] In November 1937 even Maritch issued an official protest after the Marseilles port authorities turned back a Yugoslav vessel which had arrived to pick up a consignment of twenty tanks for which the supply contract had previously been approved. By contrast, a French technical mission sent to assist in Yugoslavia's construction of fixed fortifications along the frontier with Italy during 1937–8 drew gratitude from the Belgrade War Ministry which far outweighed the importance of the assistance given.[44] Driven by the pressures of its own rearmament, France had repeatedly let the Yugoslavs down. In the first quarter of 1937, though Yugoslav exports to France increased by some 400 per cent to 118 million dinars, imports from France declined to a minuscule total of 15 million dinars. This left the Yugoslav government with declining holdings of convertible currency with which to pay for substantial war-material purchases. In December 1937 the Chautemps government conceded a bilateral commercial agreement which theoretically permitted Yugoslavia to maintain a 20 per cent surplus on its clearing account with France. This was hardly the stuff to reshape Yugoslavia's trade policy.[45]

Romania was in an analogous situation. Like its Balkan neighbours, the Romanian government was often frustrated in its efforts to secure French war material because of the restrictive quota arrangements governing exports to France. Yet Romanian oil should have given the country a crucial economic advantage over Yugoslavia. Petro-chemical resources were invaluable strategic commodities. The Quai d'Orsay, the rue Saint Dominique and the French oil concern, Petrofina Française, were anxious to increase the French share of Romania's oil exports.[46] After the conclusion of the Franco-Romanian Commercial Treaty in August 1934, it took several months of difficult negotiation to arrange further French oil purchases. The Romanian government knew that the export of refined oil generated greater profits than straightforward shipments of unrefined crude. In the event, it was agreed that a combination of crude oil and 25,000 tons of refined aviation spirit per annum were to be exported to France over a twelve-year period. An oil supply deal, initialled in September 1935 and ratified in May 1936, was intended to provide the Bucharest government with some 725 million francs with which to purchase French war material. In the same year Romania had embarked upon a fourteen-year programme of military modernization which rested upon French material supplies and technical support. The plans for completion of the original scheme were accelerated in every year from 1936 to 1939. Georges Tatarescu, Premier when the oil deal had been struck, warned the French Military Attaché, Lieutenant-Colonel Jules Delmas, on 4 November 1936 that Romania's attachment to France was bound to diminish if the French defence industry proved unable to support Romanian rearmament. French arms suppliers, Renault, Schneider and Hotchkiss foremost among them, were still reluctant to settle new supply contracts without additional state guarantees of repayment for any tanks, anti-aircraft guns or munitions delivered.[47]

The Romanian defensive position was unquestionably worsening. Fearful of intermittent Soviet demands for the return of the Bessarabian territory acquired in 1918, and hard pressed to control the disaffected Hungarian minority along its western Carpathian borders, Romania was bound to regard entry to war on behalf of France or Czechoslovakia with horror. For much of the 1920s and 1930s Romanian military expenditure was dominated by personnel costs required to cover the maintenance of the Romanian infantry. In February 1934, Delmas characterized the Romanian armed forces as little more than a large pool of manpower. At this stage, the army intended to maintain twenty-six infantry divisions. With a total population of only 18 million, it was inconceivable that Romania could both support such a large standing army and pursue a programme of rearmament. Yet the Romanians had neither automatic small-arms, motorized transport nor effective artillery. As to their air strength, though the Romanians possessed over 500 military aircraft, hardly any of these were usable, modern machines. In 1934 official estimates varied from ten to eighty aircraft that could be utilized in war with a first-class power.[48] In March 1934 King Carol asked the French War Minister Philippe Pétain to dispatch General Victor Petin to Bucharest to begin a detailed evaluation of Romania's most pressing requirements. Petin was a known Romanophile, having been chief of staff to General Henri Berthelot's French military mission to Bucharest during the First World War. Within weeks of his arrival Petin insisted that France should underpin a ten-year Romanian army re-equipment programme. This never came to fruition. In spite of the efforts of Delmas and Petin, over the next four years the French were unable to make any significant impact upon the modernization of Romania's armed forces. By mid-1938 the Romanian general staff had turned to Germany to meet a large proportion of its munitions requirements.[49]

In late 1936, Romanian co-operation was pivotal to the French Air Ministry's plans for an eastern air assistance pact. In the event that German forces occupied Czechoslovak territory, a phased withdrawal of French and Czech squadrons to Romanian airfields was envisaged.[50] In return, the Romanian authorities hoped to secure a Rambouillet-type package of financial aid and war material from France, though Vincent Auriol effectively refused this from the outset. The Bucharest government was asked to meet the 5 million franc cost of building airfields to house four French bomber squadrons along the western Carpathian frontier. It made its agreement to this conditional upon a binding assurance that French air support would be forthcoming. Despite two armée de l'air missions to Romania during the winter of 1936, and plans for parallel air-support arrangements with the Yugoslav government, these schemes were falling apart by March 1937.[51] The state of French military relations with Yugoslavia and Romania made a depressing backdrop to the proposals for a Little Entente pact.

## IV

The French project was substantially built upon Czechoslovak proposals sent to Paris in November 1936, though the idea of a France–Little Entente pact was originally the dream of the fallen Romanian Foreign Minister, Nicolae Titulescu. The French proposals were delivered to Prague, Belgrade and Bucharest on 18 January 1937, a month after Blum's son, Robert, had completed an inconclusive unofficial mission to the former two capitals.[52] Four days later, on Corbin's instruction, Roland de Margerie leaked full details of the alliance plan to Sargent. Corbin had discussed the project in outline with Eden and various central department officials during December. Although Eden had not been hostile to the idea, there was no indication of positive British support for it.[53] On 22 January, pleading that Sargent should not reveal the source of the leak, de Margerie refused to comment on the merits of the proposals, stating only that the Quai d'Orsay was convinced that British pressure could swing Belgrade.[54] This action was crucial. The details were released a week before Massigli formally delivered the draft pact to Strang at Geneva on 27 January. In the interim, a round of central department discussion took place which catalysed Foreign Office objections to the French project before Massigli even had the chance to defend it.

Among the harshest Foreign Office critics was southern department head, Owen O'Malley. His comments on 25 January were decisive:

> It is axiomatic that warm relations between France and the Little Entente entail cool relations between France and Italy. The French scheme would be certain to cause Italy to draw closer to Germany; and British support for it would prejudice the chances of improved relations between Italy and the U.K . . . It is therefore to our interest to limit our interests in Central Europe as severely as possible.[55]

Neither Vansittart, Cadogan nor Eden demurred at Sargent's conclusions, themselves drawn from O'Malley's remarks: Britain's explicit verbal guarantees to France, made during 1936, entitled London to exercise 'a definite control' over French policy in eastern Europe.[56]

This was little different from the Admiralty's advice to the Foreign Office issued in an extraordinary communication on 22 February. This was a powerful concoction of Hoare and Chatfield's francophobia. Attachment to France meant support of an encirclement strategy, the collapse of appeasement and the perpetuation of the three-power threat. The Cabinet was better advised to admit openly to Britain's withdrawal from eastern Europe. The CID amplified this argument in its debate over the viability of the Singapore strategy on 25 February. Involvement in eastern Europe risked leaving the Empire needlessly exposed, not just to German but to Japanese or Italian attack.[57]

Foreign Office confidence that it could issue stern advice to Delbos without damaging Anglo-French relations was encouraged by the Quai d'Orsay's timetable for the new eastern pacts. This stipulated that France would only increase its commitments to its alliance partners after the Little Entente was transformed into a tripartite military pact for the defence of Prague. Although it made strategic sense, by introducing a sequence to the strengthening of the eastern alliance network, the French government confirmed the prevalent international doubt that France would stand by her existing eastern obligations. Viewed from Belgrade and Bucharest, France was declining to accept the greater commitment it was urging upon others. Benes was equally frank: 'if Germany fell on Czechoslovakia and France did not come to her immediate aid, as well as [to] her partners in the Triple [Little] *Entente*, he [Benes] would have nothing left to do but go to Berlin and cry "Kamerad."'[58]

The Italo-Yugoslav treaty of friendship on 26 March 1937 confirmed the collapse in French eastern policy.[59] Acting on the latest information from Campbell in Belgrade and Pouritch in Geneva, on 6 February Eden had warned Corbin that France should accept that Yugoslav opposition to the Little Entente pact was irreversible. Stojadinović was determined to court the Axis powers. He had taken to heart Mussolini's accusation that the existing Franco-Yugoslav treaty was 'a pistol aimed at the heart of Italy'. Maritch conceded that Stojadinović's policy was the only viable course of action. In seeking friendly relations with all its neighbour states, Yugoslavia was fast approaching non-alignment.[60]

The Foreign Office was unenthusiastic about Italy's effort to woo the Yugoslavs and other key Balkan states, principally Romania and Turkey.[61] Yet, ultimately, the British were philosophical about this consolidation of Italian influence in the eastern Mediterranean. Ciano's desperation to conclude the pact at virtually any cost was taken as an indication of Mussolini's need to bolster Italian power at a time when Germany was fast encroaching into Danubian Europe and British rearmament was set to place clear water between the regional capabilities of Britain and Italy. After the brief honeymoon period following the Gentlemen's agreement, Mussolini was again becoming troublesome. Discussing Italy's position at a CID meeting on 11

February, Chamberlain had produced his baffling formula that the country be counted 'an unreliable friend'.[62]

Evidently alarmed at Britain's 1937 defence estimates, the Italians had intensified their propaganda in the Middle East and given priority to the production of aircraft and shipping for offensive action in the Mediterranean. Mussolini complained at British pestering over Italian rearmament and had discovered a vested interest in the successful colonial appeasement of Germany.[63] When it came to the point, Italy had few grounds for a genuine co-operation with Germany along the line of the Danube. As Goering admitted to Malcolm Christie on 3 February, Hitler would not tolerate any tangible expansion of Italian influence in central or south-eastern Europe. It seems, then, that there was a defensive aspect to Italian efforts to befriend Yugoslavia, Romania and Turkey.[64] The Foreign Office drew comfort from this assumption.

The French government did not see any hidden blessings in the Italo-Yugoslav treaty. Delbos even interpreted Stojadinović's abrupt conclusion of the pact as confirmation of a deeply laid plot to keep Paris misinformed. Although this was not borne out, Stojadinović's injudicious and racist slurs upon the Popular Front, and Blum in particular, were revealing.[65] In February Massigli had warned Delbos that Stojadinović thrived on the international interest in Yugoslav foreign policy:

> Pampered by London, flattered by Berlin and Rome, supported by Paris and, through the rapprochement with Bulgaria, able to use the bulk of his forces to guard the Hungarian frontier, the views of Prague matter much less; in any case, he [Stojadinović] is not inclined to compromise the immediate interests of his country for the sake of fidelity to a member of the Little Entente which is now in a highly dangerous situation.[66]

Over subsequent months Franco-Yugoslav relations continued to deteriorate as Stojadinović outgrew the Little Entente. In April, he dismissed the Little Entente conference that he had just hosted in Belgrade as 'a first class funeral'. Maritch could do little to arrest the decline.[67]

Like Stojadinović, Victor Antonescu had previously served as Finance Minister. So the Romanian Foreign Minister had also experienced the disappointments of seeking increased trade with France. But, unlike Stojadinović, Antonescu and Premier Tatarescu retained a general sympathy for France. Antonescu had, after all, served as Ambassador in Paris, a posting which produced lasting friendships with politicians as diverse as Edouard Herriot, Louis Marin and Georges Mandel. On his return to Bucharest from the Belgrade conference, Antonescu admitted to the French Minister, Adrien Thierry, that Yugoslavia had become so detached from her Little Entente partners that there remained a coalition 'in appearance only'.[68]

Antonescu was afraid that Romania would be left isolated if Yugoslavia moved closer to Italy and Britain encouraged Czechoslovakia to conclude a non-aggression accord with Germany. This added to the importance the Romanian government attached to the views of its Balkan Entente clients, Turkey above all. Doubtless influenced by the Yugoslavs, the Balkan Entente was unenthusiastic about the Little Entente pact. A new alliance network built upon the defence of central Europe would alienate Italy and undermine the rationale of a purely Balkan defensive combination.[69]

French protests to Stojadinović over his refusal to discuss the Little Entente pact at the Belgrade conference were ineffective. As Thierry put it, the Little Entente had become a hollow grouping in which each state worked to secure its own security position. Only if France could provide immediate material assistance to its allies – meaning substantial arms supplies and an unequivocal pledge of military assistance – could it prevent the coalition's disintegration.[70] When Yugoslavia's Prince Paul bowed to British pressure and deigned to meet French leaders on his return from the coronation celebrations in London in May 1937, he omitted to mention von Neurath's imminent trip to Belgrade. Goering had already aroused Anglo-French suspicion with an unscheduled 'holiday' stop-over in Bled where Prince Paul and Stojadinović promptly turned up to meet him.[71] Von Neurath's visit publicly set the seal on Yugoslavia's more cordial relations with the Axis powers. His Yugoslav hosts even helped him organize an onward journey to Bulgaria.[72] As the German government was confident of Yugoslavia's anxiety for co-operation, only the coincidence of von Neurath's later arrival in Bucharest with that of Colonel Beck and the Polish president, Ignacy Moscicki, prevented it from proclaiming Romania's increasing detachment from the Little Entente. It was hardly consistent with Nazi propaganda to admit the shared objectives of German and Polish policy towards Romania. Both were eager to consolidate bilateral relations with Bucharest at Soviet and Czechoslovakian expense.[73]

## V

Throughout 1937 and on into the following year, Hitler, Goebbels, Goering and Hess all publicly accused France and her eastern client, Czechoslovakia, of undermining the appeasement process by introducing Soviet military strength into any settlement equation. This was variously blamed for the failure of arms limitation, the collapse of an eastern pact and Germany's refusal to return to the League. In fact, Soviet Russia, much like republican Spain with which it was readily associated, was marginal to French diplomacy. Equally, the fall of the

Hodza government in Prague in mid-July 1937 derived in part from the depth of right wing opposition to Czechoslovakia's increasing reliance on the Soviet Union.[74]

Despite the vocal Nazi protests against it, the Franco-Soviet connection gradually won broader acceptance within the British government. During 1937 first the Blum government and then the Chautemps Cabinet gave the most unqualified assurances to date regarding the limited purposes of the Moscow tie. Indeed, the Front populaire was more open about its dealings with the Soviet Union than the British ever cared to be about their contacts with Rome, notably in the run-up to the Anglo-Italian agreement in April 1938.[75] Furthermore, in 1937 the development of French military co-ordination with Poland, although ultimately frustrated, did at least illustrate the diminution of Soviet importance within French defensive planning.

After a one-month postponement, on 19 January the head of the French air staff intelligence section, Commandant Loriot, led an armée de l'air mission to Poland. After agreeing a list of French desiderata with General Félix Musse, d'Arbonneau's successor as Warsaw Military Attaché, on 21 January Loriot began three days of talks with Colonel Poutchinsky, his Polish air-staff counterpart. Their discussions covered provision for French bombers to operate from Polish airfields, and the fulfilment of France's war-material pledges made under the Rambouillet agreement in September 1936. Both issues were clearly within the remit of the Franco-Polish alliance and Rambouillet itself.[76]

Since 1929 the French Air Ministry had intermittently tried to persuade the Poles and Romanians to purchase French fighters and the licences for their manufacture.[77] Throughout the 1930s the Poles produced fighter and reconnaissance aircraft modelled on French designs or fitted with French engines, notably at the Panstwowe Zaklady Lotnieze (PZL) plants at Warsaw and Lublin. But the existing French Potez and Bréguet aircraft in service in Poland had become obsolete.[78] As in the Yugoslav and Romanian cases, the Polish government had insufficient funds to undertake a modernization programme during the depression years. Loriot's mission was a partial remedy for this. He arrived in Poland less than a week after Cot approved the final statutes of the Office Français d'Exportation de Matériel Aérien, in modern parlance a quasi-governmental organization intended to advance the sales of French war material.[79]

The Loriot–Poutchinsky conversations turned on the detailed planning of radio communications, reconnaissance signalling, refuelling facilities and the allocation of specific bases within striking distance of Berlin, Saxony and Thuringia. Poutchinsky was enthusiastic. He encouraged Loriot to report to Cot that substantial progress had been made towards a firm air-force assistance agreement. If all went according to plan, this was to be crowned by the deployment of French squadrons around Poznan. Even Léon Noël shared Cot's taste for a regional air pact which he considered the least explosive means to bring about Polish–Soviet co-operation.[80] Poutchinsky paid a return visit to France in June 1937. He confirmed his francophile outlook by securing the post of Paris Air Attaché in September. Still, the talks with Loriot did not bear fruit. The head of the Polish air force, General Rayski, insisted that Polish interest in joint operational planning remained undiminished. But during 1937 Polish interest in aerial collaboration was increasingly confined to the fulfilment of the Rambouillet supply accords, specifically the acquisition of French bombs and mountings for Polish aircraft. Rayski was also anxious to train Polish bomber pilots in France. The Poles were set to create a separate bomber arm, based upon their modern medium bomber, the PZL 37, which was scheduled to begin series production in 1938.[81]

Although the French Air and War Ministries pursued technical co-operation with the Poles to a far greater extent than with the Russians, before 1939 the results were limited. At its peak in the mid-1920s, there had been a 1,500-strong French military mission in Warsaw. By late 1935 these links had grown stale. In February 1936, General d'Arbonneau sent Gauché a chilling reminder of the fate which awaited the Polish military: 'If matters remain as they are, one might say that the Polish army has but a feeble capacity for resistance against a well-equipped army – it would be almost completely ineffectual against attack by armoured divisions – and it lacks the necessary forces to take the offensive.'[82] Given the frequency of warnings such as this from Attachés in Warsaw, Bucharest and Belgrade, it is hardly surprising that the French War Ministry's evolving mobilization plans were not predicated upon concerted action with eastern European forces. Typically, discussion of these plans was scrupulously avoided by the French Attachés themselves. Although the Bucharest Military Attaché, Jules Delmas, was a particularly strong personality, none of the Attachés across eastern Europe enjoyed a rapport comparable to that which subsisted between the Prague government and the long-serving head of the French military mission to Czechoslovakia, General Louis Faucher.[83]

With Colonel Beck away from Warsaw for most of January to March 1937, the French government saw an opportunity to exploit the goodwill generated among the Polish service chiefs by Rambouillet before it ebbed away in a tide of unfulfilled promises. The flotation of a Rambouillet loan on the Paris Bourse on 9 January 1937 was a logical starting point for a new round of discussions.[84] On 13 February General Stachiewicz informed General Musse of his intention to send an army mission to France to study tank models suitable for purchase under the

Rambouillet loan. Rydz-Smigly was reportedly delighted at the Loriot mission. He wished to see it complemented by orders for the Polish army, focusing especially on light tanks mounted with 37 mm cannon. The Polish general staff was also eager to exploit a November modification to the original Rambouillet terms which increased the sum set aside for the development of Polish war industry from 200 to 250 million francs. This would be allocated primarily to the development of aero-engine and airframe factories. By June things had changed. Stachiewicz and Rydz-Smigly were complaining that Poland remained empty-handed almost a full year after Rambouillet.[85]

In seeking Warsaw's application of the accepted principles of joint Franco-Polish air operations conducted within Polish territory, the French general staff moved further away from the integration of the Franco-Soviet pact into their two-front strategy. With hindsight, it made geographical sense for Soviet, not French, bombers to operate from Poland. Although very real, the depth of Polish hostility to the Soviet Union was only a cover for the French military's own distaste for co-operation with the Red Army. As has been thoroughly demonstrated by others, General Schweisguth's condemnatory report upon the 1936 Soviet army manoeuvres in White Russia had a seismic impact upon French military planning.[86]

Though overtly political, Schweisguth's conclusions were not easy to challenge. The French did extract military intelligence from the Soviet Union. But the War Ministry was reluctant to believe it. It seemed obvious that Stalin's terror, soon to culminate in the execution of Marshal Mikhail Toukhatchevsky, was increasingly focused upon the Soviet high command. The rue Saint Dominique was reluctant to criticize Schweisguth's observations by reference to the earlier, more favourable report on Red Army capacity submitted by a deputy chief of army staff, General Lucien Loizeau, in September 1935.[87] Nor did the more balanced accounts of the Moscow Military Attaché, Lieutenant-Colonel Simon, cut much ice with the War Ministry intelligence planners. In September 1936 Simon pointed out the simple fact that the Red Army was sufficiently powerful to conduct not only the manoeuvres in White Russia that Voroshilov participated in and Schweisguth witnessed, but also simultaneous manoeuvres in the Soviet Far East and in the mountainous northern Caucasus. Simon attended the latter. He submitted a highly favourable report which emphasized the quality of Soviet motorized equipment and the aircraft employed to support it.[88]

The Military Attaché was not in tune with the thinking prevalent across the service ministries. Darlan, for example, regarded Soviet naval support as of low priority relative to co-operation with the British. The exception remained Cot's close-knit band at the Air Ministry. With

Blum's approval, a French air mission led by General Pierre Keller, Inspector-General of French air defence, had arrived in Moscow on 18 March 1937 to inspect aircraft factories and the organization of the Soviet air force. Officially, Soviet air strength stood at 4,653 machines. But the large proportion of obsolete aircraft made actual Soviet air strength more problematic. The point to note here is that the air mission reported that Soviet planning was predicated upon the need to take the offensive with blitzkrieg-style bombardments. To achieve this, Soviet industry was being geared to industrial mobilization in the immediate term, something that Schweisguth had argued was not achievable. The findings of Keller's mission did not fit in with the denigration of Soviet military capacity fashionable within the other services and among Blum's civilian ministers. In December 1937 the Czechoslovak air staff confirmed Keller's optimistic assessment of Soviet air potential during a visit by Féquant to Prague.[89]

At the height of the Czech crisis in September 1938 Féquant's successor as chief of air staff, General Joseph Vuillemin, submitted a well-known report on the efficacy of Soviet assistance. This was utilized by Gamelin and Guy la Chambre. Vuillemin's conclusions confirmed that the Air Ministry had come into line with the rest of the service establishment.[90] He cast doubt on Soviet effectiveness just as Schweisguth had done two years earlier. Reading the report, one is struck by the validity of Vuillemin's comments regarding the problems of Soviet access to Polish and Romanian airspace. These were genuine obstacles to legally sanctioned air assistance. La Chambre had made the same point to Daladier, urging that the Soviets be requested to supply the Poles and Romanians with aircraft rather than be encouraged to over-fly their airspace. Yet Vuillemin's dismissal of Soviet air strength seems hypocritical and unconvincing. The General was forced to concede a conservative estimate of 3,000 modern aircraft already in service. He accepted that the Soviet air industry, though not expanding, was able to produce 5,000 airframes and 10,000 aero-engines per annum. Knowledge of these figures was insufficient to dissuade Vuillemin from submitting a further report on 26 September which painted an alarming – and alarmist – picture of *Luftwaffe* supremacy.[91]

Looking ahead to Munich risks prejudging events. But precursors of Vuillemin's attitude are not difficult to trace in 1937. Speaking to a PCF audience on 23 January, Blum had added his voice to the EMG's opposition to a Franco-Soviet military convention. A year later at the PCF congress at Arles in December 1937, Thorez eulogized the Soviet Union just as he had done at the Villeurbanne congress in 1936. But even he did not call unequivocally for immediate staff talks.[92] At the boulevard Victor, during early 1937, Cot, Féquant and Jauneaud increasingly centred their efforts to achieve an inter-allied air-defence strategy upon Poland. They had little choice. According to the Air Minister's bitter memoirs, only Maurice Viollette had firmly supported him within Blum's inner cabinet, the Petit Conseil, when he had advocated a military accord with Moscow.[93] As Massigli had put it, at a time when the French government was distancing itself from Soviet activities in Spain, it was hardly sensible to discuss close military collaboration with Moscow. The French were poorly placed to tender forces to an eastern front. Their willingness to discuss doing so in 1937 indicates that the government placed the existent Polish and desired Little Entente alliances above a Moscow–Prague–Paris axis.[94]

Before travelling on to the Soviet Union, Schweisguth had attended Czechoslovakian manoeuvres in late August 1936. The General sought assurances from Benes that the Czechs had not made any secret military arrangements with Moscow.[95] Evidently worried at rising French military suspicion, Benes reminded General Faucher in an interview on Christmas Day 1936 that Prague's favourable attitude to Moscow was still conditioned by Polish hostility and the recognition of the possibility of a Germano-Soviet accord. Czech policy was a pragmatic response to the threats posed by dangerous neighbours and doubtful friends.[96]

On the British side, Sir George Clerk and the outspoken northern department chief, Sir Laurence Collier, agreed that the French government harboured no illusions about the worth of the Franco-Soviet pact or the possibility of a Nazi–Soviet agreement.[97] In 1935 a Soviet military mission had visited France to establish contacts with several arms manufacturers. A wide range of Soviet orders were placed during 1936, principally for artillery equipment, with arms houses including Schneider, Brandt, Renault, Hispano-Suiza and Ratier.[98] On 15 April 1937 the Petit Conseil authorized the service chiefs, Gamelin, Darlan and Féquant, to renew technical discussions with their Soviet counterparts. This was in anticipation of a limited exchange of information to which Blum attached the characteristically pacific title of 'technical covenants'.[99] But the French had been alerted to the dangers inherent in overlooking the Soviet Union in November 1936 when Ambassador Robert Coulondre presented his credentials to Mikhail Kalinin, the president of the central executive committee. In an uncomfortable meeting, Coulondre was left in no doubt that the Soviet government would only remain faithful to France while this conferred tangible benefits.[100] The Blum government did enough to keep the Franco-Soviet pact intact but little more. Far from being the prelude to full staff conversations with the Soviets, the contacts developed over the spring of 1937 were proof that no such thing would take place.

In May the army staff pointed out that the legal obstacles to the operation of the Franco-Soviet pact were a secondary consideration. Prior reference to the ailing League or to the original Locarno signatories was pointless. The decision as to whether the pact should come into effect lay with France alone. This was a responsibility the French leadership remained anxious to avoid, particularly as it risked damaging the entente. Freed from formal constraints, the EMA urged that the government should seek shelter under the anticipated British and Polish objections to a military convention.[101]

In any event, Poland and Romania were unlikely to assent to rights-of-passage agreements for Soviet forces. Antonescu characterized the Soviet Union as 'bugbear of Europe', commenting to Thierry that 'anything is preferable to Soviet assistance'.[102] The Soviet fleet was stretched to the limit by its Far Eastern, Baltic and Black Sea commitments and could not offer direct assistance to the French marine. In short, the French government was best advised to maintain the Paris–Moscow pact 'as insurance only'. By April 1937, French parliamentary criticism of the Soviet treaty had diminished. Even the Fédération Républicaine, the main right-wing party in the Assemblée, recognized that a German–Soviet détente was a bleaker alternative to the limited continuation of dialogue between Paris and Moscow.[103] On 28 May Corbin assured Vansittart that the French government would 'reduce to the smallest possible compass any further development of the Franco-Soviet Pact'.[104] By this stage Blum's government was too weak to embark on any major diplomatic initiative anyway.

## Notes

1. Baldwin papers, 124/Series B, 1936, fo. 56, Eden to letter to Baldwin, 27 Dec. 1936; PRO, T160/846/F14141/3, ICF/286, 1 May 1937.
2. Rearmament costs quickly rose beyond the original 1936 estimates, see Frank[enstein], *Le Prix*, p. 137; PRO, FO 371/20684, C695/18/17, Clerk to FO, 28 Jan. 1937.
3. DDF, 2, IV, no. 325, Massigli, 'Note de la Direction Politique', 20 Jan. 1937.
4. Moch, *Front Populaire*, p. 254.
5. SHAT, 2N23/D4, Sous direction de la société des nations, Lagarde, to Jamet, 9 June 1937; no. 4161, Cot to Daladier, 23 April 1937; Martin S. Alexander, 'A bas les marchands de canons! Efforts to

control the private manufacture and trade in arms in France during the 1930s', in M. Vaïsse (ed.), *Le Pacifisme en Europe des années 1920 aux années 1950*, Brussels, 1993, pp. 285–300.

6. PRO, FO 371/20705, C424/1/18, Phipps to FO, 18 Jan. 1937.
7. DBFP, 2, XVIII, no. 116, Van to Eden, 25 Jan. 1937.
8. PRO, FO 371/20705, C424/1/18, FO minutes, 19 & 20 Jan. 1937; DDF, 2, IV, no. 325, Massigli, 'Note de la direction politique', 20 Jan. 1937.
9. DDF, 2, IV, no. 346, François-Poncet to Delbos, 25 Jan. 1937; PRO, FO 371/20684, C695/18/17, Clerk report, 28 Jan. 1937.
10. Blum resurrected the disarmament idea in July, see SHAT, 2N23, pièce 3, CPDN, p.v., 19 July 1937.
11. Templewood papers, general correspondence, Hoare letter to Chamberlain, 17 March 1937.
12. Chatfield papers, CHT 3/1, Notes on Vansittart's 'World Situation and Rearmament', 5 Jan. 1937, fo. 193.
13. PRO, ADM 116/3596, Chatfield's comments on Craigie–Ribbentrop interview, 8 Jan. 1937. Regarding the declining British strategic position in the Far East see Malcolm H. Murfett, 'Living in the Past: A Critical Re-examination of the Singapore Naval Strategy, 1918–1941', *War and Society*, 11, 1, 1993, pp. 73–103. Regarding French allegations see CADN, Londres 285, Captain du Tour to EMM-2, 5 March 1936.
14. Chamberlain papers, NC 18/1/991, Chamberlain to sister Ida, 16 Jan. 1937; PRO, FO 371/20705, C630/1/18, Leith-Ross to Sargent, 26 Jan. 1937.
15. DBFP, 2, XVIII, no. 109, Strang record of conversations, 23 Jan. 1937.
16. PRO, FO 371/20705, C689/1/18, Ingram to FO, 28 Jan. 1937; MAE, Grande Bretagne 315, no. 197, Blondel to Delbos, 10 May 1937.
17. DDF, 2, IV, no. 307, François-Poncet to Delbos, 16 Jan. 1937; PRO, CAB 23/Cabinet 5(37), 3 Feb. 1937; FO 371/20706, C989/1/18, Phipps to FO, 4 Feb. 1937.
18. SHAT, 7N2370/D2, EMA-2, Colonel Laurent to Daladier, n.d. 1937.
19. PRO, FO 371/20706, C1316/1/18, Ovey to FO, 11 Feb. 1937.
20. DBFP, 2, XVIII, no. 310, Eden to Ovey, 18 March 1937.
21. Gauché, *Deuxième Bureau*, pp. 53–4; DDB, IV, nos. 183 & 184, de Kerchove to Spaak, 24 & 29 Dec. 1936; MAE, Grande Bretagne 315, Delbos to EMA-2, 20 May 1937.
22. DBFP, 2, XVIII, no. 226, Ovey to Eden, 26 Feb. 1937.
23. PRO, CAB 27/622, F.P.(36) 6th meeting, 10 March 1937; CAB 27/626, F.P.(36)17, Eden memo, 8 March 1937.
24. PRO, CAB 27/622, F.P.(36) 6th meeting, 10 March 1937.

25. The FO & Quai agreed that the reply destroyed the likelihood of a pact, DDF, 2, V, no. 94, Corbin to Delbos, 12 March 1937; BDFA, II, F, 23, no. 5, Clerk to Eden, 17 March 1937.
26. DDF, 2, V, no. 115, François-Poncet to Delbos, 17 March 1937.
27. CADN, Londres 263, no. 1026, Corbin to Delbos, 15 April 1937.
28. PRO, CAB 27/626, F.P.(36)21, Eden memo, 22 March 1937.
29. PRO, FO 371/20706, C2158/1/18, Clerk to FO, 17 March 1937; MAE, Grande Bretagne 314, Massigli note, 'aide mémoire Belge', 22 March 1937.
30. PRO, FO 371/20707, C2838/1/18, record of Strang–Cambon conversation, 10 April 1937, also as DBFP, 2, XVIII, no. 391.
31. PRO, FO 371/20707, C2897/1/18, record of Strang–Cambon conversation, 15 April 1937; C3158/1/18, Corbin to FO, 26 April 1937.
32. SHAT, 7N2731/EMA-2, no. 224/S, Attaché's résumé, 25 Aug. 1938; Alexander, 'In Lieu of Alliance', pp. 420–4.
33. MAE, Massigli 15, note, 'Sécurité française', 8 July 1936.
34. DDF, 2, IV, no. 281, Delbos to de Lacroix, 11 Jan. 1937; BDFA, II, F, 23, no. 2, Clerk to Halifax, 16 Feb. 1937.
35. PRO, FO 371/21136, R26/26/67, Hoare to FO, 31 Dec. 1936, R24/26/92, Campbell to FO, 31 Dec. 1936.
36. CADN, Rome 519, no. 9, Monicault, Prague, to Delbos, 6 Jan. 1937.
37. Jordan, *Popular Front*, p. 188.
38. CADN, Londres 136, no. 411, François-Poncet to Delbos, 16 March 1937.
39. SHAT, 7N3096/MMF, no. 2352/SE, Faucher, 'Rapport sur la puissance militaire de la tchécoslovaquie', 8 March 1937.
40. SHAT, 7N3202/D1, EMA-2, 'Note succincte sur l'armée Yougoslave', n.d. March 1936; 7N3203/EMA-2, 'Note de renseignements sur le nouveau matériel d'artillerie Skoda', 3 Feb. 1932.
41. SHAT, 7N3202/D1, no. 68, notes de renseignements, 'Budget de la guerre Yougoslave', 12 March 1937. Yugoslavia's 1937 defence budget totalled 2,459 million dinars. In 1938 the total was increased by 313 million dinars.
42. SHAT, 7N3202/D1, EMA-2, SAE, 'Yougoslavie', n.d. July 1938; Mile Bjelajac, 'L'influence française sur l'Armée yougoslave entre les deux guerres mondiales', *RHA*, 4, 1994, pp. 47–9.
43. SHAT, 7N7193/EMA-2, Captain Tarle, Air Attaché, to EMAA-2, 22 June 1937.
44. SHAT, 7N7193/EMA-2, Béthouart to Daladier, 18 Nov. 1937; 7N3203/EMA-2, no. 2, Béthouart to EMA-2, 3 Jan. 1938; service de missions, 'Note pour la direction du génie', 8 June 1938.
45. SHAT, 7N7193/EMA-2, no. 112, Béthouart to EMA-2, 12 May 1937;

no. 263/1, note de renseignements, 22 Dec. 1937.

46. SHAT, 7N3049/AM rapports, note by Delmas, 29 Sept. 1935; Jordan, *Popular Front*, pp. 125–6.

47. SHAT, 7N3050/AM télégrammes, no. 106/S, Delmas conversation with Tatarescu, 4 Nov. 1936; no. 58/S & no. 446/S, both Delmas to EMA-2/SAE, 24 May & 20 Nov. 1936; Maurice Pearton, *Oil and the Roumanian State, 1895–1948*, Oxford, 1981, pp. 197–8.

48. SHAT, 7N3048/EMA-2, no. 11/S, Delmas to EMA-2, 20 Feb. 1934; 7N3052/D1, no. 9/S, Delmas memo, 'L'armement de la Roumanie', 25 Jan. 1938; no. 88/S & no. 94/S, both Delmas to Daladier, 19 Sept. 1938 & 1 Oct. 1938.

49. Dov B. Lungu, *Romania and the Great Powers, 1933–1940*, London, 1989, pp. 41–3.

50. SHAT, 2B97/D2, EMAA-2, 'Projet de pacte d'entr'aide aérienne', 18 Nov. 1936.

51. SHAT, 2B97/D2, no. 786, Delbos to Daladier, 27 Nov. 1936; EMAA-2, note for Féquant, n.d. Nov. 1936; Cot to Delbos, 7 Jan. 1937; see also Martin Thomas, 'To Arm an Ally: French Arms Sales to Romania, 1926–1940', *JSS*, 19, 2, 1996, pp. 231–59.

52. For details of Titulescu's ideas and the Czech schemes see Jordan, *Popular Front*, pp. 188–95, 199–202, 230; Nicole Jordan, 'Léon Blum and Czechoslovakia, 1936–1938', *French History*, 5, 1, 1991, pp. 57–60.

53. MAE, Tchécoslovaquie 149, no. 828, Corbin to Delbos, 23 Dec. 1936.

54. PRO, FO 371/21136, R501/26/67, Sargent minute, 22 Jan. 1937.

55. PRO, FO 371/21136, R501/26/67, O'Malley minute, 25 Jan. 1937.

56. Ibid., FO minutes 29 Jan.–1 Feb. 1937.

57. DBFP, 2, XVIII, no. 198, Admiralty to FO, 22 Feb. 1937; PRO, CAB 4/25, CID 1305B, COS sub-committee memo, 25 Feb. 1937.

58. PRO, FO 371/20684, C668/18/17, Léger statement, 17 Jan. 1937; BDFA, II, F, 13, no. 125, Loraine to Eden, 3 Nov. 1937.

59. CADN, Rome 534, no. 163, Blondel to Delbos, 1 April 1937; Jordan, 'Léon Blum', pp. 60–1. The pact was composed of an exchange of letters regarding the recognition of Albanian independence, declarations over co-operation in the treatment of political refugees and the Slovene minority, and a commercial agreement.

60. DDF, 2, IV, no. 404, Corbin to Delbos, 6 Feb. 1937; BDFA, II, F, 13, no. 63, Eden to Campbell, 1 Feb. 1937; PRO, FO 371/21136, R396/26/67, FO memo, n.d.; DDF, 2, IV, no. 460, Béthouart to Daladier, 17 Feb. 1937. Maritch's comments were particularly worrying – the Yugoslav army staff remained the most francophile element within the Yugoslav establishment. See Antoine Marès, 'Les atta-

chés militaires en Europe centrale et la notion de la puissance en 1938', *RHA*, 1, 1983, p. 62.

61. PRO, FO 371/21136, R264/5/67, Loraine, Ankara, to FO, 12 Jan. 1937.

62. PRO, CAB 24/C.P.65(37)/CID, 288th meeting, 11 Feb. 1937.

63. PRO, FO 371/21157, R1908/1/22, record of Drummond–Ciano conversation, 19 March 1937; FO 371/21178, R659/419/22, Elliot–Hotblack report, 28 Jan. 1937; CAB 4/26, CID 1332B, Eden memo, 15 June 1937.

64. Papers of Group Captain M.G. Christie, Churchill College, Cambridge, section 1/5, record of interview with Goering, 3 Feb. 1937, fo. 81; MAE, Italie 270, no. 1607, Blondel to Delbos, 3 Feb. 1937.

65. DDF, 2, V, no. 154, Delbos to de Dampierre, 23 March 1937; Jordan *Popular Front*, p. 255.

66. MAE, Massigli 15, *aide mémoire*, 12 Feb. 1937, 2.

67. PRO, FO 371/21137, R2593/26/67, record of Belgrade conference proceedings, 4 April 1937; Wandycz, *Twilight*, p. 446; regarding Maritch see SHAT, 7N7193, no. 48/SC, Béthouart to EMA-2, 17 Feb. 1937.

68. MAE, Papiers 1940, Papiers Cabinet Delbos/D1, 'Roumanie – le gouvernement de Tatarescu', 13 April 1937; Regarding Antonescu's friends in France, see MAE, Roumanie 162, no. 128, d'Ormesson to Laval, 22 April 1935; for his comments to Thierry see CADN, Rome 519, no. 222, Thierry to Delbos, 31 March 1937.

69. BDFA, F, II, 13, no. 96, Sir R. Hoare to Eden, 7 May 1937; MAE, Tchécoslovaquie 149, no. 154, de Dampierre to Delbos, 2 April 1937.

70. CADN, Rome 519, no. 177, de Dampierre to Delbos, 3 April 1937 & no. 237, Thierry to Delbos, 6 April 1937.

71. PRO, FO 371/22480, R2048/2048/92, Campbell, Annual Report for 1937, 24 Feb. 1938; CADN, Rome 534, no. 267, de Dampierre to Delbos, 11 May 1937.

72. PRO, FO 371/21124, R4099/3904/7, Peterson, Sofia, to FO, 11 June 1937; CADN, Rome 534, no. 633, François-Poncet to Delbos, 22 April 1937. A Yugoslav–Bulgarian pact was concluded on 24 January 1937, see Jordan, *Popular Front*, pp. 242–3.

73. CADN, Londres 136, no. 2338, François-Poncet to Delbos, 9 June 1937. King Carol paid a return visit to Warsaw in July, see MAE, Roumanie 180, no. 49, Léon Noël to Delbos, 3 July 1937.

74. MAE, Massigli 20, note, 'Validité et portée du protocole franco-soviétique', 12 Oct. 1936; PRO, FO 371/21125, R5138/154/12, Hadow to Clifford Norton, 22 July 1937.

75. Regarding changing French views of the Russian alliance, see Jean

Delmas, 'La Perception de la puissance militaire française', in René Girault and Robert Frank (eds), *La Puissance en Europe, 1938–1940*, Paris, 1984, pp. 134–5; CADN, Londres 267, no. 1886, Delbos to Corbin, 29 July 1937.

76. SHAA, 2B104/EMAA-3, Note du Commandant Loriot, 5 Feb. 1937.
77. CADN, Bucharest 90, no. 336, Puaux to Quai, 19 Oct. 1931; MAE, Pologne 313, no. 506, Laroche to Quai, 21 Dec. 1931; MAE, Roumanie 167, Z573–4, Philippe Berthelot note, 20 Feb. 1930.
78. SHAT, 2B58/D3, EMAA-2, 'Notices sur les aéronautiques étrangères', n.d. June 1938; 2B97/EMAA-2, 'Note sur l'aéronautique polonaise', 1 July 1939. By 1931 the Polish air force included Potez and Bréguet models as well as PZL aircraft with French engines.
79. Jacques Ploquin, 'Alliances militaires et marchés d'avions pendant l'entre-deux-guerres', *RHA*, 4, 1985, pp. 43–4.
80. SHAA, 2B104/EMAA-3, Note du Commandant Loriot, 5 Feb. 1937; Léon Noël, *L'Agression*, p. 119.
81. SHAA, 2B104/EMAA-3, doc, VIII/6, Poutchinsky to Loriot, 14 June 1937 & EMAA-2, note for Féquant, 1 Oct. 1937. The PZL 37 was highly aerodynamic and could carry a 2,200 kg payload approximately 1,400 km.
82. SHAT, 7N3000/EMA-2, no. 14/S, d'Arbonneau 'Note au sujet des armements de l'armée polonaise', 3 Feb. 1936. In June 1939 Léon Noël was informed by General Stachiewicz that the Polish army would be unable to arm the greater part of its reservists once war began, see 7N3005/D1, no. 2585, Bonnet to Daladier, 15 June 1939.
83. PRO, FO 371/21094, N1522/45/38, Clerk to Collier, 8 March 1937; Marès, 'Les attachés militaires', pp. 60–72; Jackson, 'French Military Intelligence', pp. 82–7.
84. MAE, Pologne 337, no. 594, Léon Noël to Delbos, 7 Dec. 1936; DDF, 2, IV, no. 266, Léon Noël to Delbos, 9 Jan. 1937.
85. SHAT, 7N3000/EMA-2, no. 15/S, Musse report, 18 Feb. 1937; no. 54/S, Musse report, 30 June 1937; regarding Rambouillet see SAEF, B33.774, 'Collection de textes d'accord franco-polonais'.
86. Among recent historians to have commented on the Schweisguth report see Alexander, *Republic*, pp. 299–301; Jordan, *Popular Front*, pp. 206–9; Young, *In Command*, pp. 145–9; Dutailly, *Les Problèmes de l'armée*, p. 36; Adamthwaite, *France*, p. 49.
87. SHAT, 7N3123/D1, no. 346/S, Lieutenant-Colonel Simon to EMA-2, 17 May 1937. The Air Ministry intelligence section admitted in July 1937 that the Moscow Air Attaché had been unable to obtain any reliable information on Soviet air force re-equipment for over three months, see 7N3123/D1, no. 44/S, EMAA-2 rapport, 10 June 1937; Buffotot, 'The French High Command', pp. 549–52.

88. SHAT, 7N3122/D3, compte rendu mensuel no. 34, mois Août–
    Septembre 1936. General Archie Wavell, who attended the 1936
    manoeuvres on Britain's behalf, came away favourably impressed,
    PRO, Dill papers, WO 282/3, Wavell to Dill, 3 Oct. 1936.
89. Coutau-Bégarie & Huan, *Lettres et notes de l'Amiral Darlan*, doc.
    22; SHAT, 7N3123/D1, no. 1,453, Simon report, 'Mission aéro-
    nautique française', 19 March 1937; MAE, URSS 931, no. 1008,
    Lacroix to Paris, 23 Dec. 1937; Jordan, 'Léon Blum', pp. 62–3.
90. Adamthwaite, *France*, pp. 238–41; Young, *In Command*, pp. 197–
    8, 201; Maurice Vaïsse, 'La perception de la puissance soviétique
    par les militaires françaises en 1938', *RHA*, 3, 1983, pp. 18–25.
91. SHAT, 2N235/D1, no. 1994, Vuillemin report, 'Valeur de la puis-
    sance aérienne soviétique', 16 Sept. 1938; SHAA, Archive Guy la
    Chambre, Z12940, no. 662, la Chambre to Daladier, 17 Sept. 1938;
    regarding Vuillemin's view of *Luftwaffe* supremacy, see Jackson,
    'La perception de la puissance aérienne allemande', p. 82.
92. PRO, FO 371/20684, C913/18/17, Clerk to FO, 3 Feb. 1937; Jean-
    Jacques Becker, 'La Perception de la puissance par le Parti
    Communiste', *RHMC*, 31, 1984, pp. 637–40.
93. Cot, *Le Procès*, vol. II, pp. 340–1.
94. MAE, Massigli 10, Note pour le Ministre, 4 Nov. 1936; Nicole
    Jordan, 'Maurice Gamelin, Italy and the Eastern Alliances', *JSS*,
    14, 4, 1991, pp. 435–6. Jordan suggests that the French military
    feared that reliance upon Czechoslovak and Soviet support might
    push the Poles into Germany's arms.
95. SHAT, 7N3096/MMF, Schweisguth to Daladier, 26 Aug. 1936.
96. SHAT, 7N3096/MMF, Faucher report of conversation with Benes,
    25 Dec. 1936.
97. PRO, FO 371/21094, N546/45/38, Collier to Chilston, 6 Feb. 1937,
    N1522/45/38, Clerk to Collier, 8 March 1937.
98. MAE, URSS 931, Z610-2, 'Fourniture éventuelle de matériel
    d'armement à l'URSS', 16 June 1936, no. 4488, Note, 'Comman-
    des Soviétiques', 17 Aug. 1937.
99. SHM, 1BB2, c. 208/D12, Darlan note for Delbos, 20 April 1937;
    Lacouture, *Léon Blum*, p. 294.
100. MAE, URSS 931, no. 358, Coulondre to Delbos, 16 Nov. 1936.
101. DDF, 2, V, no. 480, note de l'EMA, May 1937; Jordan, *Popular
    Front*, pp. 273–6.
102. MAE, Massigli 15, *aide mémoire*, 12 Feb. 1937.
103. SHM, 1BB2, c. 208/D12, Darlan dossiers, 'Politique navale en
    générale', 20 April 1937; PRO, FO 371/21094, N1899/45/38,
    Lloyd-Thomas note, 6 April 1937.
104. PRO, FO 371/21095, N2712/45/38, Vansittart minute, 28 May 1937.

# —8—

# Exit Blum – Enter Chautemps: Entente Diplomacy, May 1937–March 1938

As the first Blum government neared eventual collapse in June 1937, the British government grew more purposeful once Chamberlain officially took over the Premiership on 28 May. Although Anglo-French relations had improved considerably over Blum's term, the British Cabinet much preferred the complexion of the new Front populaire administration led by the former Minister of State, Camille Chautemps. From June 1937 the entente relationship was increasingly fashioned in London. Yet it is difficult to argue that the Chamberlain government in any way hastened Blum's fall or determined to exploit it by imposing Britain's will upon Chautemps. Rather, the British Cabinet discovered in the new French administration a government with few independent ideas regarding the appeasement of Germany.

On 16 March 1937 a Parti Social Français meeting in the Communist-administered arrondissement of Clichy in northern Paris erupted into a night of violence. This left five dead and numerous wounded, among them André Blumel.[1] The Clichy riot and the subsequent, apparently political, judgment which exonerated PCF activists from blame for the events, undermined the second round of 'pause' cuts announced a fortnight earlier on 5 March. The Blum government never recovered its equilibrium. British influence acquired added weight in Paris because the French administration was largely paralysed by financial crisis. In the eyes of the British Cabinet and Treasury, France required a change of government and a further devaluation in order to meet the situation.

From Blum's fall in June 1937 to his short-lived return to office in March 1938, the Radical Party was the controlling force in the Front populaire. This suited London. Though not himself an obstacle to appeasement, Blum's associations with eastern collective security and Spanish Republicanism had been exploited by the German and Italian governments whenever the British had put forward proposals for a general settlement. Blum though, was not as difficult a partner as leading figures on the French parliamentary right, such as Pierre Laval and André Tardieu, were likely to be.[2] So long as inter-party hostility precluded a French 'national government' embracing both left and right, the Chautemps administration was preferable to the alternatives on offer.

Born in Paris in 1885, the son of a former Vice-President of the Senate, Blum's successor has remained a rather shadowy historical figure. Closely associated with Herriot's revitalized Radical Party after the First World War and, like Herriot, a mayor as well as a deputy, Chautemps served as Minister of Interior in the 1924 Cartel des Gauches administration. Chautemps made the Interior Ministry portfolio his own for much of the late 1920s and early 1930s, keeping the post during two brief spells as Prime Minister in 1930 and 1933.[3] This perhaps explains the elusiveness of Chautemps for international historians, and reveals why British ministers tended to like him. His concerns were always more domestic than international. Unlike Blum, he did not bring singular foreign policy ideas to the Hôtel Matignon. Seen from Britain, Chautemps was a compliant figure. Hankey liked to compare him to an affable, if ineffectual, British Liberal.[4] Chautemps was also in accord with his three senior Radical colleagues: Daladier and Delbos, still at their respective ministries, and the most important addition to the Cabinet, the new Finance Minister, Georges Bonnet. Bonnet had served in two previous Chautemps ministries in 1930 and 1933. Like his new Premier, Bonnet had built his reputation in home affairs ministries since his election in 1924 as Radical deputy for his native Dordogne. Among other appointments, he had twice served as Minister of Commerce, and had already been Finance Minister in Daladier's Cabinet of January to November 1933. More immediately, Bonnet was known to be close to Joseph Caillaux, who had orchestrated Senate opposition to Blum and Vincent Auriol's financial proposals in June 1937.[5]

# I

Three months before Blum's fall, on 6 April 1937, the Paris Financial Attaché, Rowe-Dutton, warned Eden that the French Treasury required a powerful cash injection if it was to avoid short-term bankruptcy. But the development that alarmed the Paris embassy most was the growing restiveness of the Radical Party in the wake of the Clichy disorder. Fortunately, the National Assembly was in recess throughout April, and the Matignon agreements were finally renewed at the end of that month, enabling the government to sustain its rearmament targets.[6] But by the end of May the Radicals were in open revolt over the government's borrowing plans, angered at the use of state loans to finance rearmament when Treasury reserves were nearly exhausted. On 30 April the Foreign Office got word that Hitler anticipated France's financial collapse, expecting it to clear his path in eastern Europe.[7] By May two unfortunate connections had thus been made within France and Germany, firstly between declining French financial strength and Blum's over-zealous pursuit of rearmament, and, secondly, between the anticipated fall of the French government and the utter collapse of the eastern alliance system. This threatened the schedule of British appeasement policy which depended upon German inability to see through the facade of a sustained Anglo-French interest in eastern Europe. There seemed little prospect of the smooth French Cabinet change-over that the British government hoped for.

Matters went from bad to worse in early June as the Radical Party effectively disowned government financial policy.[8] The unwillingness of French banks to lend funds to the state on the scale required led to Vincent Auriol's disastrous promulgation of plans for the socialization of credit. These were published on 9 June by the SFIO-controlled Chamber finance committee. The three managers of the exchange-equalization fund resigned in response, and a severe capital flight immediately set in.[9] From the Senate, Caillaux and his fellow elder-statesmen of the Radical Party delivered the final *coup de grâce* days later. Blum resigned from office. Technically, he could have fought on since he had yet to be voted down in the Chamber of Deputies. This had the unfortunate consequence of dividing the SFIO congress at Marseilles in July 1937.[10] Observing the French governmental crisis unfold, Sargent put Foreign Office opinion in perspective:

> Much as we sympathise with the French government in many matters and approve of their policy in a great many particulars, it is well to bear in mind . . . that their policy is likely in its ultimate results to bring about a general 'proletarianisation' of the French nation. This might well have far-reaching repercussions on this country and Europe.[11]

Tax revenue financed little of the French rearmament programme. State borrowing, Bank of France loans and Anglo-American assistance (with stringent conditions attached) tied the administration not only to domestic capital holders but also to friendly governments. Britain was pre-eminent among these. There was a certain circularity to the French borrowing requirement. A key reason for French dependence upon borrowing lay in the smaller tax base of France, and the absence of a tradition of local taxation on a comparable scale to Britain.[12] Robert Frank has pointed to the contradiction between the increased state direction in France consequent upon the rearmament plan, and the government's growing reliance upon outside institutions to finance that plan. Blum's resignation marked an acknowledgement that the SFIO could not resolve this contradiction because it was unable to win the confidence of the Bourse.[13]

In the wake of Blum's fall, Bonnet adopted a proposal agreed between Vincent Auriol and Jacques Rueff which set a three-year ceiling to defence expenditure, cutting it overall. Bonnet also devalued the franc in late June. This released the currency from the fluctuation range established by the Tripartite agreement. On 9 July he introduced a series of taxation measures intended to raise an additional 7.4 billion francs. This action was supported by his budget Director, Jean Jardel, and Labeyrie's replacement as Governor of the Bank of France, Charles Fournier.[14] In a letter sent to Bonnet on 14 July, Chamberlain welcomed the move. The Prime Minister was relieved that the new French government did not intend to use its plenary powers to reimpose exchange controls.[15]

A week earlier, Chamberlain had warned the CID that France's internal weakness precluded a French contribution to any allied defence effort in the Mediterranean. Vansittart reacted sharply to this, accusing Chamberlain of confusing France's financial crisis with a non-existent social breakdown. A reactionary Senate had ousted Blum's government, widening the rift between the Popular Front Parties in the process. Still, France was not in the ferment it had been in June 1936. Since Britain's Field Force remained unready, if anything, the French were better placed to demand more of their entente partner. Worried that Chamberlain intended to paint a picture of French military decrepitude for political ends – specifically, a renewed attempt to conciliate Mussolini – Eden gave full details of France's actual fighting strength to the defence (plans) committee on 13 July.[16] A week later, Phipps reported that Chamberlain's letter of encouragement had made 'a great impression' on the new government. The Conseil swiftly capped total defence spending for the 1938 financial year at 11 billion francs. This was 1.5 billion more than Rueff had suggested but it was insufficient to meet all the expenditure planned and approved by Blum's administration. The cut was justified on the grounds that funding on the scale previously contemplated would force a further devaluation liable to diminish the services' actual spending power.[17]

The service ministries argued among themselves over the distribution of the money rather than taking issue with the Finance Ministry over the total figure. The War Ministry came off best with an extra 1,179 million, a 28 per cent increase in funding over 1937. Cot won an additional 810 million, though this was insufficient to undertake all of the remedial measures necessary to achieve major advances in aircraft production.[18] The real loser was the marine, alone of the three services in having a new minister, César Campinchi. Although a more impressive figure than Gasnier-Duparc, Campinchi's junior status told in the division of rearmament monies. As Phipps commented, 'The new Minister appears to have brains but no ballast, as compared to his predecessor, who was all ballast but had no brains.'[19] The navy suffered a net 7 per cent cut over its 1937 funding. This was worsened by the near 30 per cent fall in the franc's purchasing power following the establishment of the free floating 'Bonnet franc' in June. Existent construction would be delayed, new construction postponed. Half of the construction voted for 1937 was not laid down until December. Of the new building scheduled for 1938, from twenty-five vessels only the battlecruiser *De Grasse* was laid down before Christmas of that year. The construction of three capital ships, five destroyers and four submarines was delayed by a full twelve months.[20]

Darlan tried to reverse the cuts using the Conseil Supérieur de la Marine presentation of its diminished 1938 estimates to illustrate the strategic folly of slowed construction. Delays in laying down major vessels would break the continuity of employment essential to keep skilled labour at the yards and arsenals. In real terms, the average cost of one metric ton of construction was expected to increase markedly in the year ahead. So the Ministry of Marine needed increased revenue even to stand still. Darlan warned that the Italian and German navies would outrank the marine by 1942, making French dominance of the western Mediterranean and the security of the North African Empire untenable.[21] During November and December 1937 the CPDN undertook a major review of French Mediterranean defence plans in view of the possibility of war breaking out within that theatre. This naturally added to the importance of France's Mediterranean fleet.[22] Darlan remained anxious lest the government avoided giving the marine extra support by pointing to British naval power. He emphasized that the British Admiralty had not undertaken any new commitments to support the French fleet. Nor was it likely to do so if the marine became relatively weaker, not stronger.[23]

Darlan did much to make up for Campinchi's junior position. In recognition of the prevailing mood within the French Cabinet, Darlan requested a 500 million supplementary credit for 1938 rather than arguing that the cuts be entirely reversed. He successfully lobbied Massigli, and through him, Delbos, in support of the credit. The 500 million was voted in November, by which time the purchasing power of the franc had fallen still further.[24] Although unintended, Bonnet's cuts left both the Ministry of Marine and the Air Ministry more dependent upon the assurance of British military support. The return to closely limited defence funding underlined the need for co-ordinated Anglo-French rearmament and a clearer division of strategic responsibility. This was not peculiar to the French side of the entente relationship. The British government also undertook a major reappraisal of rearmament costs during the latter half of 1937. The key result of this was a further prioritization of defence expenditure in favour of the RAF. The government placed still further emphasis upon metropolitan and imperial defence at the direct expense of a broader continental commitment. When Sir Thomas Inskip's defence review was debated in Cabinet in late December 1937, it became apparent that Britain would not possess the wherewithal to intervene militarily in Europe in the coming year.[25] Loath to admit it, Britain was reliant upon French military assistance to make its foreign policy credible.

In late November 1937 Chautemps led a ministerial delegation to London for talks covering common defence problems. Chamberlain took charge of proceedings in his customary, purposeful manner. In London, the visit was considered a great success. This was not because the two sides had got down to serious strategic deliberations. Quite the reverse. Before the meeting the British government had persuaded the Chautemps administration that it contributed to French security through the pursuit of a rearmament programme logically geared to the defence of Britain and its Empire. The French were clearly losing the battle to influence the direction of British strategic policy. In September even the Ministry of Marine intelligence section, usually critical of the isolationist tendencies of the Royal Navy, praised the Admiralty's 1938 spending plans and Chamberlain's ability to conserve British financial strength.[26]

## II

This rather sheepish attitude to Anglo-French defensive co-ordination was matched by a loss of momentum in French policy towards Germany. As France's eastern alliances had been conceived as a means to offset latent German strength, it is tempting to ascribe growing French subservience to Britain to the sterility of the Franco-Soviet and France–Little Entente connections rather than to the tardiness of French rearmament. The Blum government had acknowledged that the weaker France appeared, the greater became its dependence on allies.[27] But an effective defence policy was a crucial guarantee that those allies would remain true. It also enabled France to back British appeasement policy in the reasonable expectation that, should negotiations fail, the British would recognize the merits of multilateral alliances. During 1937 the logic of this approach broke down.

Stricken by financial crisis at home, as we have seen, on the European stage the Blum government suffered a series of reverses in quick succession during the spring. The western pact talks collapsed without significant compensatory increases in Anglo-French defence planning. The Belgrade Little Entente conference in April smothered the projected mutual assistance accord with France. To the north and south the French strategic position was significantly worsened by Belgian neutrality and

Nationalist advances along the Vizcaya front in Spain. The one cause for optimism was that the entente relationship had improved, though even this could not be measured in any new paper commitments.

After the collapse in May of Eden's proposals to make a multilateral guarantee of Belgian independence the starting point for wider talks with the Locarno powers, the Blum government put forward a final western pact scheme in early June. This gave ground over Germano-Italian hostility to France's claim for a free rein to fulfil her alliance obligations in the event of German eastern aggression.[28] Nevertheless the French proposal was a dead letter. Between May and July 1937 the Foreign Office could not find sufficient common ground between the Locarno powers to take the appeasement process forward. This was made manifest by the cancellation of von Neurath's planned visit to London in June, something which the Foreign Office greeted with relief.[29] In the light of virulent central department objections to Lord Halifax's trip to Germany in November, it is well to remember that, in Chamberlain's eyes, Halifax was filling a void.

In May 1937 Chamberlain played host to the Imperial Conference of Britain and the Dominions. For all its pomp, the Conference failed to build a united Anglo-Dominion front. Though the New Zealanders were ready to sanction a firmer British policy whatever the consequences, the Canadians, Australians and South Africans were not. With good reason to fear Japanese power, each of these three Dominions had a stake in the successful appeasement of Hitler. But the prospects for such negotiation did not look good. Germany appeared content to avoid negotiation, and the escalation of foreign involvement in the Spanish civil war offered Hitler and Mussolini numerous pretexts to avoid discussions. On 2 July Sargent warned Eden that the German government was well aware that France could not fight for central Europe and that Britain would not do so.[30] The Foreign Office had no coherent alternative to the CID's argument that Britain should never allow a purely notional commitment to collective security to impede direct dialogue with Berlin and Rome. Chamberlain agreed with the CID. The Chautemps government appeared willing to let Britain enter talks unencumbered by French objections.

In Berlin, François-Poncet did little to offset the influence of Britain's recently arrived Ambassador, Nevile Henderson. This was unfortunate because, as Henderson informed Strang on 5 July, 'My sole aim at the moment is to establish a clear distinction in fact, as well as drawn by Germany in practice, between British friendship with France and British support for France's eastern alliances.'[31] If the French government was resigned to the collapse of the Little Entente, there was little reason for Britain to exercise self-restraint in Berlin in deference to France's traditional position as an eastern European player. Neither Chamberlain nor Henderson believed that the German government was intent upon breaking the Anglo-French entente in addition to the eastern alliance system. François-Poncet was unable to persuade Henderson otherwise.[32] The British Ambassador increasingly looked upon his French colleague as an obstacle to successful Anglo-German discussions. Within the Berlin diplomatic community, Henderson displayed the arrogance of the *arriviste* novice that he was.

British ministers such as Halifax, Hoare and Simon, and Cabinet advisers like Hankey and Chatfield, showed little concern at the prospect of a weaker entente. They preferred to view matters in terms of a reassertion of British leadership.[33] The French and German conceptions of the Anglo-French relationship remained irreconcilable. Hitler's government was only prepared to tolerate expressions of Anglo-French unity confined to the defence of western Europe. To the French, the entente was pivotal to stability in eastern Europe as well. During Chautemps's term of office, Chamberlain's Cabinet moved closer to the German conception of the entente. This meant an acceptance of German expansion into central Europe in return for fewer concessions than had been expected during the deliberations over a western pact. Henderson was eager to act on this assumption.

Aware of the Ambassador's uneasy relationship with the Foreign Office, on 28 July Goering told Malcolm Christie that he would regard any diminution of Henderson's influence 'as a menace to peace'.[34] In fact, the Foreign Office was slow to react to Henderson's dialogue with the German leadership. On 10 October Henderson belatedly responded to central department instructions which made plain that he was not to suggest any British abandonment of interest in France or eastern Europe. By this stage the Ambassador had completed much of Chamberlain's groundwork for Halifax's impending visit to Germany. Disgruntled and significantly weakened, Eden reiterated the original Foreign Office instructions, referring them to Halifax as well. The Foreign Secretary warned that Hitler would become more dangerous if Britain appeared ready to apply pressure on France to sever its eastern ties. Neither Chamberlain, Halifax nor Henderson were inclined to listen.[35] But the sheer confusion of Hitler's and Goering's mixed messages to Halifax during his visit to Berlin and Berchtesgaden in mid-November temporarily obscured the extent of Eden's isolation.

Given that the Chautemps government was convinced that British support was vital to French victory in a *guerre de longue durée*, it raised remarkably little opposition to British plans to pursue unilateral talks with Germany. This was partly explained by two considerations. Firstly, the French government had been given conflicting information about the Halifax visit. On the one hand, it appeared that Halifax had reiterated

Britain's continued interest in central Europe, but on the other, he had restarted the quest for colonial concessions to Germany. The Quai d'Orsay was pleased about the former, and had made clear its dislike of the latter.[36] The fact that Halifax had actually made no such clear-cut statements of British policy, but had merely paved the way for Chamberlain to proceed on his own, was not understood in Paris. Reasonably enough, François-Poncet had assumed that Halifax would maintain the British effort to convince Hitler that Britain would not abandon interest in Austria and Czechoslovakia.[37]

The second explanation of French passivity lay in Delbos's pre-occupation with his imminent tour of eastern Europe, a last attempt to foster some cohesion among the disparate allies. Confusing though it may have been, the Halifax visit indicated that Britain had taken charge of the appeasement of Germany. Delbos's Balkan tour was intended to prove that the eastern alliances still counted for something. But, as Massigli had warned, the British expected Delbos to impress upon the Czech government the need for immediate concessions to the Sudeten Germans. The Foreign Office was quite prepared for Delbos to advertise the strength of the entente, but only as a means to induce the Czechs to make greater sacrifices. The French Foreign Minister visited Warsaw and all the Little Entente capitals over a two-week period in December. In a correct but otherwise ineffectual meeting with Beck, the Polish Foreign Minister saluted the improvement in Anglo-French relations but was as hostile as ever towards Czechoslovakia.[38] Between 8 and 9 December Delbos found himself in the midst of the Romanian general election campaign in Bucharest. Again, Romanian ministers stressed their interest in a strong entente cordiale as a means to side-step discussion of the moribund France–Little Entente pact. Immediately after the visit, Bucharest Military Attaché Delmas warned Daladier that it would be highly inopportune to raise the matter of rights of passage for Soviet troops.[39]

Delbos then met Stojadinović. This was only a week after the Yugoslav Premier had returned from highly publicized discussions with Mussolini and Ciano, followed by tours of Italian arms factories in Rome and Milan.[40] Stojadinović was typically ebullient. Belgrade, he said, would not abandon Czechoslovakia, not from affection, but because it was better that a general war should break out upon Czech territory than within Yugoslavia. This was humbug. Delbos summarized the allies' views of a Little Entente pact thus: 'Czechoslovakia said yes, Romania perhaps and Yugoslavia said no.'[41] Immediately after Delbos's tour, the general staffs of the Little Entente powers met for discussions in Prague. Despite the best efforts of the Czech delegation, these staff talks only produced a renewed commitment to co-ordinate a common defence strategy in response to Hungarian aggression. The Little Entente had reverted to its original narrow purpose.[42] Across the Balkans, fervent anti-communism, Nazi economic pressure and the pervasive fear of German military strength would leave Czechoslovakia isolated when a crisis arose. With customary bluntness, the Soviet government pointed out that Delbos's travels had been worthless.[43]

The failure of the Delbos visits scotched Finance Ministry proposals which posited Franco-British economic and monetary assistance to the Danubian states: Austria, Czechoslovakia, Hungary and Romania. On 17 December Monick raised the idea in conversation at the Treasury with S.D. Waley and Leith-Ross. Leith-Ross disliked the proposition that the Bank of England and the Bank of France should guarantee the exchange parity of these Danubian countries. He questioned the French capacity to lend much tangible support and doubted that enough could be done to pull any of the four states in question out of Germany's economic orbit. In south-eastern Europe, French economic diplomacy had become as ineffectual as its alliance policy.[44]

## III

By the end of 1937 the French government did not have a viable German policy to speak of. In other respects, though, the Popular Front maintained a more dogged independence. One cannot conclude that the Chautemps administration lacked an autonomous foreign policy simply by pointing to the ease with which Britain disregarded French opinion about talks with Berlin. In two key respects the Front populaire was less inclined to follow a British lead than it had been before June 1937. Firstly, the Chautemps government struck a firmer line over Spain. Secondly, it was increasingly outspoken regarding Britain's appeasement of Italy. In practice, however, this independent attitude resolved itself into a grumbling obstructionism which did neither entente partner much good.

There was no appreciable break in French policy over Spain following Blum's resignation. Anxious to reconcile the party rank and file to his resignation, Blum made firmer support of the Valencia government a precondition for continued Socialist participation in government. 'Relaxed' non-intervention was to continue until a satisfactory NIC scheme for the withdrawal of volunteers from Spain had been implemented. Since May the French had been considering the release to the Valencia government of Spanish aircraft impounded in France. In return the Republican government was requested to send captured Italian and German military equipment to France for examination.[45]

The Chautemps Cabinet continued to oppose any British efforts to regulate Mediterranean security without French involvement. The composition of the Front populaire made it impossible for either the Blum or Chautemps governments to emulate Britain's detachment in the face of obvious Axis violations of NIC plans. After the collapse of the preliminary round of discussions over volunteer withdrawal in late March, the French government issued the first in a series of threats to reopen the Pyrenean frontier in order to resupply the Spanish Republic. The short-lived naval control scheme put in place soon afterwards did little to satisfy French demands for closer surveillance of Italian and German activities in Spain.[46] At no point did Chautemps set about restoring full French diplomatic representation in Rome after the withdrawal of Charles de Chambrun in November 1936. Even the army appeared to have given up on the Italians. A week after the French Cabinet change-over, General Schweisguth recommended an intensification of covert intelligence-gathering by the Rome Military Attaché, General Henri Parisot.[47]

After unidentified attacks on the German battlecruiser *Deutschland* on 29 May and on the cruiser *Leipzig* on 19 June, the Axis powers suspended their policing duties off the Spanish coast.[48] Léger became convinced that Hitler had been persuaded to back Mussolini's ambitious intervention in Spain. On advice from Massigli, Delbos, in turn, refused to entertain British suggestions that the Axis powers be requested to rejoin the naval patrols in return for an Anglo-French grant of belligerent rights to both parties in Spain.[49] This exasperated the Admiralty in London. The Royal Navy filled the gap left by the Germans and Italians, increasing the number of British ships involved from twenty-seven to forty-five. The Admiralty blamed France squarely for the abiding tension in the Mediterranean and the responsibilities this produced. French refusal to grant belligerent rights to Franco was characterized as ideologically motivated and strategically irresponsible. Blum's ingrained hostility to the Italian regime certainly had a tighter grip on the French establishment. International observers were withdrawn from the closed Franco-Spanish border to register the growing French impatience with the frustrations of non-intervention. Much to British irritation, over the summer of 1937 French opposition to the *de jure* recognition of Italian Abyssinia also hardened. In August Delbos ignored warnings from Blondel in Rome that the French refusal to contemplate concessions to Italy would be made more conspicuous by Britain's more friendly attitude towards Mussolini.[50]

Between March and June 1937 British governmental division over the appeasement of Italy was subsumed within the more pressing difficulties presented in Spain by a widening Nationalist naval blockade, the regulation of volunteer withdrawal and the naval policing of the

Iberian coastline.[51] By the time Blum left office, Chamberlain's rising anger changed this. The Prime Minister was deeply resentful that the appeasement of Italy could not be pursued owing to problems generated by the non-intervention accord. To complicate matters further, Franco had linked his assent to volunteer withdrawal with a prior grant of belligerent rights. Since France would not consent to this, the Popular Front was made to appear culpable for Britain's inability to capitalize upon the Gentlemen's agreement. French claims that belligerent rights would benefit the Nationalist side unduly so long as France upheld its own part in non-intervention were well grounded.[52] But concomitant French warnings in July that the Franco-Spanish frontier might be reopened were unacceptable to London.

The British government still believed that the Spanish conflict should not be allowed to impede the appeasement effort. The Admiralty, the War Office and the CID refused to accept that Italy posed an irreversible threat other than as part of a coalition with Germany. To treat the Italian danger as equivalent to the menace of German or Japanese attack upon Britain and its Empire would spread British military resources too thinly.[53] This nourished the Prime Minister's appetite for substantial dialogue with Rome to match the progress being made by Henderson in Berlin. By September Chamberlain was certain that the Foreign Office tendency to let relations with Italy drift would only result in 'appallingly costly defences in the Mediterranean'.[54]

The Chamberlain and Chautemps administrations were pulling in opposite directions over Spain. The French, for example, refused to give ground over the Bank of Spain gold held in France in trust for the Republican government. Much to British annoyance, this issue generated periodic clashes on the NIC.[55] In the event, a three-month NIC deadlock over volunteer withdrawal plans between July and September dissipated Anglo-French acrimony over the volunteer question. Lacking tangible result, entente disagreements over Spain only assume lasting importance when set in the context of the resumption of Anglo-Italian negotiations. Neither the French government nor the Foreign Office was primarily concerned with the establishment of effective non-intervention in Spain. Each had utilized the Spanish situation in an unsuccessful attempt to weaken Italy by confronting Mussolini with an end to British and French indulgence towards Italian support for Franco. Instead, Chamberlain was persuaded to proceed on his own initiative, pushing along informal exchanges with Ambassador Grandi in London. These discussions began on 21 July.[56]

Chamberlain met French objections to the talks by stressing that British concessions over *de jure* recognition of Italian Abyssinia and a Mediterranean security pact would undermine Mussolini's attachment to the Axis, rekindling Italian strategic interest in central Europe into the bargain. This was expected to make Hitler more amenable to comprehensive discussions with Halifax in November.[57] These were fine objectives, but it soon became apparent that the British contemplated making concessions without prior guarantees of Italian good conduct. From the end of August, the British government disregarded French objections on the grounds that Chautemps was having to remain intransigent in order to satisfy his Socialist ministerial colleagues. Mussolini was equally dismissive. On 10 August Blondel informed Delbos that the Duce was certain that the French would rally to the British position regardless. Italy was prepared to face the consequences if France failed to do so.[58]

In one sense the British had good cause to overlook French complaints. For Britain the primary strategic objective of an Anglo-Italian settlement was to diminish the friction between the two sides in the eastern Mediterranean. After Japan took the offensive against China in July 1937, the long-stressed importance of the Suez route became still more apparent. Chatfield later anticipated the discussions with the Italians thus: 'If we have trouble with Italy the Navy can win the war slowly, but the Army and Air Force can lose it in Egypt rapidly and therefore it is the defence of Egypt which will be our main pre-occupation.'[59] It was irritating to contemplate the security of Egypt being undermined because of French hostility to Italian activities in Spain; activities which, after all, many British ministers and servicemen saw considerable reason to excuse.

## IV

Eden's alarm at the readiness of his Cabinet colleagues to back Chamberlain's Italian policy encouraged him to make the most of reports of renewed sinkings of merchant shipping in the western Mediterranean.[60] The firm Anglo-French response to this undeclared Italian submarine piracy brought a temporary halt to the dialogue with Rome. Mussolini had made four Italian submarines available to operate from Majorcan bases in order to prevent anticipated Soviet war material deliveries to Valencia. On 12 August the Admiralty intercepted an Italian signal authorizing the submarines to act without restriction. On 1 September the submarine *Iride* launched an unsuccessful torpedo attack on the British destroyer, *Havock*. On the day before this incident the Admiralty's director of plans, Tom Phillips, discussed Italy's actions with Eden. He warned Chatfield that the Foreign Secretary was determined to threaten Mussolini with retaliatory British action, backed by a reinforcement of the Mediterranean fleet.[61]

Between 10 and 14 September a conference was convened at Nyon in Switzerland to put an end to the upsurge in Mediterranean submarine attacks. As René Massigli later recalled, the French government had been eager to use this opportunity to take the Italians to task. Only Darlan sounded a note of protest. He warned Delbos on 7 September that the marine would be hard pressed to help deter additional Italian submarine activity. In exasperation, Darlan commented: 'while the government asks him to increase the activity of the fleet, the Minister of Finance asks him to reduce it.' The Admiral's plea fell on deaf ears.[62] Speaking at Velizy on 5 September Blum had condemned the German and Italian refusal to withdraw forces from Spain. He concluded that if 'a certain power' were not obliged to be so vigilant in the Far East, the peace-loving nations of Europe might have expected more support.

Another French threat to reopen its frontier helped push Eden towards greater caution. This was exemplified by the backroom arrangements made both before and during the Nyon conference. The meetings at Nyon built upon the 1936 protocol on submarine warfare. The Mediterranean states that had signed this were invited to attend.[63] In fact, a diplomatic formula was determined in advance of the conference. The British government informed Rome that, while Italy was not being accused of the recent attacks, Mussolini should know that British opinion was tending to this conclusion. To entice the Italians into concessions, Britain offered *de jure* recognition of Italian Abyssinia in return for immediate progress over volunteer withdrawal.[64] Ostensibly a conference about submarine piracy (something actually resolved in advance of the sessions), Nyon was really a vehicle to restart Anglo-Italian dialogue without attracting undue French antagonism. Eden was much closer to the French position than Chamberlain in that the Foreign Secretary regarded *de jure* recognition as the final element in a sequence of reciprocal concessions which ought to begin with Italian withdrawals from the Balearics.[65] Premature gifts to Italy would weaken British prestige within friendly states and colonial territories across the Balkans and Middle East. This remained at the heart of the differences between the two British Ministers until Eden's resignation on 20 February 1938. Massigli noted that neither Eden nor Vansittart put any faith in Italian promises.[66]

The Nyon agreements were notable in two further respects. Firstly, the conference appeared to be a striking success. Submarine activity diminished, though from intercepted cipher traffic, London knew that Mussolini had actually decided to cut his losses before the conference met. Secondly, the Admiralty and Ministry of Marine worked together efficiently in the demarcation of destroyer patrols across the western Mediterranean. Even though the Admiralty was determined to avoid the possibility of confrontation with an Italian vessel, the two sides proved that naval co-operation need not repeat the excruciating experience of the Abyssinian crisis.[67]

In the fortnight after Nyon, the French government tried to press home the humiliation of Italy by canvassing a scheme for an Anglo-French pre-emptive occupation of Minorca. Unlike neighbouring Majorca, the smaller island was still in Republican hands and free of Italian encroachment. The British government rejected the proposal, failing to realize that Massigli had suggested it as a means to prevent the Chautemps Cabinet reopening the land frontier with Spain.[68] During a brief stop-over in Paris on 21 September Eden found the French government and high command apparently united in their determination to prevent Italy taking a permanent grip upon any of the Spanish islands from Majorca to the Canaries. Darlan, especially, was adamant about this. Phipps worried that, within the Quai d'Orsay, Léger's uncontrolled Italophobia was approaching hysteria.[69]

The outcome of all this was that the British government felt bound to concede French involvement in preliminary exchanges with Italy over the Spanish situation. The French had at last forced the British to concede the linkage between the concession of *de jure* recognition and Italian volunteer withdrawal.[70] Not for long. Chamberlain instructed Lord Perth (formerly Sir Eric Drummond) in Rome to reassure Ciano that France was being temporarily admitted to the discussions simply to create a better atmosphere for direct Anglo-Italian dialogue. Chamberlain also mollified his disgruntled ministerial colleagues by pointing out that he – and not the Foreign Office – would take a closer hand in the diplomatic preparations for the talks. Meanwhile, the Minorca occupation was quietly stifled by a joint Foreign Office–Admiralty investigation into the possibility of making the island a neutral zone, policed by the entente navies.[71]

The French initiatives in the wake of the Nyon agreement had propelled Chamberlain into taking greater control of policy towards Italy, so adding to Eden's decline. This was hardly the result desired in Paris. Chamberlain was actually less extreme than colleagues, such as Hoare and Minister of Health, Sir Kingsley Wood, who were prepared to let France face the consequences of unilateral support for the Spanish Republic. Furthermore, the Prime Minister had not lost his paternalistic attitude towards Eden. Chamberlain intended to lend his Foreign Secretary the 'support and guidance' that the Foreign Office was failing to provide.[72] Eden's efforts to convince the Prime Minister of the lasting importance of the French alliance system were doomed. Still unwilling to criticize Chamberlain directly, Eden blamed the chiefs of staff for undue pessimism regarding French strength and the consequent exaggeration of Italy's importance. On 31 January 1938 he clarified his views in a remarkable letter to the Prime Minister,

> I cannot help believing that what the chiefs of staff would really like to do is to re-orientate our whole foreign policy and to clamber on the band-wagon with the dictators, even though that process meant parting company with France and estranging our relations with the United States. I believe, moreover, that there is a tendency among some of our colleagues to under-estimate the strength of France . . . I am convinced, as is Phipps and more qualified observers than myself, that [the] French army is fundamentally sound and a far better choice – if choice had to be made – than Italy.[73]

Eden's warning was ignored. Chamberlain's Cabinet acted upon CID predictions that Italy's strategic location and large air force made for a conspicuous menace to the British position in the Mediterranean basin. In a sweeping appreciation of the Italian problem in late February 1938, the chiefs of staff put their argument succinctly: the Italian threat derived from Mussolini's ability to concentrate his forces in a small area. The British would defeat Italy, but at what cost to the protection of Empire and the defence of the British Isles against Germany?[74] It was hard for Eden to deny the logic of this argument, a fact which made his objections to Italian talks appear increasingly petulant. Chamberlain's resumption of the Italian talks marked a real watershed for the Front populaire. It signalled the end of the last French attempt to reclaim the initiative in the entente relationship before the overnight radicalism of the second Blum government in March 1938. Chamberlain must be credited with a keen sense of the mood within the French Radical Party. Eden mistakenly assumed that the Radicals were united behind Delbos's conversion to Blum's views on Spain. In fact, Chautemps and Bonnet had come to realize the strategic implications of a confrontational Span-ish policy and counted upon Britain to exercise a restraining influence. Like Eden himself, Delbos was isolated from his party's mainstream.[75]

Massigli and Léger were aware that opening the French frontier would be ineffective in preventing Republican defeat. Phipps invited Hankey to Paris in October to reiterate this point with the French leader-ship. The Ambassador thought the trip a great success, congratulating Hankey on his calming influence: 'Something had to be done to stop this egging on of Corbin by A. [Eden] with subsequent turning down by Cabinet of suggestions made by the French as a direct result of that egging on. The whole thing is dangerous to the last degree, in the face of mad Mussolinis and gangster-like Hitlers.'[76] Ultimately, French obstinacy over Spain made it easier for Chamberlain to ignore Paris in the discussions with Mussolini, a strong indication of the real centre of gravity in the entente. The failure of French policy over Spain and Italy in October marked the end of the ambitious foreign policy pursued by the old guard of the Popular Front. One swan-song had yet to be sung. On 17 March 1938, much to British disgust, Blum's new government at last reopened the land frontier with Spain. This was counter-productive. The supplies which reached the Republican forces did not reverse their defeat on the Aragon front. Instead, the British were handed an ideal excuse to shut the new French Foreign Minister, Paul-Boncour, out of the final discussions for a new Anglo-Italian accord. Daladier eagerly closed the border again in mid-June.[77]

British concentration upon face-to-face diplomacy outside normal diplomatic channels relegated Eden and those of his advisers not close to the new Permanent Under-Secretary, Sir Alexander Cadogan, to the political sidelines. Though Eden conspired in the removal of Vansittart to the insignificant titular role of chief diplomatic adviser in January 1938, Corbin interpreted Vansittart's demise as part of a wider scheme to undermine Eden and the Foreign Office in general: 'In all, the [Foreign Office] departments undertake administration and not foreign policy.'[78] Eden was sensitive to Chamberlain's infringements upon his diplomatic jurisdiction. In December 1937 Mussolini had a cordial, unofficial meeting in Rome with Austin Chamberlain's widow (Neville's half-sister) Ivy. It is not hard to imagine the Foreign Secretary's irritation when it became apparent that Chamberlain placed greater store upon this than upon Eden's advice over talks with Italy. Though he put a brave face on it at the time, incidents such as this were as significant as any real differences over policy in prompting Eden's decision to resign.[79]

By December British representatives were installed with Franco's Nationalist *junta* at Salamanca. This made way for the launch of a new British scheme for volunteer withdrawal. Chamberlain was determined not to let another opportunity for détente with Italy slip by. The Prime Minister was certain how best to proceed. He was convinced that the Italian leadership dreaded a successful *Anschluss*. Furthermore the heavy costs of pacification in Abyssinia were a hostage to fortune which limited Mussolini's freedom of manoeuvre in central Europe. The imperative British requirement for secure Mediterranean communications, and its readiness to make concessions over Spain and the recognition of Italian Ethiopia, offered ample grounds for agreement.[80] Chamberlain over-estimated the residual Italian interest in blocking Germany's advance down the Danube. But his single-mindedness was further boosted by the incipient collapse of the Chautemps Cabinet in the first two weeks of the new year. Frequently, Chamberlain interpreted Foreign Office procedural suggestions regarding the Italian exchanges as a deliberate effort to slow progress rather than as a constructive effort to refine policy. Chamberlain's more direct approach yielded results. To him, Eden's abortive effort to place alleged American objections in the way of talks seemed crass.[81]

The dialogue with Rome culminated in the April 1938 Anglo-Italian agreement, the second bilateral deal of its kind concluded outside the forum of the entente. Here was *déjà vu* writ large. As with the Gentlemen's agreement, the Quai d'Orsay wasted considerable effort in its attempts to secure full information on the progress of the talks and to obtain British promises that French Mediterranean interests would not be prejudiced.[82] Between January and early March, Chautemps's Cabinet had expected that Ambassador Phipps would keep it abreast of the discussions. In fact, Phipps did little more than reiterate Chamberlain's rationale for excluding the French from the negotiations. Until France and Italy showed a willingness to discuss their differences, whether that be in regard to Spain, Tunisia or their Somaliland frontiers, it was unfair to expect Britain to miss the chance for a definitive settlement with Rome.[83]

Not surprisingly, once he returned to the Quai d'Orsay, Paul-Boncour was reluctant to back the Anglo-Italian accord, though Blondel insisted that a Franco-Italian détente could now be pursued. Massigli, too, attempted to convince Paul-Boncour that Franco-Italian relations might be improved by opening a dialogue over Spain. This was hopeless. The British had effectively permitted Mussolini to keep Italian forces in Spain until the civil war ended a year later. Rubbing salt in the wound, Ciano had refused to acknowledge France's right to renegotiate the terms of its Syrian Mandate. In early April, Corbin warned Paul-Boncour that the German government would do its utmost to foment Franco-Italian discord. He was quickly proved right. Hitler's visit to Italy in May 1938 proved the catalyst to rising Franco-Italian tension which continued to the outbreak of war.[84]

## V

In the four months before the *Anschluss*, Anglo-French relations grew more one-sided. The visit of Chautemps, Delbos and Cot to London in late November was judged successful across Whitehall largely because of the compliance of the French ministers. Chamberlain was quite effusive about Chautemps in particular. This was easily understood. The French Premier advertised his dislike of Soviet Russia, and was suitably impressed when informed that Britain was producing five times as many aircraft per month as France. Cot was humbled. He was even snubbed by Swinton's Air Ministry when Air Attaché Fournier was refused any explanation of General Milch's recent visit to London.[85] A British Air Ministry mission visited Paris in the first week of March 1938 to discuss production methods with la Chambre.[86] The staff conversations that eventually followed in the late spring were modelled on British preferences. The primordial British interest in effective air defences was striking. The Admiralty directorate of plans even stipulated in its preamble to the naval talks that the discussions were for political purposes only. The objective was to make a show of Anglo-French unity. Under no circumstances were the conversations to require any redistribution of Royal Naval forces in peacetime. As Corbin noted, the British negotiators walked a tightrope, anxious lest an unguarded remark be interpreted as a new commitment to France.[87]

When Chautemps constructed his second ministry on 18 January 1938, he did so without SFIO ministers, but with equivocal Socialist and PCF backing in the Assemblée. This government was listless, ineffective and, from a British viewpoint, easy to direct. In spite of numerous indications that Hitler would not tolerate Chancellor Kurt von Schuschnigg's efforts to preserve Austrian independence, Delbos could not obtain any clarification of the British attitude to eastern Europe. Once Blum returned to office in March, Paul-Boncour made this a priority.[88] On 24 January Monick pressed British Treasury officials to continue their support of French efforts to maintain the parity of the franc. In reply, Leith-Ross reminded the Financial Attaché that the downward pressure on the French currency originated with speculators inside France, not outside it. This was a harsh truth. The weakness of the franc stultified the new Chautemps ministry throughout its two-month existence. It passed little legislation, except a substantial pay rise for parliamentary Deputies, and collapsed as soon as the Conseil mustered the will to request decree powers to combat the continuing fall in the franc.[89] This left France without a government over the weekend of Schuschnigg's abortive referendum in Austria.

As so often with the Third Republic, the unimpressive picture of an ineffectual ministry should be treated with caution. With Chautemps's approval, between June 1937 and March 1938, Daladier and Bonnet had consolidated their influence upon policy formulation. Briefly, it had even seemed possible that Bonnet would construct a centre–right government in January to pick up the reins from Chautemps. Only Blum's one-month ministry briefly promised a change of emphasis. The collapse of the Chautemps and Blum ministries ushered in Daladier's government on 10 April. This administration enjoyed broader parliamentary support but it did not pursue a strongly independent foreign policy until Daladier adopted a combative approach to Italy in November 1938, two months after Munich. None of the French administrations in office in 1938 questioned the requirement for entente unity.[90]

Daladier had kept his customary fiefdom at the rue Saint Dominique during Blum's second ministry. As soon as this Cabinet was constructed, on 14 March Daladier received an incisive report from Gamelin on the strategic ramifications of the *Anschluss*. The General mapped out the likely progress of German expansionism into Czechoslovakia and beyond. He explained the weakness of the French strategic position, the problems of military access to Belgian territory and the dangers bound to arise if the Spanish frontier were reopened. But Gamelin was not unduly pessimistic. Above all, he stressed that French policy should be geared towards closer co-operation with Britain and Poland. When Daladier took on the Premiership in April 1938, he remained true to Gamelin's advice.[91] The consolidation of entente relations pursued by Daladier's government built upon the earlier achievements of the Popular Front. The failure to begin detailed strategic planning in the Front populaire era cannot be blamed upon the French, save insofar as the Blum government occasionally deluded itself into believing that the British could be reconciled to France's eastern alliance system. Even here, Chautemps quickly made up for this through his acquiescence in British policy towards Germany in late 1937. The strict parameters set by the British to the Anglo-French staff conversations in 1938 were counter-productive. Flushed with the apparent success of their agreement with Mussolini, the British were reluctant to discuss precise arrangements for Anglo-French operations against Italy. Yet, as transpired in 1940, it was already clear that in a confrontation between the entente powers and the Axis, it would be vital to remove Italy from the war as soon as possible.

In the months preceding the Munich conference, the entente powers did not build a common defensive front. But the Front populaire had altered the tenor of Anglo-French relations. Confrontation had given way to co-operation. Having been deeply sceptical of the merits of a centre–left coalition in France, the Whitehall establishment had come to respect the Popular Front far more than its predecessors. Phipps was not out of tune with prevalent opinion when he remarked on 25 November 1937: 'the further to the Right the [French] Government the more narrowly French, and the more short-sighted, especially towards Germany had the policy been, and the less easy has been cooperation with H.M.G.'[92] By the spring of 1938 the entente cordiale was significantly stronger than it had been when Front populaire candidates first went to the hustings.

# Notes

1. Jackson, *Popular Front*, p. 11; Bernard and Dubief, *Decline of the Third Republic*, pp. 326–7. The Parti Social Français was the reincarnation of Colonel de la Rocque's Croix de Feu after the extra-parliamentary Leagues were outlawed in June 1936.
2. Phipps papers, 2/10, Sargent to Phipps, 29 Nov. 1937; Cointet, *Pierre Laval*, pp. 212–18; François Monnet, *Refaire la République. André Tardieu: Une dérive réactionnaire (1876–1945)*, Paris, 1993, ch. xiv; William D. Irvine, *French Conservatism in Crisis: The Republican Federation in the 1930s*, Baton Rouge, 1979, pp. 95–6, 174–5.
3. Chautemps had been mayor of Tours since 1919, the same year he was first elected deputy for Indre-et-Loire. He entered the Senate in 1934, having served as Interior Minister between June 1924 to July 1926 and June 1932 to November 1933. Effectively leader of the Radical Party's right wing, he voted in favour of a Pétain government in 1940.
4. Phipps papers, 3/3, Phipps to Hankey, 25 Nov. 1937.
5. Jackson, *Popular Front*, p. 183. Bonnet entered Parliament in 1924 and obtained his first ministerial post as Under-Secretary to Premier Paul Painlevé in 1925.
6. PRO, FO 371/20689, C2674/53/17, C3405/53/17, Rowe-Dutton memos, 6 April and 6 May 1937.
7. Frank, *Le Prix*, p. 159; PRO, CAB 21/540, Munich consul, to Ogilvie-Forbes, Berlin, 30 April 1937.
8. PRO, FO 371/20686, C5170/18/17, Phipps memo, 14 July 1937; Frank, *Le Prix*, p. 161; Bernstein, *Histoire du Parti Radical*, II, ch. 1.
9. Bernard Minot, 'La Chute du premier gouvernement Blum et l'action des commissions des finances, 1936–1937', *Revue d'Economie Politique*, 1, 1982, pp. 42–6; Jackson, *Popular Front*, pp. 181–3; PRO, T177/34, Rowe-Dutton memo, 23 July 1937.
10. Irwin M. Wall, 'The Resignation of the First Popular Front Government of Léon Blum, June 1937', *FHS*, 6, 1970, pp. 546–7; Jackson, *Popular Front*, pp. 271–7.
11. PRO, FO 371/20686, C4042/18/17, Sargent minute, 10 June 1937.
12. SAEF, B12.619/D3, no. 66.922, Le Norcy memo, 'Le budget britannique et le budget français', 14 Nov. 1936.
13. Frank, 'The Decline of France' in Kettenacker and Mommsen, pp. 237–9.
14. PRO, FO 371/20690, C5427/53/17, Rowe-Dutton memo, 27 July 1937; Bonnet, *Vingt ans de vie politique*, p. 267; Frank, *Le Prix*, pp. 168–9; Jackson, *Popular Front*, pp. 183–5.

15. PRO, FO 371/20690, C5162/53/17, Chamberlain to Bonnet, 14 July 1937; SAEF, B12.636/D1, no. 67.152, le Norcy memo, 'La situation française et l'opinion britannique', 1 March 1937.
16. PRO, CAB 24/C.P.183(37), CID memo, 5 July 1937; DBFP, 2, XIX, no. 36.
17. PRO, FO 371/20690, C5230/53/17, Phipps to FO, 19 July 1937; C5427/53/17, Rowe-Dutton memo, 27 July 1937.
18. PRO, FO 371/21611, C686/686/17, Annual report for France, 1937; FO 371/21162, R6741/1/22, Strang minute, 13 Oct. 1937; Cot, *Le Procès*, II, p. 239.
19. PRO, FO 371/21611, C686/686/17, Annual report for France, 1937.
20. DDF, 2, VI, no. 293, Darlan to Campinchi, 29 July 1937.
21. SHM, 1BB2, c. 208/D2, Darlan note, 16 July 1937.
22. SHAT, 2N24, Daladier note, 12 Nov. 1937; CPDN séance, 8 Dec. 1937; 2N24/Marine, no. 149, Campinchi to Daladier, 24 Nov. 1937; Jordan, *Popular Front*, pp. 282–3; Young, *In Command*, p. 193.
23. DDF, 2, VI, no. 293, Darlan to Campinchi, 29 July 1937.
24. DDF, 2, VI, no. 354, Darlan to Massigli, 25 Aug. 1937; no. 381, Note de la sous-direction de la S.D.N., 31 Aug. 1937.
25. Young, *In Command*, pp. 193–4; Bond, *British Military Policy*, pp. 257–9; Greenwood, '"Caligula's Horse"', pp. 17–29; Peden, *British Rearmament*, pp. 134–9.
26. SHM, 1BB2, c. 94/EMG-2, bulletin no. 49, n.d. Sept. 1937.
27. Young, *In Command*, pp. 156, 166.
28. PRO, FO 371/20708, C4167/1/18, FO minutes, 15 June 1937; DBFP, 2, XIX, no. 46, Strang to Ogilvie-Forbes, 17 July 1937.
29. DBFP, 2, XIX, nos. 633, 634 and 639; PRO, CAB 23/Cabinet 32(37), 28 July 1937.
30. DBFP, 2, XVIII, no. 670, Sargent minute, 2 July 1937; Parker, *Chamberlain*, pp. 295–6.
31. PRO, FO 371/20735, C4975/270/18, Henderson to FO, 5 July 1937.
32. CADN, Londres 97, no. 761, François-Poncet to Delbos, 19 May 1937; PRO, FO 371/20735, C4975/270/18, FO minutes, 14–22 July 1937.
33. PRO, CAB 23/Cabinet 25(37), 21 June 1937, 7; FO 954/10A, Ge/37/26, Eden to Chamberlain, 7 July 1937.
34. DBFP, 2, XIX, no. 53, Henderson to Sargent, 20 July 1937; Christie papers, 1/5, record of meeting with Goering, 28 July 1937, fo. 93.
35. PRO, FO 371/20736, C7027/270/18, Henderson to FO, 10 Oct. 1937, Sargent minute, 1 Nov. 1937; Parker, *Chamberlain*, pp. 99–100.
36. MAE, Massigli 16, *aide mémoire* and record of London meetings, 27 and 29 Nov. 1937; Roberts, *'Holy Fox'*, pp. 63–73.

37. CADN, Londres, 264, no. 1715, François-Poncet to Delbos, 4 Nov. 1937; Parker, *Chamberlain*, pp. 100–1.
38. MAE, Roumanie 167, direction politique memo, 22 Nov. 1937; Pologne 380, Delbos record of Warsaw conversations, 4 Dec. 1937; BDFA, II, F, 13, no. 262, Newton to Eden, 20 Dec. 1937.
39. MAE, Pologne 380, Delbos memo, 'Visite à Roumanie', 8–9 Dec. 1937; SHAT, 7N3051, no. 125/S, Delmas to EMA-2, 30 Dec. 1937.
40. CADN, Rome 534, no. 445, Blondel to Delbos, 10 Dec. 1937.
41. MAE, Pologne 380, no. 2959, 'Entretiens de Belgrade', 14 Dec. 1937.
42. SHAT, 7N3051, Z20/S, Delmas to EMA-2, 24 Dec. 1937.
43. SHAT, N3123/D1, Lt.-Colonel Palasse, M.A. Moscow, to Daladier, 17 Jan. 1938.
44. SAEF, B12.620/D1, no. 67.730, Monick to Direction du Mouvement Général des Fonds, 17 Dec. 1937.
45. Blum demanded that a socialist Secretary of State be appointed as assistant to Bonnet to ensure that 'relaxed non-intervention' continued. Vincent Auriol's associate, Gaston Cusin, remained head of customs; Lacouture, *Léon Blum*, p. 335; SHAT, 7N2755/D1, no. 456, Morel to Daladier, 22 May 1937.
46. Stone, 'Britain, France and the Spanish Problem', pp. 134–7.
47. DDF, 2, VI, no. 142, Schweisguth report, 25–8 June 1937; Young, 'French Military Intelligence', pp. 153–4, 163.
48. CADN, Londres 206, French reports on NIS(36)542 and 556, 28 and 31 May 1937.
49. MAE, Massigli 14, Massigli memo, 1 July 1937; PRO, CAB 27/622, F.P.(36) 16th meeting, 1 July 1937.
50. PRO, CAB 27/622, F.P.(36) 15th meeting, 28 June 1937; Chatfield papers, CHT/4/1, Chatfield to Roger Backhouse, 12 July 1937; PRO, ADM 116/3522, ACNS report to Chatfield, 1 Sept. 1937; MAE, Papiers Delbos/D1, no. 319, Blondel to Delbos, 10 Aug. 1937.
51. PRO, CAB 23/Cabinet 10(37) and Cabinet 15(37), 3 March and 11 April 1937; FO 371/21173, R5490/135/22, FO minutes, 9 Aug. 1937.
52. PRO, CAB 23/Cabinet 29(37), 7 July 1937; DDF, 2, VI, nos. 196, 206 and 212, Delbos to Corbin, 7 July 1937, Delbos circular, 8 July 1937, Delbos to Corbin, 10 July 1937.
53. PRO, CAB 21/558, Haining to Deverell, 8 July 1937; CAB 23/Cabinet 30(37), 14 July 1937; Hankey papers, CAB 63/52, M.O.(37)3, Hankey note for PM, 2 July 1937.
54. Chamberlain papers, NC18/1/1020, Chamberlain to sister Hilda, 12 Sept. 1937.

55. SAEF, B33.673/D1, no. 2451, Vincent Auriol to Delbos, 12 Feb. 1937; no. 6313, Labeyrie to Vincent Auriol, 10 April 1937.
56. PRO, CAB 24/C.P.210(37), Eden memo, 2 Sept. 1937.
57. PRO, FO 371/21173, R5490/135/22, FO minutes, 9 Aug. 1937; Chamberlain papers, NC7/11/30/141, Chamberlain to Lord Weir, 15 Aug. 1937.
58. DDF, 2, VI, no. 326, Blondel to Delbos, 10 Aug. 1937.
59. Chatfield papers, CHT/4/10, Chatfield to Dudley Pound, 5 Aug. 1937; PRO, WO 33/1507, COS 691, 21 Feb. 1938.
60. PRO, CAB 4/26, appendix to 1350B, 10 Aug. 1937.
61. DBFP, 2, XIX, no. 94, note 1; PRO, ADM 116/3522, Phillips to Chatfield, 31 Aug. 1937; Malcolm Muggeridge (ed.), *Ciano's Diary, 1937–1938*, entry for 2 Sept. 1937, 8; Peter Gretton, 'The Nyon Conference – The Naval Aspect', *EHR*, 90, 1975, pp. 103–12.
62. MAE, Massigli 14, 'Instructions du Ministre', 28 Aug. 1938; Coutau-Bégarie and Huan, *Lettres et notes de l'Amiral Darlan*, doc. 26; regarding the conference see W.C. Mills, 'The Nyon Conference: Neville Chamberlain, Anthony Eden and the Appeasement of Italy in 1937', *IHR*, 15, 1993, pp. 1–22.
63. PRO, FO 371/20696, C6302/822/17, Lloyd-Thomas to FO, 6 Sept. 1937; CAB 24/C.P.208(37), record of ministerial meeting, 2 Sept. 1937.
64. PRO, CAB 24/C.P.208(37), ibid.; Edwards, *British Government*, pp. 122–4.
65. PRO, FO 371/21173, R5923/135/22, Eden conversation with Cambon, 21 Aug. 1937; DDF, 2, VI, no. 408, Corbin to Delbos, 8 Sept. 1937.
66. DDF, 2, VI, no. 453, Massigli to Delbos, 15 Sept. 1937; Norman Rose, 'The Resignation of Anthony Eden', *HJ*, 25, 4, 1982, pp. 911–31.
67. *Ciano's Diary*, entry for 4 Sept. 1937; PRO, FO 371/21404, W16802/62/41, FO meeting, 6 Sept. 1937; Gretton, 'The Nyon Conference', p. 106; Parker, *Chamberlain*, p. 111.
68. DDF, 2, VI, no. 475, Massigli to Léger, 20 Sept. 1937; MAE, Massigli 14, Massigli memo, 7 Oct. 1937.
69. DDF, 2, VI, no. 475, Massigli to Léger, 20 Sept. 1937; PRO, FO 371/20712, C7386/3/18, Beaumont-Nesbitt report, 20 Oct. 1937; Phipps papers, 1/19, Phipps to Eden, 30 Sept. 1937.
70. PRO, CAB 23/Cabinet 35(37), 29 Sept. 1937.
71. Ibid., 9–10; PRO, CAB 23/Cabinet 37(37), 13 Oct. 1937, fos. 2–9.
72. PRO, CAB 23/Cabinet(37)37, ibid.; Chamberlain papers, NC18/1/1024, letter to sister Ida, 16 Oct. 1937.

73. PRO, FO 371/21593, C362/36/17, Eden to Chamberlain, 31 Jan. 1938.
74. PRO, WO 33/1507, COS 691, 21 Feb. 1938.
75. MAE, Italie 308, no. 145, Delbos to Blondel, 13 July 1937; Phipps papers, 1/19, Phipps to Eden, 12 Oct. 1937.
76. PRO, CAB 63/52, M.O.(37)7, Hankey conversation with Léger, 11 Oct. 1937; Hankey papers, Churchill College, Cambridge, 4/29, Phipps to Hankey, 14 Oct. 1937.
77. SHAT, 2N224/D2, 'Note sur l'importance stratégique de l'Espagne', 24 April 1938; Stone, 'Britain, France and the Spanish problem', pp. 140–1.
78. CADN, Londres 264, no. 15, Corbin to Delbos, 5 Jan. 1938; record of Corbin–Vansittart conversation, 19 Jan. 1938.
79. Parker, *Chamberlain*, p. 114.
80. PRO, T273/410, Hankey to Vansittart, 3 Nov. 1937.
81. Chamberlain papers, NC18/1/1035, letter to Ida, 16 Jan. 1938; Diary entry, 19 Feb. 1938.
82. MAE, Italie 278, no. 140, Delbos to Blondel, 18 Feb. 1938; no. 607, Delbos to Corbin, 24 Feb. 1938; Italie 308, Corbin to Paul-Boncour, 7 April 1938.
83. CADN, Londres 267, no. 654, Delbos meeting with Phipps, 13 March 1938.
84. MAE, Italie 278, no. 485, Blondel to Paul-Boncour, 25 March 1938; no. 1069, Paul-Boncour to Corbin, 8 April 1938; Massigli 17, note, 'Négociations franco-italiennes', 16 April 1938; Shorrock, *From Ally to Enemy*, pp. 223–31.
85. Chamberlain Papers, NC18/1/1030a, letter to Hilda, 5 Dec. 1937; CADN, Londres 97, no. 905, Corbin to Delbos, 10 Nov. 1937; PRO, CAB 21/553, 'France – service aircraft', n.d. Dec. 1937; Adamthwaite, *France*, pp. 67–72.
86. SHAT, 2N227/D2, EMAA procès verbal, 28 March 1938.
87. PRO, ADM 116/3379, directorate of plans memo, 22 April 1938; CADN, Londres 263, no. 414, Corbin to Paris, 5 May 1938.
88. DDF, 2, IX, no. 3, Paul-Boncour to Corbin, 21 March 1938.
89. SAEF, B12.620/D1, Monick to Direction du Mouvement Général des Fonds, 24 Jan. 1938; Alexander, *Republic*, pp. 130–1.
90. PRO, FO 371/21611, C686/686/17, Annual report, France, 1937; Young, *In Command*, pp. 157–9.
91. MAE, Fonds Daladier I, Gamelin memo, 14 March 1938; CSDN, 'Note sur la collaboration Franco-Britannique', 24 April 1938.
92. PRO, FO 371/20687, C8134/18/17, Phipps to FO, 25 Nov. 1937.

# Conclusion: The End of the Popular Front Era

It is an unfortunate epitaph to the Popular Front that there was no government in place over the weekend on which Germany undertook the *Anschluss* in March 1938. The second Blum ministry was a failure. The Socialist leader left the Hôtel Matignon on 8 April after the collapse of his worthy attempts to organize a broad government of national unity. Paul-Boncour's brief return to the Quai d'Orsay had fired a resurgence of collective security rhetoric which caused alarm in London. But, without genuine PCF backing, the 1938 Front populaire bore little comparison to its 1936–7 counterparts. This was only marginally less true of French foreign policy. What then may we conclude of Anglo-French relations in the Front populaire interlude, if indeed the period was really distinctive?

Between the Rhineland crisis in March 1936 and the *Anschluss* two years later, relations between Britain and France were set on a new footing, having degenerated into mutual recrimination in the preceding era of Pierre Laval. During Blum's administration, the two powers did not develop a joint diplomatic strategy, nor did they concert regularly on all aspects of foreign and defence policy. Within the entente, Britain remained the senior partner. None the less, a closer relationship developed in the Popular Front years, and France exerted considerable, if piecemeal, influence upon key elements of the appeasement effort. The credit for this gradual restoration of Anglo-French co-operation rests principally with the first Blum government. The Front populaire coalition was the first French administration of the 1930s to structure policy upon the recognition that British support against Germany was more vital than that of all other French allies combined. It accepted that British goodwill was best won by pursuit of a coherent rearmament scheme. This was to be backed by a foreign policy which, for all its eastern alliance disappointments, placed the entente cordiale first.

In September 1936 the Blum government introduced a four-year defence programme which sought to remedy France's worsening defensive position. In the Popular Front era this re-equipment plan was undermined by financial crisis, industrial bottlenecks, the inadequacy of plant capacity, and the misguided efforts of one service arm – the armée de l'air – to build a strategic deterrent out of step with both actual air force capability and the global requirements of French military planning. Anxious to press ahead with rearmament, the first Blum government survived a year of increasing acrimony between the component parties, unions and organizations that made up the original Rassemblement populaire. Blum's economic policy, his spending plans in particular, had little hope of success without the active support of the French financial community. In the short term, this had less impact upon defence expenditure than might be imagined. By recourse to borrowing where necessary, the government met the initial costs of the rearmament plan only to find that much of the money could not be immediately spent owing to lack of productive capacity, skilled labour shortages and the restrictive labour practices the government had itself introduced.[1]

The Riom trial allegation that the Blum government failed to provide for France's defence requirements was unfair. Traumatized by defeat, the Vichy state regarded the Popular Front as an obvious scapegoat. Even so, the prosecution in this biased Vichy court could not sustain its warped allegations about the defence planning of Blum's ministers. No French government of the 1930s made greater sacrifices in pursuit of stronger defences than the first Popular Front administration. It would require a peculiar tunnel vision to remain blind to the fact that the major additions to French strength accomplished from 1938 onwards originated in the actions of the 1936–7 coalition. The parlous state of the French air force between 1936 and 1938, itself very much a product of Cot's actions as minister, should not be extrapolated onto the other services. La Chambre's energetic representation of armée de l'air needs, notably on the inter-service comité du matériel, plus the purchase of American aircraft between 1938 and 1940, meant that even the air force entered the battle for France as a credible defensive arm.[2]

In a sense, the Popular Front governments adopted a diplomatic corollary to their defence policy. The Blum and Chautemps administrations recognized that France was too weak to negotiate on equal terms with Nazi Germany. Hence, the Front populaire worked to rebuild the diplomatic bridges to Britain, so many of which had collapsed between 1933 and 1936 because of the tensions generated by the abortive Geneva Disarmament Conference and the Abyssinian crisis. It is vital to bear in mind that by January 1936 British governmental suspicion of French foreign policy had mushroomed into virtual hostility. This was particularly so within the service establishment. The behaviour of figures such as Sir Maurice Hankey, Admiral Ernle Chatfield, Sir Samuel Hoare and Lord Halifax did little to dispel French resentments of perfidious Albion.

Unlike the British themselves, or indeed Pierre Laval before them, the Front populaire governments did not employ their entente partner as a lever to coax Hitler into direct, bilateral conversations. If this suggests that France did all the giving and Britain all the taking, it does not follow that the Popular Front lacked an independent foreign policy. Blum did not ride on British coat-tails. Instead, the affability of the Popular Front governments, so much welcomed in London, was grounded on the reasoned assumption that the British appeasement effort would fail. France would work in support of the western pact, agreements over Spain and arms limitation. But this support was offered in the expectation that the 'effort of conciliation' would not succeed. Once that occurred, the British guarantee of 19 March 1936 would come into effect. The entente would be cemented into alliance since Britain would be unable to blame the collapse of its own policy upon French truculence.

British concentration upon a western pact during 1936–7 marked an unsuccessful attempt to achieve a clinical separation between the less intractable problems of a replacement Locarno, and the insoluble question of Germany's claims in eastern Europe. The failure of this policy was certainly not due to French obstacles. Indeed, the collapse of the western pact exchanges during the spring of 1937 highlighted Britain's strategic dependence upon France. Equally, although Chamberlain revived plans for colonial appeasement following Halifax's visit to Germany in November 1937, he had yet to overcome justifiable French scepticism regarding the costs and benefits of such a policy. Though *primus inter pares* within the entente relationship, Britain could not ride roughshod over France in pursuit of a bilateral settlement with Germany. To do so would have condemned Britain to an impotent neutrality in Europe, anathema to the projection of British power. French territorial integrity was, and would remain, a vital British interest.

This, of course, requires some qualification. Chamberlain certainly developed a resolve to 'go it alone' in the appeasement of Italy during 1937. Nevile Henderson's activities as Ambassador and Halifax's ill-considered visit to Berlin confirmed the Prime Minister's hankering to adopt a like approach with Germany. Even so, it was always implicit that France would have to be involved in the final stages of negotiations. During 1938 the British Cabinet increasingly imposed its will upon the Daladier government. It had not done so to the same degree in the Popular Front era. The quickening pace of Hitler's eastern diplomacy as the Czech crisis developed is insufficient to explain this. Under Blum the eastern alliances, though a declining asset, were a central part of French foreign-policy planning, collective security not merely a conference-platform phrase. Yet in the Popular Front period, these French eastern alliances disintegrated. The German threat and Italy's seduction of

Yugoslavia revealed the Little Entente for what it was: a local coalition formed for a limited purpose. An alliance designed to resist Austrian or Hungarian revisionism was ill-suited to the strategic containment of Germany's eastward expansion. Neither the French nor the Czechoslovakian governments could persuade Poland or Romania of the merits of Soviet support. Denied unequivocal British backing for its eastern policy, and unable to provide substantial economic assistance, France could not convince the eastern allies that it remained an effective counter-weight to increasing German economic, political and strategic pressure.

After March 1936 the Rhineland bridgeheads were no longer available to the French army. Military collaboration with Italy was fading from view and Belgium was no longer a compliant defensive partner. By the time the France–Little Entente pact was formally launched in January 1937, the French strategic position was significantly weakened. After the *Anschluss* French ineffectiveness became apparent. In late March 1938 renewed lobbying from Yugoslavia and Romania for the fulfilment of French arms supply contracts indicated that the eastern allies still viewed France as their principal ally of last resort. But French inability to meet these demands merely confirmed that, without outside support, the Little Entente was a hollow reed.[3]

In July 1938 Gamelin warned Daladier that, to defend itself effectively, Czechoslovakia would need to mobilize at least three classes of reservists and seek Soviet support.[4] The British government was certain to oppose both options. On 15 March Gamelin had made a similar point to Blum and Paul-Boncour within the CPDN: if France intended to defend Czechoslovakia or resist any Axis incursion from Spain, full mobilization would be essential. This was made plain to the British on 16 March in response to an earlier request for information regarding French plans for the defence of Czechoslovakia.[5] In spite of Blum and Paul-Boncour's final stand against it, the increased dependence on Britain characteristic of French policy during the Czech crisis was clearly taking shape.

Anglo-French relations, though still improving after Daladier came to office in April 1938, were not automatically close. Only the skeletal framework of a co-ordinated defence strategy had been put in place. French financial policy was considered more respectable in London, although Chamberlain and Simon's curt refusal to meet Daladier's requests for monetary talks in August 1938 confirmed the residual British disappointment at the limited economic recovery Bonnet's devaluations had achieved since June 1937.[6] The occasional British disdain for France is misleading. Britain's overseas power and British appeasement strategy were dangerously reliant upon the notoriously unquantifiable commodity of 'prestige'. So long as the British Empire appeared solid and strong it was hard to dismiss all prospects for negotiation with Germany or Italy. In reality, the security of the British Isles rested in part on the impenetrability of the French barrier to any German westward advance. Furthermore, the coalescence of German, Italian and Japanese expansionism into a three-power threat to the British Empire threatened to undermine Britain's prestige, exposing the actual indefensibility of numerous British possessions and dependencies. One cannot say that Singapore, Suez, Malta or the Australasian Dominions could not be defended, only that all of them could not be adequately guarded at any one time. Like France, in the Popular Front period Britain was very much in the early stages of rearmament. This meant that the British government could only negotiate from a position of strength with the assurance of French military backing.

While the assumption of the military support of their entente partner was central to foreign-policy formulation in London and Paris, it required French governments which tailored their diplomacy to British requirements to bring about sustained diplomatic co-operation. Both Eden and Chamberlain were well in advance of their ministerial colleagues in understanding that just such a government had come into office in May 1936. Before League sanctions were withdrawn from Italy in June 1936, Eden's preparations for this humiliating climb-down had alerted him to the prospects for closer collaboration with France once the Front populaire took office. Chamberlain was keenly interested in economic appeasement and eager to limit the diplomatic fall-out from the Spanish civil war. Both of these concerns drew his attention to the sea-change in French policy typified by the Quai d'Orsay's formulation of a non-intervention strategy in late July and Blum's discussions with Hjalmar Schacht days later.

French policy was not entirely calculated to appeal to Britain. There were four main reasons for this. Firstly, as has been said, the French leadership had less faith in the effectiveness of direct talks with Berlin. Since the British government was nevertheless determined to initiate such exchanges, the French required more precise pledges of British support in order to undercut German efforts to isolate France by means of a bilateral deal with London. Secondly, given this scepticism regarding the prospects for appeasement, it was vital to France that western European security arrangements be set in place to compensate for the destruction of Locarno in March 1936. After the failure of the western pact, the French approach was marked by constant reiteration of the German threat to Britain and occasional pressure for staff conversations. A third consideration was that the assurance of British backing was the essential precursor to a viable reorganization of the eastern alliance system. This was an objective not achieved in practice. Finally, by insisting on the need for an Anglo-French alliance, Flandin and Delbos were able to extract numerous lesser concessions from the British side.

Anglo-French misunderstandings remained. This was perhaps most notable regarding policy towards Italy and the maintenance of secure lines of communication in the western Mediterranean. There was little appreciation in Britain of how crucial the prospect of an Italian military alliance had been to the French military. Still less excusable was the British failure to integrate France properly into its Mediterranean strategy. Instead, the French marine was unknowingly being allotted increasing tasks in order to ensure the feasibility of the main fleet to Singapore ideal. It is perhaps significant that sustained opposition to Italian involvement in Spain was the one issue over which the Chautemps ministries refused to comply with British requests for greater indulgence towards the fascist powers.

Despite all the above qualifications, Front populaire diplomacy was successful in revitalizing the entente with Britain. It is crucial to avoid a prejudgment of events. French willingness to fall in with the early stages of Chamberlain's distinctive appeasement in 1936 and 1937 did not presage the humiliating French acquiescence at Munich in September 1938. During the Popular Front era, appeasement was seen by the Blum and Chautemps governments to require entente unity and sustained rearmament. Quite apart from the wish to avoid a major European war, the Front populaire administrations fell in with the appeasement effort for two sound reasons. It was essential to British goodwill and, if and when appeasement collapsed, defensive alliance was likely to follow. That this did not occur until 1939 is more a reflection of Chamberlain's remarkable tenacity than of miscalculation by the Blum or Chautemps governments. Chamberlain perpetuated into 1938 and 1939 a policy which, during the two previous years, the great majority of ministers on both sides of the Channel saw good reason to accept.

## Notes

1. PRO, T177/34, Treasury memo for Phillips, 3 Sept. 1937.
2. See SHAT, 1B6/D1, for comité du matériel minutes for 1938; regarding American equipment see Jean Monnet, *Memoirs*, London, 1978, pp. 127–36; John McVickar Haight jun., *American Aid to France, 1938–1940*, New York, 1970.

3. SHAT, 7N3097/EMA-2, Faucher, 'La Tchécoslovaquie et l'Anschluss', n.d. March 1938; 7N3202, no. 72, Béthouart to EMA-2, 8 March 1938; 7N3052/D1, no. 19, Delmas to EMA-2, 19 March 1938.
4. SHAT, 5N579/D6, no. 559, Gamelin to Daladier, 18 July 1938.
5. SHAT, 2N25/D2, CPDN procès verbal, 15 March 1938; Gamelin note, 16 March 1938; Young, *In Command*, pp. 197–201; Jordan, *Popular Front*, pp. 284–9, 316–17.
6. PRO, PREM 1/267, Phillips memo, 14 Aug. 1938; Simon to PM, 17 Aug. 1938.

# Bibliography

## Primary Sources

### British Archives

#### Public Record Office, London (PRO)
Cabinet
| | |
|---|---|
| CAB 2 | Committee of Imperial Defence minutes of meetings |
| CAB 4 | Committee of Imperial Defence B papers/miscellaneous memoranda |
| CAB 16 | Committee of Imperial Defence sub-committee papers |
| CAB 21 | Cabinet registered files |
| CAB 23 | Cabinet minutes and conclusions |
| CAB 24 | Cabinet memoranda |
| CAB 27 | Cabinet Ministerial Committee papers |
| CAB 29 | International conferences to 1939, memoranda |
| CAB 32 | Imperial Conference 1937, minutes and memoranda |
| CAB 36 | CID Joint Overseas and Home Defence sub-committee |
| CAB 53 | CID Joint Planning Staff papers |
| CAB 62 | Non-Intervention Committee memoranda |
| CAB 63 | Papers of Lord Hankey, Magnum Opus files |
| CAB 64 | Papers of Sir Thomas Inskip |

Prime Minister's Office
| | |
|---|---|
| PREM 1 | Prime Minister's Office correspondence and papers 1916–1940 |

Admiralty
| | |
|---|---|
| ADM 1 | Admiralty and Secretariat papers |
| ADM 116 | Admiralty and Secretariat cases |
| ADM 121 | Mediterranean Station records |
| ADM 167 | Admiralty Board minutes/memoranda |
| ADM 178 | Admiralty and Secretariat papers and cases, supplementary series |
| ADM 205 | First Sea Lord's papers |
| ADM 223 | Naval Intelligence papers |

# Bibliography

**Air Ministry**

| | |
|---|---|
| AIR 2 | Air Ministry correspondence files |
| AIR 6 | Air Board and Air Council records of meetings |
| AIR 8 | Records of Chief of Air Staff |
| AIR 9 | Director of Plans archive |
| AIR 19 | Air Ministry Private Office papers |
| AIR 35 | British Air Forces in France |
| AIR 40 | Air Ministry Directorate of Intelligence |

**War Office**

| | |
|---|---|
| WO 32 | War Office registered files |
| WO 33 | War Office reports/miscellaneous papers |
| WO 106 | Directorate of Military Operations and Intelligence |
| WO 208 | Directorate of Military Intelligence |
| WO 216 | Chief of Imperial General Staff papers |
| WO 258 | War Office Permanent Under-Secretary of State Private Office papers |
| WO 259 | War Office Private Office papers |
| WO 282 | Sir John Dill papers |

**Foreign Office**

| | |
|---|---|
| FO 371 | General Correspondence: Central Department, Southern Department, Northern Department, Western Department |
| FO 413 | Foreign Office Confidential Print Morocco and North West Africa |
| FO 432 | Foreign Office Confidential Print, France 1934–1956 |
| FO 800 | Foreign Office Private Office papers, 274 Orme Sargent papers, 292 Sir Ralph Wigram papers, 295 Sir Samuel Hoare Correspondence, 296 Lord Cranborne correspondence, 394 Miscellaneous Private Office papers |
| FO 954 | Papers of the Earl of Avon (Eden) |

**Treasury**

| | |
|---|---|
| T 160 | Finance Division records |
| T 161 | Supply Division records |
| T 175 | Papers collected by Sir Richard Hopkins |
| T 177 | Private Office papers/private collections: Sir Frederick Phillips papers |
| T 188 | Sir Frederick Leith-Ross papers |
| T 225 | Defence Policy and Material Provision files |
| T 273 | Edward Bridges papers |

Board of Trade
BT 59        Records of Overseas Trade Development Council
BT 90        Records of Advisory Committee to Department of
             Overseas Trade

Colonial Office
CO 967       Private Office papers
CO 968       Defence/Original Correspondence

Dominions Office
DO 35        General Correspondence

*Private Papers*
University of Birmingham: Earl of Avon papers; Neville Chamberlain
papers

University of Cambridge Library: Stanley Baldwin papers; Viscount
Templewood papers

University of Cambridge, Churchill College archive: Sir Alexander Cadogan diaries; Malcolm G. Christie papers; Baron Hankey of the Chart
diaries and papers; Leslie Hore-Belisha papers; Sir Thomas Inskip
diaries; Viscount Norwich (Duff Cooper) papers; Sir Eric Phipps papers;
Lord Strang papers; Lord Swinton papers; Lord Vansittart papers; Viscount Weir papers

Bodleian Library Oxford: Sir Horace Rumbold papers; Francis Hemming papers; Viscount Simon papers

St Antony's College, Middle East Centre, Oxford: Diaries of 1st Baron
Killearn (Sir Miles Lampson)

National Maritime Museum, Greenwich: Lord Chatfield papers

*French Archives*

*Ministère des Affaires Etrangères (MAE)*
Série Z, Europe, 1930–1940, correspondance politique
Allemagne; Espagne; Grande Bretagne; Italie; Pologne; Roumanie;
Tchécoslovaquie; URSS; Yougoslavie
Série B, 1918–1940, relations commerciales
Sous-Série B, Crédits – Assurances; Pologne; Tchécoslovaquie, 1936–
1938

Papiers d'Agents – Archives Privées:
Papiers Joseph Avenol; Papiers Robert Coulondre; Papiers René Massigli; Papiers Emile Naggiar; Papiers Léon Noël
Papiers 1940: Fonds Daladier; Fonds Cabinet, Yvon Delbos

*Centre des Archives Diplomatiques de Nantes (CADN)*
French Embassy Archives
Londres, Télégrammes/Correspondance Attachés 1935–1939
Berlin, Fonds B, Télégrammes/Correspondance Attachés 1936–1939
Rome Quirinal, Archives repatriées de l'Ambassade 1933–1939
Madrid, Fonds C, Correspondance de l'Ambassade 1936–1937
Bucarest, Télégrammes/Correspondance Attachés 1920–1943
Tokyo, Fonds A and B, Affaires de Chine/Sous Série 1932–1939

*Service Historique de l'Armée de Terre, Vincennes (SHAT)*
Cartons 2N18-22, Comité Permanent de la Défense Nationale/Haut Comité Militaire
Carton 2N56, Direction fabrication d'armement
Cartons 5N579, 5N581, Cabinet du Ministre
Cartons Série 7N: EMA-2, (deuxième bureau): Attachés reports by country: Allemagne, 1936–1938; Belgique, 1936–1938; Espagne, 1934–1938; Grande Bretagne, 1935–1940; Italie, 1934–1938; Pologne, 1930–1940; Roumanie, 1926–1940; Tchécoslovaquie, 1932–1939; URSS, 1935–1939; Yougoslavie, 1928–1938

*Service Historique de la Marine, Vincennes (SHM)*
Sous Série 1BB2 – Etat-Major Général, 1$^e$–3$^e$ Bureau, Dossiers de Darlan
Sous Série 1BB3 – Incoming correspondence
Sous Série 1BB7 – Attachés Navales, Missions Navales, Marines Etrangères
Sous Série 1BB8 – Cabinet du Ministre – Conseils, Comités, Commissions divers, CPDN procès verbaux/rapports

*Service Historique de l'Armée de l'Air, Vincennes (SHAA)*
Série B – 1B Cabinet, 2B Etat-Major de l'Armée de l'Air, 3B Directions et Services
Série C – Forces aériennes françaises d'Outre-Mer, CI Levant, CII Maroc, CIII Tunisie, CIV Extrême-Orient
Série D – Armée de l'Air de 1939 à 1945
Série Z – Private papers – Archives Guy la Chambre; Fonds Bréguet; Fonds Jauneaud; Fonds Potez; Fonds Vuillemin

# Bibliography

*Service des Archives Economiques et Financières*
Ministère de l'économie/Ministère du budget, Paris (SAEF)
Série B – Direction du Trésor/Direction des Finances Extérieures
Agence financière de Londres
Renseignements économiques et financières
Fonds Trésor – relations financières Europe Espagne; Grèce; Pologne;
Roumanie; Tchécoslovaquie; URSS; Yougoslavie

*Archives Nationales Centre des Archives d'Outre-Mer, Aix-en-Provence (ANCOM)*
Papiers d'agents: Robert Delavignette; Georges Mandel; Marius Moutet
Affaires Politiques: cartons/dossiers on the following: Allocations militaires 1930–1937; Aéronautique coloniale; Haut Comité Méditerranéen et de l'Afrique du Nord; Maroc, 1934–1938; Politique coloniale étrangère, 1929–1936; Possessions Espagnoles

## Official Collections

*British Documents on Foreign Affairs*, Part II, Series F: Europe, general editors, Kenneth Bourne and D. Cameron Watt, vols 10, 11, 12, 13, 14, 15, 21, 22, 23
*Documents on British Foreign Policy, 1919–1939*, Second Series, vols XVI–XIX, 1936–1938, edited by W.N. Meddlicott, D. Dakin, M.E. Lambert, HMSO, 1977
*Documents Diplomatiques Belges, 1920–1940*, 5 vols, edited by F. Vanlangenhove and C. de Visscher, (Brussels, 1964–6). Vols III–IV consulted.
*Documents Diplomatiques Français, 1932–1939*, Deuxième Série, 1936–1939, vols 1–V. Edited under the direction of P. Renouvin, J.-B. Duroselle, M. Baumont, Imprimerie Nationale, 1963–*et seq*
*Documents on German Foreign Policy, 1918–1945*, series C, HMSO, 1957–*et seq*
*Les Evénements survenus en France de 1933 à 1945*, Rapporte présenté par M. Charles Serre, 2 vols, Témoinages et documents, 9 vols, Paris, 1947–52
*Bulletin Officiel du Protectorat Chérifien* [Morocco] (CADN)
*Journal Officiel*, 1936
*Journal Officiel Tunisien* (CADN)

## Diaries, Letters and Memoirs

Avon, Lord, *Memoirs*, I: *Facing the Dictators*, London, 1962
Auriol, Vincent, *Hier-Demain*, vols I–II, Paris, 1945

Barnes, John, and Nicholson, David (eds), *The Empire at Bay. The Leo Amery Diaries, 1929–1945*, London, 1988

Beck, Jósef, *Dernier Rapport. Politique Polonaise, 1926–1939*, Paris, 1951

Blum, Robert (ed.), *L'Œuvre de Léon Blum*, 4 vols, especially vol. IV(I), *Les Problèmes de Politique Extérieure, 1934–1936*, Paris, 1955

Bonnet, Georges,*Vingt ans de vie politique, 1918–1938, de Clemenceau à Daladier*, Paris, 1969

Bullitt, Orville H., *For the President. Personal and Secret. Correspondence between Franklin D. Roosevelt and William C. Bullitt*, Boston, 1970

Chatfield, Lord Ernle, *It Might Happen Again: The Autobiography of Admiral of the Fleet Lord Chatfield*, vol. II, London, 1947

Cot, Pierre, *Le Procès de la République*, vols I–II, New York, 1944

Coulondre, Robert, *De Staline à Hitler*, Paris, 1950

Coutau-Bégarie, Hervé, and Huan, Claude, *Lettres et notes de l'Amiral Darlan*, Paris, 1992

Dilks, David N. (ed.), *The Diaries of Sir Alexander Cadogan*, London, 1971

Duff Cooper, Alfred, *Old Men Forget, The Autobiography of Viscount Norwich*, London, 1953

Evans, Trefor (ed.), *The Killearn Diaries, 1934–1946*, London, 1972

Flandin, Pierre-Étienne, *Politique Française, 1919–1940*, Paris, 1947

François-Poncet, André, *Souvenirs d'une Ambassade à Berlin, Septembre 1931–Octobre 1938*, Paris, 1946

Gamelin, General Maurice C., *Servir*, vols I–III, Paris, 1946–7

Gauché, General Maurice, *Le Deuxième Bureau au Travail (1935–1940)*, Paris, 1953

Gouin, Félix, introduction, *Léon Blum before his Judges at the Supreme Court of Riom, March 11th and 12th, 1942*, London, 1943

Harvey, O., *The Diplomatic Diaries of Oliver Harvey*, London, 1970

Henderson, Nevile, *Failure of a Mission, Berlin, 1937–1940*, London, 1940

Jedrzejewicz, Waclaw, *Diplomat in Paris, 1936–1939. Papers and Memoirs of Juliasz Lukasiewicz Ambassador of Poland*, New York, 1970

Jones, Tom, *A Diary with Letters, 1931–1950*, London, 1969

Keyes Papers, *Papers of Deputy Chief of Staff, Admiral Keyes*, vol. II, Naval Records Society

Leith-Ross, Sir Frederick, *Money Talks. Fifty Years of International Finance*, London, 1968

Minney, R.J. (ed.), *The Private Papers of Hore-Belisha*, London, 1960

Moch, Jules, *Le Front Populaire, Grand Espérance*, Paris, 1971

Monnet, Jean, *Memoirs*, London, 1978

Muggeridge, Malcolm (ed.), *Ciano's Diplomatic Papers*, London, 1948
*Ciano's Diary, 1937–1938*, London, 1952

Noël, Léon, *L'agression allemande contre la Pologne*, Paris, 1946
*Les illusions de Stresa: l'Italie abandonnée à Hitler*, Paris, 1975

Paul-Boncour, Joseph, *Entre Deux Guerres*, III: *Sur les Chemins de la Défaite*, Paris, 1946

Schacht, Hjalmar, *My First Seventy-six Years*, London, 1955

Simon, Viscount, *Retrospect, the Memoirs of the Rt. Hon. Viscount Simon*, London, 1952

Templewood, Viscount, *Nine Troubled Years*, London, 1954

Vansittart, Lord, *The Mist Procession*, London, 1958

Wenger, Léon, *55 ans de pétrole, 1904–1959: Souvenirs de Léon Wenger*, Paris, 1968.

## Books and Articles

Adam, Magda, 'Les pays danubiens et Hitler (1933–1936)', *RHDGM*, 98, 1975, 1–26

Adamthwaite, Anthony, *France and the Coming of the Second World War, 1936–1939*, London, 1977
'The British Government and the Media, 1937–1938', *JCH*, 18, 2, 1983, 281–97

Ader, Clément, *L'Aviation militaire*, Paris, 1990

Ageron, Charles-Robert, 'L'idée d'eurafrique et le débat colonial franco-allemand de l'entre-deux guerres', *RHMC*, 22, 1975, 446–75
'La perception de la puissance française en 1938–1939: Le mythe impérial' in Girault and Frank, 227–44

Agulhon, Maurice, *The French Republic, 1870–1990*, Oxford, 1993

Ahmann, R., Birke, A.M., and Howard, M. (eds), *The Quest for Stability. Problems of West European Security, 1918–1957*, Oxford, 1993

Alexander, Martin S.,*The Republic in Danger. General Maurice Gamelin and the Politics of French Defence, 1933–1940*, Cambridge, 1992
'The Fall of France, 1940', *JSS*, 13, 1, 1990, 10–44
'In Lieu of Alliance: The French General Staff's Secret Co-operation with Neutral Belgium, 1936–1940', *JSS*, 14, 4, 1991, 413–27
'Did the Deuxième Bureau Work? The Role of Intelligence in French Defence Policy and Strategy, 1919–1939', *Intelligence and National Security*, 6, 2, 1991, 293–333
'A bas les marchands de canons! Efforts to control the private manufacture and trade in arms in France during the 1930s', in M. Vaïsse (ed.), *Le Pacifisme en Europe des années 1920 aux années 1950*

Alexander, Martin S., and Graham, Helen (eds), *The French and Spanish Popular Fronts*, Cambridge, 1989

Andrew C.M., and Kanya-Forstner, A.S., *France Overseas. The Great War and the Climax of French Imperial Expansion*, London, 1981

Aster, Sydney, '"Guilty Men": The Case of Neville Chamberlain' in Boyce and Robertson, 233–68

Astorkia, Madeline, 'Les leçons aériennes de la guerre d'Espagne', *RHA*, 2, 1977, 145–73

'L'aviation et la guerre d'Espagne: la cinquième arme face aux exigences de la guerre moderne' in Hildebrand and Werner, 325–45

Bankwitz, Philip C.F., *Maxime Weygand and Civil–Military Relations in Modern France*, Cambridge, Mass., 1967

Bariéty, Jacques, *et al.*, *La France et l'Allemagne entre deux guerres mondiales*, Nancy, 1987

'La France et le problème de l'"Anschluss"' in Hildebrand and Werner, 553–74

'Léon Blum et l'Allemagne 1930–1938', in F.G. Dreyfus (ed.), *Les Relations Franco-Allemandes 1933–1939*, Paris, 1976

Becker, Jean-Jacques, 'La Perception de la puissance par le Parti Communiste', *RHMC*, 31, 1984, pp. 637–40.

Bédarida, François, 'La "gouvernante anglaise"' in Rémond and Bourdin, 228–40

Bell, P.M.H., *The Origins of the Second World War in Europe*, London, 1986

Bennett, G.H., 'Britain's Relations with France after Versailles: The Problem of Tangier, 1919–23', *EHQ*, 24, 1994, 53–84

Bergougnoux, Philippe, 'Le réarmement de la Marine Nationale (1934–1939)', *RHA*, 4, 1985, 26–41

Bernard, Philip, and Dubief, Henri, *The Decline of the Third Republic, 1914–1938*, Cambridge, 1985

Bernstein, Serge, *Histoire du Parti Radical. II: Crise du Radicalisme, 1926–1939*, Paris, 1982

'La perception de la puissance par les partis politiques français en 1938–1939' in Girault and Frank, 281–303

'La perception de la puissance par le parti Radical-Socialiste', *RHMC*, 31, 1984, 619–35

Bialer, Uri, *The Shadow of the Bomber: The Fear of Air Attack and British Politics, 1932–1939*, London, 1980

'"Humanization" of Air Warfare in British Foreign Policy', *JCH*, 13, 1, 1978, 79–96

'Elite Opinion and Defence Policy: Air Power Advocacy and British Rearmament during the 1930s', *British Journal of International Studies*, 6, 1980, 32–51

Bjelajac, Mile, 'L'influence française sur l'armée yougoslave entre les deux guerres mondiales', *RHA*, 4, 1994, 45–54

Blatt, Joel, 'The Parity that Meant Superiority: French Naval Policy towards Italy at the Washington Conference and Interwar French Foreign Policy', *FHS*, 12, 2, 1981, 223–48

'France and the Washington Conference', *Diplomacy and Statecraft*, 4, 3, 1993, 192–219

Bloch, Charles, 'Les relations franco-allemandes et la politique des puissances pendant la guerre d'Espagne' in Hildebrand and Werner, 429–52

Blumenthal, Henry, *Illusion and Reality in Franco-American Diplomacy, 1914–1945*, Baton Rouge, 1986

Boadle, Donald, 'The Formation of the Foreign Office Economic Section, 1930–1937', *HJ*, 20, 4, 1977, 919–936

'Vansittart's administration of the Foreign Office in the 1930s' in Langhorne, 68–84

Bodinier, Gilbert, 'Gamelin, les fortifications et les chars à travers les rapports de l'E.M.A. (1935–1939)', *RHA*, 4, 1979, 125–44

Bock, H.M., Meyer-Kalkus, R., and Trebitsch, M., *Entre Locarno et Vichy. Les relations culturelles franco-allemandes dans les années 1930*, vol. I, Paris, 1993

Bond, Brian, *British Military Policy between the Two World Wars*, Oxford, 1980

Bourdé, Guy, *La Défaite du Front Populaire*, Paris, 1977

Boussard, Dominique, *Un problème de défense nationale: l'aéronautique militaire au parlement, (1928–1940)*, Paris, 1983

Bouvier, Jean (ed.), *La France en mouvement, 1934–1938*, Paris, 1986

Boyce Robert, and Robertson, Esmonde M. (eds), *Paths to War: New Essays on the Origins of the Second World War*, London, 1989

'World Depression: Some Economic Origins of the Second World War' in Boyce and Robertson, 55–95

Brivati, Brian, and Jones, Harriet (eds),*What Difference Did the War Make?*, Leicester, 1993

Buffotot, Patrice, 'La perception du réarmement allemand par les organismes de renseignement français de 1936 à 1939', *RHA*, 3, 1979, 173–84

'Le réarmement aérien allemand et l'approche de la guerre vus par le IIᵉ bureau air français (1936–1939)' in Hildebrand and Werner, 249–324

'The French High Command and the Franco-Soviet Alliance, 1933–1939', *JSS*, 5, 4, 1982, 546–59

Caedel, Martin, *Pacifism in Britain, 1914–1945: The Defining of a Faith*, Oxford, 1980

Cairns, John C., 'A Nation of Shopkeepers in Search of a Suitable France: 1919–1940', *American Historical Review*, 79, 3, 1974, 710–43
'Some Recent Historians and the "Strange Defeat" of 1940', *JMH*, 46, 1974, 60–84

Carlton, David, *Anthony Eden: A Biography*, London, 1981
'Eden, *Blum and the origins of non-intervention*', *JCH*, 6, 3, 1971, 40–55

Castex, Raoul, 'Le problème stratégique colonial, 1939', *Marins et Océans*, 1, 1991, 207–28

Catterall, Peter, and Morris, C.J. (eds), *Britain and the Threat to Stability in Europe, 1918–1945*, Leicester, 1993

Chapman, Herrick, *State Capitalism and Working-Class Radicalism in the French Aircraft Industry*, Berkeley, CA, 1991

Charmley, John, *Chamberlain and the Lost Peace*, London, 1989

Christienne, Charles, 'L'armée de l'air française de Mars 1936 à Septembre 1939' in Hildebrand and Werner, 215–48
'L'armée de l'air française et la crise du 7 Mars 1936', SHAA, *Recueil d'articles et études, 1976–1978*, 45–68
'Le haut commandement français face au progrès technique entre les deux guerres' in Commission Internationale d'Histoire Militaire, ACTA no. 5, Bucharest, 1980
and Buffotot, P., 'L'aéronautique militaire française entre 1919 et 1939', *RHA*, 2, 1977, 9–40

Claque, Monique, 'Vision and Myopia in the "New Politics" of André Tardieu', *FHS*, 8, 1, 1973, 105–29

Clarke, J.J., 'The Nationalisation of War Industries in France, 1936–1937: A Case Study', *JMH*, 49, 1977, 411–30

Clarke, S.V.O., *Exchange-Rate Stabilisation in the mid-1930s. Negotiating the Tripartite Agreement*, Princeton, 1977

Cockett, R.B., *Twilight of Truth: Chamberlain, Appeasement and the Manipulation of the Press*, London, 1989

Coghlan, F., 'Armaments, Economic Policy and Appeasement: Background to British Policy', *History*, 57, 1972, 205–16

Cohen, Michael J., and Kolinsky, Martin (eds), *Britain and the Middle East in the 1930s. Security Problems, 1935–1939*, London, 1992

Cohen, W.B., 'The Colonial Policy of the Popular Front', *FHS*, 7, 3, 1972, 368–93

Cointet, Jean-Paul, *Pierre Laval*, Paris, 1993

Colvin, Ian, *The Chamberlain Cabinet*, London, 1971

Colton, Joel, *Léon Blum: Humanist in Politics*, New York, 1966

Constant, M., 'L'Accord Commercial Franco-Allemand du 10 Juillet 1937', *Revue d'Histoire Diplomatique*, 98, 1984, 108–42

Cornwall, Mark, 'The Rise and Fall of a "Special Relationship"?: Britain and Czechoslovakia, 1930–1948' in Brivati and Jones, 130–50

Coutau-Bégarié, Hervé, and Huan, Claude, *Darlan*, Paris, 1989

Coverdale, J.F., *Italian Intervention in the Spanish Civil War*, Princeton, 1975

Cowman, Ian, 'Main Fleet to Singapore? Churchill, the Admiralty and Force Z', *JSS*, 17, 2, 1994, 79–93

Cross, J.A., *Sir Samuel Hoare, A Political Biography*, London, 1977
*Lord Swinton*, Oxford, 1982

Crozier, Andrew J., *Appeasement and Germany's Last Bid for Colonies*, London, 1988
'Prelude to Munich: British Foreign Policy and Germany, 1935–1938', *European Studies Review*, 6, 1976, 357–81
'The Establishment of the Mandates System 1919–1925: Some Problems Created by the Paris Peace Conference', *JCH*, 14, 1979, 483–513
'Imperial Decline and the Colonial Question in Anglo-German Relations 1919–1939', *European Studies Review*, 11, 1981, 207–42

Cuvallier, Jean-Pierre, *Vincent Auriol et les finances publiques du Front Populaire*, Toulouse, 1978

d'Hoop, Jean-Marie, 'Le problème du réarmement français jusqu'à Mars 1936', in Michel, *La France et l'Allemagne*, 75–89

Dallek, Robert, *Franklin D. Roosevelt and American Foreign Policy, 1932–1945*, Oxford, 1975

Darwin, John, 'Imperialism in Decline? Tendencies in British Policy Between the Wars', *HJ*, 23, 1980, 657–79

Davis, Richard, '*Mésentente Cordiale*: The Failure of the Anglo-French Alliance. Anglo-French Relations During the Ethiopian and Rhineland Crises, 1934–36', *EHQ*, 23, 1993, 513–28

Deist, Wilhelm, *The Wehrmacht and German Rearmament*, London, 1981

Delmas, Jean, 'La perception de la puissance militaire française' in Girault and Frank, 127–40

Dennis, Peter, *The Territorial Army, 1907–1940*, Woodbridge, 1987

Dilks, David N. (ed.), *Retreat from Power. Studies in Britain's Foreign Policy in the Twentieth Century*, London, 1981
*Neville Chamberlain, I: 1869–1929*, Cambridge, 1984

Doise, Jean, and Vaïsse, Maurice, *Diplomatie et outil militaire, 1871–1991*, Paris, 1992

Döscher, Hans-Jürgen, *Das Auswärtige Amt im Dritten Reich*, Berlin, 1987

Doughty, R.A., *The Seeds of Disaster. The Development of French Army Doctrine, 1919–1939*, Hamden, Conn., 1985

Douglas, R., 'Chamberlain and Eden, 1937–1938', *JCH*, 13, 1, 1978, 97–116

Dreifort, John E., *Yvon Delbos at the Quai d'Orsay: French Foreign Policy during the Popular Front, 1936–1938*, Lawrence, KA, 1973

Du Réau, Elisabeth, *Edouard Daladier, 1884–1970*, Paris, 1993

'L'information du "décideur" et l'élaboration de la décision diplomatique française dans les dernières années de la IIIᵉ République', *Relations Internationales*, 32, 1982, 525–41

'Edouard Daladier et l'image de la puissance française en 1938', *RHA*, 3, 1983, 27–39

Duroselle, Jean-Baptiste, *La Décadence 1932–1939, Politique étrangère de la France*, Paris, 1979

Dutailly, Henri, *Les Problèmes de l'armée de terre française, 1935–1939*, Paris, 1980

'Programmes d'armement et structures modernes dans l'armée de terre (1935–1939)' in Hildebrand and Werner, 105–27

Dutter, Gordon, 'Doing Business with the Fascists: French Economic Relations with Italy under the Popular Front', *French History*, 4, 2, 1990, 174–98

Dutton, David, *Simon*, London, 1992

'Eden and Simon at the Foreign Office, 1931–1935', *Review of International Studies*, 20, 1, 1994, 35–52

Edwards, Jill, *The British Government and the Spanish Civil War, 1936–1939*, London, 1979

Ekoko, A. Edho, 'The British Attitude Towards Germany's Colonial Irredentism in Africa in the Inter-War Years', *JCH*, 14, 1979, 287–307

Emmerson, J.T., *The Rhineland Crisis, 7th March 1936, a Study in Multilateral Diplomacy*, London, 1977

Enssle, Manfred, 'Stresemann's Diplomacy Fifty Years after Locarno: Some Recent Perspectives', *HJ*, 20, 4, 1977, 937–48

Facon, Patrick, 'L'aviation dans une revue interarmes de l'entre-deux guerres: 1923–1938', *RHA*, 2, 1977, 103–12

'La visite du général Vuillemin en Allemagne (16–21 août 1938)', SHAA, *Recueil d'articles et études, 1981–1983*, 221–62

'Le haut commandement aérien français et la crise de Munich', *RHA*, 3, 1983, 110–17

Feiling, Keith, *The Life of Neville Chamberlain*, London, 1946

Ferris, John R., 'Worthy of Some Better Enemy? The British Estimate of the Imperial Japanese Army, 1919–1941, and the Fall of Singapore', *Canadian Journal of History*, 28, 1993, 223–56

'Indulged in Too Little? Vansittart, Intelligence and Appeasement', *Diplomacy and Statecraft*, 6, 1, 1995, 122–75

Fitzgerald, E.P., 'France's Middle Eastern Ambitions, the Sykes–Picot Negotiations, and the Oil Fields of Mosul, 1915–1918', *JMH*, 66, 1994, 697–725

Frank, Robert, *Le Prix du réarmement français, 1935–1939*, Paris, 1982
*La Hantise du déclin. La France, 1920–1960: finances, défense et identité nationale*, Paris, 1994
'A propos des aspects financières du réarmement français (1935–1939)', *RHDGM*, 102, 1976, 1–20
'Le Front populaire a-t-il perdu la guerre?', *L'Histoire*, 58, 1983, 58–66

Frank, Willard C., 'The Spanish Civil War and the Coming of the Second World War', *IHR*, 9, 3, 1987, 368–409

French, David, *British Strategy and War Aims, 1914–1916*, London, 1986

Fridenson, Patrick, 'L'idéologie des grands constructeurs dans l'entre deux-guerres', *Le Mouvement Social*, 81, 1972, 51–68

Fuchser, L.W., *Neville Chamberlain and Appeasement, a Study in the Politics of History*, New York, 1982

Gallagher, M.D., 'Léon Blum and the Spanish Civil War', *JCH*, 6, 3, 1971, 56–64

Gannon, F.R., *The British Press and Germany, 1936–1939*, Oxford, 1981

Geyer, Michael, 'The Crisis of Military Leadership in the 1930s', *JSS*, 14, 4, 1991, 448–62

Gilbert, Mark, 'Pacifist Attitudes to Nazi Germany, 1936–1945', *JCH*, 27, 3, 1992, 493–511

Gilbert, Martin, and Gott, Richard, *The Appeasers*, London, 1963

Girault, René, 'Léon Blum, la dévaluation de 1936 et la conduite de la politique extérieure de la France', *Relations Internationales*, 13, 1978, 91–109
'La décision gouvernementale en politique extérieure' in Remond and Bourdin, 209–27
'The Impact of the Economic Situation on the Foreign Policy of France, 1936–1939' in Kettenacker and Mommsen, 209–26
and Frank, Robert (eds), *La Puissance en Europe, 1938–1940*, Paris, 1984
and Frank, Robert (eds), *Turbulente Europe et nouveaux mondes, 1914–41*, Paris, 1988

Goldman, Aaron L., 'Sir Robert Vansittart's Search for Italian Cooperation against Hitler, 1933–36', *JCH*, 9, 3, 1974, 93–130

Goldstein, Erik, *Winning the Peace: British Diplomatic Strategy, Peace Planning and the Paris Peace Conference, 1916–1920*, Oxford, 1991

Gordon, Andrew, *British Seapower and Procurement Between the Wars*, London, 1988
'The Admiralty and Imperial Overstretch, 1902–1941', *JSS*, 17, 1, 1994, 63–85

Graham, Helen, and Preston, Paul, *The Popular Front in Europe*, London, 1987

Granatstein, J.L., and Bothwell, Robert, '"A Self-Evident National Duty": Canadian Foreign Policy, 1935–1939', *Journal of Imperial and Commonwealth History*, 3, 2, 1975, 212–33

Greene, Nathaniel, *Crisis and Decline. The French Socialist Party in the Popular Front Era*, New York, 1969

Greenwood, Sean, '"Caligula's Horse" Revisited: Sir Thomas Inskip as Minister for the Co-ordination of Defence, 1936–1939', *JSS*, 17, 2, 1994, 17–38

Grenzebach, William, *Germany's Informal Empire in East-Central Europe. German Economic Policy Towards Yugoslavia and Rumania 1933–1939*, Stuttgart, 1988

Gretton, Peter, 'The Nyon Conference – The Naval Aspect', *EHR*, 90, 1975, 103–12

Guinn, Paul, 'On Throwing Ballast in Foreign Policy: Poincaré, the Entente and the Ruhr Occupation', *EHQ*, 18, 1988, 427–37

Haggie, Paul, *Britannia at Bay: The Defence of the British Empire against Japan, 1931–1941*, Oxford, 1981

Haight jun., John McVickar, *American Aid to France, 1938–1940*, New York, 1970

Hall III, H.H., 'The Foreign Policy-Making Process in Britain, 1934–1935 and the Origins of the Anglo-German Naval Agreement', *HJ*, 19, 1976, 477–99

Hamilton, Keith A., 'A Question of Status: British Diplomats and the Uses and Abuses of French', *Historical Research*, LX, 1987, 125–9

Harris, J.P., 'Two War Ministers: A Re-assessment of Duff Cooper and Hore–Belisha', *War and Society*, 6, 1, 1988, 65–78
'British Military Intelligence and the Rise of German Mechanized Forces, 1929–1940', *INS*, 6, 2, 1991, 395–417

Harvey, Charles E., *The Rio Tinto Company: An Economic History of a Leading International Mining Concern*, Penzance, 1981
'Politics and Pyrites during the Spanish Civil War', *Economic History Review*, 31, 1, 1978, 89–104

Haslam, Jonathan, *The Soviet Union and the Struggle for Collective Security in Europe, 1933–1939*, London, 1984
'The Comintern and the Origins of the Popular Front 1934–1935', *HJ*, 22, 3, 1979, 673–91

# Bibliography

Heineman, John L., *Hitler's First Foreign Minister. Constantin Freiherr von Neurath, Diplomat and Statesman*, Berkeley, 1979

Helmreich, Jonathan, 'The Negotiation of the Franco-Belgian Military Accord of 1920', *FHS*, 3, 3, 1964, 360–78

Henderson, W.O., *The German Colonial Empire, 1884–1919*, London, 1993

Hildebrand, Klaus, *The Foreign Policy of the Third Reich*, London, 1973 and Werner, Karl Ferdinand (eds), *Deutschland und Frankreich, 1936–1939*, Munich, 1981

Hillgruber, A., *Germany and the Two World Wars*, Cambridge, Mass., 1981

Hoisington jun., William A., *The Casablanca Connection: French Colonial Policy, 1936–1943*, Chapel Hill, 1984
'France and Islam: the Haut Comité Méditerranéen and French North Africa' in Joffé, 78–90

Holland, R.F., *Britain and the Commonwealth Alliance, 1918–1939*, London, 1981

Chalmers Hood III, Ronald, *Royal Republicans. The French Naval Dynasties Between the World Wars*, Baton Rouge, 1985
'The French Navy and Parliament between the Wars', *IHR*, 6, 3, 1984, 386–403

Horn, Martin, 'External Finance in Anglo-French Relations in the First World War, 1914–1917', *IHR*, 17, 1, 1995, 51–77

Hovi, Kalervo, *Cordon sanitaire or Barrière de l'est? The Emergence of the New French Eastern European Alliance Policy 1917–1919*, Turku, 1975
*Alliances de revers: Stabilization of France's Alliance Policies in East Central Europe 1919–1921*, Turku, 1984

Howard, Michael E., *The Continental Commitment: The Dilemma of British Defence Policy in the Era of the Two World Wars*, London, 1972

Ingram, Norman, *The Politics of Dissent: Pacifism in France, 1919–1939*, Oxford, 1991

Irvine, William D., *French Conservatism in Crisis: The Republican Federation in the 1930s*, Baton Rouge, 1979

Jackson, Julian, *The Politics of Depression in France, 1932–1936*, Cambridge, 1985
*The Popular Front in France: Defending Democracy, 1934–38*, Cambridge, 1988

Jackson, Peter, 'French Military Intelligence and Czechoslovakia, 1938', *Diplomacy and Statecraft*, 5, 1, 1994, 81–106
'La Perception de la puissance aérienne allemande et son influence sur la politique extérieure française pendant les crises internationales

de 1938 à 1939', *RHA*, 197, 4, 1994, 76–87

'France and the Guarantee to Roumania, April 1939', *INS*, 10, 2, 1995, 242–72

Jeanneney, Jean-Marcel, 'La politique économique de Léon Blum' in Renouvin and Rémond, 207–32

Joffé, George (ed.), *North Africa: Nation, State and Region*, London, 1993

Joll, James, *Three Intellectuals in Politics*, New York, 1960

Jordan, Nicole, *The Popular Front and Central Europe: The Dilemmas of French Impotence, 1918–1940*, Cambridge, 1992

'The Cut Price War on the Peripheries: The French General Staff, the Rhineland and Czechoslovakia' in Boyce and Robertson, 128–66

'Léon Blum and Czechoslovakia, 1936–1938', *French History*, 5, 1, 1991, 48–73

'Maurice Gamelin, Italy and the Eastern Alliances', *JSS*, 14, 4, 1991, 428–41

Judt, Tony, *Marxism and the French Left. Studies in Labour and Politics in France, 1830–1981*, Oxford, 1986

Julien, Charles-André, 'Léon Blum et les pays d'Outre-Mer' in Renouvin and Rémond, 377–90

Kaiser, David E., *Economic Diplomacy and the Origins of the Second World War: Germany, Britain, France and Eastern Europe, 1930–1939*, Princeton, 1980

Kemp, Tom, 'The French Economy under the Franc Poincaré', *Economic History Review*, 24, 1971, 92–9

Kent, Bruce, *The Spoils of War: The Politics, Economics and Diplomacy of Reparations, 1918–1932*, Oxford, 1989

Kergoat, Jacques, *La France du Front Populaire*, Paris, 1986

Kershaw, Ian, *The Nazi Dictatorship*, London, 1989

Kettenacker, L., and Mommsen, W. (eds), *The Fascist Challenge and the Policy of Appeasement*, London, 1983

Kirkland, Faris H., 'Governmental Policy and Combat Effectiveness: France, 1920–1940', *Armed Forces and Society*, 18, 2, 1992, 175–91

Kitchen, Martin, *Europe between the Wars: A Political History*, London, 1988

Knock, Thomas J., *To End all Wars. Woodrow Wilson and the Quest for a New World Order*, Oxford, 1992

Koulakssis, Ahmed, *Le Parti Socialiste et l'Afrique du Nord de Jaurès à Blum*, Paris, 1991

Kuisel, R.F., *Capitalism and the State in Modern France*, Cambridge, 1981

Lacouture, Jean, *Léon Blum*, Paris, 1977/trans. New York, 1982

Langhorne, Richard (ed.), *Diplomacy and Intelligence during the Second World War*, Cambridge, 1985

Larkin, Maurice, *France since the Popular Front. Government and People, 1936–1986*, Oxford, 1988

Lee, Bradford A., *Britain and the Sino-Japanese War, 1937–1939: A Study in the Dilemmas of British Decline*, Stanford, 1973
'Strategy, Arms and the Collapse of France, 1930–1940' in Langhorne, 43–67

Lefranc, Georges, *Histoire du Front Populaire*, Paris, 1974

Le Goyet, Pierre, *France-Pologne 1919–1939. De l'amitié romantique à la méfiance réciproque*, Paris, 1991
'Evolution de la doctrine d'emploi de l'aviation française entre 1919 et 1939', *RHDGM*, 73, 1969, 3–41

Little, Douglas, *Malevolent Neutrality: The United States, Great Britain and the Origins of the Spanish Civil War*, Ithaca, 1985
'Red Scare, 1936: Anti-bolshevism and the Origins of British Non-Intervention in the Spanish Civil War', *JCH*, 23, 1988, 291–311

Lowe, Peter, *Great Britain and the origins of the Pacific War: A Study of British Policy in East Asia, 1937–1941*, Oxford, 1977

Lungu, Dov B., *Romania and the Great Powers, 1933–1940*, London, 1989

McDougall, Walter A., *France's Rhineland Diplomacy, 1914–1924. The Last Bid for a Balance of Power in Europe*, Princeton, 1978

McIntyre, W. David, *The Rise and Fall of the Singapore Naval Base, 1919–1942*, London, 1979

McKercher, B.J.C., 'No Eternal Friends or Enemies: British Defence Policy and the Problem of the United States, 1919–1939', *Canadian Journal of History*, 28, 1993, 257–93
'The Last Old Diplomat: Sir Robert Vansittart and British Foreign Policy', *Diplomacy and Statecraft*, 6, 1, 1995, 1–38

MacDonald, C.A., *The United States, Britain and Appeasement, 1936–1939*, London, 1981
'Economic Appeasement and the German "Moderates", 1937–1939', *Past and Present*, 56, 1972, 105–35

Maiolo, Joseph A., '"I believe the Hun is cheating." British Admiralty Technical Intelligence and the German Navy, 1936–39', *INS*, 11, 1, 1996, 32–58

Marder, Arthur J., *From the Dardanelles to Oran. Studies of the Royal Navy in War and Peace, 1915–1940*, Oxford, 1974
*Old Friends, New Enemies. The Royal Navy and the Imperial Japanese Navy: Strategic Illusions, 1936–1941*, Oxford, 1981
'The Royal Navy and the Ethiopian Crisis of 1935–1936', *American Historical Review*, 75, 3, 1970, 1327–56

Marès, Antoine, 'La faillite des relations franco-tchécoslovaques: la mission militaire française à Prague, 1926–1938', *RHDGM*, 28, 111, 1978, 45–71

'Les attachés militaires en Europe centrale et la notion de la puissance en 1938', *RHA*, 1, 1983, 60–72

Marguerat, Philippe, 'Positions économiques de la France dans la zone de la petite entente au cours des années trente', in S. Friedländer, H. Kapur and A. Reszler, *L'Historien et les relations internationales*, Geneva, 1981

Marquand, David, *Ramsay MacDonald*, London, 1977

Marseille, Jacques, *Empire colonial et capitalisme français: Histoire d'un divorce*, Paris, 1984

Martin, Jean, *L'Empire triomphant 1871–1936, II: Maghreb, Indochine, Madagascar*, Paris, 1990

Masson, Philippe, *La Marine française et la guerre 1939–1945*, Paris, 1991

'La marine française et la stratégie alliée (1938–1939)' in Hildebrand and Werner, 153–66

'Réarmement et marine française', *Revue Internationale d'Histoire Militaire*, 73, 1991, 71–80

Michaelis, Meir, 'Italy's Mediterranean Strategy, 1935–1939' in Cohen and Kolinsky, 41–60

Michel, Henri, *Le Procès de Riom*, Paris, 1979

(ed.), *La France et l'Allemagne 1932–1936*, Paris, 1980

Middlemas, Keith, *Diplomacy of Illusion: The British Government and Germany, 1937–1939*, London, 1972

and Barnes, John, *Baldwin: A Biography*, London, 1969

Mills, W.C., 'The Nyon Conference: Neville Chamberlain, Anthony Eden and the appeasement of Italy in 1937', *IHR*, 15, 1993, 1–22

Milza, Pierre, 'L'ultra droite des années trente', in Winock, 157–90

Minot, Bernard, 'La Chute du premier gouvernement Blum et l'action des commissions des finances, 1936–1937', *Revue d'Economie Politique*, 1, 1982, 35–51

Moch, Jules, *Rencontres avec Darlan et Eisenhower, I: Souvenirs sur l'amiral de la flotte française, Darlan*, Paris, 1968

*Rencontres avec Léon Blum*, Paris, 1970

Moïsuc, Viorica, 'L'écroulement des alliances de la Roumanie à la veille de la deuxième guerre mondiale', *RHDGM*, 140, 1985, 1–21

Monnet, François, *Refaire la République. André Tardieu: Une dérive réactionnaire (1876–1945)*, Paris, 1993

Moradiellos, Enrique, 'The Origins of British Non-Intervention in the Spanish Civil War: Anglo-Spanish Relations in early 1936', *EHQ*, 21, 1991, 339–64

'British Political Strategy in the Face of the Military Rising of 1936 in Spain', *CEH*, 1, 2, 1992, 123–37

'Appeasement and Non-Intervention: British Policy during the Spanish Civil War' in Catterall and Morris, 94–104

Morewood, Steven, 'Anglo-Italian Rivalry in the Mediterranean and the Middle East, 1935–1940' in Boyce and Robertson, 167–98

'Protecting the Jugular Vein of Empire: The Suez Canal in British Defence Strategy, 1919–1941', *War and Society*, 10, 1, 1992, 81–107

Morrisey, Charles, and Ramsay, M.A., 'Sir Robert Vansittart and the Defence Requirements Sub-Committee', *Diplomacy and Statecraft*, 6, 1, 1995, 39–60

Mouré, Kenneth, *Managing the Franc Poincaré. Economic Understanding and Political Constraint in French Monetary Policy, 1928–1936*, Cambridge, 1991

'"Une éventualité absolument exclue." French reluctance to devalue, 1933–1936', *FHS*, 15, 3, 1988, 479–505

'The Limits to Central Bank Co-operation, 1916–36', *CEH*, I, 1992, 259–79

Murfett, Malcolm H., *Fool-Proof Relations. The Search for Anglo-American Naval Cooperation during the Chamberlain Years, 1937–1940*, Singapore, 1984

'Living in the Past: A Critical Re-examination of the Singapore Naval Strategy, 1918–1941', *War and Society*, 11, 1, 1993, 73–103

Murray, Williamson, *The Change in the European Balance of Power: The Path to Ruin*, Princeton, 1984

'Appeasement and Intelligence', *INS*, 2, 4, 1987, 47–66

Nouschi, Marc, 'La Marine française aux débuts de la guerre d'Espagne', *Bulletin de la Société d'Histoire Moderne*, 25, 4, 1978, 15–36

Omissi, David, *Air Power and Colonial Control. The Royal Air Force, 1919–1939*, Manchester, 1990

'The Mediterranean and the Middle East in British Global Strategy, 1935–1939' in Cohen and Kolinsky, 3–20

Oprea, I.M., *Nicolae Titulescu's Diplomatic Activity*, Bucharest, 1968

Orde, Anne, 'Britain and European Reconstruction after the Great War' in Catterall and Morris, 8–14

Ovendale, R., *Appeasement and the English Speaking World*, Cardiff, 1975

Overy, Richard J., *Goering 'The Iron Man'*, London, 1984

'Göring's 'Multi-national Empire', in Teichova and Cottrell, 267–98

'Hitler's War Plans and the German Economy', in Boyce and Robertson, 96–127

'Air Power and the Origins of Deterrence Theory before 1939', *JSS*, 15, 1, 1992, 73–101

Paret, P., Craig, G.A., and Gilbert, F., *Makers of Modern Strategy from Machiavelli to the Nuclear Age*, Princeton, 1986

Parker, R.A.C., *Chamberlain and Appeasement. British Policy and the Coming of the Second World War*, London, 1993

'Great Britain, France and the Ethiopian Crisis, 1935–1936', *EHR*, 89, 1974, 269–97

'The Economics of Rearmament and Foreign Policy: The United Kingdom before 1939', *JCH*, 10, 4, 1975, 637–48

'British Rearmament 1936–1939. Treasury, Trade Unions and Skilled Labour', *EHR*, 1981, 306–43

'Perceptions de la puissance par les décideurs britanniques 1938–1939: Le Cabinet' in Girault and Frank, 45–54

Passmore, Kevin, 'The French Third Republic: Stalemate Society or Cradle of Fascism?', *French History*, 7, 4, 1993, 417–49

Pearton, Maurice, *Oil and the Roumanian State, 1895–1948*, Oxford, 1981

Peden, G.C., *British Rearmament and the Treasury, 1932–1939*, Edinburgh, 1979

'Sir Warren Fisher and British Rearmament against Germany', *EHR*, 94, 370, 1979, 29–47

'The Burden of Imperial Defence and the Continental Commitment Reconsidered', *HJ*, 27, 1984, 405–23

'A Matter of Timing: The Economic Background to British Foreign Policy, 1937–1939', *History*, 69, 225, 1984, 15–28

'The "Treasury View" on Public Works and Employment in the Inter-War Period', *Economic History Review*, 37, 2, 1984, 167–81

Peters, A.R., *Anthony Eden at the Foreign Office, 1931–1938*, Aldershot, 1986

Pike, David Wingeate, *Les Français et la Guerre d'Espagne*, Paris, 1975

Ploquin, Jacques, 'Alliances militaires et marchés d'avions pendant l'entre-deux-guerres. Le cas français (1936–1940)', *RHA*, 4, 1985, 42–50

Porch, Douglas, 'French Intelligence and the Fall of France, 1930–1940', *INS*, 4, 1, 1989, 28–58

Pordea, G.A., 'Un précurseur de l'unité européene: Nicolae Titulescu', *Revue d'Histoire Diplomatique*, 92, 1982

Pratt, L.R., *East of Malta, West of Suez: Britain's Mediterranean Crisis, 1936–1939*, Cambridge, 1975

Preston, Paul, (ed.) *Revolution and War in Spain, 1931–1939*, London, 1984 *Franco: A Biography*, London, 1993

Radice, Lisanne, 'The Eastern Pact, 1933–1935: A Last Attempt at European Co-operation', *Slavonic and East European Review*, 1, 1977, 45–64

Rémond, René, 'L'image de l'Allemagne dans l'opinion publique française de Mars 1936 à Septembre 1939' in Hildebrand and Werner, 3–16

and Bourdin, Janine (eds), *Edouard Daladier Chef de Gouvernement, Avril 1938–Septembre 1939*, Paris, 1977

Renouvin, Pierre, and Rémond, René (eds), *Léon Blum Chef de Gouvernement, 1936–1937*, Paris, 1967

Reussner, André, *Les Conversations franco-britanniques d'Etat-Major 1935–1939*, Vincennes, 1969

Reynolds, David, *The Creation of the Anglo-American Alliance, 1931–1941. A Study in Competitive Cooperation*, London, 1981

Reynolds, Siân, 'Women and the Popular Front in France: The Case of the Three Women Ministers', *French History*, 8, 2, 1994, 196–224

Rhodes-James, Robert, *Anthony Eden*, London, 1986

Richardson, R.C., and Stone, G.A. (eds), *Decisions and Diplomacy: Essays in Twentieth Century International History*, London, 1994

Roberts, Andrew, *The 'Holy Fox': A Biography of Lord Halifax*, London, 1991

Roberts, Geoffrey, *The Soviet Union and the Origins of the Second World War*, London, 1995

'A Soviet Bid for Coexistence with Nazi Germany, 1935–1937: The Kandelaki Affair', *IHR*, 16, 3, 1994, 441–60

Rock, W.R., *Appeasement on Trial: British Foreign Policy and its Critics, 1938–1939*, Hamden, Conn., 1966

Roi, M.L., 'From the Stresa Front to the Triple Entente: Sir Robert Vansittart, the Abyssinian Crisis and the Containment of Germany', *Diplomacy and Statecraft*, 6, 1, 1995, 61–90

Rose, Norman, *Vansittart, Study of a Diplomat*, London, 1978

'The Resignation of Anthony Eden', *HJ*, 25, 4, 1982, 911–31

Roskill, S., *Hankey, Man of Secrets, III: 1931–1963*, London, 1963

*Naval Policy between the Wars, II: The Period of Reluctant Rearmament, 1930–1939*, London, 1974

Rossiter, Adrian, 'Popular Front Economic Policy and the Matignon Negotiations', *HJ*, 30, 3, 1987, 663–84

Rostow, Nicholas, *Anglo-French Relations, 1934–1936*, London, 1984

Rothwell, Victor, *Anthony Eden: A Political Biography*, Manchester, 1992

'The Mission of Sir Frederick Leith-Ross to the Far East, 1935–1936', *HJ*, 18, 1975, 147–69

Sabatier de Lachadenède, René, *La Marine française et la guerre civile d'Espagne, 1936–1939*, Paris, 1993

Sakwa, George, 'The "Renewal" of the Franco-Polish Alliance in 1936 and the Rambouillet Agreement', *Polish Review*, 16, 2, 1971, 45–66

'The Franco-Polish Alliance and the Remilitarization of the Rhineland', *HJ*, 16, 1, 1973, 125–46

Salerno, Reynolds M., 'Multilateral Strategy and Diplomacy: The Anglo-German Naval Agreement and the Mediterranean Crisis, 1935–1936', *JSS*, 17, 2, 1994, 39–78

Sanson, Rosemonde, 'La perception de la puissance par l'Alliance Démocratique', *RHMC*, 31, 1984, 658–65

Santore, John, 'The Comintern's United Front Initiative of May 1934: French or Soviet Inspiration?', *Canadian Journal of History*, 16, 1981, 405–21

Schlesinger, M., 'The Development of the Radical Party in the Third Republic: The New Radical Movement, 1926–1932', *JMH*, 46, 1974, 476–501

Schmidt, Gustav, *The Politics and Economics of Appeasement. British Foreign Policy in the 1930s*, Leamington Spa, 1986

Schuker, Stephen A., *The End of French Predominance in Europe: The Financial Crisis of 1924 and the Adoption of the Dawes Plan*, Chapel Hill, 1976

'France and the Remilitarization of the Rhineland, 1936', *FHS*, 14, 1986, 299–338

Shamir, Haim, *Economic Crisis and French Foreign Policy, 1930–1936*, Leiden, 1989

Sharp, Alan, *The Versailles Settlement: Peacemaking in Paris, 1919*, London, 1991

Shay, R.P., *British Rearmament in the Thirties: Politics and Profits*, Princeton, 1977

Shorrock, William I., *From Ally to Enemy: The Enigma of Fascist Italy in French Diplomacy, 1920–1940*, Kent, Ohio, 1988

Smelser, Ronald M., *The Sudeten Problem, 1933–1938. Volkstumspolitik and the Formulation of Nazi Foreign Policy*, Folkestone, 1975

Smith, Leonard V., '"War and Politics": The French Army Mutinies of 1917', *War in History*, 2, 1995, 180–201

Smith, Malcolm, *British Air Strategy between the Wars*, Oxford, 1984

'The Royal Air Force, Air Power and British Foreign Policy, 1932–1937', *JCH*, 12, 1, 1977, 153–74

'Rearmament and Deterrence in Britain in the 1930s', *JSS*, 1, 3, 1978, 313–37

'A Matter of Faith: British Strategic Air Doctrine before 1939', *JCH*, 15, 3, 1980, 423–42

Soutou, Georges-Henri, 'L'impérialisme du pauvre: la politique économique du gouvernement français en Europe Centrale et Orientale de 1918 à 1929. Essai d'interprétation', *Relations Internationales*, 7, 1976, 219–39

'L'alliance franco-polonaise (1925–1933) ou comment s'en débarrasser?', *Revue d'histoire diplomatique*, 2, 1981, 295–348

'L'Allemagne et la France en 1919', in Bariéty, *France et l'Allemagne*

Sternhall, Z., *Ni Droite, Ni Gauche. L'idéologie fasciste en France*, Paris, 1983

Stevenson, David, *French War Aims against Germany, 1914–1919*, Oxford, 1982

Stoecker, Helmuth (ed.), *German Imperialism in Africa. From its Beginnings until the Second World War*, London, 1986

Stolfi, R.H.S., 'Equipment for Victory in France in 1940', *History*, 55, 1970, 1–20

Stone, Glyn A., *The Oldest Ally. Britain and the Portuguese Connection, 1936–1941*, Bury St Edmunds, 1994

'The European Great Powers and the Spanish Civil War, 1936–1939' in Boyce and Robertson, 199–232

'Britain, France and the Spanish problem, 1936–1939' in Richardson and Stone, 129–52

Stora, Benjamin, *Nationalistes algériens et révolutionnaires français au temps du Front Populaire*, Paris, 1987

Sullivan, Brian R., 'A Fleet in Being: The Rise and Fall of Italian Sea Power, 1861–1943', *IHR*, 10, 1, 1988, 106–24

'Italian Naval Power and the Washington Conference of 1921–1922', *Diplomacy and Statecraft*, 4, 3, 1993, 220–48

'The Italian–Ethiopian War, October 1935–November 1941: Causes, Conduct and Consequences', in A. Hamish Ion and E.J. Harrington (eds), *Great Powers and Little Wars. The Limits of Power*, Westport, Conn., 1993, 167–202

Teichova, Alice, and Cottrell, P.L., *International Business and Central Europe, 1918–1939*, Leicester, 1983

Thomas, Martin, 'French Economic Affairs and Rearmament: The First Crucial Months, June–September 1936', *JCH*, 27, 4, 1992, 659–70

'Plans and Problems of the Armée de l'Air in the Defence of French North Africa before the Fall of France', *French History*, 7, 4, 1993, 472–95

'To arm an Ally: French Arms Sales to Romania, 1926–1940', *JSS*, 19, 2, 1996, 231–59

Thompson, N., *The Anti-Appeasers. Conservative Opposition to Appeasement in the 1930s*, London, 1971

Trachtenberg, Marc, *Reparation in World Politics: France and European Economic Diplomacy, 1916–1923*, New York, 1980

Türkes, Mustafa, 'The Balkan Pact and its Immediate Implications for the Balkan States, 1930–34', *Middle Eastern Studies*, 30, 1, 1994, 123–44

# Bibliography

Turlotte, Michel, 'L'alliance polonaise à travers les archives de l'Etat-Major de l'Armée', *RHA*, 4, 1985, 70–85

Turner, Arthur, 'Anglo-French Financial Relations in the 1920s', *EHQ*, 25, 1, 1996, 31–56

Vaïsse, Maurice, *Sécurité d'abord: la politique française en matière de désarmement*, Paris, 1981

*Le Pacifisme en Europe des années 1920 aux années 1950*, Brussels, 1993

'Le procès de l'aviation de bombardement', *RHA*, 2, 1977, 41–61

'L'adaptation du Quai d'Orsay aux nouvelles conditions diplomatiques (1918–1939)', *RHMC*, 32, 1985, 145–62

Vennesson, Pascal, 'Institution and Airpower: The Making of the French Air Force', *JSS*, 18, 1, 1995, 36–67

Waites, Neville (ed.), *Troubled Neighbours: Franco-British Relations in the Twentieth Century*, London, 1971

Wall, Irwin M., *French Communism in the Era of Stalin*, London, 1983

'The Resignation of the First Popular Front Government of Léon Blum, June 1937', *FHS*, 6, 4, 1970, 538–54

'Socialists and Bureaucrats: The Blum Government and the French Administration, 1936–1937', *International Review of Social History*, 19, 3, 1974, 325–46

Wandycz, Piotr, *France and her Eastern Allies, 1919–1925*, Minneapolis, 1962

*The Twilight of France's Eastern Alliances, 1926–1936. French–Czechoslovak–Polish Relations from Locarno to the Remilitarisation of the Rhineland*, Princeton, 1988

'The Little Entente: Sixty Years Later', *Slavonic and East European Review*, 59, 1981, 548–64

Wark, Wesley K., *The Ultimate Enemy: British Intelligence and Nazi Germany, 1933–1939*, Ithaca, NY, 1985

'British Intelligence on the German Air Force and Aircraft Industry, 1933–1939', *HJ*, 25, 3, 1982, 627–48

'Three Military Attachés at Berlin in the 1930s: Soldier-Statesmen and the Limits of Ambiguity', *IHR*, 9, 4, 1987, 586–611

Warner, Geoffrey, *Pierre Laval and the Eclipse of France*, London, 1968

Watt, D.C., *Too Serious a Business: European Armed Forces and the Approach of the Second World War*, London, 1975

*How War Came. The Immediate Origins of the Second World War, 1938–1939*, London, 1989

Weinberg, G.L., *The Foreign Policy of Hitler's Germany*, vols I–II, London, 1970 and 1980

Whealey, Robert H., *Hitler and Spain: The Nazi Role in the Spanish Civil War*, Lexington, Ky., 1989

'How Franco Financed his War – Reconsidered', *JCH*, 12, 1, 1977, 133–52

'Economic Influence of the Great Powers in the Spanish Civil War: From the Popular Front to the Second World War', *IHR*, 5, 2, 1983, 229–54

Wileman, Donald G., 'P-E Flandin and the Alliance Démocratique, 1929–1939', *French History*, 4, 2, 1990, 139–73

Williamson, David G., *The British in Germany, 1918–1930: The Reluctant Occupiers*, Oxford, 1991

Winock, Michael (ed.), *Histoire de l'extrême droite en France*, Paris, 1993

Wolfe, M., *The French Franc between the Wars, 1919–1939*, New York, 1951

Wright, Jonathan, 'Stresemann and Locarno', *CEH*, 4, 2, 1995, 109–31

Young, Robert J., *In Command of France. French Foreign Policy and Military Planning, 1933–1940*, Cambridge, Mass., 1978

'The Strategic Dream: French Air Doctrine in the Inter-War Period, 1919–1939', *JCH*, 9, 1974, 57–76

'Soldier and Diplomats: The French Embassy and Franco-Italian Relations, 1935–6', *JSS*, 7, 1984, 74–91

'French Military Intelligence and the Franco-Italian Alliance, 1933–1939', *HJ*, 28, 1, 1985, 143–68

'The Use and Abuse of Fear: France and the Air Menace in the 1930s', *INS*, 2, 4, 1987, 88–109

'The Making of a Foreign Minister: Louis Barthou (1862–1934)', in M. Fry (ed.), *Power, Personalities and Politics*, London, 1992, 83–106

Zeraffa, Danièle, 'La perception de la puissance par le Parti Communiste', *RHMC*, 31, 1984, 636–57

# Index

# Index

and War Ministry, 54, 150–1
Darlan, Admiral Jean-François
  and colonial defence, 131–2
  and Italy, 57–8, 208, 217
  and Ministry of Marine, 57, 131–2
  and naval rearmament, 158, 162–3,
    167, 196, 207–8
  and Spanish civil war, 91–2, 217
Dawes Plan, 9–10, 118
Déat, Marcel, 34
Decoux, Admiral, 91
Defence Loans Bill/Act (Feb. 1937),
  146, 161–2
Defence (Plans) Committee, 146, 207
Defence Requirements Committee
  (DRC), 146
Delavignette, Robert, 129
Delbos, Yvon, 66, 181
  and appeasement, 66, 73, 128, 133–7,
    234
  and eastern alliances, 182–90, 212–13
  and rearmament, 158, 166
  and Spanish civil war, 90–1, 95–8,
    100, 103, 107, 214, 219
  appointment, 55, 60, 205
Delmas, Lieutenant-Colonel Jules,
  186–7, 193, 212
Denain, General Victor, 148
devaluation, *see* Tripartite agreement
Deverell, Field Marshal Sir Cyril, 41,
  148, 167
Devèze, Albert, 30
Dieckhoff, Hans, 38
Dill, General Sir John, 41, 156
Disarmament Conference (1932–34), 13,
  16–17, 58, 78
Dominions, 77–8, 210
Doriot, Jacques, 18
Doumergue, Gaston, 18
Drummond, Sir Eric, 99–100, 218
Duff Cooper, Alfred, 156, 159, 163
Dumanois, General Paul, 31
Dumesnil, Jacques-Louis, 57
Durand-Viel, Admiral Georges, 40, 57–8,
  92, 153–4

Eden, Anthony
  and colonial/economic appeasement,
    64, 73, 117, 119, 121–7 *passim*,
    134–6
  and First World War, 7
  and Italo-Ethiopian war, 43
  and Popular Front, 56, 60, 62, 188–9,
    207, 233
  and resignation, 217–20

and Spanish civil war, 91, 96, 101–4,
  216–20
and western pact, 66–7, 177, 180–1,
  183, 209–11
  *see also* appeasement; Foreign Office
Empire (British), 8, 11, 15, 78, 100, 156,
  233
Empire (French), 11, 32, 76, 98, 116,
  121, 125, 128–33, 208
Englis, Dr, 116
entente cordiale, 7
Etat-Major de l'Armée (EMA), 157–8,
  164, 197
Etat-Major de l'Armée de l'Air (EMAA),
  100, 150, 155, 164
Etat-Major Général (EMG), 67, 98, 100,
  195
Etat-Major de la Marine (EMM), 31, 57,
  101, 132
Etat-Major section d'Outre-Mer, 90

Faucher, General Louis, 193, 196
Faure, Paul, 55
Fédération Républicaine, 197
Féquant, General Philippe, 150–1, 165,
  167, 195–6
Field Force (British), 41–2, 145, 155–9,
  167
Finance Ministry (French), 6, 9–10, 35,
  160–1, 207, 213
First World War, 6–7, 146
Fisher, Sir Warren, 156, 158, 160
Flandin, Pierre-Etienne, 90, 129, 234
  and Italo-Ethiopian war, 44–5, 56
  and Rhineland remilitarization, 27–41
    *passim*
Foch, Marshal Ferdinand, 12
Foreign Office, 18, 27, 30, 37, 41, 43,
  64, 69, 73, 99, 102, 105, 115–9,
  127, 159, 163, 179, 189–90, 210,
  215, 220
  central department, 30, 37, 60, 67, 73,
    77, 90, 93, 118–19, 123–4, 136,
    188, 211
  southern department, 90, 93
foreign policy committee, 64, 68, 96–7,
  122–3, 125–7, 135, 181
Fournier, Charles, 207
Fournier, Lieutenant-Colonel, 167, 221
*franc Poincaré*, 10
France
  air force (armée de l'air), 31–2, 145,
    147–53, 155, 164–7, 176, 187,
    192–6, 229–30
  alliance with Britain, 3, 6

# Index

Haining, General Robert, 158
Halifax, Viscount Edward, 7, 64, 73, 181, 230
  and colonial/economic appeasement, 123, 127, 136, 210–12
  and Rhineland remilitarization, 30, 36, 40
  and Spanish civil war, 92–3, 105
  and visit to Germany (Nov. 1937), 210–12, 215, 231
Hammill, Captain, Naval Attaché, Paris, 163
Hankey, Sir Maurice, 27, 41, 64, 91, 106, 132, 156, 179, 205, 211, 219, 230
Harvey, Oliver, 29
Haushofer, Albrecht, 76
Haut Comité Méditerranéen, 90
Haut Comité Militaire (HCM), 30, 147
Henderson, Sir Nevile, 210–11, 231
Herriot, Edouard, 16, 54–5, 74, 96, 190
Hess, Rudolf, 191
Hitler, Adolf, 2, 16, 19, 27–9, 37, 60, 65–6, 68, 72, 76–7, 99, 115, 123, 125, 137, 177, 180, 205, 221, 231
Hoare, Sir Reginald, 184
Hoare, Sir Samuel, 20, 27, 60, 64, 91, 101–3, 123, 127, 162, 179, 189, 211, 218, 230
Hodza, Dr Milan, 136, 192
Hoesch, Leopold von, 67
Hopkins, Sir Richard, 63, 160–1
Hugenberg, Alfred, 65
Hungary, 12, 184, 212–13

Imperial conference (1937), 137, 210
Industrial Intelligence Centre (IIC), 66, 165
Inskip, Sir Thomas, 156, 159, 166
  Inskip review, 154, 208–9
Italo-Ethiopian war, 19–20, 39–40, 43–5, 154, 230
Italy
  and France, 43–5, 56–8, 98–100, 162, 213–21, 232, 234
  and Great Britain, 76, 89, 100–8 passim, 162, 190, 213–21
  and rearmament, 56–8, 153–4
  and Rome agreements, 19–20, 43–4
  and Spanish civil war, 91, 98–100, 213–21
  and Yugoslavia, 182, 184, 189–91
  see also Ciano; France and; Germany and; Great Britain and; Mussolini

Jacomet, Robert, 147, 149

Jamet, General Louis, 150
Japan, 15, 17, 155, 162
Jardel, Jean, 207
Jauneaud, General Jean-Henri, 95, 150, 165, 167, 195
Jeanneney, Jules, 96
Jebb, Gladwyn, 120–1, 123
Jordan, Philip, 78
Julien, Charles-André, 129

Kalinin, Mikhail, 196
Keller, General Pierre, 195
Keppler, Wilhelm, 65
Kerchove, Comte André de, 71
Kopke, Minister-Director, 67
Köster, Ronald, 67
Krosigk, Count Schwerin von, 65

La Chambre, Guy, 148, 150, 155, 166, 195, 221, 230
Labeyrie, Emile, 70, 161
Lacroix, Victor de, 76
Laroche, Jules, 12, 72
Laval, Pierre, 17, 19–20, 25, 35, 39, 44, 204, 229
League of Nations
  and Rhineland remilitarization, 29, 40
  raw materials enquiry, 115, 125, 134
  Union, 7
  see also Italo-Ethiopian war
Leeper, Rex, 119
Léger, Alexis, 32, 59–60, 67, 71, 73, 90–1, 94–5, 97–8, 107, 214, 218–19
Leith-Ross, Sir Frederick, 10, 75–6, 116, 118–19, 121–4, 134–6, 179, 222
Lelong, General Albert, 120, 158–9
Lever, E. H., 117–18
Leygues, Georges, 58, 153
Little Entente, 12, 32–3, 60, 178–80, 182–91, 196, 209–10, 212–13, 232
  see also Czechoslovakia; France; Romania; Yugoslavia
Litvinov, Maxim, 17, 27
Lloyd George, David, 6
Lloyd Thomas, Hugh, 127
Locarno treaties (1925), 3, 9, 12–14, 25–6
Loizeau, General Lucien, 194
London conference (July 1936), 68–9
London declaration (Feb. 1935), 37, 47n.18
London naval treaties (1930/1936), 35, 45, 57, 145
Loraine, Sir Percy, 108
Loriot, Commandant, 192–4

# Index